MESSIAH
in the
PASSOVER

MESSIAH
in the
PASSOVER

THE STAFF OF CHOSEN PEOPLE MINISTRIES

Edited by Darrell L. Bock and Mitch Glaser

*This book is dedicated to the faithful staff
of Chosen People Ministries who labor
day in and day out for the salvation of Israel.*

*May the Lord give them
strength, vision, courage, and joy!*

*Clean out the old leaven so that you may be a new
lump, just as you are in fact unleavened. For [Messiah]
our Passover also has been sacrificed. Therefore let
us celebrate the feast, not with old leaven, nor with
the leaven of malice and wickedness, but with the
unleavened bread of sincerity and truth.*

—1 Corinthians 5:7–8

CONTENTS

NOTE TO THE READER AND ACKNOWLEDGMENTS

*T*his book is a labor of love! Like so many other significant achievements, if you asked us how long it took to produce this volume, Darrell and I would have to respond, "A lifetime!" I was raised in a more traditional Jewish home, and Darrell Bock, who also is Jewish by birth, has been plumbing the depths of the life of Jesus far more deeply than I ever could.

However, the book did actually take almost two years to produce. Our contributing authors first composed their work and then we all met together in Los Angeles for three days of peer review where we critiqued one another's chapters, chuckled at one another's mistakes (especially those created by Microsoft Word's auto-correction feature), and prayed with and for one another. Our fervent hope is that the Lord would use this book to glorify the "Lamb of God who takes away the sin of the world" (John 1:29).

OUR THANKS TO YOU AND YOUR FAMILY

Most of all, we are grateful to the Lord and to our beloved Messiah Jesus, whom we also call Yeshua, which is His proper Hebrew name. We are also thankful for each disciple of the Messiah who reads this book because by doing so, you are expressing interest in the Jewish roots of your faith. We have written this particularly for you who know Him because He abides with you and will always be with you and in you (Matt. 28:20; John 14:17).

We are also so thankful for each skeptic or spiritual seeker who reads this book—whether you are Jewish or Gentile, and whether you read it out of curiosity or because someone dared you to, or for any other reason—because when all is said and done, our heart's desire and prayer to God for you is that you draw closer to God though the Messiah.

So whoever you are, dear reader, we want to acknowledge our gratitude to you, as you and your family are the very reason we took the time to produce this work.

OUR THANKS TO CHOSEN PEOPLE MINISTRIES
We are also grateful to Chosen People Ministries, the ministry that allows us to serve the Lord among the Jewish people. It also provides us with the inexpressibly precious opportunity to make "Messiah in the Passover" presentations at local churches and to lead Messianic Passover Seders at Messianic congregations. I presently serve as the president of Chosen People Ministries and Dr. Bock serves as a board member. Together we praise God for His faithfulness to this ministry and the opportunity to serve Him among the Jewish people.

Chosen People Ministries was founded in 1894, shortly after a Hungarian immigrant named Rabbi Leopold Cohn came to know the Lord in New York City. One of the objections Rabbi Cohn had before he accepted the Lord—and one that is so difficult for most Jewish believers in Jesus to overcome—is that he truly believed that if he accepted Jesus he would no longer be Jewish. Yet, nothing could be further from the truth. When I came to faith in Jesus the Messiah, I finally understood how faith in Him supplies the key to the Jewish identity I had always known and had sought to understand more fully. As the Bible came alive in a new way, the Exodus and the celebration of the Passover all became more meaningful when I recognized that these great events and others in our Scriptures pointed to the coming of the Messiah who died and rose to set us free from sin and death.

Passover, the subject of this book, is a powerful reminder that being Jewish and believing in Jesus go hand in hand. For this and many other reasons, we are grateful to our Messiah Yeshua for being the Passover Lamb who not only takes away the sin of the world, but who takes away our sins and puts them as far away from us "as the east is from the west" (Ps. 103:12).

OUR THANKS TO MANY, MANY PEOPLE
There are many people who have contributed to this volume.

I would of course like to thank the authors for their excellent contributions to the book. Their research, writing capabilities, and dedication have been impressive all the way through the process.

I also want to thank those who contributed valuable editorial input, particularly for style, and with other essential elements. I also offer sincere thanks to our proofreaders—some of whom are on our board and staff. A special thank-you to board member Marion Wells for her diligent and thorough edits and for her participation in the peer review sessions in Los Angeles. I am also grateful for the help of Alan Shore, one of our long-term staff members, who helped in some very critical areas.

I am also grateful for the extra effort exerted by two of our contributing authors and Chosen People Ministries staff members, Brian Crawford and Robert Walter, who provided exhaustive scrutiny of footnotes, original sources, and theological content. They also developed the appendices and contributed to the excellent glossary. We would never have completed the project without their help.

My sincere thanks also to the Chosen People Ministries Publications Department led by Nicole Parramore, including graphic designers Maralynn Rochat Jacoby and Lois Gable Ruedinger.

The Scripture index was prepared by a team that included Elisabeta Pindic and Jeannie Goldstein. We are so thankful for their efforts.

We also wish to thank Matt Hennecke, president of MANNA Bible Maps, for his group's assistance in providing several high quality maps for the back of the book.

A special thank-you goes to Paul Brinkerhoff of Grace and Truth Communications, our "super editor" who was so helpful and encouraging along the way. I think we have made him into an honorary Messianic Jew!

We also want to extend especially warm thanks to my assistant, Jacqui O'Rhea, who managed an exhaustive number of logistical necessities to prepare the book for publication.

Many thanks as well to Julia Freeman and the Chosen People Ministries Church Ministries staff who schedule thousands of presentations at local churches that enable us to teach so many people about the magnificent truths of Messiah in the Passover. Likewise, our thanks go out to the many pastors and ministry leaders who allow us to conduct "Messiah in the Passover" presentations for their congregations.

We must not forget the role of our mentors from previous generations, including Dr. Daniel Fuchs and Harold Sevener, who trained hundreds of Chosen People Ministries' staff to love the Passover and to teach these truths of redemption to others. Their work in the twentieth century helped shape our efforts in the twenty-first.

I also want to thank the Chosen People Ministries Board of Directors for their patience, understanding, and encouragement to make the truths of the Messiah in the Passover known through our ministry.

I know that Dr. Darrell Bock was supported as usual by his wife, Sally, who stands by his side in all of his many diverse projects . . . thanks, Sally, for keeping your brilliant husband on track!

Finally, I want to add a special thank-you to the beautiful mother of my children, Dr. Zhava Glaser, who helped with the concept of this book, wrote a wonderful chapter, and was deeply engaged in the book's editing. Among many other things, she served as our resident Hebrew expert, contributed to the glossary, coordinated the formulation of the various indices, and lovingly took it upon herself to do the subject index and index of other ancient and medieval writings, which we believe is one of the best parts of the whole book!

Mitch Glaser
New York City
April 2017

CONTRIBUTORS

Darrell L. Bock is Executive Director of Cultural Engagement and Senior Research Professor of New Testament Studies, Dallas Theological Seminary. He has earned recognition as a Humboldt Scholar (Tübingen University in Germany) and as author of over forty books, including well-regarded commentaries on Luke and Acts, studies of the historical Jesus, and work in cultural engagement as host of the Seminary's Table Podcasts (www.dts.edu/thetable). He was president of the Evangelical Theological Society (ETS) for 2000–2001, is a consulting editor for *Christianity Today*, and serves on the boards of Wheaton College and Chosen People Ministries. His articles appear in leading publications, and he often is an expert for the media on New Testament issues. He has been a *New York Times* best-selling author in non-fiction and is elder emeritus at Trinity Fellowship Church in Dallas. When traveling overseas, he will tune into the current game involving his favorite teams from Houston—live—even in the wee hours of the morning. He is a proud father of two daughters and a son, and is also a grandfather.

Michael Cohen was raised in a conservative Jewish home from San Fernando Valley, California. He attended Hebrew School as a boy and after his Bar Mitzvah, he excelled as a student of history. During his late teens and early twenties, Michael veered away from Judaism, while occasionally returning to Jewish traditions, but could find no comfort or guidance. Upon graduating from college, Michael met Lisa, a young Jewish believer in Jesus. After reading a copy of the New Testament she gave him, Michael accepted Jesus as his Messiah. He later married Lisa and completed a Masters of Arts in Intercultural Studies with a Jewish emphasis from Moody Theological Seminary in Chicago, Illinois. Michael has served as deacon, elder, and teacher in a Messianic congregation for over twenty years. Currently, Michael and Lisa serve with Chosen People Ministries in Southern California, and have five sons.

Brian Crawford received a call to share the Gospel with Jewish people after visiting Israel in 2005, and has served with Chosen People Ministries in Brooklyn, New York, since 2011. Brian's focus in ministry is Messianic apologetics—the defense of the faith toward a Jewish audience. He is the

Project Director for Chosen People Answers, a soon-to-be-released online community focused on making a case for Yeshua as the Messiah of Israel. Brian received a Master of Divinity from the Charles L. Feinberg Center for Messianic Jewish Studies—a partnership between Biola University's Talbot School of Theology and Chosen People Ministries. He is currently pursuing a Doctorate of Ministry in apologetics at Biola University. Brian has been married to Liz for nine years, and they have two young children.

Larry Feldman has been working with Chosen People Ministries since 1974. He currently is the Southwest Area Director for both Chosen People Ministries and the Messianic Jewish Alliance of America (MJAA). He has also been serving as the president of the MJAA since 2015. He has planted or helped in establishing seven Messianic congregations from New York to California. Larry earned an Advanced Jewish Studies Degree from Moody Bible Institute as well as a Master of Theology from Dallas Theological Seminary with highest honors in Old Testament and Semitic Languages. Larry has been a Messianic Jew since 1972 and has been married to Fran for over forty years. He is currently leading the Messianic congregation he founded in 1997 called Shuvah Yisrael (Return, O Israel), located in Irvine, California.

Richard H. Flashman is a seasoned pastoral leader and currently serves as the Chaplain, Director of Field Education, and a professor at the Charles L. Feinberg Center for Messianic Jewish Studies—a partnership between Biola University's Talbot School of Theology and Chosen People Ministries. Rich was raised in a Jewish family in Newton, Massachusetts, and came to faith soon after college. Rich was searching for answers and one of his peers shared the Gospel with him and challenged him to read the Hebrew prophets. After reading Isaiah 53, Rich could not deny that Jesus was the Messiah and accepted Him as his Lord and Savior. Soon after, God called Rich to full-time ministry. After earning a Master of Divinity and Master of Theology from Trinity Evangelical Divinity School, Rich, with his wife, Michelle, and their three boys, went on to pastor two EFCA churches in Connecticut for twenty-seven years. During that time Rich earned a Doctor of Ministry degree in Christian Leadership at Gordon Conwell Theological Seminary. Rich currently leads the only English-speaking Messianic congregation in Brooklyn along with two other missionaries. Additionally, Rich leads the southern Connecticut branch of Chosen People Ministries.

Mitch Forman was raised in a traditional Reform Jewish home near Boston. He attended the University of Massachusetts before pursuing a culinary career. Mitch went on to work in some of the finest hotels and restaurants in Boston and San Francisco, achieving his goal of cooking alongside the best chefs in the world. In 1987, Mitch came to faith in Jesus after talking with a Christian coworker about the Bible. He then became involved with Jewish evangelism over the next twelve years, from San Francisco to New York City.

In 2002, Mitch and his family returned to Boston, where he began teaching classes focused on the Jewish background of the Scriptures. He was also involved in the founding and leadership of Beth Yeshua Messianic Congregation in Newton, which is the heart of Boston's Jewish community. Mitch currently serves as the Vice President of U.S. Ministries for Chosen People Ministries, overseeing all recruitment, training, mentoring, and leadership of the entire U.S.-based missionary staff. Mitch is married to Kina, and they have two daughters and a son.

Richard E. Freeman was born and raised in Brooklyn, New York, in a very traditionally Jewish but nonreligious family. In 1973 Rich married his wife, Julia, who was from an Italian Catholic background. God reached Rich through Julia's spiritual pilgrimage, but not before Rich's Christian supervisor at work shared the Gospel with him. Rich received Yeshua as his Messiah in January of 1983. In September 1994, Rich earned a Master of Divinity degree from Conservative Baptist Seminary of the East, now part of Bethel Theological Seminary. He went on to earn a Doctor of Ministry degree from Gordon-Conwell Theological Seminary. Rich teaches on various topics such as Jewish evangelism, Messianic prophecy, end-time prophecy, the Church and Israel, the feasts of Israel, and more. He currently serves as the Vice President of Church Ministries and Conferences as well as the Southeast Regional Director for Chosen People Ministries. Rich and Julia have three children and five grandchildren and live in West Palm Beach, Florida.

Mitch Glaser is the President of Chosen People Ministries in New York City. He has been extensively involved in Jewish evangelism in several countries and was instrumental in helping to establish a congregation among Russian Jewish immigrants in New York. He is the corecipient of *Christianity Today*'s Award of Merit in the Apologetics/Evangelism category for 2009 for the book *To the Jew First: The Case for Jewish Evangelism in Scripture and History*, coedited with Darrell L. Bock. He is also the coauthor of *The Fall Feasts of Israel* and has written many articles for Christian periodicals and has taught at leading evangelical schools such as Fuller Theological Seminary and Moody Bible Institute. Mitch earned a Master of Divinity degree in Old Testament Studies at the Talbot School of Theology and a Doctor of Philosophy in Intercultural Studies at Fuller Theological Seminary. Mitch and his wife have two daughters.

Zhava Glaser serves with Chosen People Ministries and is a professor at the Charles L. Feinberg Center for Messianic Jewish Studies—a partnership between Biola University's Talbot School of Theology and Chosen People Ministries. Dr. Glaser teaches entry level Biblical Hebrew as a living, spoken language, as well as advanced Hebrew exegesis courses in Old Testament (Torah, Nevi'im, and Ketuvim). She also teaches Jewish History and Jewish Ethics, and is an editor and the coauthor of *The Fall Feasts of Israel* published by Moody

Press. Born in Argentina to Jewish parents, Zhava has traveled widely throughout the world. She speaks fluent Spanish, English, Portuguese, and Hebrew, and has a reading knowledge of French, Catalan, and Ladino. She earned a Master of Arts from the Fuller Theological Seminary School of World Mission, a Master of Arts and a Master of Philosophy from Hunter College, and completed a Doctor of Philosophy from the City University of New York. Dr. Glaser is a member in good standing of the Association of Jewish Studies, the National Association of Professors of Hebrew, and the Evangelical Theological Society. Zhava and her husband, Mitch, have two daughters.

Rachel Goldstein-Davis grew up in a Messianic home and watched her parents faithfully serve the Lord among the Jewish community. This instilled a passion for praying for and reaching out to her Jewish people, and she felt called to commit her life to full-time outreach. Rachel received her undergraduate degree from Moody Bible Institute in 2002 in Jewish Studies and Bible as well as later a Master's degree in Old Testament Studies from Alliance Theological Seminary. She joined the staff of Chosen People Ministries and served for five years in New York City. She loves to disciple children and youth, teaching young people to share their faith confidently with their Jewish friends. She also coordinates conferences for young Messianic believers around the globe as well as organizing short-term mission trips to Israel. In 2007, Rachel moved to Israel and received her citizenship, and is now serving at the Jerusalem and Tel Aviv Messianic Centers. Once in Israel, she met Steve Davis, a British Jewish believer who also felt the call from the Lord to live and serve in Israel. They have been married since June 2010 and have two young boys.

Gregory Hagg is a Professor of Bible Exposition at Talbot School of Theology, and serves as Program Director and a professor in the Charles L. Feinberg Center, which offers an accredited Master of Divinity in Messianic Jewish Studies through Biola University. This program, which is designed to provide excellent biblical and theological training for those who are reaching out to the Jewish people, is a partnership between Biola University's Talbot School of Theology and Chosen People Ministries. Gregory earned a Master of Arts from New York University, a Master of Theology from Dallas Theological Seminary, and then a Doctor of Philosophy from New York University. He also serves as a Vice President of Chosen People Ministries.

Gordon Law has been connected with Chosen People Ministries since 1999. He earned a Master of Divinity from Moody Theological Seminary, a Master of Theology from Trinity International University, and a Master of Arts in Religious Studies from Hebrew University of Jerusalem. Gordon has served in various ministry positions such as pastor in a Chinese church, missions mobilizer, seminary lecturer, and Holy Land tour guide. He loves to bring groups to Israel to learn about the Land and the people there. He resides in

New York with his wife and two children. His family always has a heart of sharing the love of Yeshua with Israelis as well as other Jewish people.

Olivier Melnick is a proficient writer and a bold evangelist. Born into a secular Jewish family in France and the son of a Holocaust survivor, Olivier is passionate about sharing his faith with his Jewish people and warning the public about rising tide of antisemitism in Europe and the West. Olivier has authored the book *They Have Conspired Against You*, which teaches readers to recognize and fight worldwide antisemitism. Olivier has also written *The Rabbi's Triad*, an evangelistic thriller. Olivier is a guest commentator on *WorldNetDaily* and is the Northwest Regional Director of Chosen People Ministries. He also serves as a board member of Chosen People Ministries in both the U.S. and France. Olivier is married to Ellen, and they have two children.

Scott P. Nassau leads a congregational plant in Los Angeles called "Kehila," derived from the Hebrew term meaning "community." He is passionate about shaping community where both Jews and Gentiles share Messiah's beautiful narrative of renewal through their unique stories. He has worked with Chosen People Ministries since 2001, is a Los Angeles native, and the grandson of Holocaust survivors. He earned a degree from Moody Bible Institute in Jewish Studies and a Master of Theology in Hebrew Bible from Dallas Theological Seminary. He has studied at University of Haifa in Israel and worked on coursework for a Doctor of Philosophy at Fuller Theological Seminary. In addition, he has published in academic journals. Scott is the husband to Dana and the father to three energetic kids.

Daniel Nessim has served with Chosen People Ministries since 1998. He is among the third generation of his family to believe in Jesus as Messiah and is a skilled communicator and leader, having established Chosen People Ministries' branch in the United Kingdom as well as a thriving Messianic Jewish congregation in Golders Green, the heart of London's Jewish community. Daniel has a Master of Arts in Christian Studies from Regent College. He now serves in Seattle and Vancouver, Canada where he leads a Messianic congregation. Daniel speaks extensively in the United States, Canada, and abroad, and is a member of the Society for Biblical Literature and the Evangelical Theological Society. Daniel has also written books on witnessing to Jewish people, the Gospel through Jewish eyes, and a prayer book for Jewish believers in Jesus.

David Sedaca was born in Montevideo, Uruguay, where his parents were missionaries. He is a second-generation Jewish believer in Jesus and currently serves as Vice President of Chosen People Ministries. David received his Bachelor of Arts degree in Psychology from Harvard University and went on to study Judaism at the graduate level in New York and abroad. David has over forty years' experience in ministry as both an evangelical pastor and a Messianic rabbi. His lectures at various prestigious universities in the United States and in Israel have been translated into Russian and Hebrew. His articles are published in different theological journals and Christian magazines around the world. He and his wife, Julia, presently live in Virginia Beach, Virginia. They have four children and nine grandchildren.

Robert Walter serves as the Brooklyn Branch Director of Chosen People Ministries in Brooklyn, New York. He also coleads Beth Sar Shalom Brooklyn Messianic Congregation with two other missionaries, and serves as an Adjunct Instructor of New Testament Greek at the Charles L. Feinberg Center for Messianic Jewish Studies—a partnership between Biola University's Talbot School of Theology and Chosen People Ministries. He earned a degree in Ministry from Palm Beach Atlantic University and a Master of Divinity from Talbot School of Theology through the Feinberg Center. Although neither Robert nor his wife, Joanna, is Jewish, God laid a heavy burden on their hearts to share Jesus with the Jewish people. They reside in Brooklyn with their two young children.

Cathy Wilson continues to draw Jewish and Gentile people to the Lord through performing comedic and dramatic sketches in the Phoenix metropolitan area. Although Cathy portrays Jewish characters, she grew up in a non-Jewish home in the Bronx, New York. While her home was "religious," she came to truly know the Lord during her senior year of high school. Cathy immediately applied to Northeastern Bible College in Essex Fells, New Jersey, and graduated in 1974 with a Bachelor of Arts in Biblical Literature. Cathy and her husband, Bob, lead a Jewish ministry team at Scottsdale Bible Church in Arizona. She trains the team to educate the Church about the Jewish roots of Christianity and to share the Gospel with Jewish people in the Phoenix area. Cathy has initiated a partnership between Scottsdale Bible Church and Chosen People Ministries to create Beth Sar Shalom, a monthly Messianic fellowship that invites Jews and Gentiles to worship the God of Abraham, Isaac, and Jacob together, through Jesus the Messiah.

FOREWORD

What does a major Jewish feast have to do with the destiny of the world? The short answer is—more than you would think.

The Feast of Passover commemorates God's deliverance of the people of Israel from their bondage to Pharaoh at the time of the Exodus, which is considered to be the major salvation event in the history of Israel. It occurs in the context of God's covenant promise to Abraham and continues the plan of deliverance and hope for the earth's nations that is explicitly spelled out in Genesis 12. The Passover demonstrates how God acts in and through His chosen people. This book explores the link between the Passover and subsequent acts of God that have opened the door for all people to enjoy the blessings bestowed upon the children of Israel.

The Passover celebrates God's actions in Egypt and points to later demonstrations of God's saving power in the land of Israel and the development of Jewish and Christian traditions that teach these truths throughout history. This book explores these links from every historical, theological, and liturgical angle. The marvelous thing about the Passover is that it not only commemorates a milestone of the past, but also connects us to a glorious future. Believers will be affirmed knowing they worship a God who keeps His promises and remains ever faithful. The Passover is a picture of God's love and salvation. It is a story of forgiveness, deliverance, hope, and reconciliation. The redemption of Israel from Egyptian slavery points us towards an even greater story of deliverance through the promised Messiah of Israel.

In sum, the Passover is a gripping account of God's goodness. We hope you enjoy this study and that it opens up for you a greater appreciation of what God was about when He caused death to pass over the children of Israel, persuading Pharaoh to at last let God's people go. That deliverance cleared the way for God to deliver more than a single nation. This book tells that story.

Darrell L. Bock

INTRODUCTION
WHY STUDY THE PASSOVER?

MITCH GLASER

There are many reasons why followers of Jesus the Messiah—whether Jewish or Gentile—should deepen their understanding of the Old Testament Scriptures and Passover in particular. Perhaps the best way to explain this is to refer to a great passage in the New Testament where the Apostle Paul (Rabbi Saul) writes a letter to his half-Jewish son in the faith, Timothy, and explains the value of the Old Testament Scriptures.

The Apostle writes,

> All Scripture is inspired by God and profitable for teaching, for reproof, for correction, for training in righteousness. (2 Tim. 3:16)

In this instance Paul describes the law as "inspired by God," which may be more literally translated "breathed by God." If you hold your hand to your mouth and speak, you'll notice immediately that you feel breath upon your hand with every syllable uttered. This is a wonderful picture of the way in which God's inerrant Word is communicated through the biblical authors while being inspired by the Holy Spirit.

The Law (Torah) is therefore profitable or useful for "teaching" (also sometimes translated "doctrine"), for "reproof" (learning what is wrong), for "correction" (learning what is right), and for "training in righteousness," where Paul uses the Greek word that usually refers to a child and therefore implies that the apostle is speaking of the ways in which parents train their children for life.

The five books of Moses include so much of the biblical information that a person needs in order to live in a way that pleases God. However, our motivation for applying the Law to our lives should not be that we would earn salvation by our efforts, but that we would grow into mature men and women who reflect the character of Christ.

Think about it for a moment with me. The five books of Moses include the creation account as well as the calling of Abraham and his sons to become a nation living in a promised land. These first five books of the Bible also include the Exodus, the laws given to the Jewish people at Mount Sinai, the sacrificial system, the role of the priests and the prophets, the lessons learned in the wilderness, and so much more! We would all agree that the five books of Moses—the Torah—are the very foundation for our faith.

Another very critical element of God's instruction for men and women in the Torah is the description of the seven great festivals of the Jewish people— mostly found in Leviticus 23. Each of these great festivals points to something unique about the planning character of God, reflecting His sovereignty over the past, present, and future. The festivals look back on the history of Israel, are often linked to the agricultural cycle, and point forward prophetically to the Messiah in the fulfillment of all of God's promises to the Jewish people.

The Jewish holidays not only include teaching but also special sacrifices that are made, such as the waving of sheaves, the baking of bread, the building of booths, and the blowing of the shofar (ram's-horn trumpet). The seven great festivals of Israel are replete with object lessons that help us better understand the story of redemption. These object lessons, woven into the very fabric of the feasts, enable the Israelites to "get their hands a little dirty" and to not merely hear or listen, but to *do* and *participate* so that the lessons of the festivals became ingrained in their very souls. It's no secret to modern experts on the process of learning that it is not merely children who learn better by doing—but adults do as well. Participating in the activities makes these lessons unforgettable.

This is the foundation for the Passover: it is a festival filled with op- portunities for participation in the remembrance of our great deliverance from Egypt. We were told to recount the story year after year so that new generations of Jewish people would never forget what God did in delivering the people of Israel from Egypt. There are symbols, given from Sinai that were part of the Torah, and instructions to the Jewish people on to how to observe the Feast. Jewish traditions have also grown up around these biblical injunctions to further help the Jewish people remember this most formative and critical event of the nation's history.

It is wonderful to observe the Passover because there are so many invalu- able lessons preserved in the festival for the people of God. Jesus celebrated the Passover with His disciples in light of His sacrifice for our sins. Similarly, Christians throughout the world, in one way or another, remember Jesus and give thanks for His sacrificial death through the Lord's Supper, also called Communion or the Eucharist.

When Christians celebrate the Passover, however, we grow in our under- standing of the Old Testament, affirm the Jewishness of the Gospel, deepen our understanding of the Lord's Supper, build community with fellow Chris- tians, and develop a common experience that will enable us to better com- municate the Gospel to our Jewish friends.

Most of all, when Christians celebrate the Passover, in one way or an- other, we are passing along the glorious message of redemption to future generations and linking our children and grandchildren to the Exodus. This will help our children develop a sense of continuity between the Old and New Testaments and between prophecy given and prophecy fulfilled. This will build the faith of our children, giving them greater assurance that what the Bible said about the future has and will come to pass.

THE ORGANIZATION OF THE BOOK: SOMETHING FOR EVERYONE

This book has something for everyone interested in the Jewish roots of the Christian faith and in becoming better equipped to tell their Jewish friends about Jesus. I hope you will be interested in reading every chapter, but we understand that you might find some chapters to be quite basic and others to be advanced. I believe you will glean great value from every chapter, but if you view the book as a reference volume that you keep coming back to, then you might read some of the material now and save other chapters for a future time.

The book has been organized into five parts to take you on a journey through Scripture so that you may learn what the Bible teaches about Passover and the Exodus. Part 1 of the book focuses on the biblical and theological issues related to the Passover throughout the Old and New Testament. We begin with the Hebrew Scriptures and then move into the days of Jesus Messiah, including His death, life, and resurrection, and the role that Passover now plays in the life of the Body of Messiah, both in the New Testament Scriptures and the present day.

Part 2 will help you understand the importance of the Passover in both Jewish and church history, including the unfortunate use of the Passover as a tool to persecute the Jewish people. Our journey to understand the profound linkages between the Passover, the Exodus, and Jesus the Messiah takes us from the Early Church to later church history and into our current day. We focus not only on the ways in which Jesus fulfills the Passover, but also on the ways in which the Church continues to experience the Seder, which is fulfilled by observing the Lord's Supper. On our journey, we also look at the various controversies regarding the Passover throughout this period and focus attention on the theological and practical implications the Passover can have today in the lives of Christians and Messianic Jews.

Part 3 of the book looks at the Passover in light of Jewish tradition, and I hope this will give you further insight into the Jewish view of the Passover.

Part 4 will equip you to use the Passover to communicate the message of Messiah in the Passover to your Jewish friends.

Part 5 of the book provides all you need to celebrate Passover in your home or church, including a Messianic Family Haggadah (guidebook with readings for the Passover Seder), recipes, and even lessons for your children. This final part of the journey allows us to explore some of the many opportunities to experience and participate in the celebration of Passover. With the biblical and theological foundations coupled with the historical and traditional and Gospel-centered perspectives on the Passover, we can pray for opportunities to serve and bless others as well as to witness the glad and rich celebration of Messiah in the Passover to our family and friends.

At the back of the book you will find a number of appendices, including helpful lists, charts, and maps, along with a glossary, recommended reading list, bibliography, and indexes to help you better understand and use the material included in the book. We pray that the entire work will inspire your participation in celebrating the Passover in your own home or congregation, Bible study or home group, or even Sunday school class or homeschool group. Additionally, we have created a Messiah in the Passover website, www.messiahinthepassover.com, that will enhance your experience of the book. The website includes additional materials that will further equip and guide you and your family to celebrate this great festival of Passover.

Even if you never take part in a Passover celebration, we believe the information presented in this volume will enrich your life by helping you better understand your Jewish heritage in the Messiah.

THE BIBLICAL FOUNDATIONS FOR THE PASSOVER

We have organized the book in a way that takes into consideration both the traditional Jewish and Christian views of the Old Testament canon. Even though the two are much the same, they are organized differently.

The Hebrew Scriptures

There is a Jewish acronym for the Old Testament canon—*Tanakh (TNK)*. The three letters refer to the *Torah*, the *Nevi'im*, and the *Ketuvim*.

The five books of Moses—known by the Hebrew word *Torah*—are the same in both the Hebrew Bible and Christian Old Testament (see appendix 1). These include the books of Genesis, Exodus, Leviticus, Numbers, and Deuteronomy.

The *Nevi'im* refers to the "Prophets," which are divided in the Jewish canon between Former and Latter Prophets. The Former Prophets include Joshua, Judges, and Samuel in the books of First and Second Samuel and First and Second Kings. The Latter Prophets include Isaiah, Jeremiah, Ezekiel, and what Christians call, "the Minor Prophets," which Jewish people simply call, "the Twelve." This corpus of Scripture includes the books of Hosea, Joel, Amos, Obadiah, Jonah, Micah, Nahum, Habakkuk, Zephaniah, Haggai, Zechariah, and Malachi.

The *Ketuvim*, which translated means "the Writings," encompasses the Psalms, Proverbs, Song of Songs, Job, Ruth, Lamentations, Ecclesiastes, Esther, Daniel, Ezra-Nehemiah, and the books of First and Second Chronicles, which are united in one book entitled "The Chronicles." Within the Ketuvim, Jewish people recognize internal subgroups such as the Megillot—or in English "The Scrolls,"—which includes the Song of Songs, Ruth, Lamentations, Ecclesiastes, and Esther.

Those books usually associated with the Apocrypha were generally not included in the Jewish canon. The Bible used in most synagogues as the

source of our modern translations of the Hebrew Bible is based upon the
Hebrew Masoretic text. This text was composed by the Masoretes, a term referring to Jewish scholars in the seventh through tenth centuries who copied
the texts, added the vowels to the Hebrew, and in their meticulous practices
of copying the text ensured the accuracy of the Hebrew canon.

For our purposes, this book follows a combination of the Protestant and
Jewish canons.

The New Testament

We follow a similar path in approaching the New Testament and pay
special attention to the Jewish backgrounds of the New Testament so that we
can better understand the linkage between Jesus and the Passover. Therefore,
we will journey through the Gospels and then the New Testament Epistles,
again highlighting the links between Passover and the Messiah. We will keep
in mind the themes of promise and fulfillment and first-century Jewish un-
derstandings, which will enable us to see the New Testament through Jewish
eyes. Our goal is to better understand our Savior Himself and the ways in
which He celebrated the Jewish holidays.

THE USE OF RABBINIC SOURCES

It is nearly impossible to understand Jewish life, culture, and history
without coming to grips with the critical role of Jewish religious tradition.
The Jewish people are like the proverbial pulling of the loose thread from
a garment—if you begin tugging on your understanding of the Jewish
people in one area, you will eventually discover that this area is attached to
another. Perhaps the common visible thread, which held the Jewish people
together for centuries, is the attachment of religious tradition to almost
every area of Jewish life.

This tradition is found in what is known as the Talmud, which includes
two major sections: the Mishnah and the Gemara. Jewish religious tradition
is also found in the vast number of commentaries on the Torah as well as
many other genres of religious literature: devotional books, manuals of spiritual discipline, and many similar works.

You will notice in various chapters in this book that Jewish religious tradition is explained, especially in relation to the Passover. We have also dedicated an entire chapter that surveys the discussions of the Passover within
traditional Jewish religious literature (see chapter 10). It is our hope that
this will enable you to better understand the Jewish people, Jewish religious
practices, and how this impacts the Passover—especially the understanding
of Jesus and the disciples.

THE LAST SUPPER AND JEWISH TRADITION

One of the critical questions addressed in this book is, "How similar
was the Last Supper celebrated by Jesus and His disciples to the modern-day
Jewish Passover?"

Is today's Passover celebration a transparent window into the way in which Jesus and His disciples celebrated Passover? Did Jesus observe the same Jewish traditions as Messianic Jews like myself who grew up in a Jewish home?

One of the immediate challenges we have to make clear is that the first part of the Talmud, the Mishnah, was compiled in written form during the third century C.E. The Gemara was compiled at the beginning of the sixth century C.E. Therefore; the New Testament could predate these important Jewish works by 150 years or more.

This century-plus gap in Jewish religious history makes us question whether or not the Mishnah in particular may be read back into the Last Supper—especially, the tractate Pesahim, which is all about the Passover and from which Jewish people developed the *Haggadah*, the Jewish guidebook for Passover.

On the other hand, we also understand that the traditions written down in the Mishnah were at one time oral. The term *Mishnah* comes from the Hebrew word meaning "to repeat," and you will learn more about this critical Jewish document in Dr. Zhava Glaser's chapter on rabbinic literature and the Passover. We are simply not used to oral traditions having weight or authority, as our modern culture is dependent upon written documents. However, this written predominance is particularly a Western idea as many cultures today in various parts of the world still grant significant authority to oral tradition, even though they might also have written documents that are important as well.

Oral tradition was tremendously important in Israel, along with written documents of course, like the Bible itself. The writing of documents actually became more important between the first and fifth centuries, which is why the Mishnah was compiled in written form in the third century C.E. Yet, we still recognize that the written Mishnah nevertheless "repeated" traditions that were earlier transmitted orally.

So we ask ourselves again, "How much of our modern Passover Seder, as detailed in Jewish tradition, did Jesus and the disciples observe?"

The clear answer to this question is, "We do not know." Additionally, we understand that this question is not only important for the Passover but for the entirety of the New Testament since it was penned within a Jewish historical context. In fact, whatever principles we determine regarding the role of Jewish tradition in first-century Jewish life—especially in the words and activities of Jesus and His disciples—will help guide us in understanding not only the Passover, but also many portions of the New Testament. There is no question that the New Testament is a very Jewish book and that in order to understand it properly, we must do our best to understand the culture and context of the time, which is both religiously and culturally Jewish.

In general, we have taken a very cautious approach and will try and understand the Jewish backgrounds of the New Testament as best we can and not simply presume that the mishnaic tractate Pesahim or today's Passover

Haggadah can simply be read into the Last Supper. Yet, we point out where we do find striking parallels between the religious customs observed by Jesus and His disciples at the Last Supper with later Jewish religious developments, and so many of our authors will suggest that these traditions could have been practiced during the Last Supper.

We cannot assume that every author writing in this volume will be in agreement as to the degree that the later Jewish traditions can be read into the Last Supper. The editors of this book believe that it will be valuable for readers to see these multifaceted opinions and then come to their own conclusions.

There is an old Jewish joke that most Jewish people are well familiar with. It's usually told as an aphorism with a twinkle of the eyes and a smile: "Where there are two Jewish people, there are three opinions." Quite frankly, I do not always like Jewish jokes as sometimes they express prejudice towards the Jewish people. But in this instance, I believe the joke expresses a profound truth that is critical to understanding the book you are about to read. Jewish religious tradition prides itself on having a variety of viewpoints on the same issue, and Jewish people view this as healthy. This reflects our approach to the challenge of understanding the level at which later Passover traditions may be read into the final Passover of Yeshua the Messiah.

We do not want you to be confused, but it is important to understand that there is a variety of opinion within Jewish tradition, as you will see throughout the chapters of this book. Where possible, we have tried to align the various positions of the authors, but you should expect to find differing viewpoints. In summary, there is not just one answer to the question, "What traditions did Jesus and the disciples observe during the Last Supper?"

Our hope is that your reading of this book will be the beginning of a lifelong journey in exploring the ways in which Jewish religious tradition helps you better understand the life and times of Jesus the Messiah.

PASSOVER AND THE EXODUS

You will notice as you read through the book that the authors often equate the Exodus with Passover. This is common and makes sense as the Exodus was the basis for the Passover. But we must remember that these are two separate events that are often intertwined in Scripture.

Some scholars use the term "the Egyptian Passover" in reference to the first Passover event that is directly tied to the Exodus event, and in particular to the slaying of the lamb in Exodus 12. The celebration of subsequent Passovers Seders, however, is a celebration of a very different event—though linked by a common origin and therefore having very similar themes. It is important as you read this book that you keep these original and subsequent events separate in your own understanding. Essentially, the Exodus refers to the redemption event, and the Passover refers to the retelling of the Exodus story! The first Passover is unique in that it prepared the way for the Exodus that occurred in history.

PASSOVER AS A SOURCE OF TYPES, SYMBOLS, AND PROPHECIES

The Exodus, the first (Egyptian) Passover, and subsequent Passovers are often used by the biblical authors to point towards a greater redemption. This is sometimes accomplished in the Scriptures through literary types, symbols, and prophecies. However, the Bible student must take great care in the ways biblical types and symbols are understood. There is no question that the Exodus and the first Passover look forward to similar but greater events, but care must be given in the interpretation of the various composite elements of the Exodus event. We should refrain from reading prophetic fulfillment into every aspect of the festival.

It is best, first of all, to understand the Exodus and first Passover as the participants might have viewed them at the time of the event. When interpreting prophecy, we should always consider the way in which the original hearers might have understood the prophetic word—even when the prophecy refers to future events the hearers might not expect nor understand. I am sure that the Israelites who were delivered from bondage did not realize that the lambs slain for the redemption of the firstborn nor the Exodus itself would have additional meaning in reference to an understanding of salvation or of the work of the future Messiah (1 Peter 1:10–12).

Yet the Lord would fill these original events with greater meaning at a later day. But this fulfillment could obviously only be understood in retrospect. For example, we would not suggest that the Israelites slaughtering the lamb for the first Passover in any way knew that the lamb would find ultimate fulfillment in the shed blood and sacrifice of Jesus. Yet in hindsight we know this is true, which leads us to the second principle of interpretation we would suggest you to consider.

A second rule of thumb is to view Passover and the Exodus as a type seen through the lens of the New Testament writers. Because the Apostles Peter, John, and Paul refer to various elements related to the observance of Passover as a foreshadow of the Messiah, we have a solid, biblical basis for looking back at these great events in the Old Testament and viewing them as types, symbols, and prophecies of events to come. Perhaps one of the clearest passages in the New Testament that helps us see this principle at work is in 1 Peter 1:18–19:

> . . . knowing that you were not redeemed with perishable things like silver or gold from your futile way of life inherited from your forefathers, but with precious blood, as of a lamb unblemished and spotless, the blood of Christ.

Our authors will help you discern how the Bible uses the Exodus and the Passover as types so that you will be careful not to go beyond the text, because we cannot simply interpret every detail as prophecy or we might find ourselves forcing Scripture to mean something that was never intended, just so it fits with a pattern we envision ourselves.

One might ask the question, "Did Moses have the sacrifice of Jesus in mind when he asked the children of Israel to offer a spotless, unblemished lamb and smear the blood of the lamb on the lintel and doorposts of their homes on the night when the firstborn of Egypt were judged?" This remains to be seen as we journey through this volume, but for now, you might consider the following: it seems that the writers of the New Testament understood the Passover and the sacrifice of a lamb in this Messianic way—especially John the Baptist who cried out, "Behold, the Lamb of God who takes away the sin of the world" (John 1:29). Yet there is much more to be uncovered!

Some of our authors believe that the way the lamb was selected is also prophetic of the schedule Jesus kept during the last week of His life and that the choosing and testing of the lamb and the time of the lamb's sacrifice follow the dates of the Jewish calendar as well, making the calendar itself prophetic.

Many scholars also see the the seven days of Unleavened Bread fulfilled in the perfect, sinless life Jesus lived before He was crucified. How purposeful was God in linking the Messiah to the Jewish calendar? Most believers in Jesus see these links, but how can we know that seeing the feasts fulfilled in Jesus to this degree is a correct biblical interpretation? These are just some of the questions we will try to answer throughout this book.

Some of your ideas about the Passover will be reaffirmed in reading this book, and in other areas you will be challenged! Our prayer is that you will be open to the Lord and to the Scriptures and read the chapters with an open Bible, using great discernment so that you will learn more and that your faith will grow through better understanding the redemption we enjoy through Jesus the Messiah.

THE FESTIVALS AS A ROADMAP TO REDEMPTION

It is as impossible to study the Passover in a vacuum, as it is the first festival among the seven great holy days detailed by God in Leviticus 23. It would be difficult to understand Passover without the associated festivals of Unleavened Bread, First Fruits, and the Feast of Weeks. These four festivals make up the first section of the festivals listed in Leviticus 23 and fall within the first few months of the Hebrew calendar. The final three festivals—the Feast of Trumpets, the Day of Atonement, and the Feast of Tabernacles—are observed in the seventh month of the Jewish calendar, which is a lunar calendar, not a solar calendar like our own.

We have utilized a number of charts and illustrations for you to better understand Passover and you would do well to take a quick look at the chart that describes the Hebrew months (see appendix 2).

The seven great festivals of the Jewish year—and the weekly Sabbath—look back at a great event in biblical history, are often tied to the agricultural calendar of Israel, and call for various ceremonies and sacrifices to bring attention to the theme of a given festival. They also seem to point to a greater fulfillment. Leviticus 23 itself does not inform us of this greater fulfillment, but other Scriptures in the Old and New Testaments do.

As you will see in reading through the various chapters, Passover is clearly used by the biblical authors to point to something greater. Commonly, the first four spring festivals are thought to point to the first coming of Jesus and the last three festivals in the seventh month are usually associated with His second coming. Once again, we understand this from later passages in the Old and New Testaments. You will not find this taught in the earlier chapters of the Torah—including Leviticus 23—as we understand this in retrospect through the words of Jesus and the actions of the writers of the New Testament. As you will read, Passover is the clearest and most common festival to be understood by the New Testament writers as being fulfilled in the person and work of Jesus. Yet the other festivals are alluded to in various ways as well.

ENJOY THE FESTIVAL AND THE BOOK

Will many Jewish believers in Jesus be celebrating Passover this year? Of course! As believers in Jesus, the festivals are more meaningful to us than ever before—especially Passover. We hope you and your family will find a way to celebrate the Festival as well.

Eating matzah and avoiding bread during the Feast of Unleavened Bread is a powerful reminder of Jesus's sinless nature, purity, and innocence. We are reminded of our need to live pure and holy lives before God as well. Then there is the Passover Seder itself, enabling us to have a new and exalted view of Jesus, the Lamb of God who takes away the sin of the world. When we find the hidden piece of matzah called the *afikoman*, we can hear echoes of our Savior's voice reverberating through time as He tells His disciples at the Last Supper, "This is My body which is given for you; do this in remembrance of Me" (Luke 22:19). As we drink the four cups of the fruit of the vine, we will be especially drawn to the third cup when He said to His disciples, "This cup which is poured out for you is the new covenant in My blood" (Luke 22:20).

Passover is more important to us now as believers in Jesus than it was for many of us who grew up in traditional Jewish homes. Passover has its natural and glorious fulfillment in Jesus the Messiah—the Lamb of God who takes away the sin of the world.

This book should be viewed as a reference book filled with a variety of information about the Passover. We will cover the Scriptures of the Old and New Testaments, other ancient writings, church history, Jewish traditions, and then help you learn how to celebrate a Messianic Seder yourself—recipes included! Finally, we will also help you learn how to share the message of the Gospel through the Passover.

May the Lord bless you as you dig into the Jewish roots of your faith and learn more about the wonderful heritage you have been given through your faith in the Jewish Messiah.

PART 1
BIBLICAL FOUNDATIONS

1
PASSOVER IN THE TORAH

ROBERT WALTER

*T*he earliest chapters of Genesis record God's initial dealings with humanity. He creates Adam and Eve, enjoys close fellowship with them, seeks them out after they had willfully disobeyed in the Garden of Eden, and promises to send a deliverer to redeem humankind and restore creation from chaos to peace. The thread of this promise is woven into all of the earliest events in Genesis, as if the Patriarchs are rehearsing the great deliverance that God will later bring about.

PASSOVER IN GENESIS

In Genesis, Egypt is consistently portrayed as "a place that needs to be gotten out of, by God's help, for the sake of preserving God's people."[1] And His ultimate goal is to bring them into the Promised Land. This has caused some scholars to suggest that Genesis was actually written with Exodus in mind, as a prelude to show God's choosing of Israel as His people and to demonstrate that He is the supreme God, two vital elements in the Exodus account.[2] While there are no specific mentions of the Passover in Genesis, there are allusions to the Exodus. Therefore, as we embark on this study of the Passover in the Torah it's important to examine these Genesis passages to gain a greater understanding of the Passover's Exodus context.[3]

Abram

The first of these occurrences in Genesis is in the account of Abram. God makes a covenant with Abram in Genesis 12:1–3 where He calls him to get up and go. Abram is to follow God to a specific Land and is promised that he will be made into a great nation and receive a great name, and that through him all the families of the earth will be blessed. In Genesis 15, God

---

1. Peter Enns, *Exodus*, NIV Application Commentary (Grand Rapids: Zondervan, 2000), 285.
2. Enns, *Exodus*, 285.
3. For a more detailed overview of the Exodus as a paradigm for salvation as found in Genesis, see Enns' comments on Exodus 13:17–14:31 in Enns, *Exodus*, 279–89.

further establishes the covenant, promising to provide him a son, and giving boundaries for the aforementioned Land. This text also provides the first hint pointing to the Exodus:

> God said to Abram, "Know for certain that your descendants will be strangers in a land that is not theirs, where they will be enslaved and oppressed four hundred years. But I will also judge the nation whom they will serve, and afterward they will come out with many possessions. . . . Then in the fourth generation they will return here . . . ." (Gen. 15:13–16)

Perhaps to show His sovereign faithfulness to His promises, or to indicate the troubled future that Abram's descendants would endure, God chooses to reveal to Abram certain details about the Exodus. His descendants will be oppressed and enslaved, strangers in a foreign land for four hundred years. God himself will judge the nation oppressing them. The descendants will leave that foreign land with many possessions and return to the Land of Promise. There is no mention of the Passover, but there is a prediction of national deliverance and return to the Land, two major themes in the Exodus from Egypt.[4]

Joseph

Perhaps the strongest foreshadowing of the Exodus in the Torah is found in the life of Joseph. In Genesis 37–50, we learn that Joseph is beloved by his father, rejected and hated by his brothers, sold into slavery for silver, wrongly accused, and convicted of crimes. Though he is blameless, he enters the depths of suffering in an Egyptian prison. It is from that lowest point that God turns Joseph's situation around, raising him from the pit and exalting him to a position that is answerable to Pharaoh alone.

Later in the account, famine strikes the region and Joseph encounters his brothers face to face, this time possessing the authority and ability to strike them down for what they had done to him. He instead shows mercy. As the brothers stand awestruck and afraid, Joseph comforts them with his understanding of God's sovereign hand at work in all that has happened. Joseph assures them,

> Now do not be grieved or angry with yourselves, because you sold me here, for God sent me before you to preserve life. . . . God sent me before you to preserve for you a remnant in the earth, and to keep you alive by a great deliverance. (Gen. 45:5, 7)

---

4. It should be noted that the covenant event of Genesis 15 between God and Abram, and the covenant event of Exodus 20 between God and Israel at Sinai have striking similarities. Sailhamer points out a number of these: (1) the similar wording of Genesis 15:7 and Exodus 20:2, "I am the LORD your God who brought you out of . . . ," introducing the covenant action of God that appeals to an earlier act of divine salvation; (2) fire and darkness accompanying God's presence at Sinai (Exod. 19:18; 20:18; Deut. 4:11) compared with the fire and darkness of Abram's vision (Gen. 15:12, 17); and (3) the common thread of the Exodus from Egypt that joins the two covenants (Gen. 15:14). See John H. Sailhamer, "Genesis" in *The Expositor's Bible Commentary: Genesis–Leviticus*, rev. ed. (Grand Rapids: Zondervan, 2009), 1:173–74.

In Joseph's view, God has used his trials for good. He highlights three results of his suffering: (1) the preservation of life, presumably for Egypt and others; (2) the preservation of a remnant, best explained as the Hebrew people; and (3) the coming of a great deliverance, which most likely points to the Exodus from Egypt.[5] Joseph later provides a similar reflection as he gives his brothers final instructions before his death:

> As for you, you meant evil against me, but God meant it for good in order to bring about this present result, to preserve many people alive. . . . I am about to die, but God will surely take care of you and bring you up from this land to the land which He promised on oath to Abraham, to Isaac and to Jacob. . . . God will surely take care of you, and you shall carry my bones up from here. (Gen. 50:20, 24–25)

Here Joseph reiterates God's sovereignty throughout his trials, which has resulted in the preservation of life for many people, both Egyptians and descendants of Jacob. He also begins to prophesy concerning God visiting His people at a future time to bring them out of Egypt and into the Promised Land. We again see the redemptive pattern of the Exodus presented to us in Genesis as Joseph appeals to the covenant promises that God made to the Patriarchs.[6]

The Genesis–Exodus Bridge

As the story unfolds in the early chapters of Exodus, it is important to note the ongoing connections between the Genesis and Exodus narratives. There are three particular points that warrant mention, as they tie Joseph's experiences in Egypt and his dying words in Genesis 50 to the Passover and Exodus more than 400 years later. First, the word for "take care of" or "visit" in 50:24–25 is a form of the Hebrew verb, פָּקַד *paqad*. The connotation is that God's presence will be with Israel as He will visit them with the intent to aid and change their fortunes. Moving forward, this same Hebrew word is only used at key points throughout the Exodus narrative to describe God taking action to deliver. It is used in Exodus 3:16 when Moses is commissioned to go to the leaders of Israel and announce that God has remembered His people and *taken note of* their afflictions. In Exodus 4:29–31, as Moses and Aaron address the elders and proclaim that God has *taken note of* their afflictions, the people believe, bow low, and worship God. And in Exodus 13:19, as the exhumed bones of Joseph are being carried off with the redeemed nation, Moses quotes Joseph's dying words

---

5.   While this final point on the "great deliverance" can be seen as finding its fulfillment in the rescue from the current famine in Joseph's time, the preservation of the covenant family carries with it the purpose of future promise fulfillment, especially in the Exodus. Hamilton suggests as much in Victor P. Hamilton, *The Book of Genesis: Chapters 18–50*, New International Commentary on the Old Testament (Grand Rapids: Eerdmans, 1995), 576. This view also makes sense when comparing the parallel statements of Joseph in Genesis 50:20, 24–25, with the preservation of life and a remnant of 45:5 paralleling what Joseph says brought about "this present result" in 50:20; and the "great deliverance" of 45:7 paralleling God's future "visit" in 50:24–25.

6.   See Genesis 12:1–3; 15:18–21; 26:3–5; 35:12.

from Genesis 50:25. It appears that Moses understood that Joseph's prophetic words were coming to pass. We can surmise with a certain level of confidence that the author of Exodus uses פָּקַד, *paqad*, in these key texts to demonstrate the promise-fulfillment relationship and build a bridge between the patriarchal narratives of Genesis and the redemptive Passover event in Exodus.[7]

Next, the word for "to bring up" in Genesis 50:24–25 is the Hebrew verb עָלָה, *'alah*, which Joseph uses to indicate how God *will bring* Israel *up* from Egypt and also how the Israelites *will bring* Joseph's bones with them at their deliverance. The word is used a number of times in the Exodus narrative to refer to God's intentions to set Israel free and *bring* His people *up* to the Land, most notably in Exodus 3:8 as He speaks to Moses from the burning bush.

Lastly, the first biblical mention of the three Patriarchs—Abraham, Isaac, and Jacob—all together is found in Genesis 50:24. In combining the three, Joseph encapsulates the covenant promises that God has made to them and begins to prophesy how God will fulfill those promises by visiting and transferring Israel from Egypt to the Promised Land. Joseph casts the hope of the Patriarchs onto the deliverance from Egypt as he predicts the Exodus (cf. Heb. 11:22). Just like the limited use of the word פָּקַד, *paqad*, so also the only mention of the three Patriarchs together is included at the end of Genesis, which later appears at key points in the Exodus narrative (Exod. 2:23–25; 3:6–8, 16–17; 6:1–5, 8).

Words matter and it appears that leading up to the redemption experienced through the Exodus, פָּקַד, *paqad*; עָלָה, *'alah*; and "Abraham, Isaac, and Jacob" are used to demonstrate the promise-fulfillment relationship between Joseph's dying words and the redemptive events of the Exodus. It's safe to say that with his dying words, Joseph stands as the covenantal bridge between the family under the leadership of the Patriarchs and the nation under the leadership of Moses. His words set the stage for how God would take redemptive action, visit His people to set them free, and transfer them from a place of bondage to a place of freedom.

Passover in Exodus

The first five chapters of Exodus trace the path toward the great deliverance that will ultimately come at the first Passover. Israel has grown in number while living in Egypt, and their situation takes a turn for the worse when a new Pharaoh arises who knows nothing of Joseph (Exod. 1:8). Great persecution and affliction ensues for Israel, and in the midst of it, Moses is born. God sovereignly chooses and prepares Moses from birth to serve as the redemptive figure through whom He will fulfill His promises. Israel's cries are heard by God and

---

7. See Bruce K. Waltke, with Cathi J. Fredricks, *Genesis: A Commentary* (Grand Rapids: Zondervan, 2001), 627; and Claus Westermann, *Genesis*, trans. David Green (New York: T&T Clark, 2004), 324; and K. A. Mathews, *Genesis 11:27–50:26*, New American Commentary (Nashville: Broadman & Holman, 2005), 1B:930. Also, for the rabbinic tradition that views פָּקַד, *paqad*, as a sort of password passed on from generation to generation in Egypt, see note on Genesis 50:24 in Nosson Scherman, ed., *The Chumash: The Torah, Haftaros and Five Megillos*, ArtScroll Series (Brooklyn, NY: Mesorah Publications, 1993), 289.

He begins to take covenant action (2:23–25). He speaks with Moses from the burning bush, and gives him a divine mission to go to Pharaoh and the elders of Israel to proclaim Israel's liberty (3:1–22). When the elders hear Moses' report, they immediately believe and worship (4:29–31). Pharaoh, on the other hand, questions the identity, nature, and character of the God of Israel and hard-heartedly refuses to acquiesce to God's bidding (5:2). Under the duress of increased labor, even Israel begins to question Moses' intentions (5:21).

The Four Promises

As the now distressed and confused Moses seeks understanding and insight from God, God answers by pointing to what He is about to do. In Exodus 6:6–7 we read:

> Say, therefore, to the sons of Israel, "I am the LORD, and *I will bring you out* from under the burdens of the Egyptians, and *I will deliver you* from their bondage. *I will also redeem you* with an outstretched arm and with great judgments. Then *I will take you* for My people, and I will be your God; and you shall know that I am the LORD your God, who brought you out from under the burdens of the Egyptians." (emphasis added)

The four highlighted promises serve as the basis for the four cups used during the traditional Jewish celebration of the Passover Seder. Jewish sources interpret these four promises as the backbone of the entire Passover experience, each one representing a stage in the progressive unfolding of Israel's redemption.[8] The first two promises, that God will bring Israel out and deliver His people from Egyptian bondage, speak of how He will physically transfer Israel from Egypt to the Promised Land,[9] and in the process change the status of His people from slave to free.

The third promise is that God will redeem Israel. The Hebrew verb גָּאַל, *ga'al*, used here can carry the sense of repurchasing something that once belonged to you. It points to a transaction between parties where the purchaser pays a price, and as a result takes ownership and possession of that which is purchased.[10] Likewise, through the Passover, God will pay a price (the Lamb) to repurchase Israel His firstborn (Exod. 4:22) from slavery, taking ownership and possession of His people and bringing them into the Land.[11]

The fourth promise is that God will take Israel to Himself. The Hebrew verb לָקַח, *laqach*, used here is found over one thousand times in the Old Testament and means "to take, or receive," but often its nuance is determined

8. See note on Exodus 6:6–7 in Scherman, *The Chumash*, 319.

9. See Kaiser's comments on the use of "to bring out" in Walter C. Kaiser Jr., "Exodus," in *The Expositor's Bible Commentary: Genesis–Leviticus*, rev. ed. (Grand Rapids: Zondervan, 2012), 1:394.

10. R. Laird Harris, "גָּאַל," *Theological Wordbook of the Old Testament*, ed. R. Laird Harris, Gleason L. Archer, and Bruce K. Waltke (Chicago: Moody Press, 1980), 1:300.

11. See Kaiser's comments on the use of גָּאַל, *ga'al*, in Kaiser, "Exodus," 1:394.

by the words with which it is used.[12] Here God takes Israel to be His people; He will be their God. This promise ultimately points to the close, special relationship that God and His people will enjoy beyond their redemption.[13] Christian and rabbinic sources view this promise being fulfilled at Sinai when God "takes" Israel, entering into a covenant contract, even a "marriage," with His people as they accept His Torah.[14]

As we keep reading, we see that there are two more promises in Exodus 6:8 that refer directly to God bringing Israel into the Promised Land and giving His people the Land as a possession:

> *I will bring you* to the land which I swore to give to Abraham, Isaac, and Jacob, and *I will give it to you* for a possession; I am the Lord. (emphasis added)

To summarize the six promises in Exodus 6:6–8, the first three (bring you out, deliver you, redeem you) relate to Israel's condition in Egypt before the crossing of the Red Sea, and the fourth promise (take you to Myself), plus the fifth and sixth promises (bring you to the Land, give Land as a possession) relate to Israel's experience beyond the crossing of the Red Sea.

Faithful Obedience and the Promises

When we consider divine promises, it is important to ask a couple of questions: When God makes us a promise, what is our responsibility? What are we to do with that promise? Pause to think about that for a moment. The simple answer is to believe. We are to believe and have faith that God will indeed come through on the promise that He has made. In light of the fact that the redemptive act at Passover is based on God's promises to the Patriarchs, to Moses, and to all Israel, we conclude that faith has always been a key element in redemption. From the moment the promises are mentioned in Exodus 6 through the crossing of the Red Sea in Exodus 14, the faithful obedience of Israel is on display as God faithfully fulfills His promises (see Heb. 11:28–29).

The Passover

The tenth and final plague begins the climb to the Torah's redemptive crescendo. In Exodus 11 God pronounces judgment upon Egypt, namely through the slaying of all firstborns in the land. God then gives the specifics of the final plague to Moses in three sections in chapters 12 and 13. He describes how Israel is to observe the first Passover in Egypt (12:1–13), how His people are to observe it throughout their future generations (12:14–20; 13:1–16), and who is to observe it (12:42–49). Moses then relays God's instructions to Israel (12:21–27), and we see the event unfold as God has described (12:28–41).

---

12. Walter C. Kaiser, "לָקַח," *Theological Wordbook of the Old Testament*, 1:1125.
13. Douglas K. Stuart, *Exodus*, , New American Commentary (Nashville: B&H, 2006), 2:172.
14. See note on Exodus 6:6–7 in Scherman, *The Chumash*, 319.

The Israelites are to choose a one-year-old, unblemished male lamb, bring it into their homes to examine it from the tenth day to the fourteenth day of the first month. When twilight on the fourteenth comes, each household will sacrifice their lamb, take its blood in a basin, dip hyssop into the blood, and apply the blood to the lintel and two doorposts of their home, remaining inside the home for the remainder of the night. They will roast the entire lamb and eat it in haste, with unleavened bread and bitter herbs, burning whatever remains the following morning.

This is Israel's moment of truth. All of the promises of deliverance for God's people are narrowing down to this moment. The blood of the Passover lamb is the hinge upon which their fulfillment turns. They have received the instructions; now the people have to exercise their faith that God will come through. By faith they have to examine and slay the lamb. By faith they have to take its blood and put it on their doors. By faith they have to wait upon the Lord. The blood stands as a testimony to their faith in God's redemptive promise and power.

That night the destroyer slays the firstborn of every human and beast in Egypt. When it comes to the homes marked by the blood of the lamb, God promises to "pass over" (פָּסַח, *pasach*) those homes. This verbal form of the noun פֶּסַח, *pesach*, where we get the name "Passover," appears only four times with this sense in the Tanakh (Exod. 12:13, 23, 27; Isa. 31:5). Elsewhere, it can be translated as "to have compassion," "to protect," "to skip over," or "to hedge, straddle." Some scholars suggest a more protective nuance in these passages and see God as protecting the entrances of the homes, not allowing the destroyer to enter.[15] A passage like Exodus 12:23 makes more sense then, as it reads:

> For when the Lord goes through to smite the Egyptians, He will see the blood
> on the lintel and the two doorposts, and the Lord will *protect* the door and not
> let the Destroyer enter and smite your home.[16] (emphasis added)

This view ultimately puts God in a more active position as defender. Rather than skipping over and passing homes by, He is instead standing between the plague and the faithful, between the judgment and the redeemed, with the shed blood serving as the basis for His sparing the firstborn males of that home. This is why we believe that the blood of the lamb is a prophetic portrait or type of the "Lamb of God" to come.

The next morning Pharaoh arises and expels Moses and Israel from Egypt. The first three Exodus 6 promises have been fulfilled. Israel's redemptive price is paid with the blood of the lamb. She is released from bondage, and promptly departs that land, with Joseph's bones in tow, plundering the Egyptians of silver and gold as she leaves.

---

15. Baruch A. Levine, *Leviticus*, JPS Torah Commentary (Philadelphia: Jewish Publication Society, 1989), 156; Mark F. Rooker, *Leviticus*, New American Commentary (Nashville: Broadman & Holman, 2000), 3A:285.
16. Translation quoted from Levine, *Leviticus*, 285.

As Israel departs Egypt, Pharaoh's heart is hardened and he pursues Israel with the intent to enslave the people once again. God leads Israel to the Red Sea, protecting and guiding His people with the pillar of cloud by day and fire by night. The Egyptian army draws closer to the seemingly vulnerable Israelites, when God steps in and executes one final act of judgment and deliverance. As Pharaoh and the Egyptian army are held at bay by the pillar of fire, God miraculously parts the Red Sea, allowing Israel to cross over on dry ground. Pharaoh gives chase through the sea, the waters envelop the army of Egyptians, and the people of Israel watch their former oppressors finally defeated as their corpses are washed upon the shore.[17] Israel rejoices greatly as the people enjoy their first taste of freedom and nationhood.

PASSOVER IN THE TORAH BEYOND THE EXODUS

The Passover and Exodus have become a reference point in the nation's history and identity throughout the rest of the Torah. Often when specific commandments are given in Exodus, Leviticus, Numbers, and Deuteronomy, God is referred to with a qualifying reference to how He has brought Israel out of Egypt.[18] These books also chronicle the development of the annual memorial celebration of the Passover. Specific guidelines for when, where, and how to observe the Passover are laid out and warrant further attention as they impact much of what we read in the rest of Scripture.

Passover in Leviticus

Leviticus 23 lays out the annual cycle of God's appointed times that the people of Israel are to observe throughout their generations. The list of these appointed times includes the weekly Sabbath, followed by four specific celebrations in the spring and three in the fall. Passover is the first of these annual feasts mentioned. Leviticus 23:4–8 reads:

> These are the appointed times of the LORD, holy convocations which you shall proclaim at the times appointed for them. In the first month, on the fourteenth day of the month at twilight is the LORD's Passover. Then on the fifteenth day of the same month there is the Feast of Unleavened Bread to the LORD; for seven days you shall eat unleavened bread. On the first day you shall have a holy convocation; you shall not do any laborious work. But for seven days you shall present an offering by fire to the LORD. On the seventh day is a holy convocation; you shall not do any laborious work.

---

17. While Exodus 14:28 does not explicitly mention whether or not Pharaoh himself was in the sea, Psalm 136:15a suggests that he may have been. It states, "But he overthrew Pharaoh and his army in the Red Sea."
18. See Exodus 16:6; 18:1; 20:2; 29:46; 32:11; Leviticus 11:45; 19:36; 22:33; 25:38; 26:13; Numbers 15:41; 20:16; 21:5; 23:22; 24:8; Deuteronomy 4:20; 5:6, 15; 6:12; 7:18–19; 8:14; 9:26; 13:5, 10; 16:1; 20:1; 26:8; and 29:25.

With the central elements of the lamb and unleavened bread both commemorating the Passover event in Egypt, there is some uncertainty as to whether or not the Passover and Feast of Unleavened Bread refer to two separate appointed times or if they refer to the same appointed time. They seem to be held as distinct in Leviticus 23:4–8. However, many scholars view them as distinct celebrations that are joined together and used interchangeably very early on.[19] One Jewish view sees more of a grammatical distinction and suggests that the term "Passover" refers to the specific offering and the "Feast of Unleavened Bread" to the appointed time itself.[20] The Passover sacrifice will be offered at twilight on the fourteenth, which in Jewish tradition is somewhere between 3:00 and 3:30 P.M. (m. Pesaḥ. 5:1), and then prepared and eaten during the festive meal that follows as the evening of the fifteenth is ushered in. The earliest portions of Scripture show more of a distinction between the two, while they are clearly merged in Deuteronomy and consistently referred in this way afterwards.[21]

This helps us better understand the place of Passover in the shaping of Israel's national worship, as the first and seventh days will be Sabbaths marked by holy gatherings, with Israel making daily burnt offerings during that time. Also, each of these appointed times has both a material and spiritual significance. The feasts are tied to the various agricultural harvest times when Israel will offer the best fruits, produce, and livestock and thank God for providing for them.

The celebration during these eight days highlights some of the great themes of Scripture, including sanctification, repentance, atonement, and God's presence with His people. Through these appointed times the nation will gather together to honor God for His bountiful spiritual and material provision, making the connection between Israel's relationship with God and the bounty produced by the Promised Land.

---

19. Rooker, *Leviticus*, 285. On the separateness of the two festivals, see J. Licht, s.v. *"pesaḥ,"* in *'Entsiklopediah Mikra'it* (Jerusalem: Mosad Bialik, 1950–88), 6:523–24; A. Rofé, *Mavo' le-sefer Devarim* (Jerusalem: Akademon, 1988), 38–40; Nahum M. Sarna, *Exodus*, JPS Torah Commentary (Philadelphia: Jewish Publication Society, 1991), at 12:14–20 (p. 57). For examples of how the two were used interchangeably by the time of the New Testament, see Luke 22:1, 7, and Mark 14:12.

20. For comments on the traditional Jewish view, see Levine, *Leviticus*, 156. The ArtScroll translation of Leviticus 23:5–6 (Scherman, *The Chumash*) is also informative of this view. It reads, "In the first month on the fourteenth of the month in the afternoon is the time of the pesach-offering to Hashem. And on the fifteenth day of this month is the Festival of Matzos to Hashem; you shall eat matzos for a seven-day period."

21. For specific mentions of Passover and Unleavened Bread in the Old Testament, see Exodus 12:1–13, 14–20, 21–28, 40–51; 13:3–10; Leviticus 23:5–8; Numbers 28:16–23; Deuteronomy 16:1–7; Ezekiel 45:21; Ezra 6:20–22; 2 Chronicles 30:2–15; and 35:17. A case could be made that the command in Exodus 12:14 for Israel to celebrate the Passover as a "feast" (חג, *chag*) shows the intent to combine them from the inception, due to the limited use of this term when paired with specific appointed times. Normally, in the Passover context only Unleavened Bread is designated as a feast. They become more clearly fused beginning in the Leviticus 23 portion. See Jacob Milgrom, *Numbers*, JPS Torah Commentary (Philadelphia: Jewish Publication Society, 1990), 371.

These appointed times contain prophetic significance as well, and we find major events take place on or around them in the New Testament. Yeshua's death, burial, and resurrection all take place in relation to the Passover, Unleavened Bread, and the Feast of First Fruits. The outpouring of the Holy Spirit occurs during the Feast of Shavuot (Pentecost). In the context of Leviticus 23, Passover is the first of the annual appointed times. It reminds the children of Israel of their deliverance from Egypt and points forward to ultimate deliverance from sin through Yeshua, "our Passover" (1 Cor. 5:7).

Passover in Numbers

Interestingly, Numbers 9:1–14 records the Torah's only mention of Israel's observance of the Passover beyond Egypt. This section also mentions an added measure of grace for those who are ritually unclean and unable to observe the Passover at the prescribed time. Instead of observing it on the fourteenth of the first month, they will celebrate it on the fourteenth of the second month. This tradition became known as *Pesach Sheni* (Second Passover), and we see it observed in the Bible only during the time of Hezekiah (2 Chron. 30:1–27). It's also important to note that this exception only applies to the Passover sacrifice on the fourteenth and not to the observance of the weeklong Feast of Unleavened Bread, which is probably the strongest biblical evidence that shows the two as distinct.[22] They are otherwise viewed as one and the same.

Later in Numbers 28–29, specific details are provided for how Israel is to offer particular sacrifices at the various prescribed times. These include the regular daily, the weekly Sabbath, the monthly New Moon, and the different annual festival sacrifices. The daily burnt offerings to be offered during the seven days of Passover, as mentioned in Leviticus 23:8, are expanded upon in Numbers 28:16–25. Each day two bulls, one ram, and seven male lambs will be offered as whole burnt offerings (עֹלָה, *'olah*), along with their accompanying grain offerings. Unlike the Passover lamb offered on the fourteenth, these burnt offerings are not to be eaten by the priests or the people.

The people will also offer one goat as a sin offering (חַטָּאת, *chatta't*) to make atonement (Num. 28:22), which is eaten by the priests only. This atoning sin offering is most likely meant to assure the ritual purity of the people as they worship, and is distinct from the Passover lamb offered on the fourteenth.[23] According to Numbers 29:39, these special festival sacrifices are in addition to the daily votive, freewill, burnt, grain, drink, and peace offerings. These festival sacrifices serve as the basis for the Rabbinic tradition developed later regarding the *hagigah* sacrifice, referring to the one Lamb offered for the entire nation.[24]

---

22. Milgrom, *Numbers*, 371.
23. Milgrom, *Numbers*, 242.
24. See chapter 10, "Passover in Rabbinic Writings," by Zhava Glaser; see also Joseph Tabory, *JPS Commentary on the Haggadah: Historical Introduction, Translation, and Commentary* (Philadelphia: Jewish Publication Society, 2008), 9–10.

Passover in Deuteronomy

In Deuteronomy 16:1–17, we find three components of Passover addressed: (1) the sacrifices offered during Passover and Unleavened Bread; (2) the specific location where the nation will offer these sacrifices; and (3) that Passover will be one of the three pilgrim feasts, along with *Shavuot* (Weeks) and *Sukkot* (Tabernacles). Each of these demonstrates how the Passover became more of a national celebration as Israel entered the Land.

The sacrifices mentioned in 16:1–4 use wording that is unique compared to the previous passages under discussion. Here the Passover offering is to be taken "from the flock and the herd" (v. 2), which will include sheep, goats, and oxen. The Passover offering is also the object referred to in verse 3, where the text states that "seven days you shall eat with it unleavened bread." This implies that the Passover would be eaten for seven days. If the Passover offering is to be a sheep or goat (Exod. 12:5), and offered only on the fourteenth and completely consumed before the next morning (Exod. 12:10; Deut. 16:4), then how do we reconcile what's stated here in Deuteronomy? There is no clear answer other than suggesting that the word "Passover" is being used as a general umbrella term under which all of the special festival and daily sacrifices fall, including the burnt offerings and peace offerings mentioned in Numbers 28–29.[25]

This portion also mandates that Israel celebrate and offer the Passover at a specific location. Here it is designated as the place where the LORD your God chooses to establish His name. This phrase is used a number of times in Deuteronomy (12:5; 14:23; 16:2, 6, 11; 26:2), looking ahead to Israel's conquest and settlement of the Land when worship will be centralized in one location. Clearly Jerusalem is in view, as 2 Chronicles 12:13 states later, since the Tabernacle and Temple will be located there. In that place God's presence will be manifest as he draws near to the people and they draw near to Him.

Finally, in Deuteronomy 16:16–17 we see that Passover is one of the three pilgrim feasts, along with Shavuot and Sukkot, when all the males are to go up to Jerusalem to bring their offerings, not coming "empty-handed":

> Three times in a year all your males shall appear before the LORD your God in the place which He chooses, at the Feast of Unleavened Bread and at the Feast of Weeks and at the Feast of Booths, and they shall not appear before the LORD empty-handed. Every man shall give as he is able, according to the blessing of the LORD your God which He has given you.

There are a number of similarities between the Deuteronomy 16 passage and Exodus 23:14–19 and 34:18–25. Looking at all three sections together we learn that Israel is to eat unleavened bread for seven days to remember the Exodus from Egypt (Exod. 23:15; 34:18; Deut. 16:3), offer the blood of the

---

25. This explanation may also help in interpreting John 18:28. See chapter 5, "Passover in the Gospel of John," by Mitch Glaser.

sacrifice without unleavened bread and leave none of its fat overnight (Exod. 23:18; 34:25; Deut. 16:4), and rest on the seventh day (Exod. 34:21; Deut. 16:8). Only Exodus 34:19–20 contains the additional command to redeem the firstborn of every womb, memorializing the tenth plague.

Perhaps the most important point here is that Passover/Unleavened Bread, Shavuot, and Sukkot are each designated with the word usually translated "feast" (חג, *chag*), but more is literally "pilgrimage." This designation, which is also used for only these three appointed times in Leviticus 23, implies an actual journey that a worshipper takes to a specific cultic site.[26] With the command in each section not to come empty-handed, and cast in the context of Deuteronomy, these three pilgrim feasts portray God as Israel's sovereign King, and the pilgrim Israelite males as His humble servants visiting His residence to pay homage.[27] That Passover is included as one of these pilgrimages at such an early stage in Israel's covenant history again emphasizes how the focus of Passover observance shifted from individual homes to a national celebration in Jerusalem as time went on.

PASSOVER AND REDEMPTION IN THE TORAH

This "great deliverance" of Israel from Egypt is a blueprint for how God redeems His people throughout Scripture. In this section we will briefly look at how the pattern found in the Torah is fulfilled for individual believers in Yeshua today, and even points to the final redemption of the nation of Israel in the future.

Personal Redemption through Yeshua

God has used the shed blood of the spotless lamb to purchase and regain ownership of the enslaved Israelites, as their true owner. It is precisely this pattern that is followed in the New Testament. Yeshua, God's only begotten Son, bursts onto the scene to pay the necessary redemptive price with His own blood, and to proclaim liberty and set free those enslaved to sin—transferring them from the kingdom of darkness into His kingdom. The sacrificial death of Yeshua is brimming with Passover connections. John declares that Yeshua is the "Lamb of God who takes away the sin of the world" (John 1:29). The death, burial, and resurrection of Yeshua all took place during the Passover / Unleavened Bread week.[28] And Paul boldly declares, "The Messiah, our Passover Lamb, has already been sacrificed" (1 Cor. 5:7 MSG).

The entire New Testament portrayal of Yeshua's sacrifice also seems to follow the pattern of the four promises from Exodus 6:6–7 outlined above.

---

26.   Levine, *Leviticus*, 156.
27.   Jeffrey H. Tigay, *Deuteronomy*, JPS Torah Commentary (Philadelphia: Jewish Publication Society, 1996), 159.
28.   For further details on Yeshua's death during the Feasts of Passover / Unleavened Bread, see chapter 4, "Passover in the Gospel of Luke," by Darrell L. Bock, and chapter 5, "Passover in the Gospel of John," by Mitch Glaser.

Through Yeshua, God sets His people free from slavery to sin, brings His people out from under the burdens of sin, and pays the redemptive price for sin. Even the later promise from Exodus 6:8 of God taking His people to Himself and bringing them into the Promised Land serve as a template for the experience of the New Covenant believer as we are His possession as well, being guided toward our promised inheritance (Eph. 1:14).[29]

Israel's National Redemption through Yeshua

There is a method of Bible interpretation known as *typology*, or pattern fulfillment. It suggests that Old Testament ideas, events, objects, or people serve as a pattern for a greater fulfillment that comes later in God's redemptive history.

It appears that Israel's national redemption at Passover may serve as a type for both the redemption experienced by believers and also for Israel's future national redemption through Yeshua. Crucial to this suggestion is viewing the Joseph narrative in Genesis and Passover narrative in Exodus as bound together in one continuous narrative that holistically points to the larger redemption achieved through the Messiah. We can trace the events from Joseph through the Passover and compare them to the Messianic ministry of Yeshua to help flesh out this idea.

Both Jewish and Christian sources view Joseph as a type of the Messiah. While the New Testament does not explicitly refer to Joseph as a type, many Christian sources point out the numerous parallels between Joseph and Yeshua, highlighted by God's use of the suffering of each to achieve His purposes.[30] In Jewish thought, the concept of the *Mashiach ben Yosef* (Messiah son of Joseph) took shape during the Talmudic era, between 200 and 500 C.E. In rabbinic theology, this Messianic figure is believed to suffer and die in the eschatological battle between the people of Israel and their enemies, only to be resurrected by the kingly messiah figure, *Mashiach ben David* (Messiah son of David), at the inauguration of the Messianic age (b. Sukkah 52a). In both views, Joseph serves as a suffering-servant-type figure.

With this in mind, we can highlight some key points in the Joseph and Exodus narratives. First, Joseph is rejected by his brothers because of his prophetic dreams that foretell his exaltation and their submission to him. As a result, he suffers greatly but rises to prominence due to God's sovereign hand working to preserve life, to preserve a remnant, and to bring about a great deliverance (Gen. 45:5, 7; 50:20, 24–25). The rejection of Joseph ultimately results in God's covenant people leaving the Promised

---

29.   I suggest that going through the waters of baptism relate to, and, in a way, reenact the crossing of the Red Sea (1 Cor. 10:2); and the parallels between the giving of the Torah at Sinai and the giving of the Spirit in Acts 2 are too many to mention here, but they reinforce the similarities shared by those redeemed by the lamb in Egypt and those redeemed by Yeshua.

30.   For example, see comments in K. A. Mathews, *Genesis 11:27–50:26*, outline section XII, "Jacob's Family: Joseph and His Brothers (37:2–50:26)."

Land and residing in a foreign land for more than 400 years. As mentioned above, with his dying words Joseph utters a statement of prophetic hope and promise for Israel. The chosen people will not remain in Egypt, but instead God will reverse their exile. Through the Passover, Israel experiences a national redemption and deliverance. Israel is freed from slavery and brought back to the Promised Land.

There are striking similarities between this outline and the outworking of the New Covenant through Messiah's two comings. Like Joseph, Yeshua is beloved by the Father. Just as Joseph is rejected by his brothers because of his exalted role,[31] Yeshua goes to His own and His own do not receive Him, instead rejecting His claim to be Messiah (John 1:11; Mark 14:62). In John 15:25, Yeshua describes this rejection as "baseless hatred," claiming that it fulfills what is written in Psalm 69:4 (verse 5 in the Hebrew Bible).

Just as he has done with Joseph, God has sovereignly used the suffering of Yeshua to bring blessings and life (Acts 4:17). And just as Israel's leaving the Promised Land is somehow related to Joseph's rejection by his brothers and the redemptive role he eventually plays in Egypt, so the nation of Israel has experienced exile from the Promised Land as a result of their leadership's rejection of the Messiah Yeshua.[32] Within a generation of Yeshua's rejection by Israel's leadership, the Second Temple was destroyed in 70 c.e., and the Jewish people were dispersed as the Romans leveled Jerusalem in 135 c.e. Interestingly, one of the primary reasons given by Rabbinic sources to explain this expulsion of the Jewish people from Israel is the "baseless hatred" each man had for his neighbor (see b. Yoma 9b). There is truth in that statement, as evidenced by the many factions of Jewish people during the Second Temple period. Further the Jewish leaders were guilty of a far greater *baseless hatred* of the one who claimed to be the promised Messiah.

Thankfully, for the past two thousand years God has not left Israel without hope. Just as Joseph transmitted words of hope about a visit from God and a great deliverance for His people, so too there are a number of words of hope for the nation of Israel in the New Testament beyond their rejection of Messiah. In Matthew 23:37–39 (cf. Luke. 13:34–35), Yeshua asserts that Jerusalem will see Him again when she greets Him with blessings. In Acts 3:19–21, Peter looks forward to the return of Yeshua and the full restoration of all things as God told through the holy prophets of old, a reality that includes the fulfillment of all of Israel's national promises. And in Romans 11:25–27, Paul clearly speaks of the future redemption that the nation of Israel will experience at the return of Yeshua.

Joseph's words of hope find fulfillment through the blood of the lamb at Passover as Israel is set free from Egypt and brought back to the Promised Land. The New Testament's words of hope will find fulfillment through the blood of

---

31. Sailhamer notes that Joseph's brothers rejected him specifically because they despised his dreams, which cast them as bowing down to Joseph. See Sailhamer, "Genesis," 274.
32. Michael L. Brown, *The Real Kosher Jesus* (Lake Mary, FL: FrontLine, 2012), 55.

Yeshua our Passover Lamb when the nation of Israel returns to the Land and is redeemed by His blood (Deut. 30:1–10; Ezek. 37:1–14; Rom. 11:25–27). This includes the redemption already provided through Yeshua in the first coming, characterized by many nations experiencing the blessings of the New Covenant, and it will find its completion when God visits once again to release the nation of Israel from bondage to sin at the second coming of Messiah. God will once again use what was meant for evil to bring about a great deliverance for Israel.

Joseph	Yeshua
Beloved by his father (Gen. 37:3–4)	Beloved by the Father (Matt. 3:17)
Rejected by his brothers (Gen. 37:18–35)	Rejected by His own (Luke 19:14; John 1:11; 15:24–25)
Suffering yields preservation of life for nations (Egyptians, Israelites, etc.) (Gen. 45:5, 7; 50:20, 24–25)	Suffering yields life for nations (John 3:16; Rom. 11:11–12, 15)
Suffering yields preservation of remnant of Hebrew people (Gen. 45:5, 7; 50:20, 24–25), albeit exiled from Promised Land	Suffering yields preservation of remnant of Jewish believers (Rom. 11:5), albeit exiled from Promised Land
Suffering sets the stage for great deliverance for nation of Israel, and visit from God (Gen. 45:5, 7; 50:20, 24–25)	Suffering sets the stage for future great deliverance for nation of Israel, through return visit from God (Matt. 23:37–39; Acts 3:19–21; Rom. 11:25–27)
Israel's national redemption through the Passover (Exod. 12–13)	Israel's national redemption through Yeshua "our Passover" (Rom. 11:25–27)

CONCLUSION

The Passover is the fundamental act that defines the very meaning of redemption in the Torah. It is the story of how God sets His people free from slavery and bondage, how He reacquires that which is His, and how He brings His people to Himself to enjoy a close covenant relationship. As members of the New Covenant, we have much to consider when we read, study, and celebrate the Passover. Not only are we looking back to this event as a remembrance of what God did for Israel in the past, and what God has done for us through Yeshua, but we are also rehearsing what God will do at the Messiah's return. We are looking ahead to that glorious moment when the nation of Israel, that for so long has rejected the Messiah, will experience its ultimate release from sin, slavery, and death.

The Passover as described in the Torah has become the pattern whereby all of Israel will understand the meaning of redemption. The national redemption of the Jewish people from Egyptian bondage looks forward to a greater redemption that has come through the sacrifice of the Lamb of God, who takes away the sin of the world. Therefore, the entirety of the Exodus may be viewed as a type of what was to come and has now come to be. The Exodus and the Passover are the redemptive reference point for the Jewish people throughout the ages and are even viewed in this way by the Messiah Himself in the Gospels.

Our journey continues as we now turn to the historical books of the Old Testament, the *Ketuvim*, or the Writings, and we shall look at the way the Passover is observed in this great section of Scripture.

2
PASSOVER IN THE WRITINGS

RICHARD H. FLASHMAN

The Ketuvim, or the Writings, are part of the Tanakh, or Hebrew Bible (otherwise known as the Old Testament canon), and mostly are written in Hebrew. The title *Tanakh* is an acronym of the letters for the traditional subdivisions of the Masoretic Text: Torah (תּוֹרָה, the Five Books of Moses), Nevi'im (נְבִיאִים, the Eight Books of the Prophets), and Ketuvim (כְּתוּבִים, the Eleven Books of the Writings)—hence *TaNaKh*, twenty-four books in all. The Writings, the final subdivision of the Tanakh, consist of eleven books grouped as follows: the Poetic Books (known as *Sifrei Emet*[1]), including Psalms, Proverbs, and Job; the Five Scrolls (*Hamesh Megillot*) consisting of the Song of Songs, Ruth, Lamentations, Ecclesiastes, and Esther; the remaining books are Daniel, Ezra–Nehemiah (which are one book in the Hebrew Bible), and Chronicles.

The Torah (the Law) is the preeminent section of the Hebrew Bible for most religious Jewish people, yet the Ketuvim is also regarded as divinely inspired and as such is a legitimate source of authority in traditional Judaism. While the Torah tells the story of the first Passover, the Ketuvim unfolds the impact the Passover event has on succeeding generations of Jewish people in the biblical story. Specifically, the Ketuvim reveals the influence the Exodus and the first Passover had on Jewish life and religious practice throughout the Old Testament era.

THE CELEBRATION OF PASSOVER IN THE KETUVIM: CHRONICLES AND EZRA

There are just three instances noted in the Ketuvim when Passover is celebrated. The first is during the reign of King Hezekiah in approximately 725 B.C.E. The next celebration is led by King Josiah in 622 B.C.E. The third is led circa 515 B.C.E. by religious leaders of exiles who have returned to Judah

---

1. *Sifrei Emet* is an acronym of the Hebrew titles for the Poetic Books: תְּהִלִּים, Tehillim (Psalms), מִשְׁלֵי, Mishlei (Proverbs), אִיּוֹב, 'Iyyob (Job), which spells the Hebrew word for "firmness, faithfulness, truth" (אֱמֶת, *emet*).

from Babylon. These celebrations are usually responses to some type of major event in the story of the Jewish people.

Hezekiah's celebration occurs in the context of his purification of the Temple after the many years of political and spiritual neglect by his father, King Ahaz. Josiah's celebration is initiated by Josiah's response to the apostasy of his father, King Amon. Josiah begins seeking God, purging idolatry from the Southern Kingdom of Judah, and repairing the Temple. In the process, Hilkiah the priest discovers the lost Book of the Law, and with Josiah's encouragement the people keep the Passover in obedience to God's command. Finally, the returning exiles celebrate the Passover after completing the Second Temple circa 515 B.C.E., some seventy years after the Babylonians destroy it.

Hezekiah Celebrates the Passover (2 Chron. 30:1–31:1)

The nation endured disaster during the reign of Ahaz. In sixteen years, he brings the nation to the brink of ruin. Had it not been for the Lord's intervention through the prophet Oded, all might have been lost (2 Chron. 28:9–15).

Ahaz's reign fails miserably, and at his inglorious death his body is not even buried in the royal tombs of Judah's kings. When King Hezekiah comes to power at twenty-five years old, he recognizes his father's failures and leads a renewal movement within Judah. He methodically repairs the Temple, beginning with its doors, and by the sixteenth day, the Temple is restored, repaired, and consecrated. Immediately Hezekiah offers sacrifices for the kingdom, the sanctuary, Judah, and for all Israel (2 Chron. 29:20–24). He reestablishes Temple worship, enlisting singers, musicians, and the use of trumpets. The people rejoice at what God had done and at the miraculous speed with which it has happened.

Hezekiah is also determined to celebrate the Passover, despite the fact that the proper date of observance, beginning at twilight of the fourteenth day of Nisan, has passed. Yet Hezekiah is so zealous for the Lord that he does not want to wait a full year to celebrate this vital remembrance of Israel's redemption. So he celebrates Passover in the second month of the Jewish calendar, the month of Iyyar, on the date given in Numbers 9:10–11 for extenuating circumstances. In that passage, the Lord permits those who are not ceremonially clean for a legitimate reason (e.g., touching a dead body or being away on a distant journey) to celebrate the Passover on the fourteenth day of the second month beginning at twilight. Hezekiah utilizes this Mosaic exception and applies it to his contemporary situation. He then moves forward with the celebration by inviting all Israel and Judah, from Beersheba to Dan, for the Passover celebration in Jerusalem.

Hezekiah's Passover proclamation is met with derision in some quarters of the Northern Kingdom of Israel (2 Chron. 30:10). Yet "some men of Asher, Manasseh and Zebulun humbled themselves and came to Jerusalem" (v. 11), thereby admitting that Jerusalem was the proper place to worship the Lord.

The people of Judah come *en masse* to Jerusalem for the feast. After the removal of Ahaz's pagan incense altars in the Kidron Valley, the Passover lambs are slaughtered on 14 Iyyar, as allowed by the Lord according to Moses in Numbers 9:9–13.

> Then the LORD spoke to Moses, saying, "Speak to the sons of Israel, saying, 'If any one of you or of your generations becomes unclean because of a dead person, or is on a distant journey, he may, however, observe the Passover to the LORD. In the second month on the fourteenth day at twilight, they shall observe it; they shall eat it with unleavened bread and bitter herbs. They shall leave none of it until morning, nor break a bone of it; according to all the statute of the Passover they shall observe it. But the man who is clean and is not on a journey, and yet neglects to observe the Passover, that person shall then be cut off from his people, for he did not present the offering of the LORD at its appointed time. That man will bear his sin.

The zeal of the people puts the priests and Levites to shame, and they quickly consecrate themselves for Temple service (2 Chron. 30:15). However, in their zeal to eat the Passover, most of the men of the Northern Kingdom are unable to consecrate themselves, yet they still want to sacrifice the Passover lamb, which would be contrary to the Law of Moses to do in an unclean state (v. 17).

This creates a ceremonial crisis, and the Levites step in to sacrifice the lambs on behalf of the unconsecrated Israelites. Recognizing this unique situation, Hezekiah does not hesitate but cries out to the Lord, asking Him to look past the Israelites' violations of the sanctuary rules and pardon the men who are truly seeking after him. The Chronicler tells us that "the LORD heard Hezekiah and healed the people" (v. 20; cf. 7:14). In his magnificent grace, God "bends His own rules" on behalf of those who set their heart to seek God (2 Chron. 30:19). Hezekiah recognizes that the Lord sees the heart and that our motives and attitudes are most important to Him.

The Spirit of God is present with the worshippers for this great feast. They continue for seven full days and decide they will continue for seven more days, as the Lord is filling them with such great joy. The priests and Levites fulfill all their vital roles: singing, playing musical instruments, praising God, eating their assigned portions, and making the appropriate fellowship offerings each day. The whole assembly rejoices; nothing like it has been seen since the days of Solomon. God hears the prayers of the priests and Levites and all are blessed!

At the end of the fourteen days of celebration, a revival movement has begun and spreads throughout the land. Israelites from Ephraim, Manasseh, Issachar, and Zebulun are overcome with religious fervor and go out to the towns of Judah and Benjamin in the South and Ephraim and Manasseh in the North, destroying all evidence of paganism. Sacred stones are smashed, Asherah poles cut down, and the high places destroyed (2 Chron. 31:1).

Passover turns out to be a marvelous success—helping a godly king bring about extensive and profound spiritual revitalization to a people suffering for years under apostate leadership.

Josiah Celebrates the Passover (2 Chron. 35:1–19)

Josiah is also in the kingly line of Judah. Like Hezekiah, he takes the throne after the disastrous reign of his predecessors. His grandfather King Manasseh undoes most of Hezekiah's reforms, reestablishing the "detestable practices" of the Canaanites in Judah. In fact, the Chronicler tells us that Manasseh and the people of Judah do even more evil than the pagan nations the Lord has driven out of the land. Eventually, Manasseh is carried off into Assyrian exile where he repents of his evil rule.

God hears Manasseh's prayers and restores his kingdom, and he does all he can to reverse his evil influence on Judah and lead his people back to God. Unfortunately, his change of heart is too late to have an influence on his son Amon, who after Manasseh's death takes up his father's pre-repentant evil ways and reintroduces the idolatry and detestable practices of the Canaanites. He is soon assassinated and his eight-year-old son Josiah becomes king.

In the eighth year of his reign, when Josiah is sixteen years old, he begins to seek the God of his father David. At twenty years old, he purges the land of its pagan idols and practices. Six years later, in the eighteenth year of his reign, he turns his attention to the restoration of the Temple that the previous kings have allowed to fall into disrepair. During this massive restoration project, Hilkiah the High Priest finds "the book of the law of the LORD" that has been given to Israel through Moses (2 Chron. 34:14).[2] The book is quickly brought to King Josiah and read aloud in his presence.

The good king is overwhelmed. He tears his robes in contrition, humbles himself before God, and weeps, realizing that the people of Judah are unfaithful to the covenant God has made with them. Josiah has the Book of the Law read publicly at the Temple, and the king renews his commitment to the covenant[3] and to following the Lord and keep his commands with all his heart. The people follow Josiah and pledge themselves to the Lord as well (34:29–32).

Josiah cleanses the land of its idolatry, and the people of Judah serve the Lord all the days of Josiah's life. In light of all this, Josiah reinstates a biblically faithful celebration of the Passover in Jerusalem.

And what a magnificent Passover it is! Josiah is determined and able to celebrate the Festival properly and on the correct date, unlike the celebration under King Hezekiah (2 Chron. 30:15, 17–20).[4] The Levites are instructed by Josiah to bring the sacred ark back into the Temple[5] and consecrate themselves in order to serve the people by slaughtering the lambs.

King Josiah provides the Passover lambs himself. He gives 30,000 sheep and goats from his own flocks, and 3,000 cattle from his own herds.[6] The

---

2. The book discovered by Hilkiah the priest was, most likely, the book of Deuteronomy.

3. God will punish Judah, but not in Josiah's lifetime, because his heart is responsive to the Lord when he hears what is written in the book of the Law (2 Chon. 34:26–28). Once again, it must be understood that God is faithful to His covenant with Abraham and will ultimately give the Land and blessings to the Jewish people. However, He will also judge the Jewish people on the basis of the Mosaic covenant, which is conditional upon their obedience (Rom. 11:11–29; Zech. 12:10–13:1; Ezek. 36:22–37; Deut. 30:1–20).

4. The year of Josiah's celebration of the Passover is 622 B.C.E., 103 years after Hezekiah's celebration.

5. The ark of the covenant, after probably having been removed for safekeeping during the evil days of Amon, is now returned to the Temple for the priestly duties in preparation for the Passover.

6. As with Moses, David, Hezekiah, and others, Josiah's generosity inspires others to give as well (2 Chron.

Passover has not been observed with such great splendor since the days of Samuel the prophet (2 Chron. 35:18).[7] None of the kings of Judah, not even David and Solomon, has celebrated the Passover so faithfully. Josiah's celebration of Passover becomes the gold standard for Israel. He is a true son of David, an anointed one of God who sets the Temple in order (v. 20) and is arguably one of the greatest kings of Israel since David.

The Returning Exiles Celebrate the Passover (Ezra 6:19–21)

The consecrated priests and Levites lead the final celebration of the Passover in the Ketuvim for the exiles returning from the Babylonian captivity. Cyrus has issued a decree in 538 B.C.E. for the Jews to return to Israel and rebuild the Temple of God. The first exiles return to Jerusalem, led by their civil leader Zerubbabel, a descendant of David, and their high priest, Joshua.

They begin to build the altar of the Lord in the month of Tishri (September-October) 537 B.C.E., after about three months of being back in the land. They offer both morning and evening sacrifices immediately. Since it is Tishri, they soon celebrate the Feast of Tabernacles, offering all the prescribed sacrifices. They continue offering sacrifices for the next year at all the prescribed times, although the foundation for the Temple of the Lord has not yet been laid.

But in the second year of their return, 536 B.C.E., in the second month,[8] they begin the work of rebuilding the Temple of the Lord in Jerusalem (Ezra 3:8–9). They lay the foundation amidst great celebration, which could be heard far away (vv. 10–13). But after laying the foundation, opposition arises to the building of the Temple. The work is stopped for sixteen years. It is not until 520 B.C.E., through the civil leadership of Zerubbabel, the preaching of the prophets Haggai and Zechariah, and with the eventual permission of King Darius I (6:1–12) that the building of the Temple resumes.

On the third day of Adar (February-March), 516 B.C.E., about seventy years after the destruction of the First Temple, the Second Temple is completed. It is immediately dedicated to the Lord. Then, forty days later on the fourteenth day of the first month of Nisan (March-April), 515 B.C.E., the exiles celebrate the Passover. It is a great celebration! The people are earnest in seeking the Lord, separating themselves from the unclean practices of their pagan neighbors. The priests and Levites do their jobs faithfully. The people eat the Passover, and for the seven days following celebrate the Feast of Unleavened Bread. They are filled with joy, not only because their celebration of Passover has been restored, but because they have seen the miraculous hand

---

35:8–9). Some commentators have a hard time with the enormous size of Josiah's offering, thinking it unlikely for so many animals to be available for such a sacrifice. But with Josiah's advanced planning and the spirit of revival sweeping the entire nation, the numbers seem reasonable. In fact, they are insignificant compared to the 120,000 sheep and 22,000 cattle that Solomon offered to the Lord at the dedication of the Temple nearly 350 years earlier (1 Kings 8:63; cf. 2 Chron. 7:5).

7. Or perhaps earlier, "from the days of the judges who judged Israel" (2 Kings 23:22).

8. The month of Iyyar (later called Ziv), the same month that Solomon began to build the first Temple (1 Kings 6:1).

of God, the God of Israel, changing the heart of the pagan King Darius as he assists them in completing the Temple of the Lord (Ezra 6:21).

Once again Passover is commemorated as a memorial of God's deliverance over Israel's enemies. This time it is the opposition to the rebuilding of the Temple that has been overturned by the powerful hand of God. The Lord is still fighting for His people "with a mighty hand and an outstretched arm" (Deut. 26:8).

Clearly, it is the celebration of the Passover that demonstrates the faithfulness of God's people at critical times in their history. Celebrating the Passover becomes the vital expression that the people's hearts are now right with God. The religious and spiritual reformations under Hezekiah and Josiah are both crowned with the celebration of Passover. The returning exiles express their gratitude for the Lord's restoration of His people to the Land and for the rebuilding of the Temple. In humble acknowledgment of these miracles, they celebrate His Passover.

PASSOVER IN THE PSALMS

We will now briefly look at a few of these beautiful and poetic praises to the One who delivers His chosen people from bondage.

Psalm 77

One of the great Passover/Exodus psalms is Psalm 77, a lament describing the anguish of an Israelite worshipper struggling to remain faithful to the Lord in the midst of personal pain.[9]

The psalm begins with a cry for help (vv. 1–2), which causes the author to recall God's presence in former times (vv. 3–6), which is so typical of the Psalms—especially those of lamentation. The writer asks the question, "Will the Lord reject forever?" (v. 7).

The question leads the psalmist to remember the power of God and His mighty deeds of long ago. He realizes that the way out of despair is to meditate on the mighty deeds of God Most High (vv. 10–12). And so we must ask ourselves, what are the mighty deeds the psalmist recalls that give him comfort and confidence in the midst of great distress?

Clearly, the writer turns to the events of the Passover and the Exodus as his source of comfort and solace. He writes, "Your way, O God, is holy; what god is great like our God? You are the God who works wonders; you have made known Your strength among the peoples. You have by Your power redeemed Your people, the sons of Jacob and Joseph" (vv. 13–15).

The language of his recollection is unmistakable. It is the "outstretched arm" of God who says to his people "I will redeem you" (גָּאַל, ga'al) from Egyptian bondage (Exod. 6:6; cf. Deut. 7:8; 9:26). And it is that same mighty arm, which is available to him as one of "the sons of Jacob and Joseph" (Ps. 77:15), that "redeems" him from his current distress. The psalmist

---

9.   Willem A. VanGemeren, "Psalms" in *The Expositor's Bible Commentary* (Grand Rapids: Zondervan, 1991). 5:499.

is able to face great distress by remembering the deliverance of God that took place during the Passover.

Psalm 80

The same is true for the experience of the community as seen in Psalm 80. The setting for Psalm 80 seems to be the last years of the Northern Kingdom of Israel. The threat of Assyrian captivity is looming large.[10] Their situation was dire.

It is a threat felt in the Southern Kingdom of Judea as well, for if the North falls, then the South will be next. The psalmist calls out to God on behalf of the people of Israel: "You removed a vine from Egypt; You drove out the nations and planted it" (v. 8). The psalmist uses the vine/vineyard metaphor to comfort his distressed nation. He recalls God's goodness to Israel in rescuing them from Egyptian bondage and establishing them in the Promised Land as a great nation. His message to the reader is clear: the same God who has loved and rescued us before is willing and able to rescue and bless us in our current crisis.

The psalmist's lament to God is simple: Israel is "Your vine," You have uprooted us from a barren place (Egypt), through the Passover/Exodus event, and then replanted us in Canaan, a fertile Land of Promise, and made us fruitful. How can You abandon us now to Assyria? Return to us, restore us, rescue us and we will be fruitful once again. We are the root You planted!

Then the metaphor changes and he writes, we are "the son whom You have strengthened for Yourself" (v. 15). Like Moses (Exod. 32:11–14), the psalmist appeals to Passover and the covenant relationship God established with His chosen people. Yet, unlike Moses' appeal at the first Passover, the petition to save the Northern Kingdom from the Assyrians will be denied for God's greater purposes. The God of redemption is also the God of justice and judgment on a rebellious people.

The Jewish people will need a greater Passover to be restored once and for all. The psalmist seems to grasp that: "Let Your hand be upon the man of Your right hand, upon the son of man whom You made strong for Yourself" (Ps. 80:17). But it will come too late for the rescue of the Northern Kingdom at this time.

Psalm 105

The psalmist praises God in Psalm 105 as the "Lord of history."[11] He is described as faithful to the covenant he made with Abraham to make his descendants a great nation (v. 42). The writer recounts the providential care of God by focusing on the Passover/Exodus event in detail (vv. 24–41).

---

10. For evidence of an imminent threat from Assyria, see the prayer for God's mercy on Israel, Joseph, Ephraim, Benjamin, and Manasseh (Ps. 80:1–3), and the LXX's historical superscription "concerning the Assyrian" (VanGemeren, "Psalms," 523–24).

11. Claus Westermann, *The Psalms: Structure, Content and Message* (Minneapolis: Augsburg, 1980), 26.

God is viewed in this psalm as having providentially protected His people during the Passover and in keeping the covenant he made with Abraham. Israel is exhorted to give thanks and make known to the nations the good works He has done and to sing praises, glory in His holy name, look to Him, seek His face, and remember the wonders He has done and the judgments He has pronounced (vv. 1–6).

Once again we are reminded of what God did for Israel through the Passover and that therefore Israel should remain faithful to the Lord. He was faithful to Israel through the redemption He accomplished at the first Passover, and so we should be faithful to Him by keeping His statutes and commandments (vv. 43–45).

Psalms 135–136

Similar themes are repeated in Psalms 135 and 136. In Psalm 135, a hymn of descriptive praise, the people of Israel, through their ministers, are exhorted to "praise the LORD" (vv. 1–4) and "bless the LORD" (vv. 19–21) because of God's mighty acts of redemption on their behalf.

Pharaoh had held Israel captive and enslaved in Egypt. But like a mighty warrior, the Lord "smote," or struck down, the firstborn of Egypt with the sign and wonder of a terrible plague (vv. 8–9). Nations opposed Israel as they made their way into the Promised Land, so the Lord struck down those nations as well (vv. 10–11). The Passover teaches us that the Lord fights for His people. Why? Because we are His chosen people and His treasured possession (v. 4), and He will "judge His people" with the sense of vindicating them (v. 14).

In Psalm 135, the Passover/Exodus event serves as the irrefutable proof of the Lord's goodness, sovereignty, greatness, and His covenantal faithfulness to His people (vv. 3–6).

Again, a similar theme emerges in Psalm 136, a psalm known in Jewish tradition as the "Great *Hallel*" (הַלֵּל, "praise"). The reader is exhorted to give thanks to God (vv. 1–3) for His great works in creation (vv. 4–9) and redemption of His people Israel through the Passover (vv. 10–22). Israel must remember to thank God not only in times of distress, but at all times, because "His lovingkindness is everlasting," mentioned by the psalmist twenty-six times.

Psalm 81

In Psalm 81, the reader is exhorted to worship God because He has defeated Egypt on behalf of His people (v. 5). He has set them free from their hard labor (v. 6) and rescued them (v. 7a), but they still rebelled (v. 7b). They have worshipped Him at first but then bowed down to alien gods. They have slipped into idolatry and apostasy, even claiming a "calf idol" has rescued them (Exod. 32:4). He is the God of the Passover; He has brought them out of Egypt (Ps. 80:10), and the people of Israel should have worshipped and obeyed Him. He deserves our loyalty (vv. 11–13).

The Egyptian Hallel *(Psalms 113–118)*

Psalms 113–118 are known as the "*Hallel*," or more specifically the "Egyptian *Hallel*." They are psalms of joyful thanksgiving for the redemption the Lord has provided for His people Israel. These songs of thanksgiving are sung in the synagogue at many Jewish celebrations including Sukkot, Hanukkah, Shavuot, Israel Independence Day, and most importantly for our purposes, on the first day of Passover.

These psalms are also an important part of the Passover Seder. At the Seder the *Hallel* is recited in two parts: Psalms 113–114 before the meal, and Psalms 115–118 after the meal. In the Talmud, various origins for the chanting of the *Hallel* at Passover have been claimed. Some commentators say it started with Moses and the people of Israel. Others say it was the prophets who instituted the *Hallel*. But the Talmud does tell us with more certainty that it was recited by the Levites in the Temple (t. Pesahim 95b), and it was also chanted on Passover Eve while the Pascal lambs were being slaughtered (m. Pesahim 5:7).[12]

It became part of the synagogue service at an early stage and in the talmudic period, after the destruction of the Second Temple in c.e. 70, it was added to the end of the evening service for Passover. Only the "half" *Hallel* is recited during the six subsequent days of the Passover and on the New Moon.[13] Some say it's out of sadness for the fate of the Egyptians, others because the sacrifice did not vary in those days.

It is not difficult to see why this section of sacred worship has been added to the Passover remembrance. Rich with the themes of rescue, redemption, and Messianic expectation, it serves as an appropriate and joyful expression and exclamation point to the holy day. If the Hallel psalms were sung in Yeshua's day at Passover, it is likely that the last song Yeshua sang on earth was Psalm 118 (Matt. 26:30, Mark 14:26). "Give thanks to the LORD, for He is good, for His lovingkindness is everlasting" (Ps. 118:29). And with that, Yeshua turned to face the horror and abandonment of the cross. Hallelujah, what a Savior!

A Psalms Summary

Clearly, the Passover has had a major influence on the spiritual life of Israel throughout biblical history. Over and over, the psalmist exhorts us to remember the "mighty hand" and "outstretched arm" of the Lord in redeeming Israel from Egyptian bondage through the Passover (Deut. 26:8). He is the one who rescued Israel from bondage at the first Passover, in keeping with His promises to Abraham, so He is to be praised and worshipped (Pss. 105, 135, 136).

Passover is a constant reminder to Israel that God's love will never fail and that He will be loyal to His chosen people even when we fail. At the end

---

12. Information in this section along with primary talmudic source citations are as quoted in "*Hallel*," *EncJud.* 8:279–80.
13. "*Hallel*," *EncJud.* 8:279–80. The "half" *Hallel* is known as the *Chatzi Hallel*, which is the "full" *Hallel* less the first eleven verses of both Psalms 115 and 116.

of it all, He is the one who turns our hearts to Himself and thereby fulfills the fullness of His covenant promises made to the Patriarchs (Rom. 11:28–29).

THE SONG OF SONGS

Finally, though we are unable to give further space to the topic, the Song of Songs is read in the synagogue service and the Seder every Passover. While its literal translation appears to have no relationship to the Passover, the beauty of its language has convinced many Jewish and Christian commentators of a hidden, deeper meaning to the song, which extolls the beauty of God's covenant relationship with Israel.

CONCLUSION

Whereas Jewish tradition considers the Ketuvim to be of lesser importance than the Torah, this body of biblical literature that we believe is as inspired as the rest of the Hebrew canon helps us better understand the story of the Bible, and especially the Passover. In the Ketuvim we see the central role of the Passover in both the individual and communal worship of the Jewish people. The Passover event has become the great example of God's plan to rescue, redeem, and restore His people as individuals and as a nation. In addition, it is in the Ketuvim that we see the significance of the Passover celebration to the religious life of the community, for in seasons of renewal and spiritual revival, the community expresses newfound spiritual passion by gathering to remember the Passover.

In the Ketuvim we see the Passover celebrated as a vital indication that the people of God are back on the right track. Like a married couple returning to the place of their engagement, so the children of Israel return to the Passover celebration to recall the Lord's great love for them. It is also the Ketuvim that provides the Passover celebration with some of its most beloved biblical expressions. We have good reason to believe that Yeshua himself sang the Egyptian *Hallel* (Pss. 113–118) just before he walked to Gethsemane and His eventual death on the cross for our sins (Matt. 26:30). Those psalms reflect the great redemptive themes of the Passover and continue to be an essential and beloved part of its celebration for over two millennia.

Passover in the biblical history of Israel and the Jewish people has been a thermometer or barometer gauging the warmth of the people's hearts toward God. During periods of apostasy or exile its observance has fallen off, and the three key national observances of the holy day recorded in the Writings represent periods of repentance, revival, and restoration. It is significant that Passover has been used to spiritually energize the Jewish people and become a means of bringing individuals and the nation itself back to God. In a sense, it is this replaying of the original Passover when the people were in Egypt that reminds the Jewish people of His love, power, and purpose for the chosen nation. The festival also looks forward to the ultimate Messianic redemption that will one day turn the heart of the nation back to the Lord forever.

3
PASSOVER IN THE PROPHETS

GORDON LAW

*W*e have reviewed the biblical foundations for the Passover in both the Torah and the Writings, and we now turn our attention to what can be learned about the Passover from the Prophets of Israel.

The definition of which books of the Hebrew Bible belong in "the Prophets" is different in the Jewish and Christian canons (see appendix 1).[1] As mentioned in the introduction to this volume, Jewish tradition identifies three sections in the Hebrew Bible: the Torah (Five Books of Moses), the Prophets, and the Writings. The Prophets contain two subgroups, the Former (or Early) Prophets and the Latter Prophets. The Former Prophets include the narrative books of Joshua, Judges, 1 and 2 Samuel, and 1 and 2 Kings as found in Christian Bibles. The Latter Prophets include the books of Isaiah, Jeremiah, Ezekiel, and the twelve so-called Minor Prophets, or in Jewish tradition simply "the Twelve." This portion of Scripture includes the books of Hosea, Joel, Amos, Obadiah, Jonah, Micah, Nahum, Habakkuk, Zephaniah, Haggai, Zechariah, and Malachi.

One of the most important figures of the Passover Seder, the Prophet Elijah, is found in both 1 Kings as well as in the book of Malachi. Although these two books are usually viewed as being in two different categories in the Christian canon—the Historical Books (1 Kings) and the Prophets (Malachi)—the Jewish canon includes both books among the Prophets. Consequently, as we investigate the background of the Passover in the Prophetic Books, we will follow the Jewish canon as we examine Elijah's link to the Passover Seder.

THE LIFE OF ELIJAH THE PROPHET
The name Elijah (אֵלִיָּהוּ, *Eliyyahu*) means "The LORD is my God."[2] He is a fascinating figure in both Jewish and Christian literature because he was

---

1. For more discussion of the books of the Hebrew Bible, see the introduction to this volume and the opening section of chapter 2, "Passover in the Writings," by Richard H. Flashman.
2. Walter Brueggemann, *1 & 2 Kings*, Smyth & Helwys Bible Commentary (Macon, GA: Smyth & Helwys, 2000), 207.

taken up to heaven instead of dying in the usual manner (similar to Enoch in Genesis 5:24). He was called by the Lord to oppose the false gods worshipped by King Ahab and Queen Jezebel (1 Kings 16:31–34). He was one of two significant prophets in the Northern Kingdom, along with his disciple Elisha. They were both used by God to pronounce judgment upon the false prophets and false gods and to demonstrate His supremacy over this world.

Elijah is first introduced at the beginning of 1 Kings 17. The author provides only a minimal introduction, perhaps because he expected his audience to already be familiar with Elijah. The prophet is described as a man of obedience to God's Word. He is directed by God to enter the wilderness, separating himself from all normal life-support systems to live in a context of extreme vulnerability east of the Jordan and is commanded to rely on the Lord's provision for his food and drink (vv. 3–6).

God first provides for Elijah through the miracle of ravens bringing him food. Later, God commands Elijah to go to Zarephath (vv. 8–9), a town in a region loyal to the false god Baal. Yet even there, God directs a widow in this foreign and hostile territory to provide for Elijah. The woman trusts in the God of Israel and does as Elijah instructs. Soon after this, the widow's son becomes ill and dies, but Elijah prays and raises the child from the dead (vv. 17–24). The widow confesses her faith in Elijah's God, the prophetic word is confirmed, and the God of Israel is shown to be the giver of life.[3] Besides highlighting the faithfulness and obedience of this widow, the biblical author links Elijah to a life of miraculous events.

The most well-known miracle of Elijah involves the prophet's confrontation with the prophets of Baal on Mount Carmel (1 Kings 18:20–40). Elijah condemns the false prophets for their idolatry. Then, after the false prophets fail to bring fire from heaven after appealing to their false gods, Elijah prays for their hearts to be turned back to God (vv. 36–37), and a fire comes from heaven consuming both the offering and the altar itself. This was a powerful demonstration of God's power, which also served to establish the authority of Elijah as a true prophet. Elijah proved that Baal was not merely dead or incapacitated.[4] The false god simply did not exist.[5] The God of Israel is affirmed through 1 Kings 17–18 as the one true God who is sovereign over all things.

Despite this victory on Mount Carmel, the evil Queen Jezebel pursues Elijah to kill him (1 Kings 19). Elijah then flees to Mount Horeb (v. 8), which is another name for Mount Sinai (Exod. 24:15–18; cf. 1 Kings 8:9; Mal. 4:4 [3:22 in the Hebrew Bible]). Elijah spends forty days and nights traveling to the mountain of God, which brings to mind how Moses spent

---

3. August H. Konkel, *1 & 2 Kings*, NIV Application Commentary (Grand Rapids: Zondervan, 2000), 297.

4. Harry E. Shields, "1 Kings," in *The Moody Bible Commentary*, ed. Michael Rydelnik and Michael Vanlaningham (Chicago: Moody Publishers, 2014), 507.

5. Or, with the Apostle Paul in 1 Corinthians 10:19–20, we may rest assured that the false god is merely a demon who has no power in and of itself.

forty days and nights upon the mountain of God (1 Kings 19:8; cf. Exod. 24:18). However, Elijah's experience of the divine presence is different from that of Moses. When God appeared to Moses on the mountain, he did it in the context of a storm, with thunder and lightning, fire, smoke and earthquake (Exod.19:18; Deut. 4:11–12). In contrast, Elijah experiences similar natural wonders but finds God in an unexpected way.

> So He said, "Go forth and stand on the mountain before the LORD." And behold, the LORD was passing by! And a great and strong wind was rending the mountains and breaking in pieces the rocks before the LORD; but the LORD was not in the wind. And after the wind an earthquake, but the LORD was not in the earthquake. After the earthquake a fire, but the LORD was not in the fire; and after the fire a sound of a gentle blowing. (1 Kings 19:11–12)

Whereas God spoke to Moses with awe and power, God spoke to Elijah through a gentle sound. The parallel between Moses and Elijah is unmistakable, although Elijah's experience is different. Because of his similarity to Moses, Elijah is considered one of the greatest of all Israel's prophets. However, Elijah's importance goes beyond his earthly life, which did not end with death.

ELIJAH THE PROPHET IN JEWISH TRADITION

Elijah is a prominent figure in Jewish and biblical tradition. It is Elijah who stands up to the evil King Ahab for allowing his pagan wife to introduce Baal worship in Israel.

Elijah has a place set aside for him at every Passover Seder, and traditionally, at the circumcision of an eight-day-old male baby.[6] The Talmud and medieval Jewish lore depict particular instances in which Elijah visits the righteous to reveal secrets of the Torah and Jewish people in distress.[7] Jewish tradition—probably dating back to the time of Jesus—likewise dictates that Elijah must come back (perhaps on one of his many visits to earth) and herald the news of the coming Messiah.

---

6. Joseph Telushkin, *Jewish Literacy: The Most Important Things to Know about the Jewish Religion, Its People, and Its History* (New York: W. Morrow, 1991), 77–79.
7. Telushkin, *Jewish Literacy*, 77–79. One example of a time when Elijah is believed to help the Jewish people is during the event of male circumcision: "One of the attendees is given the honor of placing the baby on the chair of Elijah as the *mohel* [the ritual circumciser] chants, 'This is the seat of Elijah . . .' The *mohel* also asks that Elijah stand to his right and protect him, so nothing will go wrong during the circumcision: 'This is the Seat of Elijah the Prophet, may he be remembered for good. For Your deliverance I hope, O Lord. I have hoped for Your deliverance, Lord, and I have performed Your commandments. Elijah, angel of the Covenant, here is yours before you; stand at my right and support me. I rejoice in Your word, like one who finds great spoil. Those who love Your Torah have abounding peace, and there is no stumbling for them. Happy is the man You choose and bring near to dwell in Your courtyards; we will be satiated with the goodness of Your House, Your Holy Temple'" (Dovid Zaklikowski, "The Chair of Elijah and Welcoming the Baby," *Chabad.org*, http:// www.chabad.org/library/article_cdo/aid/144123/jewish/The-Chair-of-Elijah-and-Welcoming-the-Baby.htm).

From the pages of the Bible to modern-day Jewish tradition, Elijah is linked to Israel's redemption and is held in high esteem by religious Jewish people. Perhaps most notable is his bodily accession to heaven, which to many is proof of his ability to come and visit Jews on earth, throughout the generations. Second is his thirst for righteousness—namely in calling out Ahab for his apostasy; his complete dependence on God—precisely when he calls out the prophets of Baal (1 Kings 18:38); and his execution of the pagan priests of Baal (v. 40).

Likewise, his other two miracles—multiplying food and resurrecting the dead—identify him as a miracle worker and as playing a key role in the future Messianic redemption.[8] Furthermore, the people's words in 1 Kings 18:39 ("The LORD, He is God; the LORD, He is God") are included as part of the concluding liturgy at Yom Kippur (Day of Atonement) services.

The role of Elijah at the Passover Seder is significant and linked to his serving as the forerunner of the Messiah himself. This is why a place setting, including a cup of wine (the well-known cup of Elijah) is placed on the table as part of the Jewish family's effort to bring Elijah to the table. Of course, the hope is not simply for Elijah but even more for the one he will bring with him, even the Messiah himself.

So we ask the question, why pour a cup for Elijah at a Seder?[9] The four previous cups—each for the "Four 'I Wills,'" based on what God says he will do for His people in Exodus 6:6–7, are completed according to Jewish tradition:

> Say, therefore, to the sons of Israel, "I am the LORD, and *I will bring you out* from under the burdens of the Egyptians, and *I will deliver you* from their bondage. *I will also redeem you* with an outstretched arm and with great judgments. Then *I will take you* for My people, and I will be your God; and you shall know that I am the LORD your God, who brought you out from under the burdens of the Egyptians." (emphasis added)

The fifth cup grows out of the fourth and final cup we drink and is a further expression of hope for future redemption, which is attested to in verse 8:

> *I will bring you* to the land which I swore to give to Abraham, Isaac, and Jacob, and *I will give it to you* for a possession; I am the LORD. (emphasis added)

The cup of Elijah signifies anticipation of a final future fulfillment of God's promises to His people. This fifth cup of the Passover Seder looks to a future time when Israel is in the Land and the Messiah comes, alludes to

---

8. Some modern Jewish scholars see the connection between Elijah and Jesus, at least in a literary way; for instance, see Telushkin, *Jewish Literacy*, 77–79. Also see Naftali Silberberg, "Why Is Elijah the Prophet Invited to the Seder?," *Chabad.org*, http://www.chabad.org/holidays/passover/pesach_cdo/aid/504495/jewish/Why-Is-Elijah-the-Prophet-Invited-to-the-Seder.htm.

9. See Silberberg, "Why Is Elijah the Prophet Invited to the Seder?" For the earlier discussion of God's promises in Exodus 6:6–8, see chapter 1, "Passover in the Torah," by Robert Walter.

future redemption (this is why we do not drink the cup), and comes right before the *Hallel* (praising of God, reciting from Psalms 113–118).

ELIJAH'S RETURN AS FORERUNNER FOR THE MESSIAH IN MALACHI 4

The role of Elijah in relation to Moses is found at the conclusion of Malachi, the last book of the twelve Prophets and final chapter of the Old Testament in the Christian canon. The reference to Moses in Malachi 4:4 is a reminder to the entire nation that they remain obligated to the covenant given by God to Moses at Mount Horeb.[10] The book of Malachi also concludes with the prediction of Elijah's return:

> Behold, I am going to send you Elijah the prophet before the coming of the great and terrible day of the LORD. He will restore the hearts of the fathers to their children and the hearts of the children to their fathers, so that I will not come and smite the land with a curse. (Mal. 4:5–6)

This text is important since it encourages Israel to look for a future appearance of Elijah. His life did not end when he was taken up into heaven (2 Kings 2:11); according to Malachi, he still has a role to play in Israel's future. In subsequent Jewish and Christian tradition, the return of Elijah is expected before the coming of the Messiah. Elijah's translation to heaven from earth only heightened the speculation about Elijah's role in the last days, as some biblical interpreters, especially based upon his appearance at the Transfiguration, believe that Elijah will appear again during the season of Israel's future suffering mentioned in Jeremiah 30:7, "the time of Jacob's distress."

It is a mystery of Scripture as to why this happened to Elijah as it had to Enoch before him. However, in Elijah's case, the Scriptures affirm this expectation of Elijah's reappearance in the last days. In Malachi 3, the prophet foretells the coming of one identified as, "My messenger" to prepare the way for Messiah (v. 1). The similarities between Malachi 3:1 and 4:5–6 suggest that Elijah is that messenger of the covenant.

> "Behold, I am going to send My messenger, and he will clear the way before Me. And the Lord, whom you seek, will suddenly come to His temple; and the messenger of the covenant, in whom you delight, behold, He is coming," says the LORD of hosts. (Mal. 3:1)

> Behold, I am going to send you Elijah the prophet before the coming of the great and terrible day of the LORD. He will restore the hearts of the fathers to their children and the hearts of the children to their fathers, so that I will not come and smite the land with a curse. (Mal. 4:5–6)

---

10. Konkel, *1 & 2 Kings*, 309.

The messenger's mission reinforces both the pronouncement of judgment for sin (3:1–5; 3:16–4:3) and the hope that by returning to God, judgment will be averted (3:7–11). Malachi 4:6 anticipates Elijah's powerful effect upon the people of Israel in the last days as when he urged Israel to confess that the Lord alone was God (1 Kings 18, esp. vv. 21–24, 36–37).[11] Since the last phrase of Malachi 4:6 included the threat of destruction, there is a tradition in Jewish liturgy to repeat Malachi 4:5 again after reading 4:6, thus concluding the public reading on a strong and hopeful note.[12]

According to the New Testament, the ministry of Elijah indeed prepares the way for the first coming of the Messiah. Jesus Himself claims that John the Baptist fulfills the role prepared for Elijah (Matt.11:10; Luke 1:17). John is presented as that one who heralded the ministry of Yeshua the Messiah (Matt.11:11–15; Mark 9:11–13; Luke 1:17).

In discussing the return of Elijah, we need to make one thing clear: the Bible does not teach reincarnation. This notion of rebirth of a soul in a new human body is a Hindu concept that is foreign to the Bible. We do not believe that John the Baptist is literally Elijah. We simply affirm that John fulfills an Elijah-like ministry, preparing the way for the coming of the Messiah. Jesus applies the passages in Malachi to John in a very first-century Jewish fashion. The writers of the New Testament, most of whom were Jewish, often used prophecy to explain their situation and to draw back the heavenly curtain in order to show that the experiences of the early disciples were in fact predicted in Scripture as either a type of what was to come or to reflect a step towards a greater fulfillment. But this does not mean that the original intent of the prophecy is totally fulfilled in thus being quoted. The meaning and significance of biblical prophecy unfolds in the course of time as circumstances develop and certain events occur, which later we may recognize as part of the flow of redemptive history.

Based upon this view of the *prophetic unfolding*, at times in stages, it is reasonable to expect that we will see more of Elijah as we draw closer to the second coming of the Lord. Elijah's role at the second coming will be a more literal fulfillment of what was predicted by Malachi. The Gospels hint that there is "more to come" from Elijah as he literally reappears in person with Moses at the Mount of Transfiguration (Mark 9:2–8).

The sobering words of the prophet Malachi in chapter 4 call the attention of all who are willing to accept the reality of coming judgment. The New Testament teaches us that the fullness of judgment will be initiated at the return of Jesus. Jesus will judge the living and the dead (1 Peter 4:5; 2 Tim. 4:1). It will be a dreadful day for the enemies of God. It is the day of God's wrath, when his righteous judgment will be revealed

---

11.   M. Daniel Carroll, "Malachi" in *Eerdmans Commentary on the Bible*, ed. James D. G. Dunn and John W. Rogerson (Grand Rapids: Eerdmans, 2003), 734.

12.   Adele Berlin and Marc Zvi Brettler, eds., *The Jewish Study Bible* (New York: Oxford University Press, 2004), 1261.

and the Lord God will repay each person according to what that person has done (Rom. 2:5–9).[13]

The Jewish people have waited for Elijah for many years, but his coming, like that of the Messiah Jesus, was not what was expected. John, the "new Elijah," was sent by God to introduce the Jewish people to the Redeemer who would arrive with humility rather than the grandeur expected. The Jewish people alive at the time of Yeshua unfortunately missed the coming of both the great prophet Elijah and the greater prophet Jesus the Messiah.

At Passover, Jewish people continue to fan the flames of hope—expecting Elijah to come, bringing with him the Messiah—and if not, then refocusing this hope to the following year affirmed in singing the final song of the Passover, "Next Year in Jerusalem." In other words, if Elijah did not come this year, then we know he will come next Passover. The hope for Elijah reflects the hope Jewish people have in every generation for the coming of the Messiah.

Followers of Jesus the Messiah know that one like Elijah did come and the expected Messiah came as well, only in humility and not in the glory expected. He died for our sins as the Lamb of God and rose, conquering death, only to be held by heaven until the time is right and He returns to reign on His rightful throne. And we expect Elijah to reappear and again prepare the way for the Lord's return. Until then we will continue to celebrate the Passover meal and sing our final song of hope—לְשָׁנָה הַבָּאָה בִּירוּשָׁלַיִם!, *L'shanah HaBa'ah B'Yerushalayim!* "Next Year in Jerusalem!"

ELIJAH AND THE FIFTH CUP

Although the prophet Elijah does not factor into the Exodus story, he is featured prominently in the traditional Passover Seder. But why was Elijah brought into a celebration that is based on the Exodus? A strong case could be made that Elijah was included in the Passover Seder because of his parallels with Moses:

Moses	Elijah
A prophet of God	A prophet of God
Opposed the royalty of his age (Pharaoh) and delivered the word of God	Opposed the royalty of his age (Ahab and Jezebel) and delivered the word of God
Confronted idolatrous worship (the golden calf) while on Mount Sinai	Confronted idolatrous worship (of Baal) while on Mount Carmel
Received revelation from God on Mount Sinai after 40 days and 40 nights	Received revelation from God at Mount Horeb (Sinai) after 40 days and 40 nights

---

13. Anthony R. Petterson, *Haggai, Zechariah & Malachi*, Apollos Old Testament Commentary 25 (Nottingham, UK: Apollos; Downers Grove, IL: InterVarsity Press, 2015), 388.

Let us summarize the ways in which Elijah plays a key role in the cel-ebration of the Passover Seder. First of all, it is a long-standing tradition to set up an extra seat at the dining room table in anticipation of his return. After all, he would need someplace to sit!

Also, there is a fifth ceremonial cup of wine prepared for the Passover dinner, called the cup of Elijah. This is a very important part of the Passover Seder and takes up quite a few pages in the modern Haggadah. This portion of the liturgy, which is focused on Elijah, also provides one of the great musi-cal moments in the Passover service, with the family singing a moving and melancholic song inviting Elijah to sit at the table and enjoy the feast with them. A cup of wine is filled for Elijah but left untouched by the participants in the Seder if he does not come. The filled cup points to the hope of a coming Redeemer and Messiah who will gather the Jewish people and bring them back to the Land of Israel and establish God's kingdom as promised by the great prophets of Israel: Isaiah, Jeremiah, Ezekiel, and others. Therefore, Elijah represents the great Messianic hope of the Jewish people.

Traditionally, the Jewish children open the front door and summon Elijah to the Seder to fulfill his ministry of preparation for greater things to come. The leader of the Seder, representing the family, sits facing the door in order to welcome Elijah to the Seder table. If the room cannot be arranged in this way, the leader will simply turn his face to the door when Elijah is welcomed near the final stage of the Seder. Very often, the children will be sent to the front door to call upon Elijah's name, making sure he hears their invitation to join the family in celebrating the redemption from bondage.[14] Either way, the front door is opened to welcome Elijah. Some have suggested that originally the door was held open throughout the entire Seder. However, during the Middle Ages, when it was dangerous to do so, the door was kept closed.[15]

There is a Jewish legend that says "when Elijah comes, all unsolved ques-tions will be answered" and Elijah is also believed to wander from town to town to bring hope in time of distress. For the Jewish people, the anticipa-tion of Elijah's coming brings hope and joy in a variety of times of helpless-ness and distress.[16] Ultimately this hope will culminate in the coming of the Messiah, whom Elijah will announce before he comes.

CONCLUSION

The Passover Seder not only looks back to the Exodus, but also looks for-ward to the coming redemption, when the Jewish people will be redeemed from the Diaspora and brought back to the Land of Israel in a new Exo-dus. This looking back to look forward is so often a part of various Jewish

---

14. Ruth Fredman Cernea, *The Passover Seder: An Anthropological Perspective on Jewish Culture* (1981; Lanham, MD: University Press of America, 1995), 45.
15. Isaac Klein, *A Guide to Jewish Religious Practice* (1979; New York: Jewish Theological Seminary of America, 1992), 129.
16. Cernea, *The Passover Seder*, 125.

traditions and the synagogue; and though Elijah does not factor into the Exodus story, his life parallels the life of Moses and he is expected to return some day at the vanguard of God's plan for the end of days and the establishment of the Messianic kingdom.

However, as believers in Jesus—the Messiah of Israel—the Jewish people's eager expectation for Elijah and the Messiah should only increase our burden for Israel's salvation. Jewish people have correctly interpreted the Scriptures in expecting Elijah to come before the Messiah, and yet the coming of both the forerunner and the Messiah Himself has eluded recognition by most Jewish people in the first century and today.

Elijah exemplifies what it means to trust God in the face of adversaries, which should encourage us to pray for the salvation of Jewish people. We should pray that our Jewish friends and family will understand that John the Baptist fulfilled the first part of Elijah's ministry, but that there is more to come. Jesus, the Lamb of God who takes away the sin of the world, has already come once to save humankind and will come again as both judge and king. The great joy of celebrating Passover is that the Festival encourages us not only to remember what God did in the ancient Exodus, but also to delight in what He did at the first coming of the Messiah, which gives us great hope and anticipation for the Messiah's second coming.

In conclusion, may we offer this prayer, "Oh Lord and Savior, Yeshua our King, we pray you might redeem the remnant of Israel, and draw their hearts to You, the one who brings ultimate redemption to Israel and the nations. Amen."

4

PASSOVER IN THE GOSPEL OF LUKE

DARRELL L. BOCK

*T*he events of the Last Supper are critical as it is the basis for what is commonly known as the Lord's Supper or Communion. The Apostle Paul
considers this meal to be important as he makes direct reference to the words
spoken by Jesus at the table, which most Christians today hear regularly.
(1 Cor. 11:23–25).

However, the issues related to this meal are numerous and complex,
leading to a host of debates and discussions, each of which could fill this
chapter.[1] However, our concerns are narrow.

We will attempt to answer the question, "What does the first-century
Jewish background of the Passover holiday contribute to our understanding
of what Jesus did with His disciples at this evidently special meal?" Specifically, we will need to establish if a Passover or Passover-like meal took place,
what can be known about the way in which it was celebrated, and how Jesus
transformed this celebration by His words and actions.

Luke explicitly associates the Last Supper with the Passover meal and
the Feast of Unleavened Bread (Luke 22:1, 7, 15). He does this because the
two feasts come back to back and were often combined or discussed together
with either name used for the whole (Ezek. 45:21; Matt. 26:17–18; Mark
14:1, esp. 14:2). Flavius Josephus, the first-century Jewish historian, writes
"the feast of unleavened bread, which we call the Passover" (*Antiquities of the
Jews* 14.21).[2] The Passover connection is also seen in Mark's use of the terms

---

1. Perhaps the most complete recent discussion is by I. Howard Marshall, "The Last Supper," in *Key
Events in the Life of the Historical Jesus: A Collaborative Exploration of Context and Coherence*, ed.
Darrell L. Bock and Robert L. Webb, Wissenschaftliche Untersuchungen zum Neuen Testament
247 (Tübingen: Mohr Siebeck, 2009), 481–588. What is amazing about this one-hundred-page
article is how many issues are compressed into this discussion.
2. Similarly, see Josephus, *Antiquities of the Jews* 2.317; 17.213; and 20.106; see also *Jewish War* 5.99,
where Josephus says Unleavened Bread starts on Nisan 14, which is Passover.

in Mark 14:1, 12, where he similarly refers to both celebrations. This is an important observation to make as we prepare to discuss the topic.

As is common within the Jewish community today, one could use "Passover" or "Unleavened Bread" in reference to any part of the eight days of this period (Lev. 23:5–6). Yet, the Synoptic Gospels' timing for Passover seems to differ from John's, who links the day of Jesus's crucifixion with Passover, a connection that could make the Passover mentioned by John's Gospel lag a day behind the Synoptic Gospels (John 13:1; 18:28; 19:14). This seeming difference in timing has been vigorously discussed in New Testament studies throughout the years and is our first topic of concern in this chapter.

Our second concern is to decide if the meal described in Luke chapter 22 is actually a traditional Passover Seder. The celebration of the Passover goes back centuries as other chapters in this book show. But the more controversial question is whether specifically a Passover Seder was celebrated or merely a liturgically structured meal with multiple cups. And if it was a Seder, where can we find more conclusive information regarding the meal, elements, symbolism, and traditions observed that evening at that particular first-century time? We will examine whether or not Jesus observed a defined Seder, the nature of its internal elements and symbols, such as the cups mentioned in the account, and if what Luke describes is generally consistent with the elements of the Passover meal. So we are asking two questions: (1) Was this a Passover meal? (2) If it was a Seder, do we know enough about the Seder at that time to suggest what took place when?

The Seder question introduces the question of indiscriminately viewing the Passover in Jesus's time through the lens of Jewish tradition developed centuries later. We are referring specifically to the mishnaic tractate Pesahim (10), developed around 200 c.e. as the earliest rabbinic source of information about the traditions of the Seder. Certainly we must be careful not to read the modern Seder, found in the traditional Haggadah, into the events of Luke chapter 22. However, there might very well be some traditions that parallel and have persisted through time. Being conclusive will be difficult as we have very limited historical resources about the Passover Seder from the first century.

Whatever we think about these two issues—(1) the Synoptic-John chronological issue around the exact timing of Passover and (2) about the question of a specific Passover and its accompanying Seder—the association of this meal with this time period in general is full of significance. Interestingly, even those who think the meal was not a Seder or some type of Passover meal recognize the shadow cast by the Passover season over the Last Supper. The Passover's proximity to the meal colors what is said and done in chapter 22 of Luke, no matter how some of the details might be understood. Part of the beauty of this issue is that, as complex as some of the details are that we shall cover, the larger outline is still fairly clear. This is because Passover was a prescribed feast leading into a week's celebration whose symbolism was well established by the time Jesus sat down with His disciples for this event (Exod. 12:1–49).

Regardless of how this meal aligns with the mishnaic Seder or today's Passover celebrations, Jesus clearly connects it to the Passover and gives the symbolism of the evening a greater meaning. So what Jesus does with the Passover imagery will be our third stopping point and will conclude our look at the Passover in Luke 22.

THE TIMING AND NATURE OF THE MEAL: ON OR BEFORE PASSOVER?

How do we explain the seeming discrepancies in chronology between the Synoptics and John's Gospel? The Apostle John appears to speak of the Last Supper as happening a day before the Passover lambs were slaughtered (John 13:1; 18:28; 19:14), while Mark 14:1 and 12 place the meal on the Passover. In fact, John 19:14 speaks of Jesus's trial with Pilate being on the day of preparation for the Passover, while 18:28 speaks of the Jewish leaders not entering Pilate's Praetorium for fear of becoming defiled and thus unable to eat the Passover. If John's dating is correct, Jesus's meal might not even have been a Passover meal, as the Last Supper would have been held a day before the Passover, *if* John 18:28 is referring to the Passover sacrifice and meal. It is dealing with the *if* that drives the options people suggest.

Three major options are suggested to bring the references in line. Option 1 argues that one writer is referring to the season as a whole either in terms of general timing (usually John) or in some symbolic way (either the Synoptics or John). Option 2 is an appeal to distinct calendars with Jesus on His own Passover schedule in the Synoptics distinct from the official calendar that John appeals to.[3] Option 3 makes an appeal to a Passover-like meal or a Passover meal taken early.[4]

At the center of the discussion are several contested elements. Is there evidence of a Passover meal in the descriptions? Is there a case for the use of multiple calendars? How do we explain the remarks made in John, especially 18:28, that in light of the Passover, the Jewish leaders did not want to contract uncleanness during Jesus's examination by Pilate? We will consider these elements next.

Two of John's references are to the Passover in general in 13:1 and 19:14. The reference in 13:1 is generic, simply noting that before the time of the Passover feast Jesus knew His time to depart this world had come. This reference does not help us with our question. On the other end of the passage sequence stands John 19:14, which says, "It was the day of the preparation for the Passover" as Pilate presents Jesus to the crowd after examining Him.

---

3. For example, the study by Annie Jaubert, *La date de la Cène: Calendrier biblique et liturgie chrétienne* (Paris: Lecoffre, 1957); English translation: Annie Jaubert, *The Date of the Last Supper*, trans. Isaac Rafferty [Staten Island, NY: Alba House, 1965]), argues that Jesus followed the distinct calendar of the Dead Sea Qumran community. However, no evidence really exists for Jesus following this separatist sect on matters in general, much less on matters tied to the calendar.

4. For details on an array of options, see Marshall, "The Last Supper," 552–60.

This is after the Last Supper in the Synoptics and the Upper Room discourse in John. One of the issues here is that John does not present a discussion of the meal and its liturgy at all. This does not mean that John does not hold to a Last Supper meal because by the time he wrote, this practice had been formalized into the Lord's Table (1 Cor. 11:23–26, plus the traditions that fed into the Synoptic portrayals). John simply chose not to present it, probably because it was an already well-known event in the Church.

The phrase in John 19:14 could mean one of two things: the day of preparation for the Passover meal itself, placing it in tension with the Synoptic timing, or it is shorthand for the day of Sabbath preparation during Passover week, as the Sabbath begins with sundown on Friday night leading into Saturday. The additional reference to the Passover points to a sacrifice during the time of Passover and could refer to other sacrifices tied to that feast, either daily sacrifices (Deut. 16:2–8)[5] or the *hagigah* (Num. 28:18–19). The Synoptics show this latter meaning of preparation day for the Sabbath in other texts (Matt. 27:62; Mark 15:42; Luke 23:54).[6] Part of what is complicating the discussion of this event is that the Sabbath of a feast week is a High Sabbath, a kind of twofer holiday, doubly sacred because it is a Sabbath tied to a feast.

This last reference is the most crucial for our discussion. I cite the controversial part of John 18:28, "They did not go into the governor's residence so they would not be ceremonially defiled, but could eat the Passover meal" (NET). The avoidance behavior in this verse takes place as the examination of Jesus by Pilate begins. The leaders do not want to contract uncleanness by going into a Gentile's residence. Most take this location to be the tower of Antonia, the fortress where Pilate stayed when he was in Jerusalem that also housed the troops protecting the city. This location overlooked the Temple complex from the northwest corner of the Temple mount in such a way that the troops could see Temple activity without defiling the Temple space proper. Only closed spaces like these were thought to create an environment where one could contract uncleanness, as colonnades were in the open air and viewed as not having the same level of risk (m. Ohalot 18:7–10). Uncleanness in such a case lasts for a week, because of the belief that Gentiles did not take proper care of the dead (Num. 19:14). Issues tied to uncleanness were important because contamination would preclude these priests from observing any part of the feast.[7] Other forms of uncleanness lasting for a day could be related to the presence of yeast (m. Pesahim 1.1; 2.1) or to contaminated road dust from foreigners (m. Berakhot 9.5). They wanted to avoid

---

5. Mishnah, Pesahim 5.1 alludes to the timing of the sacrifice on Passover day, but points to the fact that other sacrifices were taking place throughout this period. This passage alludes to the sacrifices tied to the daily times of prayer.

6. Leon Morris, who will argue in contrast to the view taken in this chapter for John's Passover chronology, also accepts that the reference here in John 19:14 is to the Friday before the Sabbath ("the Friday of Passover week") versus a Passover reference; *The Gospel according to John*, New International Commentary on the New Testament (Grand Rapids: Eerdmans, 1971), 800.

7. Morris, *John*, 763.

these possibilities in any form and so they remained outside. Pilate kindly came out to address them.

For our purposes it is the seeming reference to eating the Passover meal in John 18:28 that contains the difficulty. If this is the Passover meal, then John and the Synoptics are not in sync, since Luke 22:15 presents Jesus as eating the Passover with the disciples (also Mark 14:12). New Testament and Johannine scholar Dr. Leon Morris defends John's chronology, and his explanation is worth noting. He first cites an observation: "That the expression could apply to the Passover plus the feast of unleavened bread is, in my opinion, clear."[8] He then goes on to say, "That it could be used of the feast of unleavened bread without the Passover, which is what is required if John 18:28 is to be squared with the theory, is not."[9] So, for Morris, John must be referring to the Passover meal. Passover has to be in the reference for him. If Morris is correct, then what do we do with the references in Mark and Luke? Morris opts for Jesus's use of a different, more sectarian calendar to solve the seeming contradiction. Above, it was suggested that the evidence for the use of a different calendar is not strong.

But what are we to do if the reference is to the High Sabbath Passover *season* sacrifices? Morris never mentions this possibility, yet the chronology permits it with an expression already shown to be ambiguous. Passover is not excluded here, and can be referred to because the holiday colors the whole week. The sentence is not merely specific to the Passover sacrifice at the beginning of the feast, but refers to any of the events tied to the opening of the celebration. Morris is seeing a technical term that involves a reference to a specific meal that in fact may have been used more broadly in terms of other events tied to the week.

However, the reference to the Passover can be used of a period of time, covering the entire week, with more than one meal eaten during that entire season, any part of which could be called Passover. The term in such contexts is being used in a popular, less technical way, a kind of shorthand to point to what kicked off this special time and an event that worked as kind of a shadow over the whole week.

All of these options would require cleanliness during this time, especially as people approached a Sabbath.[10] The internal chronology within John itself also may suggest this broader use of the phrase and a timing like that of the Synoptics. If, while noting the array of events, we simply count back from

---

8. Morris, *John*, 689.
9. Morris, *John*, 689.
10. John 19:31 might seem to raise questions about our claim about ambiguity, as it refers clearly to the day of preparation and does not call it Passover. But we are still in the Passover day at this point of the story, and now the issue is getting the body off the cross before the Sabbath actually comes. The aside in the verse that this Sabbath was a "great one" is the allusion to the Passover High Sabbath. It was the Passover season that made this Sabbath an even more special day than a normal Sabbath. Passover is still indirectly in view even in 19:31. John may be only using a shortened form here.

Nisan 14 to the six days "before the Passover" that John 12:1 mentions, then Nisan 14 *is* the day of Passover (Thursday night/Friday day) *within* John's Gospel just as the Synoptics present it.[11] What makes the chronology work in this way in John is that we also are dealing with a late-day meal in John 12,[12] which by the counting and description looks to be an evening meal held on Friday night, Nisan 8, rather than a late afternoon meal.

So we are contending that the Synoptics and John are in agreement and the confusion comes from failing to see (1) that the reference to Passover is to the entire eight days referred to as the Feast of Passover / Unleavened Bread and (2) that reference to eating Passover meals could refer to the Passover meal at the start of this period, but also to the sacrifices that are offered on the next sacred day–especially the Festival (hagigah) sacrifices.

If this is correct, then all the other discussions about different calendars or other kinds of meals kept in the shadows of the Passover are no longer necessary. This means we can now consider the issue of the Seder used in relationship to the meal.

THE SEDER AND THE LAST SUPPER

Although the Synoptics seem to be clear that this is a Passover meal (Mark 14:12 and Luke 22:15), we might examine some other indications that this is true. We have a meal in Jerusalem (all Gospels), at night (Matt. 26:20; Mark 14:17; Luke 22:7 with 22:14; John 13:2; all Gospels), a reclining meal that points to a special occasion (John 13:12), singing hymns

---

11.   One has to work back one event at a time to the events of John 12 using both the Synoptics and John's hints about dating and timing of events to get here, but it does work. The details on this argument are found in the companion chapter in this volume, chapter 5, "Passover in the Gospel of John," by Mitch Glaser. Complexity exists, and being dogmatic is not permitted. Even Morris says that the alternative I am contending for and that he rejects "cannot be ruled out as impossible" (*John*, 779). Morris in adopting the chronology of John that argues for Jesus observing the Passover on a different calendar, something that Qumran shows is possible (Morris, *John*, 779–85). This explanation is also conceivable, but I see it as less likely (see n. 3 above). Other explanations tied to a simple association with the Passover time could work by arguing that the Synoptics have painted a meal with the symbol of the season and Jesus turning a meal into a Passover-like event. This approach rests on an excessive skepticism about our sources and understates the chronological links we have pointed out.

12.   There is another issue wrapped up in this discussion, as the evening meal in John 12 where an anointing occurs is placed next to a note that we are six days before the Passover in John. Virtually all agree that the anointing in John is the same as the one in Mark 14 that is placed in a context where both Mark 14 and Matthew 26 have just mentioned that we are two days from the Passover. However this chronological note has to do more directly with the plotting by the leaders (Mark 14:1; Matt. 26:2), not the meal as described in Mark 14:3–9 and Matthew 26:6–13. So John's six-day note on the timing may well be correct. The meal in the Synoptics is simply introduced in Mark 14:3 and Matthew 26:6 with a note about it being held while Jesus was in Bethany. If originally these events of plotting and the anointing meal circulated independently in the tradition, then this beginning for the meal does not give a specific date and time to the event and John's timing is likely more precise. The Synoptics prefer a more topical arrangement where the anointing woman senses Jesus's peril given the leaders' desire to be done with Jesus. The plot has been juxtaposed to an earlier meal.

pointing to the *Hallel* psalms (Pss. 113–118) of the meal (Matt. 26:30; Mark 14:26), the presence of interpretation of the elements of the bread and wine (Synoptics), and remarks tied to giving to the poor (Matt. 26:9; John 13:29) since the giving of alms were a part of the Passover season.

When one discusses the Seder, the source of recorded tradition is found in the Mishnah (m. Pesahim 10), compiled around 200 c.e. This mishnaic tractate suggests that the Seder uses four cups of wine during the meal. The order of the cups is as follows: a blessing with the first cup of wine; the recitation between the father and the son reviewing the events of Exodus with the second cup of wine; the consumption of the food with the third cup of wine; and the singing of the *Hallel* psalms with the fourth cup of wine. Scholars have associated Jesus's remarks in various ways, tying them to the second, third and fourth cups. The third cup is the more common association.[13]

However, as we mentioned earlier, it is hard to determine if this tradition dates back to the time of Jesus. That the Seder we have in the Mishnah goes back to Jesus's time is less than certain because we do not have any references or sources contemporary to Jesus or predating him that give any details about any Seder.[14] Some lines in Pesahim 10 clearly have a post-destruction of the Temple perspective showing them to come after Jesus's time as it refers back to "in the time of the Temple." They speak about what took place in the Temple before the Temple's destruction, given that the end of Pesahim 10.3 talks about the pre-destruction practice in terms of the sacrifice, not merely the uttering of the Seder.[15] In fact, the Seder's language itself has no direct reference to a sacrifice, which those who regard the Seder as a post-Temple (after 70 c.e.) liturgical construction take as more evidence of it being a later development. Nevertheless, the three essentials of the meal according to Pesahim 10.5 are (1) to discuss the Passover event of God passing over the houses as he judged (Exod. 12), (2) the symbolism of the unleavened bread (picturing redemption; Exod. 13:7–9; Deut. 16:3), and (3) the symbolism of the bitter herbs (picturing the bitter life in Egypt; Exod. 12:8; Num. 9:11). As the listing above shows, all of these symbols are explicit in the Torah. These elements seem to be included in the Seder mentioned in Luke chapter 22.

Adding to this uncertainty about the level of developed Jewish Passover tradition present at the Last Supper is that Matthew and Mark only refer to one cup and one taking of bread, while Luke alone mentions two cups. The

---

13. Marshall, "The Last Supper," notes that the third cup is the most common view (544 n225). Dissent on this comes from Rabbi D. M. Cohn-Sherbok, "A Jewish Note on τὸ ποτήριον τῆς εὐλογίας," *New Testament Studies* 27, no. 5 (1981): 704–9, who argues for the fourth cup, while Phillip Segal, "Another Note to 1 Corinthians 10:16," *New Testament Studies* 29, no. 1 (1983): 134–39, considers Cohn-Sherbok's arguments and opts for the second cup.

14. I have in mind here the writer of the OT pseudepigraphal book of Jubilees, Josephus, or Philo, who simply do not address the topic.

15. Baruch M. Bokser, "Was the Last Supper a Passover Seder?" *Bible Review* 3, no. 2 (1987): 24–33, argues that the Seder we have in the Mishnah is post destruction of the Temple.

Seder itself has four cups. So it becomes very hard to be conclusive about what exactly took place and in what order. The variety of views tied to which of the four cups in particular is present at the Last Supper shows the difficulty here (see note 13 above).

The New Testament does not focus on the details of the ancient Seder nor the traditions associated with the event, but rather on the association between the Passover and the deliverance of the nation from Egyptian slavery. In Exodus 12:27 the gathered family is told, "It is the Passover sacrifice to the LORD, for He passed over the houses of the Israelites in Egypt when He struck the Egyptians and spared our homes" (HCSB).

This first-century scene involving Jesus certainly included a meal with elements recalling the Exodus and reflected whatever liturgy was in place at the time, even if we do not know all the details. The Exodus is clearly the background for the Passover meal. It appears very likely to have been a Passover meal, but exactly what kind of Seder attached to it, along with how the individual elements were viewed, is not as clear.

This brings us to our third topic, Jesus's recasting of this meal and its longstanding significance.

THE SIGNIFICANCE OF JESUS RECASTING THE MEAL

One of the unique features of the Lucan portrayal of the Last Supper is the potential mention of multiple cups, an issue tied to a famous problem about the exact wording of the original Lucan text. That question is whether Luke 22:19b–20 is an original part of Luke's Gospel.[16] The longer version of the text picks up from the mention of "this is My body," shared with the other Synoptics, and adds to it, 'being given for you. Do this in remembrance of me.' And the cup likewise after dinner, saying, 'This cup is the New Covenant in my blood, being shed for you'" (author's translation). Thus the longer version does several things: (1) it makes the point about a substitutionary sacrifice for both the bread and the cup ("for you"), (2) it calls for a repetition of the observance ("Do this in remembrance of me"), (3) it makes for the use of multiple cups unique to Luke, and (4) it explicitly ties Jesus's act to the New Covenant ("new covenant in My blood").

The major reason to accept the longer reading is that its manuscript evidence is extensively distributed across key early witnesses and most textual families.[17] Another feature is that there are next to no variants for the longer reading, while the shorter version appears in various forms. Multiple variants are often an indication of later changes, that is, the introduction of a variety

---

16.   The problem is covered in detail by Marshall, "The Last Supper," 529–41. He works through several internal arguments. I will only focus on the external evidence in this chapter.

17.   This includes strong Alexandrian and Byzantine support, a rare but important alliance. Here we have $\mathfrak{P}^{75}$, A, B, as well as E, G, H, and N. The only family presenting the shorter text involve the Western texts. The only Greek witness to the shorter text is the sometimes idiosyncratic D, a manuscript that often goes its own way in giving readings of the Greek. Textual families are manuscripts that belong together because they show the same shared readings in many places.

of attempts to fix the text. It also would be odd for the scribes to make an addition that goes in a direction away from the mention of a single cup shared with Matthew's and Mark's versions. So multiple cups looks original because of its uniqueness, since a scribe would tend to bring texts into agreement and so act to remove the differing number of cups. It also would be odd to have an original version with no words said over the cup that relate to Jesus's death. If the longer text is original, as we are arguing, then the multiple cups are part of what points to a special Passover meal.

What makes this meal so different is that Jesus not only refers to the Exodus and ties the meal to Israel's history, but also completely recasts the meal as a vehicle for describing His coming death as a substitutionary sacrifice. The Lucan reference "for you" points to the substitutionary nature of the sacrifice. In Mark 14:24 Jesus speaks of his shed blood given "for many," an allusion to Mark 10:45, presenting the idea that Jesus will die as a "ransom for many." This is in fact a very likely Messianic allusion to Isaiah 53:12, where the Servant bears the sin of the many.[18]

In the Lucan version, the bread is His body and the wine pictures His blood shed for His disciples. Whether Jesus spoke of "the many" as in Mark 14:24 or of the sacrifice being "for you" as in Luke 22:19–20, the point is crystal clear, as Jesus is about to die as an offering made on behalf of others.[19] The allusion to establishing a covenant (Mark 14:24) or a new covenant (Luke 22:20) also assumes a sacrifice and the shedding of blood (Heb. 9:15–22) to inaugurate a covenant.[20]

So in both versions the meal is portrayed as a commentary on Jesus's forthcoming work, which is the ultimate act of deliverance the Passover anticipated. What started as Israel's deliverance, God also had in mind the ultimate blessing for the world (Gen. 12:1–3). In places within the meal and service where you would naturally expect to hear about the deliverance of Israel through the first Exodus, we see Jesus pointing His disciples to His substitutionary death for sinners—a second and even greater Exodus deliverance.

---

18.   On Mark's meaning, see Darrell Bock, *Mark*. New Cambridge Bible Commentary (Cambridge: Cambridge University Press, 2015), 342–43. Paul also refers to this meal as a part of Early Church tradition in 1 Corinthians 11:23–26. Paul's version mirrors that of Luke on the issue of the death being "for you." Matthew 26:26–28 is the other Synoptic account of this meal. Matthew's version is similar to Mark's with the death being "for many."

19.   Such variations in wording at the same point of an event are not uncommon in the Gospels, but they are not a problem, since a writer can choose to quote or give the force of what is meant. So such differences may simply make explicit what was implicit. The core point in both versions is the same. In speaking of Jesus's act for the many, Mark surely was including His death for the disciples, just as the disciples are but a portion of those Jesus intended to die for on the cross. On this phenomenon in the Gospel accounts, see Darrell L. Bock, "Precision and Accuracy: Making Distinctions in the Cultural Context That Give Us Pause in Pitting the Gospels Against One Another," in *Do Historical Matters Matter to the Faith? A Critical Appraisal of Modern and Postmodern Approaches*, ed. James K. Hoffmeier, Dennis Magary (Wheaton: Crossway, 2012), 367–82.

20.   Again, the difference here is not significant. The only covenant left to establish when Jesus spoke was the eschatologically hoped for New Covenant. Luke makes explicit what Mark says implicitly.

Now an important question arises: Who has the right to transform the meaning of a Feast prescribed by the Torah? The Passover liturgy became part of Israel's historical narrative and had been developing continually since the Exodus as previous chapters in this book have shown.[21] The focus of course in those developments was always the Exodus from Egypt. Yet Jesus takes matters for His disciples further than expected by such customs. He does not simply look back on the original deliverance from Egypt, but rather takes center stage Himself and turns the gaze of His disciples to a new and greater act of deliverance. In this He claims rightful authority over the sacred calendar, not by subtraction but by addition. Jesus also adds to the symbolism of the celebration of Passover and by doing so claims authority over Jewish tradition, similar to His claiming to be Lord of the Sabbath (Luke 6:1–5). Jesus declares Himself to be the full realization of the Passover. He contends that the symbols of the meal have their fulfillment in His sacred work.

This is a significant Christological and soteriological claim. It also is an assertion about His role to Israel and the world involving the hope of eschatology. Jesus is about to fulfill hidden hopes residing in the hearts of His chosen people for ages. Jesus's death would bring a greater salvation than the Exodus and initiate the New Covenant predicted by Jeremiah the prophet (Jer. 31:31–34).

The Messiah's fresh approach to the symbolism of the Seder is also a claim to greater authority over divine acts and deliverance. The disciples sat down to this meal expecting to again look back on what God did, but were now urged to see their Master in a new light as the Sacrificial Lamb, the penultimate peak of God's program having revelatory authority over the divine calendar and Jewish tradition.[22] In this Jesus claimed far more authority than any rabbi before or after Him.

Passover transformed becomes a statement about God's ultimate act of deliverance. Jesus's coming death and resurrection reflects God's vindication of the claims made at His final meal. Jesus reveals His right to create revelation, as God Himself did when He inaugurated the Feast in Exodus 12. The Last Supper becomes a commentary on what God was doing in and through the work of the Messiah. The Last Supper is a commentary rooted in the history of Israel presenting Jesus as the Savior. He uniquely stands at the very nexus of God's plan for saving a broken world.

CONCLUSION

The question of Luke's portrayal of the Last Supper as a Passover meal is both complex and subject to a variety of difficult questions. We only touched on some critical concerns enabling us to better understand the significance

---

21. To develop liturgy around the same event is common in Israelite worship. This book is showing as much about the Passover imagery. However, the extension of liturgy is not what we have here with Jesus. We have fresh symbolism built around a distinct event.

22. We say "penultimate" because after the death comes resurrection, which is the guarantee of everything claimed about the death.

of Jesus's statements in these final moments with His disciples. We believe it was a Passover meal and that the significance of the event is often underappreciated, regardless of how one views the degree to which His Seder meal reflected the later written traditions found in the Mishnah.

We may now ask ourselves, "What does it mean if some of these historical judgments about the Last Supper, its details, or its specific chronology, are wrong?" Ironically, it means little. Many scholars who do not see a Passover meal here still view the Passover as relevant to understanding the backdrop for Jesus's activities at the event.[23] The actions would perhaps not have the same intensity as if a more traditional understanding of a Passover meal was accepted, but His choice to add fresh symbolism, connected to the Passover, should still be viewed as a bold innovation.

All that has been said would apply regardless. Jesus was giving the Passover season deeper significance. A new deliverance, a fresh Exodus, had come. However, if what we have argued is the case, and we are witnessing a Passover meal of some sort, then Jesus's act may be viewed as doubly provocative. His pointing to a new and greater salvation as well as new revelatory authority over salvation and the Feast will only add to the majesty of His person.

All of this means that when we celebrate the Passover with Jesus in mind we are considering two events: (1) one linked to Israel and God's deliverance of the Jewish people from Egypt to begin the journey to the Promised Land and (2) the act of God forgiving our sin and vindicating Jesus through His resurrection and ascension, thereby distributing gifts of salvation to those who trust in His divine work (Acts 2:16–39). Of course, we also can recall that in doing this God fulfilled promises made to Israel that also were about how the people of Israel were a source of blessing for the world through their Messiah. The two events (Exodus and Cross) are powerful bookends. They represent the foreshadowing and the fulfillment. God validates Jesus's once-for-all atoning sacrifice through His resurrection and ascension. In doing so, He shows the ultimate point of the original Exodus for the world.

Passover calls upon God's people to look back. This is a blessing and spiritually enriching for the Jewish community. But when Jesus's followers better understand the Passover, then we are able to affirm our connection to all that Jesus proclaimed at this meal. He is with us as we celebrate the Feast. Whether we recall this during a Passover Seder or at the Lord's Table, we proclaim the Lord's death until He returns and completes what He started at this meal with His disciples (1 Cor. 11:26). To participate in this celebration is to engage in a covenant affirmation. He has initiated the New Covenant with all of its benefits, because He is Lord of the Passover, the Lamb of God, and the One to whom Passover pointed all along.

---

23. A good example of such an approach is Jonathan Klawans, "Was Jesus's Last Supper a Passover?" *Bible Review* 17 (2001): 24–33, 47, http://www.biblicalarchaeology.org/daily/people-cultures-in-the-bible/jesus-historical-jesus/was-jesus-last-supper-a-seder/, who argues against the meal being a Passover meal and yet the proximity of the meal to Passover would not be dismissed as a mere historical coincidence.

5
PASSOVER IN THE GOSPEL
OF JOHN

MITCH GLASER

The Gospel of John is critical to understanding the "Jewish story of Jesus." Many scholars argue that the Gospel of John was primarily written to Gentiles, perhaps because of its relatively later 90 C.E. date of authorship as well as for a variety of textual reasons. However, the Gospel of John really should be viewed through a Jewish lens. The book's author, John, is himself Jewish and one of the earliest disciples of Jesus. Traditionally, and without argument, he is thought to be the author of the Gospel that bears his name in the New Testament as well as the epistles First, Second, and Third John, along with the book of Revelation. John lives longer than any of the other Apostles, according to Early Church tradition, and he dies as an exile in the late first century on the island of Patmos in the Aegean Sea.

John's firsthand experience with Jesus gives him great insight into the details of Jesus's life. He travels with the Messiah, hears His sermons, and is perhaps the one described in his Gospel as "beloved." He is present at the foot of the cross, unlike his peers, and given the task of caring for Mary, the mother of Yeshua (John 19:26–27).

If anyone knows the fine details of Jesus's life, it is John. He is present with Jesus at every Jewish festival the Savior celebrated. Perhaps this is why we learn many new details from John regarding the Feast of Tabernacles as well as some unique aspects of the last Passover supper of Jesus—especially the teaching of the Savior during that meal, generally referred to as the Upper Room Discourse.

John mentions Passover quite often in his Gospel. In his very first mention of Jesus, John the Baptist refers to Him as "the Lamb of God who takes away the sin of the world!" (John 1:29). We may assume that his original hearers understood this comment in light of the Passover. John describes three different Passovers observed by Jesus: the first Passover in John 2:13; the second Passover in John 6:4; and the final Passover, which is the focus of this chapter, found in John 11:55, 12:1, and 13:1, with additional references in John 18:28 and 19:14. It should also be noted that Luke tells us that John was asked by Jesus to make preparations for this final Passover meal (Luke 22:8–13).

John provides unique information about the last week of Jesus's life and therefore his description of the last days of Jesus as related to this final Passover will be briefly surveyed in this chapter. We will also explore the timing of the crucifixion and resurrection of Yeshua and attempt to sync the last week of the Savior's life described in the Synoptic Gospels (Matthew, Mark, and Luke) with that of the Gospel of John. Certain textual clues linked to the third Passover in John give us further insight into the above.

THE FINAL WEEK OF JESUS'S LIFE AND OLD TESTAMENT PROPHECY

Often referred to as His Passion, this last week is the most eventful of Jesus's short life. Certainly, it is the most significant from a human perspective, as it includes His death and resurrection—the penultimate moment of human history. His final week, according to John, also includes various teachings, which are unique to this Gospel such as His Upper Room Discourse, which taught on the Holy Spirit, High Priestly Prayer, etc. The last week of the Jesus's life is also significant because many Old Testament prophecies were fulfilled during this week, especially those involving His atoning death and resurrection.

The agenda, goals, and purposes of His last week are outlined in both the Old and New Testaments and driven by the necessity for Jesus to fulfill all that is predicted about Him in the Law, the Prophets, and the Writings, as well as His own predictions in the Gospels.[1] In particular, three Old Testament passages heavily influence the agenda of the Messiah's last week on earth: Isaiah 53, Daniel 9:24–26, and Leviticus 23. These texts create a path for what Yeshua would do and when He would do it.

1. Isaiah 53—The prediction of the Messiah's suffering, death, and resurrection, along with Israel's response to His message.

---

1. Gospel harmony studies by biblical scholars such as A. T. Robertson, *A Harmony of the Gospels for Students of the Life of Christ: Based on the Broadus Harmony in the Revised Version* (New York: George H. Doran, 1922), are especially helpful in understanding the last week of Jesus's life as their works attempt to harmonize the various Gospel passages in chronological order. For a more recent Greek-English edition of a harmony of the four Gospels, see Kurt Aland, ed., *Synopsis of the Four Gospels: Greek-English Edition of the Synopsis Quattuor Evangeliorum,* 12th ed. (Stuttgart: German Bible Society, 2001). Another helpful book in this regard is by Harold Hoehner, *Chronological Aspects of the Life of Christ* (Grand Rapids: Zondervan, 1977). See also the classic by Alfred Edersheim, *The Life and Times of Jesus the Messiah,* 2 vols. (London, Longmans, Green: 1883). This magnum opus is admittedly somewhat difficult to read, though it contains a wealth of valuable information as Edersheim, a Jewish believer in Jesus, shows the interplay between the Gospels and first-century Jewish life. We cannot assume, however, that material written as part of the Mishnah two hundred years later was precisely followed in the first century C.E. An earlier book by Alfred Edersheim, *The Temple: Its Ministries and Services* (London: Religious Tract Society, 1874), is also very helpful in understanding the Jewish backgrounds of the Gospels.

2. Daniel 9:24–26—The prediction of the Messiah's death as detailed in the prophecy of the seventy weeks.
3. Leviticus 23—The pattern of the Messiah's passion as revealed through the Passover, which will especially influence the last week of Jesus's life.

The Jewish Festivals found in Leviticus 23 appear to be prophetic types and in one way or another are fulfilled in the person and work of Jesus. We view the first four "spring" festivals as fulfilled in His first coming and the three additional "fall" festivals as fulfilled in His second coming.[2]

Additional Old Testament prophecies such as Psalm 22 and Zechariah 12:10 also help to paint a prophetic portrait of our Messiah's last days on earth. As the Apostle Peter writes,

> As to this salvation, the prophets who prophesied of the grace that would come to you made careful searches and inquiries, seeking to know what person or time the Spirit of Christ within them was indicating as He predicted the sufferings of Christ and the glories to follow. (1 Peter 1:10–11)

There is no doubt that the Savior of the world was born to die in order to fulfill many direct prophecies and types, especially that of the Lamb of God—a direct comparison to the Passover lamb whose blood was smeared on the doorposts of the Israelites to protect their firstborn males from the tenth plague of the Exodus story.

The Apostle John, in the book of Revelation, describes Jesus as "the Lamb who has been slain" (Rev. 13:8). The Apostle Peter adds that we "were not redeemed with perishable things like silver or gold…but with precious blood, as of a lamb unblemished and spotless, the blood of Christ. For He was foreknown before the foundation of the world, but has appeared in these last times for the sake of you" (1 Peter 1:18–20).

The predicted role of Jesus as the suffering and sacrificial Lamb of God who will die for sin and rise from the grave is not peripheral to the plan of God, but rather is at the very heart of who Jesus is and what He came to accomplish. Isaiah had already used the prophetic imagery of the Passover lamb in his well-known chapter 53.

> He was oppressed and He was afflicted,
>   yet He did not open His mouth;
> like a lamb that is led to slaughter,
>   and like a sheep that is silent before its shearers,
>   so He did not open His mouth. (Isa. 53:7)

---

2. See Mitch Glaser and Zhava Glaser, *The Fall Feasts of Israel* (Chicago: Moody Press, 1987).

THE GOSPEL OF JOHN AND EVENTS OF JESUS'S LAST WEEK

There is considerable discussion regarding the chronology of the last week of Jesus's life. Attempts by scholars to harmonize John's Gospel with the Synoptics abound. We will primarily focus on the Last Supper and attempt to understand what took place, when the meal occurred, whether or not it was a Seder, and the importance of what Jesus taught during this final meal. Prior to looking day-by-day at the events of Jesus's last week, we will note what the term *Passover* can refer to as it is used in Scripture as well as review a Jewish reckoning of time in terms of what constitutes a day, that is, when it starts and when it ends.

THE PASSOVER SEASON, THE PASSOVER, AND THE OFFERING OF THE PASSOVER

For our study of Jesus's last week, it is critical to understand the three ways the term *Passover* is used in the Gospels, which will shed some light on the ways the Passover events in the Synoptic Gospels align with the Gospel of John. We will also note the sense of *Passover* as a Jewish festival.

A Season

First of all, Passover is referred to in the Scriptures as a *season*. This includes the seven-day festival of Unleavened Bread as well as the one-day Passover event (Lev. 23:5–8). It is helpful to view the Passover as a season that perhaps even goes beyond the eight days of the combined Feasts of Passover and Unleavened Bread described in Leviticus 23. The Passover season has many different elements to it, including a first-century tradition of Jewish men coming to Jerusalem to be purified, as John notes in his Gospel: "Now the Passover of the Jews was near, and many went up to Jerusalem out of the country before the Passover to purify themselves" (John 11:55).

A Meal

The term *Passover* is also used in reference to the Passover meal. This meal developed throughout the centuries and became the vehicle by which the Jewish people fulfilled the decree of Moses to remember the Passover event. The details and liturgy for this home-based service are found in the *Haggadah*, the biblical-liturgical ceremony used to retell the story of the redemption of the Israelites from Egypt. We are suggesting that Jesus and His disciples used a more primitive and undeveloped form of this guide and that the Seder was observed in John 13 as it was in Luke 22 and Matthew 26.[3]

---

3. For more on Jesus's Last Supper with His disciples related to the celebration of Passover in the Gospel of Luke, see the companion chapter in this volume, chapter 4, "Passover in the Gospel of Luke," by Darrell L. Bock.

The Sacrifices

Finally, the word *Passover* is also used of the Passover sacrifices; including the specific Passover offerings (Num. 28:16–24; Deut. 16:5), the daily offerings known as *Tamid* (Num. 28:23; Exod. 29:38–42), and the *hagigah* offerings offered at all three pilgrim Festivals (Exod. 23:14–17). Alfred Edersheim, the great Messianic Jewish commentator of the nineteenth century, summarizes as follows: "Thus the sacrifices which every Israelite was to offer at the Passover were, besides his share in the Paschal lamb, a burnt offering, the *hagigah* (one or two), and offerings of joyousness—all as God had blessed each household."[4]

An Aliyah Festival

Passover is also one of the three *aliyah* festivals when Jewish men "go up" (עֲלִיָּה, *aliyah*) to Jerusalem to celebrate the Festival on behalf of their family or village. In addition to *Pesach* (Passover), the other two pilgrimage (*aliyah*) festivals are *Shavuot* (Pentecost) and *Sukkot* (Tabernacles).

> Three times in a year all your males shall appear before the LORD your God in the place which He chooses, at the Feast of Unleavened Bread and at the Feast of Weeks and at the Feast of Booths, and they shall not appear before the LORD empty-handed. (Deut. 16:16)

JEWISH DAYS: EVENING AND MORNING

John undoubtedly lived according to the Hebrew calendar—as did the other Apostles, all of whom were Jewish. Most dates noted in the Gospels should be viewed through the lens of the Hebrew calendar. The Apostles observed the calendar in the same manner as any other first-century Jew and began their days of the week at twilight (lit., between the two evenings)—not sunrise. This is obvious from the establishment of the Passover and Feast of Unleavened Bread.

> In the first month, on the fourteenth day of the month at twilight is the LORD's Passover. Then on the fifteenth day of the same month there is the Feast of Unleavened Bread to the LORD; for seven days you shall eat unleavened bread. (Lev. 23:5–6)

A DAY-BY-DAY LOOK AT THE LAST WEEK OF JESUS'S LIFE

With a sense of how the term *Passover* is variously used in John's Gospel and the rest of Scripture as well as how a day is reckoned according to the Hebrew calendar, we now consider the unique insights the Gospel of John provides into the day-by-day chronology of the last week of the Messiah's earthly life (see appendices 8 and 9).

---

4. Edersheim, *The Temple*, 187.

Nisan the Eighth—Friday: Six Days before the Passover

John 12:1 is critical in establishing the chronology for this final week.

> Jesus, therefore, six days before the Passover, came to Bethany where Lazarus
> was, whom Jesus had raised from the dead.

Before Jesus enters Jerusalem for the last time, He visits His favorite family in Bethany on the sixth day before the Passover. We know that Bethany is the home of Lazarus, Mary, and Martha and is located on the slopes of the Mount of Olives, nearby to Jerusalem. John writes in 11:18, "Now Bethany was near Jerusalem, about two miles off." According to tradition, Bethany was an outpost for festival pilgrims to rest from their journey, especially those who were sick and needed medical help and time to recover. Bethany is also the home of Simon the Leper.

In the Apostle John's account, the Messiah's visit to Lazarus' home took place "six days before the Passover," which was the eighth day of Nisan, as Passover fell on the fourteenth day of the Hebrew month Nisan (see Lev. 23:5–6 quoted above). The dinner Jesus attends at the home of Lazarus is probably a Sabbath dinner, taking place on Friday night. We may assume that Jesus arrives in Bethany during the daytime, on the eighth of Nisan, as travel is impossible on the Sabbath (Saturday).

Nisan the Ninth—Saturday: Five Days before the Passover

This Sabbath meal observed on Friday evening occurs on the beginning of the ninth of Nisan. Several critical events take place during this Sabbath meal. Mary, who somehow knows that Jesus is going to die, anoints the Lord with burial perfume (John 12:2–8; cf. Matt. 26:6–13; Mark 14:3–9). Judas contests the use of the expensive perfume as he allegedly wants to use the money for the poor, but actually he is a thief and plans to keep the money for himself (John 12:6–7). Jesus will identify Judas as His betrayer during the Passover Seder (John 13:26; Luke 22:3–6).

Enemies of Jesus and Lazarus are among the group gathered in Bethany that weekend. This group of Jewish leaders is already plotting to seize Yeshua as His popularity among the common people has been growing. They are also going to arrest Lazarus. At this point, John writes,

> Now the chief priests and the Pharisees had given orders that if anyone knew
> where He was, he was to report it, so that they might seize Him. (John 11:57)

And then he says further,

> The large crowd of the Jews then learned that He was there; and they came [to
> Bethany[5]], not for Jesus's sake only, but that they might also see Lazarus, whom

---

5. For more on the movement of the crowd to Bethany, see Thomas L. Constable, "Notes on John,

He raised from the dead. But the chief priests planned to put Lazarus to death also; because on account of him many of the Jews were going away and were believing in Jesus. (John 12:9–11)

This tension intensifies during the last week of Jesus's life, culminating in His crucifixion. However, we should assume that the Sabbath day, the ninth day of Nisan, came and went quietly, including the usual rest and worship on the Sabbath for Jesus, His disciples, and hosts.

Nisan the Tenth—Sunday: Four Days before the Passover

The "action" picks up on Sunday, the first day of the week, and involves what has become known as the Triumphal Entry. John writes,

> On the next day the large crowd who had come to the feast, when they heard that Jesus was coming to Jerusalem, took the branches of the palm trees and went out to meet Him, and began to shout, "Hosanna! BLESSED IS HE WHO COMES IN THE NAME OF THE LORD, even the King of Israel." (John 12:12–14)

John uses the phrase "the next day" in verse 12 to refer to the day after the Sabbath; that would be Sunday, the first day of the week. Therefore, the following events take place on the tenth day of Nisan—beginning on Saturday night and continuing until twilight on Sunday.

The Choosing of the Lamb

On the tenth of Nisan the Jewish family will choose a Passover lamb from among their flock to be sacrificed on the fourteenth day of the month. During this four-day period, the lamb is observed and tested to make certain it is in good health and also is pure, without any blemish. As Moses writes,

> Speak to all the congregation of Israel, saying, "On the tenth of this month they are each one to take a lamb for themselves, according to their fathers' households, a lamb for each household. Now if the household is too small for a lamb, then he and his neighbor nearest to his house are to take one according to the number of persons in them; according to what each man should eat, you are to divide the lamb. Your lamb shall be an unblemished male a year old; you may take it from the sheep or from the goats. You shall keep it until the fourteenth day of the same month, then the whole assembly of the congregation of Israel is to kill it at twilight." (Exod. 12:3–6)

On "Palm Sunday," Jesus presents Himself as the Lamb of God, chosen by God before the foundation of the world (1 Peter 1:20; Rev. 13:8b). During

---

2017 Edition," *Sonic Light*, http://www.soniclight.com/constable/notes/pdf/john.pdf, PDF file, comments on 12:9 and 12:10–11 (p. 233).

the remainder of the week, He will endure fierce temptations, tests, and threats against His life and prove Himself to be pure and holy, worthy and blameless.

He is presented both as the Lamb to be slain and the King to be enthroned, but not in the manner the majority of Jewish people expect. By entering the Holy City on the foal of a donkey as a humble king, the Messiah fulfills the prophecy of Zechariah 9:9 (Matt. 21:10–17), which the disciples fully understand after Jesus is glorified (John 12:16).

His entering the city as a king, even in humility, helps explain the actions of the multitudes as they cut palm branches and spread them before Him. This may have been a premature celebration of Tabernacles, which is understandable because according to the Prophet Zechariah, faithful Jews and Gentiles will celebrate Tabernacles in the Messianic kingdom (Zech. 14:16–21). The people greet Jesus as He enters the Holy City by quoting from Psalm 118:25–26, a kingdom psalm. The rabbis tell us that this is the psalm that will be uttered by the nation of Israel in welcoming King Messiah.[6]

The palm branches are usually used to cover the Sukkot booths, the small booths the Jewish people are commanded to build in obedience to the laws given by Moses regarding this holiday. Tabernacles are also associated with the Messianic kingdom and the Messianic king in both Scripture and Jewish tradition. So it makes some sense that the Jewish people welcoming Jesus into Jerusalem associate His coming into Jerusalem with the Feast of Tabernacles. The general Jewish population, however, is probably less familiar with these passages in the Bible, which speak about His coming in humility to die an atoning death, such as the prophet describes in Isaiah 53. In effect, the Jewish people who gathered on "Palm Sunday" may have believed they were welcoming the Messianic King to Jerusalem.[7]

Nisan the Fourteenth—Thursday Evening through Friday Afternoon

After Sunday, the tenth day of Nisan, Jesus and His disciples are involved in a number of events in and around the vicinity of Jerusalem, presumably walking the two miles from Bethany and later returning in the evening. Harmonizing all the details in some instances can be very challenging given the limited but notable differences when comparing parallel passages in the Synoptics themselves as well as with John's Gospel. But as our purpose pertains to the Passover in John's Gospel, it best to move past the various interim events and focus on what is about to happen on the evening of Nisan the fourteenth.

---

6. For an in-depth discussion of the kingdom orientation of the text and its use in relationship to the Feast of Tabernacles, see Andrew C. Brunson, *Psalm 118 in the Gospel of John: An Intertextual Study on the New Exodus Pattern in the Theology of John*, Wissenschaftliche Untersuchungen zum Neuen Testament 2, 158 (Tübingen: Mohr Siebeck, 2003), 40–50.

7. For additional information on the Messianic connections to and significance of Israel's Feasts in general and the Feast of Tabernacles (*Sukkot*) in particular, see chapters 1–2, 13–17, and the conclusion in Glaser and Glaser, *The Fall Feasts of Israel*.

The Last Supper

The chronology of events continues on the fourteenth day of Nisan, which is why we suggest that this is the date of the Last Supper. According to Leviticus 23:6, the Feast of Unleavened Bread begins the following day, on the fifteenth of Nisan, and lasts for seven days. However, these two Festivals were combined in the Jewish mind at the time of Jesus as is the case today. Regarding these Feasts, Alfred Edersheim notes in his book, *The Temple: Its Ministries and Services*,

> But from their close connection they are generally treated as one, both in the Old and in the New Testament; [Matt 26:17; Mark 14:12; Luke 22:1] and Josephus, on one occasion, describes it as "a feast for eight days" [*Ant.* 2.15, 1; but cf. 3.10, 5; 9.13, 3].[8]

The Passover Service

The meal Jesus celebrates is an early form of the traditional Passover Seder. The meal observed that evening includes many of the usual elements of the Seder observed by Jewish people today: the breaking of the *matzah*, the reclining of the participants, the taking of four cups—only two of which are named in the Gospels—the bitter herbs—the washing of the hands, etc. These elements are further explored in other chapters in this book.

We will highlight the Seder observances described by the Apostle John in his Gospel. These include the washing of feet rather than hands, the reclining of the participants, and the dipping of the *sop* (either unleavened bread or a vegetable dipped into some type of liquid), which was given to Judas Iscariot, by which Jesus identified His betrayer (John 13:21–30).

The Passover Seder of Jesus also provides the background for His teaching recorded in chapters 13–17, usually referred to as the Upper Room Discourse. The Last Seder takes place in the Old City, in a large upper room (ἀνάγαιον μέγα, *anagaion mega*, Luke 22:12), which Luke has previously described as a "guest room" (Luke 22:11). It very well may have taken place late into the evening as that would have allowed time for Jesus and the disciples to have made the proper sacrifice of a lamb at the Temple.

Again, it must be restated that it is difficult to determine which traditional observances associated with the mishnaic or contemporary Seder Jesus and His disciples observed. The text suggests that though primitive, certain traditions still observed by Jewish families today may have been already included as part of Jesus's Passover meal (see appendix 4).[9]

---

8. Edersheim, *The Temple*, 177.

9. In *The Eucharistic Words of Jesus*, Joachim Jeremias comments further on the nature of the Passover-like meal Jesus and His disciples observed: "There are other traces of the synoptic chronology in the fourth gospel, especially in the account of Jesus's last supper (John 13:2ff.). The fact that John depicts here the same meal as that described in Mark 14:17–25 par. is shown by the betrayal scene (John 13:18–30, cf. Mark 14:18–21 par.) as well as by the ensuing walk to Gethsemane (John 18:1ff., cf. Mark 14:26ff. par.). Some of the remarks made by John presuppose that this was a passover meal. According to John

The Examinations

The Sanhedrin arrest and then examine Jesus in order to collect evidence for a trial by Pontius Pilate, the Roman prefect (governor) of Judaea (26–36 C.E.), who was under the emperor Tiberius. In a rejoinder written in response to the idea that the Jewish leaders put Jesus on trial, Darrell Bock argues that Jesus was examined and not tried; the Jewish leaders were collecting evidence for Pilate.[10] Moreover, when Pilate later tells them to take Jesus and judge Him according to their own law, the Jewish leaders are prepared and say they lack judicial authority to put anyone to death (John 18:31). Bock said, "This is an examination to gather evidence for Pilate, *not* a trial. They could not issue a verdict and deliver a sanction for the verdict. This use of the Jewish jurisprudence is misleading."[11] The illegalities of the alleged trials of Jesus by the Jewish leaders have unfortunately become a basis for historic antisemitism.

Before Annas (John 18:12–14, 19–24)

The only mention we have of this "hearing" for Jesus before Annas is found in the Gospel of John and may be viewed as a private inquiry. Annas, the former High Priest, is the father-in law-of Caiaphas, the current High Priest. Annas also keeps the title of High Priest, which was not uncommon practice. He hears Jesus's story, rejects His innocence, and sends Him to Caiaphas.

It is possible that Annas and Caiaphas were in the same house, which, if the current archaeological identification of the house is accurate, is about a forty-five-minute walk from the Garden of Gethsemane (see appendix 9). In any case, these examinations take place within close proximity to one another, which is why they could have easily been completed during the night and into the early morning—in time for Jesus to be crucified on Friday.

Before Caiaphas and the Sanhedrin (Mark 14:53–65; 15:1; Luke 22:66–71)

Jesus's appearance before Caiaphas and the Sanhedrin is also a religious inquiry. There is virtually no information given in the Gospel of John about this "trial." Caiaphas simply sends Jesus to Pontius Pilate for an appearance before the governor in the Praetorium, which is a forty-five-minute walk

---

also the Last Supper, as we have seen, took place in Jerusalem despite the overcrowding of the holy city by the passover pilgrims (cf. John 11:55; 12:12, 18, 20). According to John also the Last Supper was held at an unusual hour: it lasted into the night. According to John also Jesus celebrated this meal with the closest circle of his disciples. According to John also the Last Supper was a ceremonial meal: those who took part in it reclined at table. According to John also when the meal was over Jesus did not return to Bethany but went to a garden on the other side of the Kidron valley. In this connection we must also consider John 13:10: the meal was taken in a state of levitical purity; further 13:29: the supposition of some of the disciples that Judas was either to purchase necessities for the imminent feast or to distribute alms may also indicate that it was passover night." Joachim Jeremias, *The Eucharistic Words of Jesus* trans. Norman Perrin, rev. ed., New Testament Library (New York: Scribner, 1966), 81–82.

10.   Darrell Bock, "Blasphemy and the Jewish Examination of Jesus," *Bulletin for Biblical Research* 17, no. 1 (2007): 53–114, https://www.ibr-bbr.org/files/bbr/bbr17a03.pdf.

11.   Dr. Darrell L. Bock, telephone conversation with author in the course of editing this chapter.

back across the Valley of Kidron to the Jaffa Gate. Again, close enough to allow for the morning crucifixion.

According to theologian and biblical scholar D. A. Carson, "Archaeologists differ as to whether this headquarters was Herod's palace on the western wall, or the Fortress of Antonia (named after Mark Antony) northwest of the temple complex and connected by steps to the temple's outer court (*cf.* Acts 21:35, 40)."[12]

Before Pilate—Two Appearances (John 18:28–38; Luke 23:1–7, 13–25)

Jesus's two appearances before Pontius Pilate are the civil inquiry, as the Romans did not allow the Jewish people to judge their own community members (see b. Sanhedrin 2a, 52a; y. Sanhedrin 41a).

> Therefore when Pilate heard these words, he brought Jesus out, and sat down on the judgment seat at a place called The Pavement, but in Hebrew, Gabbatha. Now it was the day of preparation for the Passover; it was about the sixth hour. And he said to the Jews, "Behold, your King!" So they cried out, "Away with Him, away with Him, crucify Him!" Pilate said to them, "Shall I crucify your King?" The chief priests answered, "We have no king but Caesar." (John 19:13–16)

John also describes the time in question as "early" ($\hat{\eta}\nu$ δὲ πρωΐ, *en de proi*, "it was early"; John 18:28), indicating that the trial before Pilate in the Praetorium takes place in the early hours of the morning (Mark 15:1).

Before Herod (Luke 23:6–12)

The trial before Pilate the governor takes place in two parts, between which Jesus is sent to Herod Antipas, who was in Jerusalem visiting from Galilee during the time of the Feast. Herod finds no reason to convict Jesus of political crimes and sends Him back to Pilate.

The Friday Crucifixion

It appears that the crucifixion occurs at 9:00 AM the next morning on the fourteenth of Nisan—Friday. Once again, we must remember that the Jewish day of the fourteenth began the evening before. Jesus dies at 3:00 PM around the time of the afternoon sacrifices, which are being offered in the Temple.

Both Gospel writers John and Mark note the hour when the crucifixion begins. And though they seem to disagree on the hour, the following explanation seems to harmonize the differences.

John's sixth hour and Mark's third hour (Mark 15:25) can be harmonized if we understand John's use of the sixth hour as Roman (see John 1:39; 4:6, 52) and Mark's use of the third hour as reflective of a more Jewish

---

12. D. A. Carson, *The Gospel According to John*, Pillar New Testament Commentary (Leicester, UK: Inter-Varsity Press; Grand Rapids: Eerdmans, 1991), 588.

context. Roman timekeeping begins at midnight, whereas first-century Judaism tells time beginning with sunrise (m. Berakhot 1:2).[13] So the Jewish method begins the day around 6:00 AM (also see John 1:29, 4:6, 52).

John affirms the timing of early morning when he mentions that the rooster crowed after Peter's denial (John 18:27), which the informed reader will easily understand as an early morning event. The Gospel of Mark does the same by referring to the crowing of the rooster as well (Mark 14:72). Therefore, both John and Mark both describe the crucifixion verdict decided at about 6:00 AM and the crucifixion beginning at 9:00 AM, Friday, the fourteenth day of Nisan.

We believe Jesus died on that Friday afternoon, noting that the Gospels indicate there is an urgency to remove the bodies and prepare Jesus's body for burial in view of the approaching Sabbath (John 9:31, 38–42).

> When evening had already come, because *it was the preparation day, that is, the day before the Sabbath*, Joseph of Arimathea came, a prominent member of the Council, who himself was waiting for the kingdom of God; and he gathered up courage and went in before Pilate, and asked for the body of Jesus. (Mark 15:42–43, emphasis added)

Mark uses the Greek term παρασκευή, *paraskeuē*, "preparation," which usually refers to Friday—the day before the Sabbath. Biblical scholar Harold Hoehner also argues for a Friday crucifixion:

> Jesus predicted that He would die and be raised on the third day (Matt. 16:21; Mark 8:31; Luke 9:22). When one reads these events in the Gospels, one clearly receives the impression that Jesus rose on the third day. Jesus's body was laid in the tomb on the evening of the day of preparation (Friday), the day before the Sabbath (Matt. 27:62; 28:1; Mark 15:42; Luke 23:54, 56; John 19:31, 42). The women returned home and rested on the Sabbath (Saturday, Luke 23:56).[14]

Therefore, Friday, the fourteenth of Nisan, seems to best fit the facts of the New Testament and the prophetic and typological expectation that the

---

13. Professor Lewis A. Foster explains the differences between Jewish and Roman timekeeping: "The Jews calculated the passage of days from sunset to sunset. Thus their day began at 6 o'clock in the evening, though they numbered their hours of the day from 6 A.M. This differed from the Roman method, which measured days from midnight to midnight. The difference is reflected in the Gospel narratives. Mark describes the time of Jesus's crucifixion as the 'third hour' (Mark 15:25), but the Gospel of John notes the time of his earlier condemnation as the 'sixth hour' (John 19:14). The difference is reasonably accounted for by recognizing that Mark uses the Jewish method (third hour = 9 A.M.) and John employs the Roman designation (sixth hour = 6 A.M.)." Lewis A. Foster, "The Chronology of the New Testament," in *Expositor's Bible Commentary: Introductory Articles*, ed. Frank E. Gaebelein and J. D. Douglas (Grand Rapids: Zondervan, 1979), 1:594.
14. Hoehner, *Chronological Aspects of the Life of Christ*, 71.

Messiah will die as the Lamb of God whose blood covers our sins in the same way the blood of the lamb in Exodus 12 covered the doorposts of the homes. We will not build the case for the Friday crucifixion upon typology; however, the textual evidence still points to a Friday crucifixion.

Joachim Jeremias, the German scholar who wrote the excellent book *The Eucharistic Words of Jesus*, likewise affirms the Friday crucifixion:

> All four Gospels agree that the day of Jesus's death was a Friday (Mark 15.42; Matt. 27.62; Luke 23.54; John 19.31, 42). The Jewish day was reckoned from sunset to sunset, *this Friday* (from 6 p.m. on Maundy Thursday to 6 p.m. on Good Friday) includes the whole of the Passion in its narrower sense: the Last Supper, Gethsemane, arrest and trial, crucifixion and burial (Mark 14.17–15.47; Matt. 26.20–27.61; Luke 22.14–23.56a; John 13.2–19.42); all the four evangelists agreed also on this point.[15]

The reason some believe the crucifixion takes place on Thursday grows out of efforts to argue for Jesus remaining in the grave for three literal twenty-four-hour days. However, the chronological details as presented in the Gospels do not substantiate a Thursday death, and therefore, it appears that the issue of the literal three days and nights must be solved in a different way.

The Passover Offerings and the Moment of Messiah's Death

Jewish tradition indicates that the Passover lamb is to be sacrificed around 3:00 PM on the fourteenth of Nisan, which is Friday afternoon (m. Pesahim 5:1).[16] However, we learn from Josephus that upwards of three million Jewish people were present in Jerusalem during the days of the Feast, so it is likely that the initial sacrifices took quite some time to perform.[17] If true, this would mean that Jesus, the Lamb of God, was crucified during the same period of time the Jewish people were offering their lambs at the Temple.

Nisan the Sixteenth—Sunday Morning

The Resurrection

We are suggesting that Jesus is crucified on Friday, Nisan the fourteenth, and rises from the dead on Sunday, Nisan the sixteenth. This allows for the Passover described by John to be observed on the beginning of Nisan the fourteenth—the last Thursday evening of Jesus's life.

---

15. Jeremias, *The Eucharistic Words of Jesus*, 15–16.
16. This particular Passover sacrifice is not easily found in the Bible but is described in great detail in the Mishnah, which was written a few hundred years later and remains one of our best sources for Jewish information at the time.
17. Josephus, *Jewish War* 2.280. Elsewhere, Josephus says that over 250,000 lambs were sacrificed for Passover. He says that the lambs were sacrificed from 3 PM until 5 PM, but this would require over 2,000 lambs sacrificed per minute, which is unlikely. In any case, Yeshua's death was taking place during the time of these sacrifices (*Jewish War* 6.424).

The argument against this position is founded on the assumed necessity of having Jesus's body remain in the grave for three literal, twenty-four-hour days. The verse usually quoted on this topic is found in Matthew 12:40,

> For just as Jonah was three days and three nights in the belly of the sea monster, so will the Son of Man be *three days and three nights* in the heart of the earth. (emphasis added)

However, Mark describes the event in Mark 8:31 as simply "after three days":

> And He began to teach them that the Son of Man must suffer many things and be rejected by the elders and the chief priests and the scribes, and be killed, and *after three days* rise again. (emphasis added)

Again, Paul, in his Gospel formula penned in 1 Corinthians 15:3–4, pinpoints "on the third day":[18]

> For I delivered to you as of first importance what I also received, that Christ died for our sins according to the Scriptures, and that He was buried, and that He was raised *on the third day* according to the Scriptures. (emphasis added)

The above passages do not necessarily demand three twenty-four-hour days. Yet how then can these passages be harmonized? It is our understanding that in first-century Jewish thinking, any part of a day is counted as a day for the purpose of fulfilling ritual obligations.[19]

A passage often quoted to bolster this view is found in the Jerusalem Talmud. Rabbi Eleazar ben Azariah (lived ca. 100 C.E.), who was the tenth

---

18.   Also see Matthew 16:21; 17:23; 20:19; Luke 13:32; 24:46.

19.   On the question of counting any part of a day as a day with respect to fulfilling ritual obligations, Hoehner (*Chronological Aspects of the Life of Christ*, 74n17) references b. Pesahim 4a, which is as follows (quoted from the Babylonian Talmud, Judeo-Christian Research, http://juchre.org/talmud/pesachim1.htm#4a):

> A certain man used to say, "Judge my case." Said they, This proves that he is descended from Dan, for it is written, Dan shall judge his people, as one of the tribes of Israel. A certain man was wont to go about and say, "By the sea shore thorn-bushes are fir-trees." They investigated and found that he was descended from Zebulun, for it is written, Zebulun shall dwell at the haven of the sea. And now that it is established that all agree that "or" means evening, consider: according to both R. Judah and R. Meir, leaven is forbidden from six hours and onward only, then let us search in the sixth [hour]? And should you answer, The zealous are early [to perform] religious duties, then let us search from the morning? For it is written, and in the eighth day the flesh of his foreskin shall be circumcised, and it was taught: The whole day is valid for circumcision, but that the zealous are early [to perform] their religious duties, for it is said, And Abraham rose early in the morning!—Said R. Nahman b. Isaac: [It was fixed] at the hour when people are found at home, while the light of a lamp is good for searching. Abaye observed: Therefore a scholar must not commence his regular session in the evening of the thirteenth breaking into the fourteenth, lest his studies absorb him and he come to neglect his religious duty.

in the descent from Ezra the priest, stated: "A day and night are an *Onah* ['a portion of time'] and the portion of an *Onah* is as the whole of it."[20]

A first-century Jewish view of time allows for Jesus to be raised "on the third day," as Paul and Mark both describe.[21] The Jewish people at the time would have understood the principle that a part of the day is counted as a day in terms of ritual purification. The reference to Jonah's time in the belly of the "sea monster" (great fish) is used by Jesus to describe what was about to happen to Him by comparing it to a well-known story in the Hebrew Bible. Jesus, however, is not necessarily making a case for an exact parallel regarding three twenty-four-hour days.

The Sunday resurrection, on the first day of the week, seems to affirm the Friday crucifixion as well, and the Gospels, especially Luke 24:13 and 21, point to a Friday crucifixion. If the premise is accepted that Jesus died on Friday and rose on Sunday, then the resurrection may well have happened on the Festival of First Fruits, which took place on the day after the Sabbath.

> Speak to the sons of Israel and say to them, "When you enter the land which I am going to give to you and reap its harvest, then you shall bring in the sheaf of the first fruits of your harvest to the priest. He shall wave the sheaf before the LORD for you to be accepted; on the day after the sabbath the priest shall wave it." (Lev. 23:10–11)

In 1 Corinthians 15:20, the Apostle Paul seems to view the resurrected Jesus as "the first fruits of those who are asleep," which is likely linked to his understanding that the waving of the sheaf of grain (the first fruit) takes place on Sunday as well, affirming the typology of the passion: Jesus dies as the Lamb of God and rises as *Messiah the first fruits* (v. 23). Paul, a well-trained first century Pharisee, would have understood these parallels and points them out under the inspiration of the Holy Spirit, especially to his Jewish readers.

THE ARGUMENT AGAINST THE MEAL IN JOHN 13 BEING A PASSOVER SEDER

The passage that causes some to question whether or not the meal in John 13 was a Passover Seder is found in John 18:28. John mentions the concern of the Jewish leaders about defilement that would keep them from eating the Passover.

---

20. Quoted in Hoehner, *Chronological Aspects of the Life of Christ*, 74. Hoehner's footnote to the quotation reads: "Jerusalem Talmud: Shabbath ix. 3; cf. also Babylonian Talmud: b. Pesahim 4a."

21. For example, see references cited in Eric Lyons, "Did Jesus Rise 'On' or 'After' the Third Day?," *Apologetics Press*, 2004, http://apologeticspress.org/apcontent.aspx?category=6&article=756. Also see Michael R. Licona, *The Resurrection of Jesus: A New Historiographical Approach* (Downers Grove, IL; Nottingham, England: IVP Academic; Apollos, 2010), 324–29.

Then they led Jesus from Caiaphas into the Praetorium, and it was early; and they themselves did not enter into the Praetorium so that they would not be defiled, but might eat the Passover.

If we understand the use of the term "eat the Passover" in this verse as a reference to the Seder meal celebrated earlier on Thursday night, the beginning of Nisan the fourteenth, then there does seem to be a potential chronological contradiction. However, we must remember that Passover was viewed as a season and not always as one event.

John identifies this event as taking place on "the day of preparation for the Passover" (John 19:14), which was the Friday of Passover week.[22] Even if they did celebrate the supper on Thursday night, the leaders would still need to remain pure as John 19:14 implies (cf. 18:28; 19:31, 42), since there were additional sacrifices to be made that week, including the *hagigah* offerings. These were freewill offerings and could be offered at any time, but only if the one making the offering is ritually pure and untainted by leaven. Edersheim affirms this idea,

> But on one point the law was quite explicit—Chagigah might not be offered by any person who had contracted Levitical defilement [Pesahim 6.3]. It was on this ground that, when the Jews led "Jesus from Caiaphas unto the hall of judgment," they themselves went not into the judgment-hall, lest they should be defiled, but that they might "eat the Passover" (John 18:28).[23]

The question of what would have defiled them is intriguing. Was it simply related to their concern with entering a Gentile home or institution? This is probably not the case. It is more likely that the Jewish leaders were concerned with the possibility of encountering leaven in the Praetorium, which would have defiled them. If they were defiled, then they could not offer the *hagigah* Passover sacrifice with their family, which was then also eaten.[24]

---

22. Carson (*The Gospel According to John*, 588) reasons, "Hence *paraskeuē tou pascha* probably means "Friday of Passover week" (*cf.* also notes on v. 31). In this view, John and the Synoptics agree that the last supper was eaten on Thursday evening (*i.e.* the onset of Friday, by Jewish reckoning), and was a Passover meal."

23. Edersheim, *The Temple*, 218.

24. The following lengthy comment (with bracketed whole or partial footnotes per the original) by Edersheim (*The Life and Times of Jesus the Messiah*, 2:567–58) on the *hagigah* (or *Chagigah*) offerings in light of John 18 and 19 is worth considering:

> The point is of importance, because many writers have interpreted the expression "the Passover" referring to the Paschal Supper, and have argued that, according to the Fourth Gospel, our Lord did not on the previous evening partake of the Paschal Lamb, or else that in this respect the account of the Fourth Gospel does not accord with that of the Synoptists. But as, for the reason just stated, it is impossible to refer the expression "Passover" to the Paschal Supper, we have only to inquire whether the term is not also applied to other offerings. And here both the Old Testament [Deut. 14:1–3; 2 Chron. 35:1–2, 6, 18] and Jewish writings [e.g., Pesahim] show, that the term *Pesach*, or "Passover," was applied not only to the Paschal

The Foot Washing

We understand that the Seder observed by Jesus and His disciples was probably more primitive and not as well developed as what is described two hundred years later in the mishnaic tractate Pesahim,[25] or found in the Haggadah, the guide to our modern Passover Seder. However, some traditions linked to the Passover Seder appear in both Luke 22 and John 13 and run parallel to the Passover of Jesus, the Passover in the Mishnah, and our modern-day Passover as well.

The Washing of Hands Is Foundational to Foot Washing

The modern Haggadah calls upon participants to wash their hands twice for the sake of establishing ritual purity. The first ritual handwashing is called in Hebrew *Urchatz* (lit., "washing" or "cleansing"). In this instance, water is poured from a cup, once over each hand without reciting a blessing in preparation for taking the greens, either parsley or lettuce, which is part of the traditional Seder meal.

The second handwashing is called *Rachtzah* (lit., "to wash or bathe"), and it is done a little later in the Passover service just prior to eating the matzah (unleavened bread). This time a blessing is spoken when pouring the water over the hands:

> Blessed are You, Lord our God, King of the Universe, who has sanctified us with His commandments and commanded us to wash our hands.

These washing traditions harken back to those linked to ritual purity found in the Torah and in particular to various commandments associated with the priesthood and Temple offerings, especially the preparation of the priests for their duties (Lev. 8:6; 16:24–25).

Lamb, but to all the Passover sacrifices, especially to what was called the *Chagigah*, or festive offering (from *Chag*, or *Chagag*, to bring the festive sacrifice usual at each of the three Great Feasts). According to the express rule (Chag. i. 3) the *Chagigah* was brought on the first festive Paschal Day. [יום מוב הראשון של פסח, etc.] It was offered immediately after the morning-service, and eaten on that day—probably some time before the evening, when, as we shall by-and-by see, another ceremony claimed public attention. We can therefore quite understand that, *not* on the eve of the Passover, but on the first Paschal day, the Sanhedrists would avoid incurring a defilement which, lasting till the evening, would not only have involved them in the inconvenience of Levitical defilement on the first festive day, but have actually prevented their offering on that day the Passover, festive sacrifice, or *Chagigah*. For, we have these two express rules: that a person could not in Levitical defilement offer the *Chagigah*; and that the *Chagigah* could not be offered for a person by some one else who took his place (Jer. Chag. 76 *a*, lines 16 to 14 from bottom). These considerations and canons seem decisive as regards the views above expressed. There would have been no reason to fear "defilement" on the morning of the Paschal Sacrifice; but entrance into the *Prætorium* on the morning of the first Passover-day would have rendered it impossible for them to offer the *Chagigah*, which is also designated by the term *Pesach*.

25.   Pesahim is the tractate of the Mishnah that discusses the Passover.

Ceremonial washings are linked to many other aspects of Jewish religious and community life.[26] Jewish people are required to ritually wash every morning, before every meal, and in preparation for marriage, the Sabbath, and various rituals related to holiday observance.[27]

These washings are sometimes limited to the hands and at other times designed for the entire person as we see in the case of the *mikvah*,[28] which requires the immersion of the whole body.

Again, our modern Passover Seder rituals developed over centuries and cannot be "read into" the Passover Seder of Jesus. In this instance, however, it seems that the washing of the disciples' feet should be associated with the liturgy of the Last Supper rather than the common washing of feet when entering a guest's house. Most obvious of all is that the disciples are already sitting at the table and engaged with dinner when the foot washing begins.[29] As John writes,

> During supper, the devil having already put into the heart of Judas Iscariot, the son of Simon, to betray Him, Jesus, knowing that the Father had given all things into His hands, and that He had come forth from God and was going back to God, got up from supper, and laid aside His garments; and taking a towel, He girded Himself. Then He poured water into the basin, and began to wash the disciples' feet and to wipe them with the towel with which He was girded. (John 13:2–5)

Jesus decides to wash the feet of His disciples rather than their hands in order to teach them about true humility, suggesting that true spirituality is not simply a matter of performing rituals correctly but a matter of the heart. The lessons in humility demonstrated and then taught through changing the handwashing into a foot washing are dramatic and powerful. John continues,

> So when He had washed their feet, and taken His garments and reclined at the table again, He said to them, "Do you know what I have done to you? You call Me Teacher and Lord; and you are right, for so I am. If I then, the Lord and the Teacher, washed your feet, you also ought to wash one another's feet. For

---

26. For more on ritual washings from a Jewish perspective compared with Christian baptism and Muslim ritual washings, see the following brief but excellent responses provided by writers representing each of these faith traditions, respectively: David Arnow, Mary C. Boys, and Muhammad Shafiq, "What Role Does Washing Play in Our Traditions?," Exodus Conversations, n.d. (ca. October 2013), http://exodusconversations.org/questions/what-role-does-washing-play-in-our-traditions/.

27. Elijohu Blasz, *Code of Jewish Family Purity: A Condensation of the Nidah Laws in an Abridged Form*, trans. Committee for the Preservation of Jewish Family Purity, 14th ed. (Brooklyn, NY: Committee for the Preservation of Jewish Family Purity, 1987), http://www.israel613.com/books/TAHARAT_HAMISHPACHA-E.pdf.

28. For an in-depth article on the *mikvah* written from a Jewish perspective, see Rivkah Slonim, "The Mikvah," TheJewishWoman.org, n.d. (ca. April 2004), http://www.chabad.org/theJewishWoman/article_cdo/aid/1541/jewish/The-Mikvah.htm.

29. Craig S. Keener, *The Gospel of John: A Commentary*, 2 vols. (Peabody, MA: Hendrickson, 2003), 2:906.

I gave you an example that you also should do as I did to you. Truly, truly, I say to you, a slave is not greater than his master, nor is one who is sent greater than the one who sent him. If you know these things, you are blessed if you do them. (John 13:12–17)

The Mishnah and Talmud contain considerable numbers of rabbinic teachings emphasizing the importance of humility.[30] We can only imagine that some of this teaching regarding humility was already fixed in the mind of Jesus and known by first-century Jews. We find similar thoughts about humility in the words of Jesus himself spoken during the Sermon on the Mount, especially as gleaned from the first three beatitudes: "Blessed are the poor in spirit, for theirs is the kingdom of heaven. Blessed are those who mourn, for they shall be comforted. Blessed are the gentle, for they shall inherit the earth" (Matt. 5:3–5).

Reclining at the Table

Once again, we have good evidence that this meal is a Seder because, as Carson suggests in his commentary on John, the "reclining" posture itself during the meal hints at this: "In short, the posture of Jesus and his men is a small indicator that they were in fact eating the Passover meal."[31] The reclining posture of the disciples and Jesus Himself indicates that the meal was a "special meal," and because of the other elements mentioned and the date on which it took place, in this instance it may be seen as a Passover Seder. The weight of evidence is becoming more and more significant.

The Sop and the Betrayal

Another key to understanding this meal as the *Last Seder* of Jesus comes when Jesus indicates to His disciples that Judas is going to betray Him. In response to Peter, who asks who the perpetrator will be, Jesus answers,

"That is the one for whom I shall dip the morsel and give it to him." So when He had dipped the morsel, He took and gave it to Judas, the son of Simon Iscariot. (John 13:26)

The dipping of the "morsel" (ψωμίον, *psōmion*) likely refers to one of the various "dippings" that are part of the Seder. It could refer to the dipping of the greens (parsley or lettuce); or the matzah dipped into the bitter herbs or into the *charoset* (the sweet mixture of apples, nuts, and honey used to symbolize the sweetness of redemption in the midst of the bitterness of slavery). Carson again comments,

The Evangelist may well be thinking of an early point in the paschal meal when bitter herbs were dipped into a bowl of fruit puree, the *harōset* sauce of dates, rai-

---

30.   Keener, *The Gospel of John*, 2:906–7.
31.   Carson, *The Gospel According to John*, 473.

sins and sour wine. This "sop" Jesus passed to Judas Iscariot. That Jesus could pass it so easily suggests Judas was close by, possibly on his left, the place of honour.[32]

We might not know which dipping Jesus is referring to exactly, but clearly this is an unusual action for a regular meal, though not so for a Passover Seder.

CONCLUSION

The Gospel of John is critical to understanding the role of Passover in the life of Jesus. The Messiah used the Passover as a backdrop for describing His suffering and redemptive death. He taught His disciples profound truths during the Last Supper, and initiated the New Covenant (Jer. 31:31–34) and Communion, along with a corpus of teaching usually called the Upper Room Discourse recorded in John chapters 13–17.

Additionally, the information we glean from John's chronology of the events surrounding the Passover helps us to better understand the details of the last week of Jesus's life. We believe that Jesus celebrated His last Passover supper on Thursday night, the beginning of the fourteenth day of the Hebrew month Nisan, was crucified the following day, Friday (in Jewish reckoning, still the fourteenth of Nisan), and rose on the third day, which was Sunday, the sixteenth of Nisan. His resurrection proves him to be the Savior of the world, conquering both physical and spiritual death.

Understandably, we have barely scratched the surface of the lessons to be learned from the ways in which John wove the themes of Passover throughout the entirety of his Gospel (John 21:25), expressed so clearly by John the Baptist who, seeing his cousin approaching the Jordan River, cries out, "Behold, the Lamb of God who takes away the sin of the world!" (John 1:29)

And indeed—Yeshua is *our* Passover Lamb, if put our trust in Him as our Messiah!

---

32.   Carson, *The Gospel According to John*, 474.

6

PASSOVER AND THE LORD'S SUPPER

BRIAN CRAWFORD

*O*nce we leave the Gospel accounts of the Passover and come to 1 Corinthians, we find ourselves in the unusual position of going back to the future. Although the Gospels are the written accounts of Yeshua's life, it is likely that they were not written down until after the Apostle Paul penned the letter of 1 Corinthians in 54 or 55 c.e.[1] Consequently, even though the historical setting of 1 Corinthians is *later* than the Gospels, the letter contains our *earliest* written reports of Yeshua's Passover Seder and the Early Church's celebration of Communion.[2]

FIRST CORINTHIANS, THE PASSOVER EPISTLE

Paul refers to or alludes to Passover in three separate sections of 1 Corinthians, each of which we will investigate further below. This recurring Passover theme is striking due to Paul's silence on the matter in his other letters. Why did Paul have Passover on his mind in this letter? The most likely reason

---

1. For the dating of the Gospels, see P. L. Maier, "Chronology," in *Dictionary of the Later New Testament and Its Developments*, ed. Ralph P. Martin and Peter H. Davids (Downers Grove, IL: InterVarsity Press, 1997), 187–88. For the dating of 1 Corinthians, see D. A. Carson and Douglas J. Moo, *An Introduction to the New Testament*, 2nd ed. (Grand Rapids: Zondervan, 2005), 448; Anthony C. Thiselton, *The First Epistle to the Corinthians: A Commentary on the Greek Text*, New International Greek Testament Commentary (Grand Rapids: Eerdmans, 2000), 32; C. K. Barrett, *The First Epistle to the Corinthians*, Black's New Testament Commentary (London: Adam & Charles Black, 1968), 5; and Joachim Jeremias, *The Eucharistic Words of Jesus*, trans. Norman Perrin, rev. ed., New Testament Library (London: SCM Press, 1966), 188. Citations of *The Eucharistic Words of Jesus* in this chapter refer to the SCM Press edition.
2. However, see Jeremias, *The Eucharistic Words of Jesus*, 186–89, where he identifies Mark as recording the earliest version of Yeshua's eucharistic words, despite Mark being written after 1 Corinthians. According to Jeremias, "Mark with his numerous semitisms stands linguistically nearest to the original tradition" (188).

is due to the season of his writing.[3] At the end of his letter, Paul tells his readers that he "will remain in Ephesus until Pentecost" (1 Cor. 16:8), the Greek name for the Jewish Feast of Weeks, which occurs fifty days after Passover in May/June (Lev. 23:15–16). Additionally, he tells them that he hopes to come to Corinth "soon" (1 Cor. 4:19). The combination of these time markers makes it very likely that Paul wrote his letter in the spring, before Pentecost, and near the time of Passover.

Other material encourages us to consider the real possibility that Paul and his Corinthian audience were celebrating Passover in a manner that pointed to the Messiah. Early Church sources report that the second-century churches in Paul's region celebrated Passover and Messiah's crucifixion on the fourteenth of Nisan.[4] Some second-century believers even claimed that the Apostles themselves encouraged the celebration of this Messianic Passover.[5]

PAUL AND THE FEASTS

Some think that if a church celebrates Passover, this contradicts Paul's teachings elsewhere on the Feasts. Paul is the one who called the dietary laws, the Feasts, new moons, and Sabbaths "a mere shadow" compared to "the substance," which belongs to Messiah (Col. 2:16–17). He is the one who chastises the Galatians for observing "days and months and seasons and years" (Gal. 4:10). How can Paul celebrate the old Jewish Feast of Passover when the Messiah has already fulfilled the Feast?

This misconception may be dismissed by a closer look at the intended audience of these passages. In both Colossians and Galatians, Paul's primary audience is Gentile believers. In Colossians, Paul is addressing those who were uncircumcised in their flesh (Col. 2:13). Paul encourages the Gentile Colossians to disregard Jewish critics who *require* them to observe special days, since Gentiles were never obligated by God to follow the Mosaic calendar. In Galatians, Paul is addressing Gentile believers who are choosing to get circumcised in order to be justified before God (Gal. 5:2–6). He tries to dissuade them from undergoing this rite lest they forfeit Christ Himself and the justification He achieved on their behalf (v. 2).

There is nothing in these passages that speaks against *Jewish* believers celebrating the Feasts, or anything that speaks against Gentiles celebrating them with a heart of faith. In fact, Paul's wording in Colossians 2:17 implies that the "shadows" still have present-day importance because he uses the present-tense verb ἐστιν, *estin*—"Things which *are* a mere shadow of

---

3. Thiselton, *The First Epistle to the Corinthians*, 407–8.
4. See Eusebius, *Ecclesiastical History*, 5.23 (*Nicene and Post-Nicene Fathers, Series 2* 1:241–42). For a discussion of the chronology of Yeshua's final week of life, see chapter 5 in this book, "Passover in the Gospel of John," by Mitch Glaser.
5. See Polycrates' letter to Victor in Eusebius, *Ecclesiastical History*, 5.24 (*Nicene and Post-Nicene Fathers, Series 2* 1:242–44). He identifies the Apostles Philip and John as the originators of the Passover observances in Asia Minor, and then identifies six others, including himself, who have retained that practice until Polycrates' own day.

what is to come" (emphasis added). Many commentators ignore the present tense and jump to the conclusion that the Jewish observances *were* shadows that have been made obsolete.[6] But Paul did not believe that the Feasts were a thing of the past, but rather a shadow with present-day anticipatory features.[7] Celebrating the shadow without the substance of Messiah would be foolish, and celebrating Messiah without the shadow would be adequate for the Gentile Colossians, but Paul's use of the present tense shows that he sees continuing value in the shadows, including the Feasts. This continuing importance of the Feasts will explain other passages, indicating that Paul continued to keep the Feasts.[8] In Paul's mind the Feasts still hold significant relevance to believers. With Paul's positive stance towards the Feasts in mind, let us now return to 1 Corinthians.

MESSIAH, OUR PASSOVER (I COR. 5:6–8)

The context for 1 Corinthians 5:6–8, our first of three Passover-themed passages in this epistle of the Apostle Paul, is that the Corinthian church was accepting the presence of an unrepentant sexual deviant in their midst, and accepting him in prideful arrogance (5:1–2). Paul's first response is to exhort the church to take decisive action against the offender, casting him out from the church community (vv. 2–5). However, it is relatively easy to expel an unbeliever from the church; it is much harder to deal with the sin in the hearts of believers. For this reason, Paul pivots to draw a principle from the Passover in 1 Corinthians 5:6.

After calling the Corinthians "arrogant" (5:2), he again warns them, "Your boasting is not good" (v. 6). This remark signals that Paul is no longer addressing the sin of the sexual offender, but rather the pride of the church community that was boasting about retaining him. Paul continues, "Do you not know that a little leaven leavens the whole lump of dough?" (v. 6) Paul's reference to leaven may arise from two parallel directions. First, leaven ferments and puffs up bread just as human pride puffs up a person with sin.

---

6. On the issue of ignoring implications of the present tense verb in Colossians 2:17, Martha King cites Bible commentators F. F. Bruce and Peter T. O'Brien as saying that the shadows "were only temporary." Similarly, Ralph P. Martin says that "their observance is antiquated." Also, N. T. Wright says, "Now that the reality is here, there is no point in holding on to things which are only a shadow." Martha King, *An Exegetical Summary of Colossians*, 2nd ed., Exegetical Summaries 12 (Dallas: SIL International, 2008), 180.

7. Jeremias remarks, "Rather oddly, the Church took over only two of the great feasts in the Jewish calendar, namely, the Passover and Pentecost, but not Tabernacles." The omission of Tabernacles need not be surprising if we consider that Paul believed that some of the shadows still pointed forward to unfulfilled "things to come." Perhaps, in the Early Church's mind, Tabernacles was not emphasized because its fulfillment awaits a future era (Zech. 14, Rev. 21:3). Joachim Jeremias, "πάσχα," *(pascha) Theological Dictionary of the New Testament*, ed. Gerhard Kittel and Gerhard Friedrich, trans. and ed. Geoffrey W. Bromiley (Grand Rapids: Eerdmans,1968), 5:901.

8. See Acts 20:6, 16; and 27:9. See also Reidar Hvalvik, "Paul as a Jewish Believer: According to the Book of Acts," in *Jewish Believers in Jesus: The Early Centuries*, ed. Oskar Skarsaune and Reidar Hvalvik (Peabody, MA: Hendrickson, 2007), 143–45.

Both Paul's contemporaries and later Jewish rabbis use leaven as an analogy for pride.[9] Secondly, if Paul is writing near the time of Passover, then the thought of leaven would be at the forefront of his mind as a Jewish believer (Exod. 12:19). Consequently, Paul's use of the leavening theme is a vivid word-picture that speaks to the time and situation of his audience.

In contrast to the greater sin of the sexual offender, the Corinthians' sin of boasting may be just "a little leaven," but it still makes the whole dough unfit for Passover. The analogy is that the sin of pride has infected the whole Corinthian church, which is inconsistent with their justification in Messiah. Paul clearly believes that the Corinthians are saved and justified in Messiah because he calls them "unleavened" (1 Cor. 5:7). Their status as sinless, righteous, and pure in God's eyes through Messiah is a fact in Paul's mind; however, the Corinthians' prideful actions are springing from "the old leaven" of "malice and wickedness" (v. 8), that is, their old sinful nature. The only proper response is to remove the pride from their midst like the Jewish people remove the leaven from their homes at Passover.

In the second half of verse 7, Paul gives the reason *why* the Corinthians are "unleavened" and righteous believers: "For Christ our Passover also has been sacrificed." The Passover sacrifice of Yeshua is the only reason why the Corinthians have clean hearts. Yeshua's sacrifice is greater than any previous Passover lamb, providing complete atonement for all-time to all who believe (John 1:29; 1 Peter 2:24). The Corinthians have already been redeemed by the blood of the Lamb, but their boasting is taking them back to Egypt. Paul commands the Corinthians to turn back from that treacherous road and to instead clean out the leaven of pride and thereby celebrate the Festival of Passover correctly.

Many interpreters see the figurative language in this passage and assume that the reference to "the feast" (1 Cor. 5:8) must be figurative as well. "Celebrate the feast," or "keeping the festival," means holy living or consecrated lifestyles or some other universalized notion that removes the context of actual Passover observance.[10] But we need not jump to an exclusively spiritual meaning here. We have previously argued that believers did celebrate a Messiah-focused Passover in the Early Church and that Paul was writing in the spring, during Passover season. Both points should lead us to consider that Paul has an actual Passover festival in mind here. We must remember that

---

9. The Jewish philosopher Philo, Paul's contemporary, makes the connection in at least two places: *On the Special Laws* 1.293 and Fragments from an Unpublished Manuscript in the Library of the French King. According to Ronald L. Eisenberg, *JPS Guide to Jewish Traditions*, "The Rabbis regarded *hametz* [leaven] as the symbol of the evil inclination. The 'yeast in the dough' (the evil impulse that causes a ferment in the heart) prevents human beings from carrying out the will of God (Ber. 17a). *Hametz* also represents human haughtiness and conceit. Just as leaven puffs up dough, so human arrogance cause[s] us to believe that we, not God, control our destiny." Ronald L. Eisenberg, *The JPS Guide to Jewish Traditions* (Philadelphia: Jewish Publication Society, 2004), 269.

10. Ronald Trail, *An Exegetical Summary of 1 Corinthians 1–9* (Dallas: SIL International, 2008), 211. Thiselton, *The First Epistle to the Corinthians*, 406.

Paul was still *Sha'ul*,[11] and that he continued to identify himself as a Pharisee from the Diaspora (Acts 23:6). The Apostle viewed himself as still Jewish (Acts 22:3) and as part of the Messianic remnant (Rom. 11:5). In such a case, Paul is exhorting the church to enter the Passover season with as much zeal to remove sin from their midst as his fellow Jews are zealous to remove leaven from their homes. Believers in Yeshua, made unleavened through His sacrifice, should not approach the fourteenth of Nisan, the yearly reminder of their redemption, without living in accordance with their new nature.

FELLOWSHIP WITH THE LORD THROUGH COMMUNION (1 COR. 10:14–22)

The second Passover passage we will consider, 1 Corinthians 10:14–22, does not derive its Passover themes from Old Testament observance, but rather from Yeshua's use of the Passover to institute the celebration of Communion.[12] This is the earliest written reference to believers participating in "the cup of the Lord" (v. 21; cf. v. 16) and "the bread that we break" (v. 16).[13] Paul does not explain the Passover origin of these practices here since they are already so integrated into the Corinthians' rhythms. Paul assumes that his audience knows what he is referring to.

"The cup of blessing" has a blessing spoken over it (v. 16a), which may have been the same blessing as recorded in the Mishnah: "Blessed are You, O Lord our God, King of the Universe, the Creator of the fruit of the vine" (m. Ber. 6:1). In this passage, Paul emphasizes that the Corinthians are united together in fellowship, "a sharing" (κοινωνία, *koinōnia*), when they participate in the Lord's Supper. Κοινωνία, *Koinōnia*, refers to a "close association involving mutual interests and sharing."[14] Just as the Jewish people who sacrifice at the Temple are made participants or "sharers" (κοινωνοί, *koinōnoi*) with the God of "the altar" (v. 18),[15] so too the Corinthians are united together in fellowship or "a sharing" (κοινωνία, *koinōnia*) in the blood of Messiah (v. 16a) and in the body of Messiah (v. 16b). The practice of Communion is meant to foster an attitude of brotherhood and

---

11. Many believe that *Saul* (Hebrew, שָׁאוּל, *Sha'ul*; Greek, Σαῦλος, *Saulos*) was Paul's Jewish name, which he left behind once he "converted" to Christianity. This narrative, although popular, is not correct. As late as Acts 13:9, Paul is still called "Saul." The simple solution is that *Saul* was his Hebrew name, and *Paul* (Greek, Παῦλος, *Paulos*; Latin, *Paulus*) was his Greek/Latin name. The Apostle was known by both names in different contexts.
12. See in the next section the discussion of 1 Corinthians 11:23–26 and the Lord Yeshua's use of the Passover to institute the celebration of Communion, also witnessed in the Gospels (Matt. 26:26–29; Mark 14:22–25; Luke 22:14–23; cf. John 13:21–30).
13. See note 1 above for the dating of 1 Corinthians and the Gospels.
14. "κοινωνία," in Frederick W. Danker, Walter Bauer, William F. Arndt, and F. Wilbur Gingrich, *Greek-English Lexicon of the New Testament and Other Early Christian Literature*, 3rd ed. (Chicago: University of Chicago Press, 2000), 552.
15. "The altar" is Paul's Jewish substitute for the name of God. Many Jews used the name of God sparingly due to the commandment to not use his name in vain (Exod. 20:7; Deut. 5:11). The technical term for this is *circumlocution*.

unity within the community of believers, reminding all that they are spiritual brothers and sisters who have been united with God and each other through the sacrifice of Yeshua.

Paul draws out the practical implications for the Corinthians in verses 19–22. If participating in "the table of the Lord" means that believers are united with the Lord, then why are they practicing things that make them participants or "sharers" (κοινωνοὺς, *koinonous*) with demons (v. 20)? Believers should run from such practices because being united with the Lord excludes any other kind of religious participation. Believers cannot adopt the worship of foreign religions and anti-Yeshua worldviews without provoking the Lord to jealousy (v. 22), which has serious consequences as shown in the narrative of the Exodus and wilderness wanderings in the Torah (1 Cor. 10:1–13).

Although Paul does not refer to the idea of the New Covenant here, it surely influences his exhortations. It is by means of the New Covenant in Messiah's blood that believers are brought into fellowship with the Lord and are betrothed to Messiah, and we await a great marriage supper in the last days (Rev. 19:6–9). Marriages are exclusive, admitting no foreign lovers. So too with the New Covenant. Messiah Yeshua owns the hearts and deserves the total affections of His people, and the cup and the bread are His reminders to us that we are united with Him and no other.

THE TRADITION AND APPLICATION OF COMMUNION (I COR. 11:17–34)

The third Passover-themed passage we will consider is 1 Corinthians 11:17–34. After a brief aside from the previous discussion, Paul returns to the subject of Communion and Passover in verse 17. In this section, he expands upon his exhortation to unity in 1:10 by addressing a particularly shameful expression of factionalism in the Corinthians' practice of Communion. Paul acknowledges that there will always be factions whereby true believers may be distinguished from believers in name only (11:19), but that is not the factionalism that grieves him. Paul has heard that the Corinthians' practice of Communion has turned into a frenzy where some overeat, some go hungry, and some get drunk (v. 21). This frantic and factionalized atmosphere is not at all reflective of a supper named after the Lord Yeshua (v. 20). Instead of Communion being an opportunity for fellowship and worship, the church is sinning by disrespecting itself and humiliating the poor among them (v. 22). The Lord's Supper is not the appropriate place for partying and drinking.

The Early Tradition of Communion (1 Cor. 11:23–26)

After establishing the grounds for his rebuke, Paul transitions to remind the Corinthians in verses 23–26 of the solemn origins of Communion and why their practice of it was so inconsistent with the Lord Yeshua. "For I received from the Lord that which I also delivered to you," says Paul, the Pharisee (11:23; cf. Acts 23:6). Before we continue to the content of the message Paul received from the Lord, we must first recognize the particularly Jewish pairing of "received" with "delivered," which is reflective of Paul's Pharisaic background.[16] In ancient Jewish understanding, the authority of the teacher came not from his charisma or his success, but from his office as a conduit for official tradition.[17] With this introduction, Paul is preparing to remind the Corinthians of the tradition that he did not invent himself, but which he received "from the Lord."[18]

The tradition begins by referring to the night when the Lord Yeshua "was betrayed" (1 Cor. 11:23). Most English translations use the word "betrayed" here, which is certainly appropriate, but the Greek word ($\pi\alpha\rho\alpha\delta\iota\delta\omega\mu\iota$, *para-didomi*) is the same as the one just used for the tradition Paul "delivered." Just as tradition is "handed over," so too Yeshua was "handed over." However, the use of this word probably harkens back to the Greek version of Isaiah 53, where the same word is used to describe the Messiah being "given over" for our sins (Isa. 53:12 LXX).[19] Consequently, the early believers probably understood Judas' act of betrayal as a fulfillment of the prophecies in Isaiah 53.

On the night that Yeshua is handed over, he takes bread, gives thanks, and breaks it (11:23–24). It is possible, but not certain, that this bread is the *afikoman* bread that figures so prominently in later Jewish Passover tradition. Whether or not this is the *afikoman*, Yeshua gives a radical new meaning to the bread: "This is My body, which is for you" (1 Cor. 11:24). These very few words are overflowing with meaning. We must note that Yeshua says these words about His own human body of flesh and blood. He also says these words in the context of a Passover Seder in which food and other elements have memorial and symbolic meanings. The unleavened *matzah*, called "the Bread of Affliction," is not literally affliction and not literally sinless, but representative and symbolic of affliction and sinless purity.

When we consider Yeshua's actual body and the memorial nature of Passover, this should lead us to view the bread of Communion in a similarly symbolic way. The bread is Yeshua's body in symbolic form, not in nature. We should also note in verse 24 that Yeshua's body is "for you [all]" (plural pronoun). This is a beautiful reminder once again of Isaiah 53, but with the audience and speaker reversed. In Isaiah 53, the Prophet Isaiah speaks on behalf of believing Israel about the Messiah who was "pierced through for

---

16. On this verse Thiselton (*The First Epistle to the Corinthians*, 867) says, "'Received' and 'handed on' in 11:23 (cf. 15:1–3) were virtually technical terms in Jewish culture for the transmission of important traditions . . . (cf. m. Abot 1:1)."

17. Gerhard Delling, "$\pi\alpha\rho\alpha\lambda\alpha\mu\beta\acute{\alpha}\nu\omega$," (*paralambánō*) *Theological Dictionary of the New Testament*, 4:12–13.

18. This is probably a reference to Paul receiving the tradition about the Last Supper from other believers or from disciples who were present at the Last Supper. This is strengthened by the nearly verbatim wording in 1 Corinthians 11:24 and Luke 22:19. He probably does not mean that he received the tradition about the Last Supper through direct revelation.

19. The Greek version of Isaiah 53:12 is $\kappa\alpha\grave{\iota}$ $\delta\iota\grave{\alpha}$ $\tau\grave{\alpha}\varsigma$ $\dot{\alpha}\mu\alpha\rho\tau\acute{\iota}\alpha\varsigma$ $\alpha\dot{\upsilon}\tau\tilde{\omega}\nu$ $\pi\alpha\rho\epsilon\delta\acute{o}\theta\eta$, *kai dia tas hamartias autōn paredothe*, which means "and because of their sins he was given over" (author's translation). Alfred Rahlfs, *Septuaginta: With Morphology*, electronic ed. (1935; Stuttgart: Deutsche Bibelgesellschaft, 1996), ad loc.

our transgressions" and "crushed for our iniquities" (v. 5), but now it is the Messiah who is speaking to Jewish believers—His disciples. Yeshua confirms what Isaiah has declared previously: the Messiah's death will be "for us."

Yeshua continues, "Do this in remembrance of Me" (1 Cor. 11:24).[20] Just like the celebration of the original Passover was meant to be a memorial (Exod. 12:14), so too is the fulfilled Passover of Communion. The Lord wants his followers to see the bread of Communion as a reminder of Him, just as the lamb and bitter herbs were reminders of the Exodus. By partaking of the broken bread, we are to remind ourselves of the broken Messiah who gave Himself for our sins. Any partaking of the Communion bread without remembering the sacrifice of Yeshua is an affront to Yeshua Himself, as Paul explains in the verses that follow.

The tradition continues by saying that Yeshua gave a new meaning to the cup of the Passover Seder (1 Cor. 11:25), just as he did with the bread (v. 24). The tradition only mentions the cup "after supper," which most likely refers to the third of four Passover cups, the cup of redemption. This cup is the only one mentioned because of its supreme importance in the life of a believer. Yeshua says, "This cup is the new covenant in my blood" (v. 25). Here, the symbolic nature of the Communion is made most apparent. The cup in a Passover Seder is filled with wine—not blood—and yet it is given symbolic meaning. The origin of wine at the Passover Seder is shrouded in mystery,[21] but in Jewish culture, wine symbolizes "the essence of goodness" when used appropriately.[22] Here, Yeshua is saying that this cup of wine symbolizes His own blood, which inaugurates the New Covenant that had been foretold by Jeremiah (Jer. 31:31–34). What had been prophecy to Jeremiah is now reality through Yeshua's blood.

The tradition concludes, "For as often as you eat this bread and drink the cup, you proclaim the Lord's death until he comes" (1 Cor. 11:26). We learn several things from this remark. First, Paul and the early believers expect congregations to celebrate Communion often. We cannot tell *how often*—that decision is left up to the congregation itself—but it needs to be part of the life of the congregation. Secondly, the practice of Communion is an act of proclamation—a visible, tangible exclamation of the work of Yeshua in the lives and hearts of believers. Why? The bread and the wine have embedded within them the message of the Gospel! Although unbelievers should not be admitted to Communion, they should be able to see the practice of Communion in the life of a congregation and thereby be exposed to the proclamation of the Gospel. Thirdly, the practice of Communion encourages

---

20. These words τοῦτο ποιεῖτε εἰς τὴν ἐμὴν ἀνάμνησιν, *touto poieite eis tēn emēn anamnēsin*, are identical to the Greek of Luke 22:19, showing that Luke and Paul are drawing on common tradition.

21. The earliest reference to wine used at Passover is in a pre-Yeshua pseudepigraphal book, Jubilees 49:6.

22. Judah David Eisenstein and Emil G. Hirsch, "Wine," *The Jewish Encyclopedia: A Descriptive Record of the History, Religion, Literature, and Customs of the Jewish People from the Earliest Times to the Present Day*, ed. Isidore Singer (New York; London: Funk & Wagnalls, 1906), 12:533, http://www.jewishencyclopedia.com/articles/14941-wine.

a forward-thinking hope in the return of our Lord Yeshua. Practicing Communion is not merely about remembering the Lord's death, but also being eagerly expectant about celebrating Communion "until he comes."

According to Jewish tradition, the Messiah is supposed to arrive on the night of Passover.[23] This understanding was retained by the early believers, since we learn from extrabiblical Christian sources that there was an annual tradition of fasting until midnight on Passover, staying up late in case Yeshua returned![24] As to be expected, this Messianic anticipation about the yearly Passover also made its way into Communion. According to the first-century Messianic Jewish work the *Didache*, or the "Teaching of the Twelve Apostles," the Early Church ended their Communion prayers with the Aramaic phrase, "Maranatha!" (Did. 10.6), which means, "O Lord, Come!" Paul also uses this word at the end of this Passover epistle (1 Cor. 16:22). This early remnant of Jewish-Christian liturgy depicts how Communion was intended to be an eager expectation of the Lord Yeshua's return.

The modern Jewish Passover Seder shares in this eager expectation for the future. A Seder does not merely look backward to the Exodus event, but rather, every Jewish family hopefully proclaims at the end of the Seder, "Next year in Jerusalem!" The season of Passover is the season of redemption, yesterday and tomorrow, as both Paul and the modern Seder remind us.

The Tradition Applied (1 Cor. 11:27–34)

Now that Paul has reminded the Corinthians of the solemn origin of Communion, he turns in 1 Corinthians 11:27–34 toward the factionalized congregation to apply its meaning to their situation. He concludes that partaking of Communion "in an unworthy manner" makes the participant "guilty of the body and the blood of the Lord" (11:27). This is a severe accusation that no believers should want to be true about themselves. Yeshua is our Lord and our Messiah and our Bridegroom—we should do all we can to avoid participating in Communion "in an unworthy manner." What does this mean?

This phrase cannot mean "celebrating Communion with sin in your life." Likewise, it cannot mean "celebrating Communion when you are unworthy of it." Not a single believer is worthy of the grace of God—that's why it's freely given grace—and all believers continue to struggle with sin. Our sins do not disqualify us from taking Communion; rather, our acknowledgment of our sin is what leads us *to* take Communion! We need to be reminded of our Savior who redeemed us from the power of sin and who gave us the Spirit to progressively sanctify us from our sinful nature. If we think

---

23. Commenting on Exodus 12:42, the Rabbi Ishmael ben Elisha school of *midrash* says, "In that night were they redeemed and in that night will they be redeemed in the future." Jacob Z. Lauterbach, trans., *Mekilta de-Rabbi Ishmael*, 2nd ed. (Philadelphia: Jewish Publication Society, 2004), 1:79. See also *Targum Neofiti* to Exodus 12:42, and *Targum Pseudo-Jonathan* Exodus 12:42.

24. Jeremias, *The Eucharistic Words of Jesus*, 123.

that we need to be sinless to partake of Communion, then not only do we have a works-based view of God and salvation, but we also have disqualified everyone from ever partaking of Communion themselves.

Instead, Paul uses an adverb in the Greek to say that we should not partake of Communion "unworthily," that is, in a way that dishonors or shames the noble meaning of Communion itself.[25] The bread and the wine receive their symbolic meaning from the Lord Yeshua himself, so dishonoring Communion is a personal attack on the Lord himself. Because of this, "let a person examine himself" (1 Cor. 11:28 ESV), says Paul, to ensure that each of us is properly honoring the Lord of the Communion in the practice of Communion. Anyone who does not properly "judge the body rightly" only brings judgment upon oneself (v. 29). Judging the body rightly or "discerning the body" (ESV) can refer to acknowledging the body of Yeshua in the memorial bread, or it can refer to recognizing the unity of the congregation as the body of Messiah (cf. 10:16–17). Either way, the Corinthians' lack of self-reflection and self-judgment has led God to bring weakness, illness, and even death upon some members of the congregation (11:30). According to Paul, just as God judged Israel for neglecting him (10:1–13), so too God will bring earthly consequences upon a congregation that dishonors the Lord in Communion. This might sound unbelievable and superstitious to many people today, but "[s]uch an attitude reflects the extent to which the modern world has lost the biblical understanding of God's transcendence and fearsome holiness."[26] God takes His holiness and the actions of His Son seriously; therefore the misuse of Communion can bring with it severe divine consequences.

"But," Paul says, "if we judged ourselves rightly, we would not be judged" (1 Cor. 11:31). Believers need not come under the temporal judgment of God, if only they would self-judge themselves before coming to the Communion Table. Are we properly honoring the work of Yeshua? Are we remembering the sacrifice of His body and blood? Are we acting in fundamental unity with the other believers around us? These are the kinds of questions that every believer should ask himself or herself upon coming to the Lord's Table. God wants us to judge ourselves so He does not have to do it against our will. Even so, Paul says, God's judgment of believers serves a redemptive purpose (v. 32). God disciplines His people to keep them from being condemned along with the world. Like a loving Father, He brings

---

25. The word for "unworthily" (ἀναξίως, *anaxiōs*) is used only here in the entire New Testament. However, other Greek sources use the word. The Jewish apocryphal work 2 Maccabees talks about a man of noble birth who is abused "in a way unworthy of his own nobility" (2 Macc. 14:42). Rick Brannan, Ken M. Penner, Israel Loken, Michael Aubrey, and Isaiah Hoogendyk, eds., *The Lexham English Septuagint* (Bellingham, WA: Lexham Press, 2012), ad loc. Plato uses the word in *Apology of Socrates* 38, and Herodotus uses it in *Histories* 7.10.5. In all these cases, the word is used to describe actions that dishonor or shame the nobility of someone or something that deserves better.

26. Roy E. Ciampa and Brian S. Rosner, *The First Letter to the Corinthians*, Pillar New Testament Commentary (Grand Rapids: Eerdmans; Nottingham, UK: Apollos, 2010), 557.

temporal punishments upon His children so they can learn wisdom and properly inherit their eternal destiny with Him.

With all of this tradition and admonition complete, Paul now gives some concluding applications that remind the Corinthians of where they started. They are not practicing the *Lord's* Supper but rather a corruption of it. This is inconsistent with the reality of Communion and the reasons for it. "So then, my brethren," Paul concludes, "when you come together to eat, wait for one another. If anyone is hungry, let him eat at home, so that you will not come together for judgment" (11:33–34). Communion is meant to foster an atmosphere of unity and community. Instead of judgment, Communion is supposed to bring blessing.

The Corinthians were failing at this because they had forgotten the origin, purpose, and symbolism of Communion itself. They were using Communion to fulfill their own personal appetites rather than to remember the Lord and thank Him for His sacrifice on their behalf. Congregations today need to be wary of making the same mistakes. Instead, they should give Communion the solemnity and reverence it deserves, as well as foster an attitude of unity in Messiah among the participants.

CONCLUSION

Paul's first letter to the Corinthians contains rich Passover and Communion imagery that is intended to deepen the Corinthians' understanding of the Gospel (1 Cor. 5:6–8), to inspire them to spiritual unity in one body (10:14–22), and to remind them of the Passover-sacrifice basis of their unity (11:17–34). These three passages serve as a rebuke of the Corinthians' congregational life, but they can serve as precious encouragements to us. By learning from the Corinthians' failures, we can strive for a more intimate relationship with the Messiah, our Passover, who gave His body and blood for our sins, uniting us into one body for His eternal glory and praise.

Based upon these passages we should be reminded why it is important to see the Bible—especially the New Testament—through Jewish eyes and why understanding the Passover enriches our celebration of the Lord's Supper. The following five lessons are important for us to recall and for you to share with your home group or church—whether you are a pastor or a member of a congregation:

1. Nearly all of the books of the New Testament (except, perhaps, Luke's Gospel and Acts) were written by Jewish believers, who presumably continued to identify as Jews and live like Jews. This is implied throughout the New Testament. A key example of this is how greatly the Early Church struggled with the enormous changes created by the influx of believing Gentiles described in the book of Acts. This resulted in a major decision made in concert with the Holy Spirit not to require non-Jews to be circumcised or to observe the Law of Moses, aside from a few "essentials" (Acts 15:28–29).

Overlooking the Jewishness of the New Testament and most of its writers can lead to misunderstanding its message to us.

2. Paul continued to see relevance in celebrating the Feasts found in Leviticus 23, since they point to the Messiah.

3. The tradition concerning Communion in 1 Corinthians 11:23–26 is based upon ideas and events found in the Hebrew Bible and Jewish tradition. Therefore, understanding the Jewish backgrounds regarding Passover will deepen our thankfulness for what Yeshua accomplished on our behalf.

4. The practice of Communion is meant to be a visual and experiential reminder of the unity of believers with each other and with their Lord. As believers we should do everything possible to make that unity a meaningful reality by forgiving and asking forgiveness of each other and rebuking the spirit of factionalism within our own hearts.

5. On a personal level, the practice of Communion should not only look backward to the Cross in thankfulness, but should also look forward to the day that Messiah returns. Our Lord is not dead—He is risen!—and He will come to take us to His side. Communion should lead our hearts to exclaim, "Next year with Yeshua in the New Jerusalem!"

PART 2
PASSOVER AND CHURCH HISTORY

7

PASSOVER, THE TEMPLE, AND THE EARLY CHURCH

SCOTT P. NASSAU

*B*iblical scholars generally agree that Jesus celebrated the Passover with His disciples in some fashion (Luke 22:1–15).[1] It is also probable that the disciples maintained the custom within the nascent community of faith, since they still considered themselves to be part of the Jewish community and not a separate religious movement (Exod. 12:14; 13:9–10; Acts 10:28). It is not clear how long and in what manner this practice of celebrating Passover continued within the Church. In light of the ambiguity concerning the manner in which Jesus's followers continued to celebrate the Passover, this chapter will examine the Passover practices in early Judaism, the Passover customs observed within the developing Church and the events that led to the seeming abandonment of these traditions. While the early Jesus followers maintained many of the traditional Jewish customs concerning Passover, as time progressed the expanding Church reinterpreted, modified, and appropriated these practices for a new day.

CHALLENGES OF THE STUDY

Exploring the extent to which the Early Church observed any form of Passover customs has limitations. The most notable involves the scarcity of evidence to reconstruct and analyze the various Jewish traditions within the Early Church. Since many of the first followers of Jesus did not document their customs, any conclusion rests upon a significant amount of informed speculation.

The multiethnic nature of the developing community of faith only compounds the challenges. The Early Church can be characterized by an eclectic array of beliefs and practices, including a number of distinct practices favored by Jewish followers of Jesus, and others deemed more appropriate for

---

1.   Concerning the matter of the Last Supper as a Passover or Passover-like meal, see chapter 4, "Passover in the Gospel of Luke," by Darrell L. Bock.

non-Jews. We need to be careful in making broad generalizations about Christian customs and traditions practiced by the Church during this early period.

The first few centuries spawned two separate emerging traditions—rabbinic Judaism and orthodox Christianity.[2] The Jewish followers of Jesus, who were more likely to preserve traditional Jewish Passover customs, found themselves at the intersection of these two emerging traditions. The destruction of the Temple and its impact on the practice of Judaism, coupled with the diversity of Jewish expression in the first century, makes it difficult to determine whether there was any one all-encompassing form of Jewish Christianity.

RECONSTRUCTING PASSOVER CUSTOMS IN THE FIRST CENTURY

Before delving into the manner in which the Early Church observed Passover, it will be helpful to first consider how the broader Jewish community approached the holiday. The destruction of the Temple in 70 c.e. divides Jewish observance of Passover into two distinct epochs. Prior to 70 c.e. the Temple remained the locus for Jewish religious life, including the national Passover celebrations. Jewish life dramatically changed following the Roman destruction of Jerusalem and the Temple, which resulted in the further decentralization of Jewish religious observances.

Passover in the Temple

The Mishnah represents the most comprehensive collection of Jewish rules and customs addressing every area of life. It devotes an entire section, or *tractate*, to the observance of Passover.[3] While it is the most authoritative compilation of Jewish customs and practices, its composition did not occur until around 200 c.e., more than a hundred years after the devastation of the Temple.[4] It paints a fascinating picture of the Passover following the destruction of the Temple, but only provides a shadow of what Passover was like prior to its fall; therefore, the objective to reconstruct Passover customs of the first century requires other earlier sources.

Most evidence suggests that observance of Passover revolved around the Temple. The Feast of Unleavened Bread, coupled with Passover, was one of the three pilgrimage festivals in Judaism, during which God required every adult male to travel to Jerusalem to celebrate at the Temple (Deut. 16:6, 16).[5] This practice continued in Jesus's day. The Gospels record Jesus's journey to Jerusalem for the purpose of observing Passover at the Temple, both as

2. Edwin K. Broadhead, *Jewish Ways of Following Jesus: Redrawing the Religious Map of Antiquity*, (Tübingen: Mohr Siebeck, 2010), 46.

3. For a more detailed discussion about the Mishnah and its depiction of Passover, see chapter 10, "Passover in Rabbinic Writings," by Zhava Glaser.

4. The Mishnah, coupled with the Gemara, which forms the Talmud, remains the foundation for Jewish religious life today.

5. Passover and the Feast of Unleavened Bread are different but inseparable holidays, both commemorating God's deliverance of Israel out of Egypt.

a child and as an adult (Matt. 21:1; Luke 2:41–43; John 2:13; 11:55; 12:1, 12). The enormous crowds gathered in Jerusalem indicate that this custom was practiced throughout the Jewish community (John 12:12). Josephus (37–ca. 100 C.E.), the Romano-Jewish scholar and historian, describes multitudes of pilgrims in Jerusalem during the holiday (*Jewish War* 2.10, 224).

The presence of thousands of pilgrims in Jerusalem for Passover demonstrates how the Temple played a vital role in the holiday ceremonies. While the account of the first Passover in Egypt describes how each family killed their lamb within the home (Exod. 12:1–11), God later instructs the nation to offer the Passover sacrifices at a central location, namely, the Temple in Jerusalem (Deut. 16:5–6). The Mishnah indicates that this practice continued throughout the time of the Second Temple (m. Pesahim 6.1). Not only does God instruct Israel to sacrifice animals at the Tabernacle and then the Temple, but also to eat the meat within the prescribed confines (Deut. 16:7).

The Temple Scroll, found at Qumran, reinforces this custom by directing men, who are at least twenty years of age, to sacrifice the Passover offering prior to the evening sacrifice (Temple Scroll[a] 17:6–8). They then must prepare it and eat it within the Temple courtyards, before returning home the next morning (Temple Scroll[a] 17:8–9). Josephus, in an attempt to determine the number of people in Jerusalem during the festival, mentions that the priests would slay approximately 256,500 lambs (*Jewish War* 6.422–427). As a result Josephus calculates somewhere around 2.7 to 3 million people in Jerusalem on Passover at the close of the Second Temple period (*Jewish War* 2.280; 6.422–27).[6]

This would make an elaborate, multicourse meal in the home rather difficult.[7] Considering the heat, the bleating of thousands of lambs and hundreds of barrels of warm blood, the Temple was anything but quiet and pristine on Passover. Plainly speaking, it was bloody and loud with an exuberant crowd.

Typically only priests killed sacrifices, but the slaughter of hundreds of thousands of lambs is a task too vast to be conducted by the High Priest alone, or even by the priests in general. Therefore, the Passover sacrifice at the time of the Second Temple preserved the customs of the family offering by allowing the entire nation to function as priests, in order to slaughter the lamb for their family. The Mishnah records this process by explaining how each individual, "slaughtered *the Passover lamb* and a priest received the blood, handed it to his companion, and companion to his companion" (m. Pesahim 5.6, emphasis added). Josephus implies the involvement of all Israel in the process when he states that the sacrifices occurred between the ninth and eleventh hours of the day (*Jewish War* 6.423–24).[8] The short span of time, two hours, suggests everyone had to participate in the slaughter of the animals.

---

6. It is quite possible that Josephus artificially inflates and exaggerates these numbers. These numbers reflect his calculations of the Passover in 65 C.E.

7. Baruch M. Bokser, *The Origins of the Seder: The Passover Rite and Early Rabbinic Judaism* (Berkeley: University of California Press, 1984), 22.

8. The ninth and eleventh hours coincide with approximately 3:00 and 5:00 P.M. in modern convention.

Philo (ca. 25 B.C.E.–50 C.E.), the ancient Jewish philosopher from Alexandria, mentions that the killing of the Passover offering took place from midday into the evening (*On the Special Laws* 2.145), which indicates a longer span of time for sacrificing the animals. As the participants sacrificed the Passover offerings, the priests sang from the *Hallel* psalms, Psalms 113–118 (m. Pesahim 3.11). These psalms have remained a crucial part of the Passover observance throughout Jewish history and are now a central feature in the *Haggadah*, an ancient compilation of Passover liturgy telling the story of Israel's liberation from Egyptian slavery.

Even before the destruction of the Temple, sufficient evidence indicates that part of the Passover celebrations revolved around a meal in the home, including the eating of the Passover sacrifice. In the later part of the Second Temple period, Jewish law allowed for the removal of the sacrificed lamb from the Temple precincts for consumption elsewhere in Jerusalem (m. Zevahim 5.8). This is why Jesus had to observe the Passover with His disciples at a home within the city walls (Matt. 26:18–19).

Philo considers the problematic situation of those living far from Jerusalem or unable to make the pilgrimage in time for the holiday. These circumstances should not prevent the community from participating in Jewish observances. Rather Philo confers value to the Jewish home and suggests that it is possible to celebrate Passover in the home (Philo, *On the Special Laws* 2.148; *On the Decalogue* 159; *On the Life of Moses* 2.224–32). The book of Jubilees (ca. 200–140 B.C.E.), an ancient Jewish extrabiblical text, confirms many of the traditions prescribed by the Torah, but also includes drinking wine as part of the Passover rituals (Jubilees 49:6). Wine becomes a central element in later Jewish practice with the development of the *Seder* meal, which is organized around four cups of wine (m. Pesahim 10.1). In addition to the wine, it was already customary to eat the lamb, bitter herbs (*maror*), and *charoset*, which is a mixture of fruit, nuts, and wine to represent the mortar used to make bricks in Egypt.

Passover Following 70 C.E.

If one could characterize the Passover observance of the Jewish community prior to the destruction of the Temple as centralized, then the Roman demolition of the Temple certainly forced the Jewish community into a decentralized approach to Passover. While the Temple was the heart of the nation's Passover celebration prior to 70 C.E., the home has remained the focus for Passover ever since that time. Today Jewish families organize the Passover meal, referred to as the Seder, by following the Haggadah described above, but these traditions were still developing during the first few centuries.

After the destruction of the Temple, the festive meal became the heart of the Passover observance.[9] On the day prior to the start of the holiday, the family prepared for Passover by removing all remnants of leaven from the

---

9. In chapter 10, "Passover in Rabbinic Writings," Zhava Glaser provides a thorough analysis of the

home, typically by the light of a candle (Exod. 12:19; m. Pesahim 1.1). Each family disposed of or burned all leaven discovered in the search (m. Pesahim 1.5; 2.1). As the time of the dinner approached, each person refrained from eating in order to be mentally and spiritually attentive to the celebration of the Passover meal (m. Pesahim 10.1).

The celebration began with wine. It became customary to consume at least four cups of wine during the meal. The four cups of wine served as key markers, signifying the meal's progression (m. Pesahim 10.1–2, 7). Following the first cup, the participants dipped a piece of lettuce into vinegar to symbolize the bitterness of slavery in Egypt (m. Pesahim 2.6; 10.3). Following the lettuce, they broke and ate unleavened bread, reminding the nation of how they had to leave Egypt in haste (Exod. 12:39; m. Pesahim 10.3). The meal also consisted of *charoset*, a symbol of the mud for bricks, along with two other dishes. Rabbi Gamaliel, the Apostle Paul's tutor, says the most crucial elements of the Passover meal are the Passover sacrifice, the unleavened bread, and the bitter herbs (m. Pesahim 10.5). In addition to food elements, a practice developed for the younger children to ask questions concerning the uniqueness of the event. The father would answer the questions by recounting the story of Israel's deliverance (m. Pesahim 10.4–5). The meal concluded with the recitation of the *Hallel* psalms, similar to the practice in the Temple (m. Pesahim 10.6–7).[10]

Jewish tradition illustrates how Passover customs were adapted and evolved during the early centuries. Since the celebration of Passover revolved around the Temple, the destruction of the Temple forced the Jewish community to find new ways to observe Passover outside of Jerusalem. As a result, the commemoration of Passover developed into an elaborate sacred meal, observed within the home. Although the Passover meal preserved many of the earlier traditions, the community had to figure out how to celebrate the holiday in a new context, without the centralized Temple to unify and galvanize the nation (see appendices 3–4).

EARLY JEWISH FOLLOWERS OF JESUS

The eclectic nature of the early Jewish followers of Jesus contributes to the difficulty of uncovering the way the Early Church approached and observed Passover. A brief overview of the customs of the early Jewish followers of Jesus, specifically the Ebionites and the Nazarenes (ca. 70 c.e.–fourth century), establishes the context for an investigation into the Passover customs of the Early Church. There were other communities of Jewish believers in the first few centuries, but these two notable groups provide an indication

---

Passover meal and Jewish traditions that developed after the destruction of the Temple; therefore, this section will offer just a cursory overview of the Passover meal during the first few centuries.

10. For more on the Passover meal and Messianic Jewish traditions, see chapter 16, "Passover in Your Home," by Cathy Wilson, and chapter 18, "A Messianic Family Haggadah," by the Staff of Chosen People Ministries.

of both early Passover customs and the broader Church's response to these Jewish traditions.[11]

Ebionites

Irenaeus (ca. 130 C.E.–202 C.E.) is the first to mention the Ebionite community by name (*Against Heresies* 1.26.2). Some had mistakenly believed the name originated from some unidentified founder named Ebion, but the term unquestionably originates from the Hebrew term אֶבְיוֹן, *'ebeyon*, designating the "poor" or "needy." It is not clear how this term came to signify the community of Jewish believers within the Early Church, but it might refer to the members of the Jerusalem church mentioned by Paul, who collected an offering from the Gentile church for the "poor" in Jerusalem (Gal. 2:10; 1 Cor. 16:1, MSG).[12]

It is also possible that the appellation originated as a self-designation utilized by a broad community of Jewish believers and alluded to the frequent cry in the Hebrew Bible by the poor and oppressed for God's salvation, both now and in the future.[13] Even though the rich and powerful ostracize those submerged under the weight of poverty, God looks upon them with compassion and as recipients of His blessing (Luke 6:20).

Although various Church Fathers speak about the "heretical" teachings and practices of the Ebionites—including Irenaeus, Tertullian, Hippolytus, Origen, Eusebius, and Epiphanius—the primary historical material originating from any group associated with the Ebionites is limited and dubious.[14] The name *Ebionite* apparently became a designation within "patristic literature to describe those who seek to both follow Jesus and maintain their Jewishness."[15] Within the extant sources its most frequent usage carries a strong pejorative emphasis. Any attempt to reconstruct the community relies upon a certain amount of speculation, since most of what we know of the Ebionites derives from the information provided by the Church Fathers, who wanted to discredit the group as heretical.[16]

---

11. Included in the assorted portrait of Jewish followers of Jesus are the Jerusalem community that reportedly fled to Pella prior to the destruction of the Temple in 70 C.E. and both the Symachians and Elkesaites sects.
12. Broadhead, *Jewish Ways of Following Jesus*, 188.
13. Oskar Skarsaune, "The Ebionites," in Skarsaune and Hvalvik, *Jewish Believers in Jesus*, 421.
14. See David F. Wright, "Ebionites," in *Dictionary of the Later New Testament and Its Development*, ed. Ralph P. Martin and Peter H. Davids (Downers Grove, IL: InterVarsity Press, 1997), 313–17. See also Irenaeus, *Against Heresies* 1.26.2, 5.1.3; Tertullian, *Prescription against Heresies*, 30.3–5; Hippolytus, *Refutation of All Heresies* 7.34–35; Origen, *First Principles* 4.1.22, 4.3.8; Eusebius, *Ecclesiastical History* 3.27; and Epiphanius, *Refutation of All Heresies* 30.
15. Broadhead, *Jewish Ways of Following Jesus*, 188.
16. The portrayal of the Ebionites as a heretical sect by Irenaeus (*Against Heresies* 1.26.2, 5.1.3), Epiphanius (*Refutation of All Heresies* 30), Origen (*First Principles* 4.1.22, 4.3.8), and others does not mean this depiction is inaccurate. Rather, when analyzing the authenticity of the historical depiction of the Ebionites it is important to note that the majority of the extant evidence for the community derives from a group of people who sought to censure the community in their beliefs and practices.

The picture of the Ebionites, as presented within patristic writings, shows how the community followed the Gospel of the Hebrews, a Hebrew version of the Gospel of Matthew, while rejecting both the divine nature of the Messiah and His virgin birth. Rather than affirming the Messiah's eternal nature, the Ebionites believed that Jesus became the Messiah through His faithful and meticulous observance to the Torah.[17] They were accused of the heresy of *adoptionism*, which declares that Jesus became divine at His baptism.[18]

While church history has generally identified the Ebionites as a splinter sect that rejected Jesus's divine nature, it is possible that the designation originally applied to a broader community of Jewish believers, which encompassed a variety of doctrinal positions, both orthodox and unorthodox.[19] If this is the case, the information gathered concerning the observance of Passover within the Ebionite community might suggest that the observance of Passover in the Early Church was rather common and not limited to a small splinter group.

In his brief mention of the Passover observed by the Ebionites, Origen (ca. 184–253 C.E.) says that they followed the pattern of Jesus, because it behooves "us as imitators of the Messiah to do similarly" (*Commentarium in evangelium Matthaei* § 79).[20] Jesus, in turn, celebrated Passover "in the way of the Jews and also likewise the first day of the Unleavened Bread and Passover" (ibid.). At first glance, it appears that Origen commends the Ebionite community for imitating Jesus in their observance of Passover, but he expresses his displeasure with their practice, because it was his opinion that Jesus came "to those who were under the Law" in order "to lead them away from the Law" (ibid.). Origen's testimony reveals two salient factors. First, the Ebionite community observed Passover according to the customs of the larger Jewish community. This may even indicate that the observance of Passover was normative in the nascent Church, at least among Jewish believers. Second, Origen's disapproval of the Ebionite celebration of Passover illustrates his opinion that observance of Jewish feasts signifies enslavement to the Law. As a result, Origen implies that the Ebionite celebration of Passover, following the Jewish custom, is a heretical practice.[21] Origen's opinion

---

Since their intention was to discredit the Ebionites, they will likely have a tendency to emphasize the ways in which they deviated from accepted practice but omit any rationale for their beliefs.

17. Oskar Skarsaune, *In the Shadow of the Temple: Jewish Influences on Early Christianity*, (Downers Grove, InterVarsity Press: 2002), 203–6.

18. David E. Wilhite, *The Gospel According to the Heretics: Discovering Orthodoxy through Early Christological Conflicts* (Grand Rapids: Baker Academic: 2015), 41–56.

19. Origen (*Against Celsus* 5.61) seems to confirm various groups within the Ebionites. For evidence of other patristic writings supporting two separate groups of Ebionites, namely, those who affirm the deity of Jesus and those who do not, see Broadhead, *Jewish Ways of Following Jesus*, 181–82.

20. Origen, quoted here and in next two quotations as recorded and translated by A. F. J. Klijn and G. J. Reinink, *Patristic Evidence for Jewish-Christian Sects*, Supplements to Novum Testamentum 36 (Leiden: Brill, 1973), 130–33.

21. Petri Luomanen, *Recovering Jewish-Christian Sects and Gospels*, Supplements to Vigiliae Christianae 110 (Leiden, Brill, 2012), 26.

reflects a sentiment shared by other church leaders of his day and embodies the rationale for rejecting Passover observance within the Church.

On the other hand, Epiphanius (ca. 310–403) provides a different picture of the Ebionite adherence to Passover customs in the Gospel of the Ebionites, attributed to the Ebionite sect. In this account Jesus gives the disciples instruction on how to prepare the Passover meal. Jesus says to His disciples, "I have no desire to eat flesh this Passover with you" (*Refutation of All Heresies* 30.22.4).[22] This emendation of the canonical Gospel tradition illustrates the Ebionite preference for a vegetarian diet, which breaks from the Jewish custom of eating roasted lamb for the Passover meal.[23] Since Jesus satisfied the need for a Paschal Lamb (1 Cor. 5:7) and the Romans destroyed the Temple, the Ebionite sect established a rationale for breaking with the Jewish Passover tradition by following a vegetarian *kashrut*, or *kosher*, diet.[24] Eating lamb at Passover is intended to remind the nation of sacrifice of the lambs to secure Israel's deliverance from Egypt. The Ebionite breaking from this tradition demonstrates their willingness to adapt Jewish tradition in light of their recognition of Jesus as the Messiah. Jesus became the lens through which they viewed and applied Jewish tradition. This leaves a rather curious portrait of the Ebionites. On the one hand, they enthusiastically adhered to the Torah, including observance of Passover in a manner consistent with the Jewish community, but, on the other hand, their faith in Jesus led them to potentially break with Jewish tradition by following more stringent dietary restrictions.

Nazarenes

The Nazarenes likely represent a larger and more conventional community of believers. The name *Nazarenes* recalls the designation for the original Jewish followers of Jesus.[25] Initially, the identification applies to Jesus in order to distinguish Him from others bearing the same name (Matt. 26:71; Luke 18:37).[26] The first time this term refers to a particular group of Jesus's

---

22. See Craig A. Evans, "The Jewish Christian Gospel Tradition," in Skarsaune and Hvalvik, *Jewish Believers in Jesus*, 253.

23. Evans, "The Jewish Christian Gospel Tradition," 253. Eating roasted lamb for Passover reflects the Jewish custom prior to the destruction of the Temple. Ashkenazic Jewish tradition refrains from eating lamb during the Passover meal, since there is no longer a Temple, making it impossible to sacrifice a lamb for Passover in the way prescribed by the Torah.

24. Evans, "The Jewish Christian Gospel Tradition," 253. The word *kashrut* refers to the Jewish dietary laws and restrictions. The term derives from a Hebrew word meaning "fit or proper," which relates to the more commonly used term *kosher*, signifying the set of laws indicating which foods are fit to eat.

25. Broadhead, *Jewish Ways of Following Jesus*, 163.

26. It is difficult to determine how the designation "Nazarenes" developed into a term for the Jesus followers. Matthew suggests that the term "Nazarene" (Ναζωραῖος, *Nazōraios*) derives from Jesus's hometown, "Nazareth" (Ναζαρέτ, *Nazaret*; Matt. 2:23), but the linguistic relationship between the two terms is uncertain. See the discussion on the terms in Frederick W. Danker, Walter Bauer, William F. Arndt, and F. Wilbur Gingrich, *Greek-English Lexicon of the New Testament and Other*

followers occurs in Luke's account of Paul's trial before Felix in Caesarea when Tertullus accused Paul of stirring up riots as the ringleader of the "sect of the Nazarenes" (Acts 24:5). Both Jerome (ca. 347–420; *Commentariorum in Matthaeum libri IV* 27:9–10; *Epistulae* 112.13) and Epiphanius; *Refutation of All Heresies* 29) discuss a group they identify as "Nazarenes."[27] On a few occasions, early rabbinic literature utilizes the designation נוצרים, *notzrim*, (the Hebrew/Aramaic equivalent for Nazarene) when referring to the followers of Jesus (b. Avodah Zarah 6a; b. Ta'anit 27b). The Nazarenes mainly resided in the region of Beroea (the ancient name for modern Aleppo, Syria), adjacent to vibrant Jewish and Christian communities.[28]

The Nazarenes were believers who maintained their Jewish identity and continued to adhere to the Torah. Little evidence remains describing the Passover traditions of the Nazarenes, but it is possible to draw a few inferences concerning their Passover observance in light of other information known about the community. Most of the surviving information about the beliefs and practices of the Nazarenes relies on the writings of Jerome and Epiphanius during the fourth century.[29] Jerome has a rather neutral view of the Nazarenes, with both positive and critical assessments at times, but his overall portrait presents the group as a faithful community of Jewish followers of Jesus with beliefs compatible with a developing Christian orthodoxy, while also maintaining Jewish customs and adherence to the Torah.[30] They were the recipients of frequent hostility from local synagogues and engaged in an ongoing debate with the Jewish community concerning rabbinic tradition and authority.[31] Epiphanius presents a picture similar to Jerome, but with a very different evaluation. He considers the Torah observance of the Jewish believers to be heretical, which signifies a key moment in the relationship between the Jewish and Christian communities (*Refutation of All Heresies* 29.9.1–5).[32]

From this summation it is fair to assume that the Nazarenes likely celebrated Passover in one form or another, although they may have questioned

---

Early Christian Literature, 3rd ed. (Chicago: University of Chicago Press, 2000), 664–65. It is possible that Matthew connects the two as homophones, alluding to the Messianic hope in Isaiah, who anticipated a time when "a shoot will spring from the stem of Jesse, and a *branch* [נֵצֶר, *netzer*] from his roots will bear fruit" (Isa. 11:1, emphasis added; see also vv. 2–10). For a detailed discussion concerning the etymological difficulties presented by this term, see Wolfram Kinzig, "The Nazoraeans," in Skarsaune and Hvalvik, *Jewish Believers in Jesus*, 468–71.

27. Skarsaune, *In the Shadow of the Temple*, 202–3.

28. For over five centuries, the Central Synagogue of Aleppo was home to the Aleppo Codex, one of the oldest and most important Hebrew manuscripts. It is over one thousand years old and survived a fire during the anti-Jewish riots of 1947. Today, the Israel Museum in Jerusalem houses the Aleppo Codex.

29. Broadhead, *Jewish Ways of Following Jesus*, 164–79; Petri Luomanen, *Recovering Jewish-Christian Sects and Gospels*, 49–77.

30. Broadhead, *Jewish Ways of Following Jesus*, 173–74.

31. Broadhead, *Jewish Ways of Following Jesus*, 170, 174; Kinzig, "The Nazoraeans," 477–78.

32. Broadhead, *Jewish Ways of Following Jesus*, 174–79.

some of the Passover traditions of the larger Jewish community in Beroea, since they maintained a preference for the Torah over rabbinic traditions.

The assessment by Epiphanius signifies the move within the Early Church away from an observance of Passover.[33] Since he considered adherence to the Torah heresy, the Passover traditions preserved by the Nazarenes did not pass on to future generations in the Church.

Both the Ebionites and the Nazarenes illustrate a painful reality in church history. The expanding number of Gentile Christians began to view the Jewish believers in a negative light and marginalized their customs. At best, observance of traditional Jewish customs was discouraged, but by the time of the Council of Nicaea, the church rulers considered such Jewish expressions of faith heretical. This makes it difficult to reconstruct Passover customs in the Early Church. The challenge for the historian is that victorious groups characteristically push their victims out of existence and then fail to document their practices and contributions to the development of the faith. Thus the sad reality is that church leaders, after the fourth century, did not record the Jewish elements of the Early Church, essentially removing the Church from its Jewish cultural foundation.

ANCIENT FATHERS

While many church leaders objected to participation in traditional Jewish customs, because they presumed it represented "Judaizing" the Church, the Passover remained an important symbol for Jesus's deliverance of humanity through His death and resurrection. The celebration of Passover commemorates sacrifice and redemption, a concept originating in the Scriptures shared by both Christians and Jews.[34] Leaders like Hippolytus of Rome (170–235), Justin (100–165), and Polycarp (69–155) allude to the Passover in their liturgy for the Eucharist. In the last century, discovery of two remarkable treatises concerning the Passover, by Melito and Origen, illustrate how the observance of Passover played a crucial role in the way the Church related to Jesus's death.

Melito of Sardis and a Christian Haggadah

Melito was born into a Jewish home and immersed in Hellenistic culture. He served as the bishop of Sardis, a significant and wealthy city in the province of Lydia in the western region of Asia Minor. Sardis was home to sizable Jewish and Christian communities. Melito's most notable work is a retelling of the Passover, based upon the traditional Haggadah, entitled *Peri Pascha*, "concerning the Passover" (ca. 160–170 C.E.). He begins his narration

33. Ray A. Pritz, *Nazarene Jewish Christianity: From the End of the New Testament Period Until Its Disappearance in the Fourth Century*, Studia Post-biblica 37 (Jerusalem: Hebrew University / Magnes Press, 1988), 34.

34. Israel J. Yuval, "Easter and Passover as Early Jewish-Christian Dialogue," in *Passover and Easter: Origin and History to Modern Times*, ed. Paul F. Bradshaw and Lawrence A. Hoffman, Two Liturgical Traditions 5 (Notre Dame, IN: Notre Dame Press: 1999), 103.

by recounting the story of Passover as described in the Exodus, including God's instruction to Israel, the calamities experienced in Egypt, and God's deliverance of His people (*Peri Pascha* 1–33).[35] These historic events, central to Israel's purpose and identity, function merely as a model for the ultimate archetype expressed in the relationship between Jesus and His Church.[36] Thus, at the heart of his Haggadah, Melito emphasizes the celebration of the suffering of Jesus, the Passover Lamb.[37] While he recounts the Exodus from Egypt, those events for Melito are merely the backdrop to a more significant story: the death of the Messiah for the deliverance of humanity.

Melito's rendition of the Passover appears to appropriate traditional Jewish motifs about the Exodus for a new context. In the introduction to the *Hallel* prayer and prior to the second cup of the Seder, the traditional Jewish Haggadah reads, "He took us from slavery to freedom, from suffering to joy, from mourning to celebration, from darkness to great light, and from subjection to redemption. And we shall sing for him a new song: *Halleluyah*."[38] Melito echoes the traditional Jewish liturgy with a doxology comparing Jesus's victory over death to Moses' victory over Pharaoh, "This is the one who delivered us from slavery to freedom, from darkness into light, from death into life, from tyranny into an eternal Kingdom, and made us a new priesthood, and a people everlasting for himself" (*Peri Pascha* 68.) The striking parallels between the traditional Jewish Haggadah and Melito's Haggadah indicate Melito's familiarity with Jewish traditions and his dependence upon them in shaping Christian liturgy.

Melito's Haggadah also alludes to a prominent Messianic symbol in the traditional Haggadah. As part of the Passover meal it is customary to break a whole piece of *matzah* into two pieces, wrap up one of the pieces, referred to as the *afikoman*, and to hide it until later in the Seder. Although the origin of this tradition is uncertain, it was present within Jewish observance of Passover at the time of Melito, because the instructions concerning the Passover regulations in the Mishnah, which is contemporary with Melito, refer to the practice (m. Pesahim 10:8).[39] The custom likely functioned as an ancient Messianic symbol in which the broken piece of matzah represents the coming Messiah; therefore, when Jesus handed His disciples a piece of matzah at

---

35. For a translation of *Peri Pascha*, see Melito of Sardis, *On Pascha: With the Fragments of Melito and Other Material Related to the Quartodecimans*, ed. John Behr, trans. Alistair Stewart-Sykes, (Crestwood, NY: St. Vladimir's Seminary Press: 2001), 37–67. Subsequent quotations of Melito's *Peri Pascha* are from Stewart-Sykes's translation.

36. Stewart-Sykes, *On Pascha*, 34–55.

37. Stewart-Sykes, *On Pascha*, 46.

38. Quoted in Joseph Tabory, *JPS Commentary on the Haggadah: Historical Introduction, Translation, and Commentary* (Philadelphia: Jewish Publication Society, 2008), 101. Cf. Mishnah Pesahim 10:5.

39. Translating the tractate Pesahim 10:8 of the Mishnah has proven problematic for scholars, since the Greek etymology for אֲפִיקוֹמָן, *'afiyqoman*, has engendered much debate. Various proposals have included "dessert" (ἐπίκωμοι, *epikōmoi*), "after-dinner revelry" (ἐπὶ κῶμον, *epi kōmon*), and "festivities" (ἐπικώμιον, *epikōmion*).

the conclusion of the meal, He took a traditional Jewish custom and applied it to Himself by essentially announcing to His disciples, "I am the one who is to come" (cf. Matt. 23:39; 26:26). Melito, in his Haggadah, draws attention to this custom by proclaiming that "this is the one who *comes* from heaven onto the earth for the suffering one, and wraps himself in the suffering one through a virgin womb" (*Peri Pascha* 66, emphasis added). The term Melito utilizes for Jesus's coming is ἀφικόμενος, *aphikomenos*, which is reminiscent of the broken piece of matzah in the Seder, *afikoman*.[40] Melito links the identity of the *afikoman* with Jesus, who suffers as the Passover Lamb.[41]

While it appears Melito borrows from traditional Jewish liturgy in the shaping of his Haggadah, it is possible that he influenced the development of later Jewish tradition as well. One of the most memorable parts in the traditional Seder is the singing of the song "*Dayenu*," which is a Hebrew word that simply means, "It was enough for us." The liturgical song first appeared in the Haggadah some time around the ninth century, seven centuries after the time of Melito. The word דַּיֵּנוּ, *dayenu*, returns as a refrain in each stanza, recalling how God continually intervened on Israel's behalf, bestowing repeated blessings on the nation. Melito's arrangement is remarkably similar to this piece of Jewish liturgy when he addresses "ungrateful" Israel by asking, "How much did you value being formed by him? How much did you value the finding of your fathers? How much did you value the descent into Egypt, and your refreshment there under Joseph the Just? How much did you value the ten plagues? How much did you value the pillar by night, and the cloud by day, and the crossing of the Red Sea?" (*Peri Pascha* 87–88).[42]

The liturgical song "*Dayenu*" exhibits strong parallels to Melito's composition, which may be a reflection of the ongoing "Jewish-Christian dialogue" in the first few centuries.[43] Although later Jewish liturgy will incorporate Psalms 78, 106, and 136 into the Passover tradition, Melito appears to be the first to incorporate Psalm 106 into the Passover liturgy. The appearance of "*Dayenu*" as a central piece of liturgy in later Jewish tradition may illustrate the influence of Melito's work on this Jewish-Christian dialogue.

Origen and the Treatise on Passover

Origen, who was born in Alexandria a generation after Melito, also wrote extensively on the Passover in a treatise by the same title, *Peri Pascha*.[44]

---

40. Stewart-Sykes, *On Pascha*, 54.
41. Melito uses the term πάσχων, *paschōn*, to depict Jesus's suffering. For more on Melito of Sardis and the history and meaning of the afikoman tradition, see chapter 11, "Passover and the Afikoman," by Daniel Nessim.
42. Melito continues in *Peri Pascha* with the same refrain into 88–89.
43. Yuval, "Easter and Passover as Early Jewish-Christian Dialogue," 104–5.
44. For a translation of Origen's *Peri Pascha*, see Origen, *Treatise on the Passover* and *Dialogue of Origen with Heraclides and His Fellow Bishops on the Father, the Son, and the Soul*, trans. Robert J. Daly, Ancient Christian Writers 54 (Mahwah, NJ: Paulist Press, 1992). Subsequent quotations of Origen's *Peri Pascha* are from Daly's translation.

While Origen's composition is notable, it does not reveal much about how the Early Church observed Passover. The first part of his treatise comments on the Egyptian Passover, and the second section examines the spiritual impact of the holiday.

Origen departs from Melito's presentation of Passover by arguing that the Passover does not prefigure the passion of Christ; rather, they are two separate events, which should not be fused together. He backs away from the emphasis upon suffering in Passover, specifically the suffering of the Messiah. He demonstrates how the Hebrew term for the holiday does not relate to the concept of suffering but to that of a passage or the act of passing. The Hebrew term for "Passover," פֶּסַח, *pesach*, relates to a verb depicting movement from one place to another. In the case of Passover, it refers to passing over of the homes.[45] Therefore, Origen warns Christians against falsely thinking the Jewish holiday derives its name from the suffering of the Messiah.

THE PASSOVER CONTROVERSY

The critical issue surrounding Passover in the Early Church revolved around the establishment of a date when the community should commemorate the holiday. There was a strong contingent who believed the Church should observe both Passover and Jesus's resurrection in continuity with the traditional Jewish calculation for Passover, while a growing contingent had a preference for celebrating Jesus's resurrection on the following Sunday. The sacrifice of the Passover lamb in ancient Judaism occurred on the fourteenth day of Nisan. Observance of the holiday followed a specific date in the Jewish calendar, regardless of the day of the week. The Early Church in Jerusalem and the surrounding region in Asia maintained this practice, but the church in Rome detached the celebration from the Jewish calendar and began to venerate the following Sunday as the day of Jesus's resurrection.

Quartodecimanism

Within the Early Church there was a movement, referred to as *Quartodecimanism*, to celebrate Passover beginning on the evening of the fourteenth of Nisan, the date the Torah establishes as the beginning of the

---

45. The etymology of the Hebrew name for the holiday of Passover, פֶּסַח, *pesach*, is uncertain and disputed (see Ludwig Koehler, Walter Baumgartner, and Johann J. Stamm, *The Hebrew and Aramaic Lexicon of the Old Testament*, trans. and ed. Mervyn E. J. Richardson, 4 vols. [Leiden: Brill, 1994–1999], 3:947). The relationship between the verbal and the nominal form is not clear. However, there is compelling evidence to suggest that *Passover* derives from a verb meaning "to have compassion for." The Aramaic translation of Exodus 12:13 reads, "I will see the blood and have compassion on you" (Targum Onkelos Exod. 12:13). For a brief, yet fascinating and accessible explanation of this alternative reading, see Ari Z. Zivotofsky, "What's the Truth about . . . the Meaning of 'Pesach'?" *Jewish Action* (Spring 2004): 58–59, https://www.ou.org/torah/machshava/tzarich-iyun/tzarich_iyun_the_meaning_of_pesach/.

holiday (Lev. 23:5).[46] On the afternoon of the fourteenth the nation offered their Passover sacrifices (Exod. 12:6). This practice indicates that segments of the Early Church relied upon the Jewish traditions as the foundation for Christian customs. The tradition for observing Passover on the evening of the fourteenth of Nisan possibly began as an early Christian adaptation of the Jewish tradition.[47] Eastern churches in Jerusalem, Asia Minor, and Syria maintained this tradition into the fourth century.[48]

Locating Passover on the fourteenth of the month, rather than on Sunday, signifies a crucial aspect of the Early Church; they did not consider the observance of Passover to be an innovation of the Church but in continuity with a long-standing Jewish tradition. Their Passover observance also included celebration of Jesus's resurrection, although they did not consider the fourteenth to be the actual day of the resurrection. In fact, the Quartodecimans may represent a "direct continuation of the custom of the primitive Church, that the Paschal feast was indeed observed by Christians."[49] By continuing this tradition, the Early Church followed the example of Paul who "respected and regulated his life" according to the normative Jewish calendar when he eagerly sought to travel to Jerusalem for the celebration of Pentecost (Acts 20:16).[50]

Polycrates of Ephesus (ca. 195 C.E.) speaks about the long lineage of seven spiritual luminaries who preceded him: Philip and John the Apostles; Polycarp, who many consider a spiritual successor to the Apostle John in Asia Minor; Thraseas (died ca. 170 C.E.), who was both a bishop and a martyr; Sagaris (died ca. 166 C.E.), who was also a bishop and martyr; Papirius of Smyrna (died ca. 170 C.E.); and Melito of Sardis (died ca. 180 C.E.). Each of these men, along with Polycrates, celebrated the Passover on the fourteenth day, according to the rule of faith, as did his compatriots, who always observed the day when they put away the leaven (Eusebius, *Ecclesiastical History* 5.24.2–7).[51] Polycrates provides this statement as evidence for maintaining the tradition of his predecessors and as the reason why the churches in Asia Minor continued to

---

46. The name for this movement, *Quartodecimanism*, develops from the Latin term *quarta decima*, which means "fourteenth." Jewish tradition calculates the beginning of the day from the point of sundown, since the account of the creation of the world states that "there was evening and there was morning, one day" (Gen. 1:5). Today, the Jewish community observes Passover (פֶּסַח, *pesach*) as part of a weeklong celebration connected with the Feast of Unleavened Bread (חַג הַמַּצּוֹת, *chag hammatsot*). The Passover meal, known as a Seder (סֵדֶר, *seder*), typically takes place on the evening of the fifteenth of Nisan, which follows the conclusion of the fourteenth.
47. Joachim Jeremias, *The Eucharistic Words of Jesus*, trans. Norman Perrin, rev. ed., New Testament Library (New York: Scribner, 1966), 122–23.
48. Yuval, "Easter and Passover as Early Jewish-Christian Dialogue," 98.
49. Samuele Bacchiocchi, *From Sabbath to Sunday: A Historical Investigation of the Rise of Sunday Observance in Early Christianity* (Rome: Pontifical Gregorian University Press, 1977), 76.
50. Bacchiocchi, *From Sabbath to Sunday*, 76. Pentecost is known in Judaism as the Feast of Weeks (חַג שָׁבֻעוֹת, *chag shavu'ot*; Exod. 34:22).
51. Oskar Skarsaune ("Evidence for Jewish Believers in Greek and Latin Patristic Literature," in Skarsaune and Hvalvik, *Jewish Believers in Jesus*, 519–20) makes a case for the Jewish ethnicity for all seven bishops as "compatriots" (συγγενεῖς, *sungeneis*) of Polycrates.

follow the Jewish calculation for Passover, contrary to the vehement objections by Victor, the bishop of Rome, who believed the Church should celebrate on a Sunday to commemorate the resurrection of Jesus from the dead.

The emphasis for many of the Quartodecimans in their celebration of Passover was not the resurrection of Jesus but His sacrifice and crucifixion, in the same way the Jewish Passover emphasizes the death of the Paschal lamb in the redemption of Israel from Egypt (1 Cor. 5:7; John 1:29, 36). In preparation for the Passover celebration the community fasted, but the fast concluded with a feast celebrating Jesus as the Paschal Lamb. It is possible that the celebration looked at the redemptive elements of Jesus's sacrifice by anticipating the return of the Messiah, following the Jewish expectation for the arrival of Messiah at Passover.[52]

The new story invited the Quartodecimans to apply new meanings to ancient Jewish symbols.[53] The Passover lamb (פֶּסַח, *pesach*) now symbolized the sacrifice of Jesus as the Lamb of God (John 1:29, 36). The unleavened bread (מַצָּה, *matzah*) became a picture of Jesus's body in the manner He presented during His Passover celebration with the disciples (Matt. 26:26). The bitter herbs (מָרֹר, *maror*) recalled the bitter suffering Jesus endured during His trial and execution. While history has either obscured or lost many of the Quartodeciman customs associated with the observance of Passover, the ample evidence concerning the date of their celebration and the rationale behind it demonstrates how a significant part of the Early Church relied heavily upon Jewish tradition for the shaping of their customs.

Passover Sunday Observance

The dating and celebration of Passover developed into one of the more controversial subjects in the Early Church. Initially, it was just a matter of a slight disagreement between churches in the East and churches in the West, but by the end of the second century it degenerated into a contentious topic with Victor, the bishop of Rome, attempting to excommunicate the Quartodecimans by accusing them of heresy.[54] The churches in the West celebrated the first Sunday following the fourteenth of Nisan by commemorating the resurrection of Jesus from the dead (Matt. 28:1). The available evidence seems to suggest that the custom of celebrating the resurrection on the Sunday following Passover developed in Rome sometime toward the end of the first century.[55] This celebration became the foundation for what later developed into Easter.

During the next three centuries, the schism over the dating of Passover widened, highlighting the growing gap between Christianity and Judaism.

52. Paul F. Bradshaw, "The Origins of Easter," in Bradshaw and Hoffman, *Passover and Easter*, 85.
53. Yuval, "Easter and Passover as Early Christian Dialogue," 106.
54. Samuele Bacchiocchi, *Anti-Judaism and the Origin of Sunday*, (Rome, Pontifical Gregorian University Press: 1975), 85.
55. Bacchiocchi, *Anti-Judaism and the Origin of Sunday*, 86.

Rome and the churches in the West accused the Quartodecimans of "Juda-izing" the Church by primarily focusing upon the relationship between the resurrection of Jesus and Passover.[56] As the influence of the Quartodecimans waned, Emperor Constantine arranged for the first ecumenical council (325 C.E.) in Nicaea, a town located in the northwestern area of modern-day Tur-key, conveniently situated at the intersection of the East and the West.

The Council of Nicaea is most notable for articulating the relationship between Jesus and the Father and thereby delineating the boundaries of or-thodoxy with the Nicene Creed. Yet the Council also established a standard-ized observance for the date of Easter. History of religions specialist Marcel Simon notes, "It was henceforth forbidden to celebrate Easter, even with specifically Christian rituals, at the same time as the Jewish Passover."[57] Since the emperor convened the gathering of church leaders, the decisions of the conclave carried significant consequence. The Church chose to follow the directives from the emperor, who was likely attempting to consolidate his power by eliminating the Jewish traditions in church practice.

The Audians, a small Christian community in the region of Syria dur-ing the fourth century, believed that the leaders at Nicaea "abandoned the fathers' Paschal rite in Constantine's time from deference to the emperor, and changed the day to suit the emperor" (Epiphanius, *Refutation of All Heresies*, bk. 3, 70.9.3). As a result, the Church considered it heretical to observe Passover according to Jewish calculations and customs. Later that century, the Council of Laodicea reinforced the decisions of Nicaea and outlawed observance of the Sabbath or participation in Jewish festivals (364 C.E.). The councils had irretrievably wedged an insurmountable chasm between Chris-tianity and Judaism.

IMPLICATIONS

The move away from observance of Passover has significant implications for the Church. During the first few centuries of the Early Church, robust communities preserved traditional Jewish customs while faithfully follow-ing Jesus as their Messiah. Church leaders increasingly marginalized these communities, diminishing the Church's participation in Jewish practices. Melito's Haggadah switched the focus of Passover off of the Exodus from Egypt and onto the suffering of the Messiah, as the ultimate Paschal Lamb, to secure redemption for humanity. While he was right to understand the death and resurrection of Jesus as the watershed moment in human history, detachment of this event from the Jewish symbolic foundation weakens the redemptive significance. On the other hand, the Quartodeciman preserva-tion of Passover within the Jewish context amplifies the importance of Jesus's

---

56.   Broadhead, *Jewish Ways of Following Jesus*, 239.
57.   Marcel Simon, *Verus Israel: A Study of the Relations Between Christians and Jews in the Roman Empire (ad 132–425)*, trans. H. McKeating (1986; repr., London: Littman Library of Jewish Civilization, 1996), 316.

crucifixion by placing it within the ongoing narrative of Israel's redemption and setting it against the backdrop of the nation's deliverance out of Egypt.

Emperor Constantine, in a push to consolidate his power and create uniformity within the Church, outlawed the practice of celebrating Passover at the time of Jewish custom and made the observance of Easter on Sunday compulsory for all churches. While allusions to Passover traditions would remain within the Eucharistic liturgy, the Church soon lost its connection to the Passover narrative. The Eucharist, or Communion, maintains central elements of the Passover meal with the bread and wine, but without the inclusion of the remaining traditional elements, the celebration loses the powerful reminder of God's deliverance of His people from slavery, truncating the story and divorcing from it the role the Jewish people play in redemption history.

The story of Passover is the story of God having compassion on a people suffering under the oppression of slavery and providing deliverance. God instructed the nation of Israel to offer the Paschal lamb, not necessarily as a way of atoning for sin, but as the means for deliverance from injustice under Egyptian tyranny.[58] It is a story of liberation and redemption. Rabbi Jonathan Sacks, former Chief Rabbi of the United Hebrew Congregations of the Commonwealth, speaks about the importance of remembering our deliverance: "We were once strangers: the oppressed, the victims. Remembering the Jewish past forces us to undergo role reversal. In the midst of freedom we have to remind ourselves of what it feels like to be a slave."[59] Passover establishes a paradigm for deliverance in the movement of slavery to redemption, bondage to freedom.

Jesus spoke of His death from within the context of a Passover meal. Each participant retells the story as if he or she personally experienced deliverance from Egypt (m. Pesahim 10:5). As participants, the community cannot disassociate the remembering from the historical context; rather, telling the story requires thinking creatively about how the historical event has present ramifications. It is a retelling that must incorporate the Exodus event as a motif through which the community views the crucifixion of Jesus and God's ongoing involvement in the liberation of His people. The retelling is never a private event but one that occurs within community, stressing unity. Historically, the Exodus unified a diverse group of people around a singular event.

The relationship of the Early Church to Passover illustrates the progression of the developing community away from its Jewish foundation. Each year the Jewish community recites the Passover narrative and tells the story from the perspective of the first person, because each generation must see itself as the generation God delivered out of Egypt. This allows each generation to personally identify with the experience of the slaves in Egypt.

---

58. This is does not mean atonement is not a theme within the Lord's Supper, but the context for its origin suggests the theme of liberation, which emphasizes Jesus's death as a means to liberate His people from the clutches of sin (Heb. 9:15).

59. Jonathan Sacks, *Not in God's Name: Confronting Religious Violence* (New York: Schocken Books, 2015), 187.

By approaching the Jewish Passover story as a detached historical event, which separates the Exodus from its relationship to Communion, the Church has become disconnected from the continuity of God's grand narrative. The Exodus is no longer viewed as a personal experience but as an ancient event that exists in the dust of antiquity. The Church reinterpreted and modified the great Old Testament themes of the Passover and reapplied them to the suffering and sacrifice of Jesus for the restoration of a broken world, thereby rejecting the earlier chapters for the conclusion of the story. As a result, the Church has lost a precious and crucial part of its heritage and connection to its Jewish nucleus (Rom. 11:17–24). This is a lesson the Church of our present day should not and cannot afford to ignore, especially in a day when younger generations are searching for meaningful relationship to tradition and deeper historical connection.

Connecting the story of both Testaments through the Passover is one way to counterbalance the mistakes of our spiritual ancestors who intentionally severed the Church from its Jewish heritage in the Messiah. The lesson is not merely about the importance of Passover as a backdrop for God's ongoing redemptive work, but, more importantly, it is how the regular retelling of the community's ancient stories shapes and energizes the communal identity of God's people. History infuses community with meaning. Passover provides the Church with an invitation to reflect and remember. Remembering not only produces compassion for others who are presently experiencing a similar form of oppression, but it also fills the community with hope, because the trajectory of God's story always moves from bondage to freedom.

8
PASSOVER CONTROVERSIES IN CHURCH HISTORY

GREGORY HAGG

The Passover controversies form an important part of the story of church history, especially in shaping the relationship of the Church with the Jewish community. This chapter will provide an overview of only a few of the more notable controversies related to the Feast in relation to the Church's attitudes and actions. Three examples have been selected: the Quartodeciman debate, the *Novellae* of Justinian I, and the blood libels.

THE QUARTODECIMAN DEBATE (155–325 c.e.)

The Quartodeciman controversy, introduced by Scott Nassau in the previous chapter, focuses on the Early Church and the key role Messianic Jews played in the formation of the Post-Apostolic Church.[1] In this chapter we will recap some of what was detailed earlier and show the ongoing impact of this early controversy and how it shaped the Church's discussion and understanding of its relationship to the Jewish people.

As noted earlier, the term *Quartodecimans* comes from the Latin term *quarta decima*, which means "fourteenth," referring to the fourteenth day of Nisan in the Jewish lunar calendar. This, of course, is the biblical date of the beginning of Pesach, the Feast of Passover.

The early Jewish believers understood that the death of Yeshua, the Lamb of God, took place on the fourteenth of Nisan, so the celebration of His resurrection should occur in close proximity to the Passover. The obvious problem was that this date did not fall on the same day of the week each year, so the church leaders eventually required that a Sunday be selected for the date of Easter.

In a letter to the church at Philippi, Ignatius of Antioch (30–108 c.e.) says, "If any one celebrates the Passover along with the Jews, or receives the

---

1. See chapter 7, "Passover, the Temple, and the Early Church," by Scott P. Nassau.

emblems of their feast, he is a partaker with those that killed the Lord and His apostles" (*To the Philippians* 14 [*ANF* 1:119]). This was a very early indication that the parting of the ways between an emerging early Christianity and post-Temple Judaism was in beginning to be established.

Hippolytus of Rome (170–236 C.E.), who attacks the Quartodecimans in a rather combative way later in the controversy, says,

> There are others, fractious by nature, individualistic in their understanding, pugnacious over the point, who maintain that it is necessary to keep the Pascha on the fourteenth of the first month in accordance with the provision of the law, on whatever day it might fall. They have regard only to that which is written in the law that whosoever does not keep it as it is commanded is accursed. They do not notice that the law was laid down for the Jews, who in time would destroy the true Passover, which has come to the gentiles and is discerned by faith, and not by observation of the letter. By keeping to this one commandment they do not notice what was said by the apostle, namely "I bear witness to everyone who is circumcised that they are obliged to keep the entirety of the law." In other things they conform to everything, which has been handed down to the church by the apostles. (*Refutation of All Heresies* 8.18)[2]

Clearly, this is not simply a discussion of which day to observe an event. Rather, it is a polemic against the practice of Jewish believers and others who agreed with this emphasis upon the Passover.

It should be noted that before the final decision of the Council of Nicaea in 325 C.E., when Easter officially replaced Passover, there were various Church Fathers and Apostles before them who could be called Quartodecimans.

Eusebius Pamphili (ca. 264–340 C.E.) was a bishop and church historian known as Eusebius of Caesarea. His *Ecclesiastical History* is the principal source for the history of Christianity (especially in the Eastern Church) from the age of the Apostles until 324. He carefully listed many names of those who "observed the day [Easter] when the people [the Jews] put away the leaven" (*Ecclesiastical History* 24.6).[3] The names included those of the Apostles John and Philip along with Polycarp, all of whom "observed the fourteenth day of the Passover, according to the Gospel" (24.2–6). He also recorded pertinent communication concerning the Quartodeciman controversy between Irenaeus of Lyons (ca. 120–202 C.E.) and Victor I, who had become the bishop of Rome in 189 C.E. (*Ecclesiastical History* 24.9–17). To summarize that interchange as described by Eusebius, Victor had become quite harsh in his treatment of

---

2. Translation of Hippolytus of Rome, *Refutation of All Heresies*, quoted from Melito of Sardis, *On Pascha: With the Fragments of Melito and Other Material Related to the Quartodecimans*, ed. John Behr, trans. Alistair Stewart-Sykes, Popular Patristics Series 20 (Crestwood, NY: St Vladimir's Seminary Press, 2001), 83.

3. For citations of Eusebius in this section, see Eusebius, *Ecclesiastical History,* 22–25 (*Nicene and Post-Nicene Fathers*, Series 2 1:240–44).

those who continued to observe Easter on the fourteenth of Nisan. He excommunicated them! Irenaeus, even though he agreed that the resurrection should be celebrated on the Lord's Day only, reprimanded Victor for his desire to cut off whole churches of God for observing the ancient traditions. He stated that there had always been differences in the observance of days and the manner of the fast surrounding Easter. In fact, the general rule was to maintain peace between both groups. Irenaeus mentioned how Polycarp and Anicetus (in 155 C.E.) had been able to put aside their differences on the issue and commune together in peace. They evidently observed the Lord's Table together. In reflection on Irenaeus' letters, Eusebius remarked that Irenaeus was aptly named, since his name comes from the Greek word for "peace."

There is no clear evidence that the Quartodecimans were overemphasizing the death of the Lord or downplaying the resurrection. It seems rather to be a combination of both aspects in much the same way as Good Friday and Easter have come to be observed in the Church. (Many a Good Friday sermon cannot contain the truth of the Resurrection Day that follows!) However, this controversy gave rise to the complete elimination of the Judaic roots of Easter. The final decision came at the Council of Nicaea, which was called, at least in part, to resolve this issue. A synodal letter was circulated to the effect that the Church would not tolerate the position of the Quartodecimans, and the official day of observance would follow the Roman calendar, abandoning the connection with Pesach.

Emperor Constantine supported the decision and attacked the Quartodecimans. He ordered a severe persecution of those who refused to comply.[4] Furthermore, his successor and son, Constantinius, attempted "to disrupt the order of Jewish festivals and to prevent those Christians who wished to do so from celebrating Easter on the first day of Passover."[5] What is essential to keep in mind, however, is that Constantine, his son, and emperors to follow were further motivated by their anti-Jewish policies as expressed in the language of Constantinius: "To this legislator the Jews were nothing but a 'pernicious' or 'despicable sect' that used to meet in 'sacrilegious assemblies'. Such terminology was to become a permanent feature in the decrees of later Christian emperors."[6] He seems to speak not merely of Jews who reject the Messiah, but also of Jewishness in general.

THE *NOVELLAE* OF JUSTINIAN I (553 C.E.)

Although there were many other skirmishes between the growing Gentile-dominated Church and Jewish believers, one period stands out from the others.

---

4. Constantine's anti-Judaic attacks against the Quartodecimans can be found in Eusebius, *On the Keeping of Easter* (*Nicene and Post-Nicene Fathers*, Series 2, vol. 14).
5. H. H. Ben-Sasson, ed. *A History of the Jewish People*, coauthored by A. Malamat, H. Tadmor, M. Stern, S. Safrai, H. H. Ben-Sasson, and S. Ettinger (Cambridge: Harvard University Press, 1976), 350.
6. Constantinius, quoted in Ben-Sasson, *A History of the Jewish People*, 350.

Jewish people who did not "convert" became the objects of scorn and vitriol from the Church. The persecution of non-Christian Jewish people, of course, widened the gap that began with the parting of the ways in the first century.

Justinian I (reigned 527–565 c.e.), was one of the greatest emperors of the Eastern Roman Empire, but was also "a virulent and consistent persecutor of all non-Orthodox Christians, heretics, pagans, and also of Jews and Judaism."[7] He added edicts called *novellae* (lit., "new laws") to the restrictions already placed upon the Jewish people by those who preceded him (cf. Theodosius II, r. 408–450). A complete discussion of Justinian's anti-Jewish measures is beyond the purview of this chapter, but those measures included confiscation of synagogues, prohibition of Jewish participation in local governments or even holding office in their own religious communities, and refusal to sell property to be used as places of Jewish worship.

In *Novellae* 146, Justinian countered the prevailing Jewish conviction that all readings must be done in Hebrew in the synagogue. Instead, he encouraged the additional use of the Greek Septuagint (LXX) or a Latin version. He also forbade the use of the Mishnah, as the Church generally took the position that the Jewish understanding of the Bible was woefully inferior to the Church's interpretations and could lead people astray. His work *Corpus Juris Civilis*[8] combined with his anti-Judaic *novellae* "virtually fixed the status of the Jews in Byzantine society for the next 700 years."[9] His interference in the synagogue "attempted to impose a Christian interpretation of what Judaism and its holy texts should be."[10] These are important considerations as these decisions created a future anti-Jewish trajectory for the Church.

More specific to the Passover controversy was that Justinian "allegedly prohibited the celebration of Passover if its date fell before the date of Easter."[11] This may have been an early expression of a more punitive replacement theology[12] based on the undercurrent of deicide.[13] Everything in the Church was considered superior to the synagogue—the rules of Bible interpretation (hermeneutics), the rituals, the celebrations, the practices, the leadership, the sacred texts, and all that differentiated the two. Rather than building bridges, the Church under Justinian I burned the bridges of

---

7.   Andrew Sharf, "Justinian I," *EncJud*, 11:579.

8.   Justinian I, *Corpus Juris Civilis* [Body of Civil Law] (529–34).

9.   Sharf, "Justinian I," 11:579. The term "Byzantine" when used of Christianity or of society at large relates to the churches in that region using a traditional Greek rite in worship and being subject to the canon law of the Eastern Orthodox Church, the church of the Eastern Roman Empire having its center in Constantinople.

10. Sharf, "Justinian I," 11:579.

11. Sharf, "Justinian I," 11:579.

12. Punitive replacement theology argues that God replaced the Jewish people with the Church because of Israel's sins, and therefore the nation of Israel had forfeited its biblical promises. Some would argue that these promises of blessing were always focused on the Church.

13. Deicide is the act of killing God. The Jewish people were accused of this because of the participation of the Jewish leaders in calling for Jesus's death. This false charge became the basis for terrible antisemitism throughout church history.

connection with its Jewish heritage. This, of course, was hardly a way of endearing the Jewish people to the Jewish Messiah and set the stage for further disputation and controversy and increased persecution of Jewish people by the medieval Church.

THE BLOOD LIBELS (12TH CENTURY–PRESENT)

The blood libels deserve a special place in the discussion of the ongoing conflict between the Jewish community and Christianity.[14] The Jewish people were accused of murdering Christian children and using their blood to prepare the Passover *matzot*. Jewish historian Solomon Grayzel reflects on the irony of these tragic and resurgent accusations:

> It is one of the saddest aspects of Jewish experience that on the very evening when the Jew is supposed to recall the joys of freedom, he has frequently been made to feel the bitterest sorrows of exile. It is no less strange that a people so restricted in their choice of food should have been accused of eating human flesh and drinking human blood. Yet the charge has been made hundreds of times, in lands and periods which we consider fairly civilized.[15]

Modern minds recoil at the possibility that such accusations could even be made, as the alleged crime is so outrageous. Yet it is even possible that the Church inherited some of its antisemitic positions from pagan, pre-Christian history.[16] Alluding to ancient Alexandrian writers, historian James Parkes observes that some people thought that "[t]he Jews worshiped the head of an ass; and they ritually indulged in cannibalism."[17] In the Maccabean period as well, there was negative propaganda from Antiochus, the Syrian, which said "the Jews were accustomed to kidnap a Greek man . . . and later sacrifice him to their God and eat of his entrails."[18]

Similarly, superstitious ideas about the mystical power of blood were also circulated during the Middle Ages. It was thought that Jews wanted to rid themselves of diseases unique to their race by comingling the "redeemed" and "innocent" blood of Christian children with the ritual elements of the Passover meal. After the Fourth Lateran Council in 1215, the Roman Catholic

---

14. For more on the blood libels and other forms of antisemitism, see chapter 9, "Passover and Antisemitism," by Olivier Melnick.

15. Solomon Grayzel, "Passover and the Ritual Murder Libel," in *The Passover Anthology*, ed. Philip Goodman, JPS Holiday (Philadelphia: Jewish Publication Society of America, 1961), 17–18.

16. For what is perhaps the most comprehensive study in the origins of antisemitism, see James Parkes, *The Conflict of the Church and the Synagogue: A Study of the Origins of Antisemitism* (1934; repr., New York: Atheneum, 1977).

17. Parkes, *The Conflict of the Church and the Synagogue*, 16.

18. Grayzel, "Passover and the Ritual Murder Libel," 18. See also Yehuda Slutsky and Dina Porat, "Blood Libel," *EncJud*, 3:774–80. In a similar way, the same antisemitic tropes were also used against the Early Church, especially in regard to the Christian practice of Communion, which some authorities interpreted not as eating bread and wine to commemorate the sacrifice of Jesus's body and blood but as cannibalism.

teaching of transubstantiation—that the Communion bread and wine literally become the body and blood of Jesus—fostered the notion that the
blood of Jesus was flowing through the bodies of Christians. It was thought
that since non-converted Jews refused baptism, an act according to medieval
superstition that could heal disease, "Christianized blood" could effect the
same result in place of baptism. The underlying theory leading to allegations
of blood libel accused the Jewish community of "trying to . . . cure themselves by the application or the intake of the blood, the heart or the liver of a
simple, sinless Christian, a male child by preference."[19]

Although none of this was true, these lies were still perpetuated by superstitious medieval Christianity. It was not until the time of the Crusades,
however, that this libelous accusation became a frequent form of defamation.
Perhaps the first occasion was in Norwich, England, in 1144. The allegation
was as follows: "It was on the second day of Passover that the boy William
was said to have disappeared, and a number of Jews were soon accused of
having caused his death. . . . since the Jews performed the sacrifice of a
Christian every year at about the time of the original Crucifixion."[20] Interestingly, it was a "converted" Jew who evidently provided the details about the
supposed custom. Author and syndicated columnist Michael Freund says, "A
Jewish convert to Catholicism, Theobald of Cambridge, was quick to cor-
roborate the calumny, falsely claiming that rabbis and Jewish leaders would
gather each year in Spain and draw lots to decide in which country they
would kill a Christian child to use his blood in ritual practices."[21]

In the decades that followed, other such incidents were alleged which were
specifically connected with Passover. "In 1171, the Jewish community of Blois
was accused of crucifying a Christian child for Passover and tossing his body
into a local river. The entire community was imprisoned and then sentenced
to be burned to death. When the Jews were taken to the *auto-da-fe* [ceremony
for pronouncing judgment], they were told they could save themselves by con-
verting, but nearly all of them refused to do so, preferring to die and sanctify
God's name."[22]

Most of these alleged ritual murders were crucifixions. "The motif of
torture and murder of Christian children in imitation of Jesus's Passion persisted with slight variations throughout the 12th century (Gloucester, England, 1168; Blois, France, 1171; Saragossa, Spain, 1182), and was repeated
in many libels of the 13th century."[23]

Although found in its most virulent form during the Middle Ages, it should
be noted that blood-libel accusations persisted through the centuries. In Spain,

19.   Grayzel, "Passover and the Ritual Murder Libel," 20.
20.   Grayzel, "Passover and the Ritual Murder Libel," 19. See also Cecil Roth, *History of the Jews in
      England* (Oxford: Oxford University Press, 1941), 13.
21.   Michael Freund, "Passover Blood Libels, Then and Now," *The Jerusalem Post*, April 13, 2014, http://
      www.jpost.com/Jewish-World/Judaism/Passover-blood-libels-then-and-now-348382.
22.   Freund, "Passover Blood Libels, Then and Now."
23.   Slutsky and Porat, "Blood Libel," 3:775.

the Jews who had allegedly converted to Catholicism were called "Conversos"[24] and were said to collaborate with the chief rabbi of the Jewish community to crucify, abuse, and curse a child in the manner that Jesus was treated.[25]

Even when it was not directly related to Passover, members of the Jewish community were frequently accused of murdering Christians, and invariably the blood-libel charge was invoked. Such was the case when in 1840 Jews were blamed for the murder of a Capuchin monk and his servant, which became known as the Damascus Affair. The church leaders brought out various points of evidence to convince the authorities of the alleged Jewish actions, including "treatises which set out to prove the truth of the libel from the records of past accusations and Jewish sources. . . . Another way of implying the truth of the blood-libel charge was to state it as a fact without denying it."[26]

False accusations were repeatedly made against the Jews of Russia. When there were Christian victims, there were Jewish suspects, usually linked to the libel that Jews required Christian blood for one reason or another. From 1799 to the Bolshevik Rebellion of 1917, there were numerous blood libels, but the cases were dismissed for lack of evidence. While the authorities may have declared that these were unsubstantiated charges of murder, the Russian populace engaged in an unrelenting persecution of the Jewish people. "With the growth of an antisemitic movement in Russia in the 1870s, the blood libel became a regular motif in the anti-Jewish propaganda campaign conducted in the press and literature."[27]

Of particular interest is the role played by the church leaders. "The chief agitators of the blood libels were monks. At the monastery of Supraśl crowds assembled to gaze on the bones of the 'child martyr Gabriello,' who had been allegedly murdered by Jews in 1690."[28] Many of the victims were considered martyrs complete with shrines, tombs, and even subsequent canonization by the Church (declaring a deceased person an officially recognized saint), all of which served to perpetuate the lie of ritual murders by the Jewish people.

It is no surprise that the Nazi propaganda in Germany used this insidious ploy to dehumanize the Jews. Disgusting cartoons depicting Jews collecting the blood of the innocents were combined with reinvestigations of previous baseless cases in which Jews had been acquitted. This fanned the flames of German antisemitism that had been seething for centuries. Links between the antisemitism of Adolf Hitler and the writings of Martin Luther are well known and vigorously discussed. In like manner Hitler used the sad history of the blood libels to fuel his campaign against the Jews. What was a Passover controversy in church history became the grounds for slander in the political realm.

---

24. Conversos were Jewish people who converted to Christianity under pressure but continued to practice Jewish traditions clandestinely in their homes, and were the focus of the Inquisition.
25. Slutsky and Porat, "Blood Libel," 3:775. See also Ben-Sasson, *A History of the Jews*, 590.
26. Slutsky and Porat, "Blood Libel," 3:778.
27. Slutsky and Porat, "Blood Libel," 3:779.
28. Slutsky and Porat, "Blood Libel," 3:779.

It is obvious that the blood-libel component of the Passover controversy in church history has been used by Satan to instill fear, suspicion, and hatred in the hearts of influential non-Jewish people throughout the ages. What else could account for the irrationality of these charges and their wholesale acceptance by huge swaths of otherwise civilized human beings? The growing distance between the Church and its Jewish roots, lack of understanding of Jewish beliefs and practices, and other related factors created the climate in which these irrational charges maintained credibility. One of the striking features of this history is the lack of evidence and the Church's repeated official denials that there were grounds for the blood-libel slanders. In an attempt to be fair and balanced, some of those declarations by church leaders should be included here.

Even though incidents of blood-libel accusations occurred repeatedly after the first one in 1144 in Norwich, there were no papal pronouncements about them until the middle of the thirteenth century. Jewish leaders sought help from ecclesiastical leaders due to the increase in the false charges and the resulting crimes against the Jewish populace. "On May 28, 1247, Pope Innocent IV wrote to the Archbishop of Vienne, in France, pointing out that various noblemen as well as the Bishop of Trois Chateaux had perpetrated against the Jews of Valrias cruelties of a most inhuman kind."[29] A young girl had been murdered, and the Jews were blamed. They had been arrested and tortured, and their property had been confiscated. In his letter, Pope Innocent IV said this was merely a concocted story used to steal Jewish property. He demanded the release of the prisoners and the restoration of the property.

Similar attempts to end the libels were issued by the church hierarchy in the form of papal bulls of protection, "which this and later popes used to issue to the Jews. . . . that the Christians themselves were the kidnappers and the murderers and had the sole object of robbing the Jews, or taking over the property of those killed."[30] This was a most unusual strategy! Did it work, we might ask, and did these edicts and pronouncements have any effect on the peasantry? Evidently, they did little to dissuade the general populace from escalating their attacks at Passover time. Massacres and expulsions became the rule rather than the exception.

In 1422, another pope, Martin V, "accused Christian preachers of fomenting hatred of the Jews, but also spoke with horror of the libel that Jews mixed blood with the dough of the Passover *matzah*."[31] So on the one hand the pope wanted to protect the Jews, but on the other hand he perpetuated the blood-libel myth.

The children allegedly murdered for their blood were viewed as saints. For example, a Franciscan named Bernardino da Feltre accused the Jewish

---

29.   Goodman, *The Passover Anthology*, 21. See also Solomon Grayzel, *The Church and the Jews in the XIII Century: A Study of Their Relations During the Years 1198–1254, Based on the Papal Letters and the Concillar Decrees of the Period* (Philadelphia: Dropsie College, 1933), 263, 265.

30.   Goodman, *The Passover Anthology*, 22.

31.   Goodman, *The Passover Anthology*, 22.

people of blood libels, which led to the Trent blood libel of 1475 in north-ern Italy. It seems that a two-year-old child named Simon disappeared. As expected, the Jews were accused of killing him, and the whole community was arrested and tortured until "confessions" were forthcoming. Many were executed and the rest expelled. "The pope at first refused to authorize the adoration of this 'victim of the Jews', but in due course he withdrew his opposition. In 1582 the infant Simon was officially proclaimed a saint of the Catholic Church."[32] In a too-little-and-too-late response centuries later, Rome attempted to make amends. In 1965, the Catholic Church withdrew its canonization and acknowledged that a judicial error had been committed against the Jews of Trent in this trial.[33]

When we consider Europe in the sixteenth century, one might ask about the ways in which the Jewish people were treated during the time of the Protestant Reformation. It is well known that Martin Luther (1483–1546) engaged in horrible antisemitic rhetoric. He began by attacking the practices of the Church against the Jews in *Jesus Christ Was a Jew by Birth* (1523),[34] but he ended by attacking the Jews in *About the Jews and Their Lies* (1543).[35] What is little known, however, is that other Reformers maintained a much more positive relationship with the Jews.

Prior to Luther's publication of his diatribe against the Jews, "the Re-former Andreas Osiander issued an anonymous work that attacked the blood libels and their charges of ritual murder. In this pamphlet he disproves, item by item, the so-called 'proofs' of Jewish guilt and responsibility for slaying Christian children."[36] His attacks were against the Roman Church in this regard, and in spite of Luther's vicious preaching against the Jews, the anti-Jewish riots were greatly reduced in number during that time. His words may have been a glimpse of light in those dark ages due to the Reformation.

In 1540, Pope Paul III also spoke out against the rank-and-file Catholic treatment of the Jews. He believed that many Catholics were enemies of the Jews because they were blinded by avarice, which caused them to accuse the Jews of murdering children and drinking their blood. Unfortunately, even when the Roman Catholic authorities spoke against the blood libels, it had little effect on the superstitions of the people, who claimed that miracles oc-curred at the graves of the presumed martyrs. The Church could not afford to dispute the spurious miracles nor did it bother to refute the libels that surfaced over and over again.[37]

Yet another apparently positive response came from Pope Clement XIII in 1759 when he investigated accusations against the Jews of Poland and

32. Ben-Sasson, *A History of the Jewish People*, 580. See also Shlomo Simonsohn, "Trent," *EncJud*, 20:131.
33. Ben-Sasson, *A History of the Jewish People*, 580.
34. Martin Luther, *Jesus Christ Was a Jew by Birth* (Wittenberg, 1523).
35. Martin Luther, *About the Jews and Their Lies* (1543).
36. Ben-Sasson, *A History of the Jewish People*, 650.
37. Goodman, *The Passover Anthology*, 22.

declared the charges to be false. However, the process took over a decade. The wheels of progress in protecting the Jews always seemed to "grind exceedingly slowly." So even though efforts were made to thwart the antisemitism of the libels, they were slight and made little difference among the masses.[38]

CONCLUSION

The Passover controversies have remained a blight on the Church. It has been a rather one-sided affair in which the Jewish community has endured tragic mistreatment by the very people whose Savior is Jewish. In every era, the Enemy has waged war on his ancient foes, the Jewish people—from the very beginning when the importance of Passover was minimized through the changing of the calendar, to the edicts of the emperors and the popes who undermined the rightful place of Jewish tradition in the Church, to the slaughter of innocent Jewish people due to the malicious lies of the blood libels. It is incumbent therefore upon all who name the name of Yeshua to resist the temptation to turn a deaf ear to these things whenever they rear their ugly heads and spout their venomous lies. The old refrain comes to mind:

> How odd
> Of God
> To choose
> The Jews.
> But not so odd
> As those who choose
> A Jewish God
> Yet spurn the Jews.[39]

As followers of the Jewish Messiah, we must be vigilant in safeguarding God's chosen people and constantly call upon the Church and society in general to treat the Jewish people with respect. The Church, though, has an even greater responsibility. As followers of the Messiah, we are to shine the light of the Gospel so that our Jewish friends and neighbors can both hear and see the Gospel message and believe (Matt. 5:14–16; Rom. 10:14–17; 2 Cor. 4:3–5). We have centuries of darkness to overcome and so should approach this task with prayer and with our souls filled with the love of God that enables us to impart His love to the Jewish people (Rom. 5:5; 10:1). At times this will mean apologizing on behalf of our spiritual ancestors who mistreated the Jewish people. There might simply be no other way for the Church to overcome the past and "make the Jewish people jealous" of the Jewish Savior who lives in our hearts.

---

38. Goodman, *The Passover Anthology*, 22–23.
39. The first four lines of this poem are attributed to William Norman Ewer, whereas the remaining lines are attributed to Cecil Brown or Ogden Nash.

9
PASSOVER AND ANTISEMITISM

OLIVIER MELNICK

*A*s the first of the "holy convocations" of the Lord (Lev. 23:4–8) Passover has always held a special place within the Jewish lifecycle (Exod. 12–13) and provided a warm sense of family camaraderie. It is the holiday when the college kids all come home for the Passover Seder meal, which outside of Israel is eaten on the first two nights of the eight-day holiday.

It is hard to believe that such a joyful celebration could be linked to an often very destructive form of antisemitism—but it is. This chapter will briefly review the history of this tragic truth. We will show that antisemitism did not develop in a vacuum but is the result of centuries of misconceptions and misunderstandings, anchored in every human being's sinful nature and further fueled by early forms of theological anti-Judaism that gave way through the centuries to a more virulent racial antisemitism.

Former professor of medieval history at Stanford University Gavin Langmuir, in his classic work *Toward a Definition of Antisemitism*, separates between anti-Judaism and antisemitism, explaining how one builds upon the foundation of the other. Christian anti-Judaism started as the result of religious and doctrinal differences leading to various accusations without necessarily having the lethal components of antisemitism. Langmuir sees a progression from anti-Judaism to antisemitism throughout the Middle Ages, widening the original chasm and endangering Jewish people further.[1] His work helps us better understand the nature of antisemitism, its origins, and impact upon the Jewish people.

A DEFINITION OF ANTISEMITISM

At first glance it would appear that the scope of antisemitism includes anyone of Semitic descent. Literally, to be a Semite simply means that you are a descendant of those people groups commonly associated with Shem, one of Noah's three sons named in the Bible.

---

1. Gavin I. Langmuir, *Toward a Definition of Antisemitism* (Berkeley: University of California Press, 1990), 57–62, 311–52.

Noah was five hundred years old, and Noah became the father of Shem, Ham, and Japheth. (Gen. 5:32)

Noah became the father of three sons: Shem, Ham, and Japheth. (Gen. 6:10)

The family of Shem may have included well-known ancient people groups such as the Akkadians, Ugarites, Chaldeans, Arameans, and the Hebrews among others.[2] If antisemitism was defined as those from the lineage of Shem, then the term *Semite* would apply to both Jews and Arabs. Yet the term *antisemite* is not usually used to describe the hatred of Arabs but is usually limited to hatred of the Jewish people. For example, if the meaning of the word *antisemite* included Jews and Arabs, then Jordanians, who are part of the Hashemite kingdom, would be classified as Semites. In that case, if Jordanians today were hated, then they would be the recipients of antisemitism. However, this is not how the term is commonly used.

Actually, although one can easily find examples of nations that were the enemies of the Jewish people in the Bible, the word *antisemitism* is relatively new. The term was first coined in the late nineteenth century by German journalist Wilhelm Marr,[3] who in the 1870s published a pamphlet[4] entitled "The Victory of Jewry over Germandom."[5]

There might be as many definitions for antisemitism as there are for who is a Jew. Once it is understood that the word *Semite* is used differently within antisemitism and that there is a fundamental difference between the anti-Judaism of the Early Church and modern antisemitism, we can formulate a clearer definition. Given this distinction, I suggest the following definition: Antisemitism is the hatred of the Jewish people characterized by destructive thoughts, words, and/or actions against them, and further characterized by irrationality.[6]

Over time, the Christian Church grew increasingly distant from Judaism and lost the connection to its Jewish roots. This set the stage for a diminished appreciation of Judaism and the Jewish people. Eventually, this disconnect between Christianity and Judaism led to some decisions that reverberate to our present day.

---

2. For a more complete listing of the descendants of Shem, see Genesis 10:21–32; 11:10–32.

3. Richard S. Levy, comp., *Antisemitism in the Modern World: An Anthology of Texts*, Sources in Modern History (Lexington, MA: D.C. Heath and Company, 1991), 74–76.

4. Richard S. Levy, "Marr, Wilhelm (1819–1904)," in *Antisemitism: A Historical Encyclopedia of Prejudice and Persecution*, ed. Richard S. Levy, 2 vols. (Santa Barbara, CA: ABC-CLIO, 2006), 2:445–46.

5. Wilhelm Marr, *Der Sieg des Judenthums über das Germanenthum* (Bern: Rudolph Costenoble, 1879), http://sammlungen.ub.uni-frankfurt.de/urn/urn:nbn:de:hebis:30-180014998005. English translation: Wilhelm Marr "The Victory of Jewry over Germandom," in Levy, *Antisemitism in the Modern World*, 76–93.

6. For additional definitions of antisemitism, see sources such as Langmuir, *Toward a Definition of Antisemitism* (refer to n. 1); and Dennis Prager and Joseph Telushkin, *Why the Jews? The Reason for Antisemitism* (New York: Simon and Schuster, 1983).

THE COUNCIL OF NICAEA: PASSOVER OR EASTER?

One such decision of consequence was made in the fourth century by a council of the Church. We are grateful for the earlier chapter by Scott Nassau, in which he reflects upon antisemitism in the very early centuries of church history.[7] We will begin our journey a bit later with the Council of Nicaea (325 C.E.).

While the Council of Nicaea was not convened specifically to focus on the Jews, the decisions made by the bishops left an indelible mark on the Jewish psyche. After Emperor Constantine's conversion in 312 C.E., Christianity became the state religion of the Roman Empire in 380 C.E. In effect, Constantine encouraged the "Christianization" of many pagan customs in an attempt to transform them into bona fide Christian practices.[8]

Originally organized to fight the heresy of Arianism and establish a uniform Christian doctrine, the Council also decided on the construction of a unified church calendar, including the setting of a date for Easter that was not linked to the Jewish date for Passover. Until then Christians had relied on the Jewish (lunar) calendar to pinpoint the fourteenth of Nisan, the Jewish Passover, and celebrated Easter on the Sunday after Passover. They were known as the Quartodecimans ("fourteenthers," from the Latin word for "fourteen").[9]

Even though the Nicene decisions were not immediately enforced, the Council of Nicaea paved the way for greater distance and increasing animosity between the Jewish people and the growing Christian Church. Within sixteen years, another council in Antioch (341 C.E.)[10] prohibited Christians from celebrating Passover with the Jews. These actions fed the growing antipathy between Judaism and Christianity.

FROM CHURCH COUNCILS TO LEGISLATION

Soon after these councils, accusations of deicide (killing God) that amounted to blaming the Jews for Christ's death began to grow, and church leaders at that time felt an obligation to protect Christians from the Jewish people. This protection was enacted through the creation of legal codes: the *Codex Theodosianus*, or Theodosian Code (439 C.E.),[11] and the *Codex Justinianus*, or Justinian Code (534 C.E.).[12] While not necessarily always enforced,

---

7. See chapter 7, "Passover, the Temple, and the Early Church," by Scott P. Nassau.

8. William Nicholls, *Christian Antisemitism: A History of Hate* (Northvale, NJ: J. Aronson, 1993), 189–97.

9. For more on the Quartodecimans, see chapter 7, "Passover, the Temple, and the Early Church," by Scott P. Nassau, and chapter 8, "Passover Controversies in Church History," by Gregory Hagg.

10. *Encyclopædia Britannica Online*, s.v. "Council of Antioch," accessed August 31, 2015, http://www.britannica.com/event/Council-of-Antioch.

11. George Long, "Codex Theodosianus," in *A Dictionary of Greek and Roman Antiquities*, ed. William Smith (London: John Murray, 1875), 302–3, http://penelope.uchicago.edu/Thayer/E/Roman/Texts/secondary/SMIGRA*/Codex_Theodosianus.html.

12. *Encyclopædia Britannica Online*, s.v. "Code of Justinian," accessed August 31, 2015, http://www.britannica.com/topic/Code-of-Justinian.

these imperial Roman laws would affect Jewish-Christian relations for centuries to come.

Then Emperor Justinian decreed that Jews could not celebrate Passover before the Christian Easter,[13] which drove an additional wedge between the Christian Easter and Jewish Passover. This led to further persecution of the Jewish community, including forced baptisms and forced conversions, paving the way for a new generation of libelous accusations.

THE BLOOD LIBELS: CHRISTIAN BLOOD FOR PASSOVER RECIPES

Another manifestation of antisemitism that continues to this day is the accusation of blood libels against the Jewish people in relation to Passover and Easter, which Dr. Gregory Hagg discusses in the previous chapter.[14] We will seek to add some new information and further reflections on this terrible blight upon the history of the Church.

In the twelfth century, a new charge was introduced against the Jews that would be added to the list of reasons why they should be forcibly converted, ostracized, persecuted, and even killed. This new charge led to the further demonization of the Jewish people and is still being used today against the Jewish people by various antisemitic groups.

The term *blood libel* refers to the accusation that Jews kidnapped and murdered the children of Christians to use their blood as part of their religious rituals during the Passover season. More than 150 blood libels resulting in the death of Jewish people have been recorded throughout history, mostly during the Middle Ages.[15] The accusation, however, goes back to the first century when even the well-known Jewish historian Flavius Josephus wrote against this view in his work *Against Apion*,[16] in which he defends the Jewish people against the libel (2.8).[17]

As Hagg mentions earlier, the first blood libel case ever recorded came out of Norwich, England, in 1144. The dismembered dead body of a boy was found on Good Friday. The boy was later referred to as William of Norwich[18] through the testimony of a Catholic monk named Thomas of Monmouth, who provided the only record of the event. The Jewish community of

13. Edward H. Flannery, *The Anguish of the Jews: Twenty-Three Centuries of Anti-Semitism*, rev. ed., Stimulus Book (New York: Paulist Press, 1985), 68.

14. For more on the accusations of blood libels against the Jewish people, see chapter 8, "Passover Controversies in Church History," by Gregory Hagg.

15. Joshua Trachtenberg, *The Devil and the Jews: The Medieval Conception of the Jew and Its Relation to Modern Anti-Semitism*, 2nd ed. (Philadelphia: Jewish Publication Society, 2002), 140–55.

16. Flavius Josephus, *The Works of Flavius Josephus*, trans. William Whiston, 4 vols. (1974; repr., Grand Rapids: Baker, 1990), 4:208–10.

17. Trachtenberg, *The Devil and the Jews*, 140–55.

18. Léon Poliakov, *The History of Anti-Semitism*, 4 vols. (New York: Vanguard Press, 1965), 1:58; Robert Chazan, *Medieval Stereotypes and Modern Antisemitism* (Berkeley: University of California Press, 1997), 58–70.

Norwich was falsely accused of kidnapping and crucifying the Christian boy and emptying his body of blood. This libel was based on a misconception regarding the shed blood of the sacrificial Passover lambs.[19]

The statement "without the shedding of blood there is no forgiveness of sin" is biblical and based on two Scriptures:

> For the life of the flesh is in the blood, and I have given it to you on the altar to make atonement for your souls; for it is the blood by reason of the life that makes atonement. (Lev. 17:11)

> And according to the Law, one may almost say, all things are cleansed with blood, and without shedding of blood there is no forgiveness. (Heb. 9:22)

The blood of an animal sacrifice was necessary for Jewish people to atone for their sins, according to the Bible. But these sacrifices ceased with the destruction of the Temple in 70 c.e. However, the accusation that Jewish people would use the blood of a Christian child, rather than the blood of a lamb, shows the level of superstition, myth, and anti-Jewish sentiments that formed a critical part of the worldview of medieval Christianity; not to mention the Torah ban on on human sacrifice and the condemnation of child sacrifice as pagan (Lev. 18:21; Deut. 18:10).

The blood-libel accusation was never actually given as the official reason for the death of William of Norwich, yet it was generally believed by the populace and generated violence against the Jews leading to other accusations of blood libel throughout the centuries.[20] The William of Norwich murder was responsible for a crowd attacking a Jewish delegation coming to the coronation of Richard the Lionheart in 1189. The following year, most of the Jews of Norwich were slaughtered in the village. More accusations of ritual murders by the Jews followed the first one. The Jewish people were

19. Douglas Raymund Webster, "St. William of Norwich," in *The Catholic Encyclopedia*, vol. 15 (New York: Robert Appleton Company, 1912), http://www.newadvent.org/cathen/15635a.htm. Webster recounts "the story of the martyrdom as given by Thomas [of Monmouth, a monk of the cathedral priory of Norwich] and the evidence adduced by him":
> William had been in the habit of frequenting the houses of the Jews and was forbidden by his friends to have anything to do with them. On the Monday in Holy Week, 1144, he was decoyed away from his mother by the offer of a place in the archdeacon's kitchen. Next day the messenger and William were seen to enter a Jew's house and from that time William was never again seen alive. On the Wednesday, after a service in the synagogue, the Jews lacerated his head with thorns, crucified him, and pierced his side. . . . But the most telling piece of evidence and the most disastrous in its consequences was that of Theobald, a converted Jew and a monk probably of Norwich Priory. This man told Thomas that "in the ancient writings of his Fathers it was written that the Jews, without the shedding of human blood, could neither obtain their freedom, nor could they ever return to their fatherland. Hence it was laid down by them in ancient times that every year they must sacrifice a Christian in some part of the world" (Vita [et Passio], II, 2) .

20. Flannery, *The Anguish of the Jews*, 99–102.

eventually expelled from England in 1290 under Edward I and were not allowed to return until 1655 under Oliver Cromwell.

The ritual murder libel picked up momentum across the English Channel, in France and then Germany. In France, in 1187, Jews were burned for failing the water test (the accused would either sink or remain afloat while submerged in a tub of Catholic holy water, depending on whether or not they were lying). In 1329, in France, Jews were accused of mixing Christian blood to make their *charoset* (a sweet mixture eaten at Passover).[21] Fearful of reprisals, Jews of certain communities would even go as far as using white wine instead of red wine to dispel rumors of them mixing blood with their wine as they participated in their own Passover Seders, remembering the suffering of their forefathers along with the contemporary plague of antisemitism affecting them.[22]

For hundreds of years, blood libels have impacted Jewish life all across Europe, including the late eighteenth century in Poland and the late nineteenth century in France, Germany, and Russia. The 1903 Kishiniev pogrom in Russia began on the Russian Orthodox Easter because of a blood libel, demonstrating the extremely long life span of this terrible lie. The same libel can also be found in Nazi propaganda during World War II and even in a booklet entitled "Jewish Ritual Murder," which was republished in Birmingham, Alabama, in 1962, a mere fifty-some years ago.[23] Yet nowhere in the abundant Jewish literature over the centuries can we find even a trace of what could be considered the usage of Christian blood by Jews for liturgical purposes.[24]

As mentioned previously, the children of Israel were forbidden by God to make human sacrifices or to practice sorcery of any sort.

> There shall not be found among you anyone who makes his son or his daughter pass through the fire, one who uses divination, one who practices witchcraft, or one who interprets omens, or a sorcerer. (Deut. 18:10)

Already considered to be unbelievers, "Christ killers," and usurers, the Jewish people were now accused of practicing ritual murder. Charges of blood libel became the root cause for the violent death of many Jewish people in

---

21. Trachtenberg, *The Devil and the Jews*, 135.

22. Alfred J. Kolatch, *The Jewish Book of Why* (Middle Village, NY: Jonathan David Publishers, 1981), 202–3.

23. Arnold S. Leese, *My Irrelevant Defense Being Meditations Inside Prison and Out on Jewish Ritual Murder* (1938; repr., Birmingham, AL: Thunderbolt, 1962), https://archive.org/details/dudeman5685_yahoo_ MID. Originally released as two articles in the July 1936 issue of *The Fascist* (the I.F.L. or Imperial Fascist League newspaper) entitled "Jewish Ritual Murder," this booklet was later published in London by I.F.L. Printing & Publishing in 1938.

24. Richard Gottheil, Hermann L. Strack, and Joseph Jacobs, "Blood Accusation," in *Jewish Encyclopedia: A Descriptive Record of the History, Religion, Literature, and Customs of the Jewish People from the Earliest Times to the Present Day*, ed. Isidore Singer (New York: Funk & Wagnalls, 1902), 3:260–67, accessed September 1, 2015. http://www.jewishencyclopedia.com/articles/3408-blood-accusation.

the Middle Ages and thereafter. We can write off this behavior as extreme antisemitism and an irrational contempt for the Jewish people, but we also know that the accusation has a theological foundation as well. Historically, Christianity had grown more and more hostile to the Jewish people, and this created an environment in the midst of medieval superstition and ignorance to produce what may be viewed as one of the most heinous accusations against the Jewish people ever perpetrated.

HOST DESECRATION: A REENACTMENT OF YESHUA'S CRUCIFIXION

Along with the blood accusation came another fabricated story against the Jewish people that is also connected to Holy Week and the Passover season. It involves the ritual piercing of Communion wafers by Jewish people worldwide. This false claim also originated during the Middle Ages.[25]

In 1215, one of five ecumenical councils of the Catholic Church took place. These all-church gatherings often resulted in the establishment of a new church doctrine or the rebuking of a trending heresy. Much of church history can be traced and studied through its various councils, yet these gatherings had a negative impact on the Jewish community. The Fourth Lateran Council was no different. It was during this time that the Catholic Church demanded a distinctive dress for the Jews of Europe and decreed other laws that directly restricted their liberties.

One measure introduced by the Council changed the status and the safety of Jews for the next seven hundred years. New clothing laws now required Jewish people of Europe to wear a badge on their garments (later a pointed hat) to facilitate their identification on the byways of Europe.[26] Nazi Germany later picked up on the idea and took it to a new level that culminated in the marking and murder of six million Jews.

Additionally, Pope Innocent III recognized the Catholic doctrine of transubstantiation.[27] From that point on, whenever the Lord's Supper was celebrated, it was understood that the wine became the blood of Messiah and that the wafer or "Host" became His body. Consequently, it was thought that the Jewish people would desecrate Communion wafers by piercing or breaking them so that the blood of Yeshua would start pouring out, thereby allowing them to reenact the crucifixion for which they were presumed "originally

---

25. Nicholls, *Christian Antisemitism*, 239–40.

26. For illustrations and further description, see presentation by Michael Palomino, "Prosecution of the Jews: The Badge and Clothing Laws for Jews in the Middle Ages," *History in Chronology* (2007), http://www.geschichteinchronologie.com/MA/judentum-EncJud_judenfleck-u-judenhut-im-MA-ENGL.html, taken from "Badge, Jewish," in *Encyclopaedia Judaica* (1972), vol. 4, col. 62–74. See also updated article (2nd. ed., 2007) by Bernhard Blumenkranz and B. Mordechai Ansbacher, "Badge, Jewish," in *EncJud* 3:45–48.

27. See under "Transubstantiation" by Joseph Pohle, "The Real Presence of Christ in the Eucharist," in *The Catholic Encyclopedia*, vol. 5 (New York: Robert Appleton Company, 1909), http://www.newadvent.org/cathen/05573a.htm, accessed February 3, 2017.

guilty." It was also believed that the Host had supernatural powers and performed miracles when Jews tried to pierce, burn, or hide it.[28]

Of course, it is fundamentally flawed thinking to consider that the Jewish people, who did not believe in Jesus nor value the crucifixion, would even attempt to somehow reenact the crucifixion. But, again, the medieval popular Christian attitude towards the Jews was faulty from many different perspectives. The average medieval Catholic did not understand the Jewish faith and simply perpetuated the stereotypical picture of the Jewish people taught by the Church at that time. Rabbi and author Joshua Trachtenberg writes, "The charge of mutilation of the host by Jews rested upon the belief that they too accepted the dogma of transubstantiation, the most peculiarly sectarian of Christian dogmas."[29] In other words, the Jewish people were accused of tampering with and even "re-crucifying" Christ by piercing a Communion wafer. This accusation is especially far-fetched as the Jewish people certainly did not accept Catholic doctrine and neither did they observe the Lord's Supper.

The year 1243 marks the beginning of the accusations of "Host desecration" in Belitz, near Berlin, where as a result, all the Jews of the town were killed. These accusations increased throughout Europe, from Paris in 1290 to Poland and from Prague to Berlin in 1510.[30] While difficult to prove, it is widely believed that the 1306 expulsion of all Jews from France was connected to the 1290 "Host desecration" case.[31] The last report of Jewish deaths at the hands of "Christians" motivated by the Host desecration accusation was in 1631. What seemed to have led to that accusation was the fact that some red discoloring had appeared on Communion wafers. It wasn't long before the Jews were held responsible for the stains, believed to be blood. In reality, it was discovered later that a bacterium affecting certain food like these wafers was responsible for the red stains.[32]

Underlying the idea of Host desecration is the misconception that Yeshua, God in the flesh, could be murdered by a human being, Jewish or Gentile. This is patently false, as Yeshua Himself says that He gave His own life:

> For this reason the Father loves Me, because I lay down My life so that I may take it again. No one has taken it away from Me, but I lay it down on My own initiative. I have authority to lay it down, and I have authority to take it up again. This commandment I received from My Father. (John 10:17–18)

28.   "Host, Desecration of," Jewish Virtual Library, http://www.jewishvirtuallibrary.org/host-desecration-of.

29.   Trachtenberg, *The Devil and the Jews*, 110.

30.   Miri Rubin, *Gentile Tales: The Narrative Assault on Late Medieval Jews* (1999; repr., Philadelphia: University of Pennsylvania Press, 2004), 40–41.

31.   Rubin, *Gentile Tales*, 46–47.

32.   Hugo Valentin, *Antisemitism: Historically and Critically Examined*, trans. A. G. Chater (New York: Viking Press, 1936), 27.

The Host-desecration accusation led hordes of Europeans, especially Germans and Austrians, to travel from community to community in an effort to slaughter Jews. As a result, thousands of Jews from more than 140 different communities were massacred over time. Host-desecration libels resulted in entire Jewish communities being burned at the stake. One of the reasons used to justify the expulsion of the Jews from Spain in 1492 was the belief that they killed Christian children to drink their blood.[33]

THE BLACK PLAGUE

There was also the accusation that European Jews had brought on the Black Plague by poisoning the wells of Europe. The recipe for the poison was believed to contain—among other strange ingredients—the dough used to make holy Hosts. The use of the Communion wafer was again believed to be another way in which the Jewish community as a whole was condemned for repeatedly trying to bring additional suffering to Jesus Christ, whom the general "Christian" European populace believed had been originally crucified by the Jews.[34]

The Black Plague was one of the most devastating pandemics in human history. It dramatically affected European Jews, who as a result of being accused of poisoning the wells of Europe, experienced severe persecution and even death.

THE OBERAMMERGAU PASSION PLAY

Indirectly, the Black Plague was also responsible for more antisemitism through a theater production known to this day as the Oberammergau passion play.[35] In the 1630s, the small Bavarian town of Oberammergau was severely hit by the bubonic plague. Town elders promised God that if He spared Oberammergau, they would perform a passion play indefinitely, as a thank-you. The town was spared and thus began the regular performances of the Oberammergau passion play, taking place every ten years, and continuing into the twenty-first century.[36]

The plot follows the theme of Passion Week from the triumphal entry to the crucifixion to the ascension. While the story remains faithful to the biblical narrative, including the Passover in the upper room, also known as the Last Supper, the script evolved over the years and was rewritten to introduce the Jews as "Christ killers" around 1860.

In his excellent volume on antisemitism, *A Lethal Obsession*, scholar Robert Wistrich writes,

33. Trachtenberg, *The Devil and the Jews*, 134.
34. Abram Leon Sachar, *A History of the Jews* (New York: Knopf, 1965), 201.
35. James Shapiro, *Oberammergau: The Troubling Story of the World's Most Famous Passion Play* (New York: Vintage, 2007), 12–13.
36. For the official English website for the Oberammergau Passion Play 2010, see http://www.oberammergau-passion.com/.

150 PART 2—PASSOVER AND CHURCH HISTORY

The mythical Jew of the Christian Middle Ages was the product not only of blood libels, theological polemics, and antisemitic sermons, but also of mystery plays, fiction and the visual arts. The wickedness of the Jews was one of the central themes in the Oberammergau passion play in Bavaria, which enjoyed extraordinary popularity well into the twentieth century.[37]

The 1930 performance of the play was attended by Adolf Hitler and Joseph Goebbels, who enjoyed it so much that they decided to have it performed again in 1934 as the tercentennial version, including a cast mostly composed of Nazi Party members. The play continued after the war, and in 1949 it received the praise and official blessing of Cardinal Faulhaber for being consistent with Catholic doctrine, even though it was still portraying Jewish people as deceitful, evil, and murderous.[38] This changed at the Second Vatican Council in 1965 when the declaration *Nostra aetate* (Latin, "In Our Time") was released by the Catholic Church and officially exonerated the Jewish people of deicide.

The Jewish authorities and those who followed their lead pressed for the death of Christ; still, what happened in His passion cannot be charged against all the Jews, without distinction, then alive, nor against the Jews of today. . . .[T]he Jews should not be presented as rejected or accursed by God, as if this followed from the Holy Scriptures.[39]

It took time for the Oberammergau tradition to reflect this change and absolve the Jews. Finally, in the year 2000 the script was revised and even included a statement about the damage that was inflicted on Jewish people over the years because of the play's antisemitic undertones.

PASSOVER AND CONTEMPORARY ANTISEMITISM

Both the blood libels and the Host-desecration accusations continue to influence those who are anti-Jewish to this day, and this is no longer limited to Europe alone. The Christian view on Host desecration has been appropriated by Islamic antisemites as seen in the following statement made in 2013 by Egyptian politician Khaled Zaafrani: "It is well known that during the Passover, they make matzos called the 'Blood of Zion.' They take a Christian child, slit his throat and slaughter him. Then they take his blood and make their [matzos]. This is a very important rite for the Jews, which they never forgo [*sic*]."[40]

37. Robert S. Wistrich, *A Lethal Obsession: Antisemitism from Antiquity to the Global Jihad* (New York: Random House, 2010), 90.
38. Jeremy Cohen, *Christ Killers: The Jews and the Passion from the Bible to the Big Screen* (Oxford: Oxford University Press, 2007), 215–29.
39. *Nostra Aetate*, Declaration on the Relation of the Church to Non-Christian Religions, proclaimed by Pope Paul VI on October 28, 1965, http://www.vatican.va/archive/hist_councils/ii_vatican_council/documents/vat-ii_decl_19651028_nostra-aetate_en.html.
40. Quoted in "Egyptian Politician Khaled Zaafrani: Jews Use Human Blood for Passover Matzos," MEMRI TV, Clip #3873, 2:27, from excerpts [transcript included] from a TV show with Khaled

Mr. Zaafrani founded the Egyptian Justice and Progress Party.[41] While the party claims to be more secular and independent, it is still an Islamist party under the umbrella of the Muslim Brotherhood, a Sunni Islamist organization founded in Egypt in 1928. Mr. Zaafrani is not alone propagating his blood accusations. Many other leaders and clerics of the Muslim world have either joined or preceded him, such as Egyptian researcher Muhammad Al-Buheiri, who claims that Jews still use Christian blood to bake Passover matzah,[42] or former president of the American Center for Islamic Research Dr. Sallah Sultan, who also states that Jews murder non-Jews to use their blood for Passover.[43]

It would seem that in many cases the instigators are poorly informed, as in the case of Egyptian columnist Ghada Abd El Moneim, who writes of the use of human blood for Passover *and* Hanukkah and insists that it was in the preparation of "Hanukkah matzah"—a bread only used for the Passover and the Feast of Unleavened Bread.[44] The result is the same, as it continues to demonize the Jews in a way that could have been justified during the uneducated era of the Middle Ages but has no place in a twenty-first-century global community.

CONCLUSION

As we have seen throughout this chapter, what started as sectarian theological disagreements evolved into deeply rooted theological anti-Judaism, eventually leading to today's antisemitism. The misinterpretation and misappropriation of Scripture led to these abhorrent beliefs by the Church about the Jewish people. As a result, the blood-libel and Host-desecration accusations have caused terrible persecutions of the Jewish people throughout the centuries.

Antisemitism, aside from the pure evil at its core, is further characterized by irrationality—an irrationality by its proponents' use of unprovable accusations and the ensuing blind acceptance by a wide spectrum of people

Al-Zaafrani, founder of the Egyptian Justice and Progress Party, which aired on Al-Hafez TV (Saudi Arabia/Egypt) on May 12, 2013, http://www.memritv.org/clip/en/3873.htm.

41. Jocelyne Cesari, *The Awakening of Muslim Democracy: Religion, Modernity, and the State* (New York: Cambridge University Press, 2014), 137–40.

42. "Egyptian Researcher Muhammad Al-Buheiri: Jews Still Use Christian Blood to Bake Passover Matzos," MEMRI TV, Clip #1393, 7:20, from excerpts [transcript included] from an interview with Egyptian researcher Muhammad Al-Buheiri, which aired on Nile Culture TV (Egypt) on February 25, 2007, http://www.memritv.org/clip/en/1393.htm.

43. "Salah Sultan," The Global Muslim Brotherhood Daily Watch, posted by "gmbwatch," January 17, 2015, https://www.globalmbwatch.com/wiki/salah-sultan/; "Blood Libel on Hamas TV - President of the American Center for Islamic Research Dr. Salah Sultan: Jews Murder Non-Jews and Use Their Blood to Knead Passover Matzos," MEMRI TV, Clip #2443, 1:03, from excerpts [transcript included] from an address by Dr. Salah Sultan, president of the American Center for Islamic Research, which aired on Al-Aqsa TV (Hamas/Gaza) on March 31, 2010, http://www.memritv.org/clip/en/2443.htm.

44. Ghada Abd El Moneim, "Qualities of the Jews and the Impact of mating with them" [translation of Arabic; select See Translation], Facebook page, posted April 25, 2014, accessed February 3, 2017, https://www.facebook.com/photo.php?fbid=10151967027556533&set=a.461333866532.247979.619346532&type=1&theater.

not necessarily sharing similar ideologies, except when it comes to demonizing Israel. How else can we explain the outlandish accusations of ritual blood murder and Host desecration, especially when we consider the fact that nothing in the Old Testament or the Talmud prescribes the use of human blood or dead people for Jewish religious purposes?

How ironic that Passover, a Jewish festival meant to point to salvation through the Jewish Messiah, the Lamb of God, who gave Himself for us all, would be used to demonize, ostracize, and cause the deaths of thousands of Jewish people. For generations these accusations have given Jewish people a negative view of Christianity and influenced the ways in which Jewish people respond to the Gospel message, since they have been so badly misrepresented over the centuries by the Church and others.

The blood-libel and Host-desecration accusations have driven a wedge between Christians and Jews. A proper biblical approach to the Passover Feast and the people of the Book is necessary to quell past stereotypes of the Jewish people, which have been founded upon these destructive myths. This would enable today's Christians to be more sensitive to a dark past and overcome this bloody legacy with love and understanding, leading to a positive witness of the Gospel to the Jewish people.

Hopefully this chapter and the entirety of this book will help usher in a new day of fruitful and productive relationships with Jewish people, leading to a powerful and relevant witness for the Messiah who is at the very heart of the Passover celebration.

PART 3
JEWISH TRADITION
AND THE PASSOVER

10
PASSOVER IN RABBINIC WRITINGS

ZHAVA GLASER

*W*ith the destruction of the Temple in 70 c.e., Judaism by necessity had to adapt to the fact that sacrifices could no longer be made. Unable to offer sacrifices to atone for sin, the rabbis suddenly needed to face a new reality if they wanted Judaism to survive.

According to legend, Rabbi Yohanan ben Zakkai escaped from Jerusalem in 70 c.e. and established a rabbinic center of learning in the city of Yavneh on the southern coastal plain of Israel (b. Gittin 56b). From there, he and his fellow rabbis founded what is known today as rabbinic Judaism, which centered on the *Torah*[1] and rabbinic teachings rather than on the Temple sacrifices and political jurisdiction.

THE DEVELOPMENT OF RABBINIC TRADITION

When studying the Jewish roots of the Christian faith, we must be careful not to serendipitously weave together first-century and twenty-first-century Jewish traditions. We must not attempt to read medieval or modern-day Jewish practices into the time of Jesus and the disciples. Ancient Jewish literature is a vast and complex field that is often difficult to understand and must be navigated carefully. A respectful and cautious use of Jewish writings, however, can provide an enriching lens to help us see the New Testament in light of its Jewish background.

To gain an insight into how the Feast of Passover was celebrated in Jesus's day, we must turn to the oldest historical evidence. The very early history of the celebration of Passover is difficult to reconstruct; our richest source of information is in the *Talmud*, which forms the core of Jewish law. The Talmud is made up of sixty-three tractates or sections that contain the (often

---

1. The Torah refers to the five books of Moses. Note that key terms are usually italicized at first mention (sometimes a second time) even if mentioned in earlier chapters, and are generally set in roman type thereafter. Many such terms can also be found in the index and glossary at the back of the book.

divergent) opinions of thousands of rabbis on a large variety of subjects, including history, ethics, exegesis, traditional lore, and religious practice.

The central core of the Talmud is known as the *Mishnah*. Originally, rabbinic discussions of the Torah were transmitted orally and thus are known as the Oral Torah and seen as a revelation in their own right. These traditions were committed to writing by Rabbi Judah HaNasi[2] before his death around 220 C.E.[3] The rabbis quoted in the Mishnah are known as *Tannaim*, or "repeaters," because they repeated the memorized discussions of earlier rabbis. The Mishnah is concise in its language and contains many of the traditions of the Pharisees, a religious political party from the time of Jesus. Because of this, a critical reading of the Mishnah can give us an insight into how Passover was celebrated in Jesus's day.

A later commentary, the *Gemara*, recorded the attempts of subsequent rabbis to adapt the teachings of the Torah and the Mishnah into their life situation. Thus, the Gemara analyzes, expands upon, and explains the Mishnah. The rabbis quoted in the Gemara (200 to 500 C.E.) are known as *Amoraim*, or "those who say," because they talked about and expounded the teachings of the Oral Torah. Together, the Mishnah and Gemara make up the Talmud.

The Gemara actually exists in two independent compilations from the two main centers of Jewish scholarship: the Jerusalem Gemara, which forms the Jerusalem Talmud,[4] is dated 350 to 425 C.E., and the Babylonian Gemara, forming the Babylonian Talmud,[5] is dated around 500 C.E.[6] The Babylonian Talmud is much more extensive and is considered to be more authoritative regarding Jewish law; but the Jerusalem Talmud often gives us greater insight into practices in the land of Israel in the first century.

An entire tractate of the Talmud, Pesahim (lit., "Passovers"), is devoted to discussions on the Passover. The first four chapters of Pesahim address the

---

2. The term *HaNasi* means "the Prince," and is the title of this rabbi, indicating that he was a key leader of the Jewish community.
3. Judah Goldin, "The Period of the Talmud," in *The Jews: Their History*, ed. Louis Finkelstein, 4th ed., 3 vols. (New York: Schocken, 1970–71), 1:170. Solomon Schechter and Wilhelm Bacher, "Judah I.," in *Jewish Encyclopedia: A Descriptive Record of the History, Religion, Literature, and Customs of the Jewish People from the Earliest Times to the Present Day*, ed. Isidore Singer (New York: Funk & Wagnalls, 1904), 7:333, accessed February 5, 2017. http://www.jewishencyclopedia.com/articles/8963-judah-i.
4. The Jerusalem Talmud, or *Talmud Yerushalmi* (i.e., the Gemara written in Israel), is the older and actually originates from the Galilee area (Tiberias and Caesarea) rather than from Jerusalem, and because of this is also known as the Palestinian Talmud. The Jerusalem Talmud is more difficult to read and is incomplete, only covering thirty-seven of the sixty-three tractates of the Mishnah.
5. The Babylonian Talmud, also known as the Talmud Bavli but usually referred to as just "The Talmud," reflects the discussions of the Jewish academies in the Mesopotamian cities of Pumbedita and Sura, in modern-day Iraq.
6. The date of the Babylonian Talmud is a matter of debate among scholars; opinions range from 500 to 700 C.E. For further discussion on the dating of the Talmud, see H. L. Strack and Günter Stemberger, *Introduction to the Talmud and Midrash*, trans. and ed. Markus Bockmuehl (Minneapolis: Fortress Press, 1996). See also Shmuel Safrai and Peter J. Tomson, eds., *The Literature of the Sages. First Part: Oral Tora, Halakha, Mishna, Tosefta, Talmud, External Tractates*, Compendia Rerum Iudaicarum ad Novum Testamentum (Assen, Netherlands: Van Gorcum; Philadelphia: Fortress Press, 1987).

laws of leaven, chapters 5–9 tell of the laws relating to the Passover Lamb, and chapter 10 describes the laws of the actual Passover *Seder*.[7] Scholars believe Pesahim to be the kernel of what later became the Passover *Haggadah*, which gives the precise order of the Passover Seder meal.

Between the seventh and eighth centuries, the *Geonim*, the Jewish sages in ancient Babylonia, compiled a version of the Passover observance on which today's Haggadah is based. Fragments of the ninth-century prayer book of Amram Gaon, a famous Jewish leader of the time, were found in the Cairo Genizah, a collection of more than three hundred thousand bits of ancient documents preserved by chance behind a wall of the Ben Ezra synagogue near Cairo, Egypt. These fragments, which date from 870 C.E. to the nineteenth century, contain the earliest known version of the Haggadah.[8]

Also in the Cairo Genizah we have the prayer book of Saadiah Gaon, one of the greatest Jewish sages of the tenth century, containing fragments of an additional Haggadah. At this early stage, many versions of the Haggadah existed, and it was not until the invention of the printing press in the late fifteenth century that the first printed Haggadah was produced and what we have come to know as the modern Passover Haggadah began to be standardized.

THE PASSOVER SACRIFICE

If we want to learn how Passover was celebrated between the Old and New Testaments, so we can gain an insight into how the feast was observed in the time of Jesus, we need to look at ancient historical records.

The observance of Passover was instituted in the Torah and consisted of eating the Passover lamb and unleavened bread and bitter herbs. The only rule that the Torah gives for the actual eating of the Passover lamb is found in Exodus 12:11:

> Now you shall eat it in this manner: with your loins girded, your sandals on your feet, and your staff in your hand; and you shall eat it in haste—it is the LORD's Passover.

The rabbinic sages have considered this command to be applicable only to the first Passover, when the Israelites were fleeing Egypt. Passovers after that were to be festive occasions, celebrating the freedom that God had granted the Israelites and serving as opportunities for parents to instruct their children, reminding them of the story of the Exodus lest they forget that God brought them from slavery to freedom (Exod. 12:26–27; 13:8).[9]

---

7. *Seder* means "order" and refers to the order of service followed in Passover celebrations.
8. For a masterful study of the Cairo Genizah, see S. D. Goitein and Paula Sanders (vol. 6, indexes), *A Mediterranean Society: The Jewish Communities of the Arab World as Portrayed in the Documents of the Cairo Geniza*, 6 vols. (Berkeley: University of California Press, 1967–93).
9. See also b. Pesahim 114 for discussion on *karpas*, or the vegetable.

After the closing of the Old Testament, the book of Jubilees,[10] reflecting practices at the latest one hundred years before Jesus, expands on the biblical commandment. Though it is not authoritative,[11] Jubilees nevertheless gives us an insight into how Passover was celebrated before the destruction of the Temple. Chapter 49 of the book mentions that "all Israel was eating the flesh of the paschal lamb, and drinking the wine, and was lauding and blessing, and giving thanks to the Lord God of their fathers . . ." (Jubilees 49:6).[12] Thus we see that the Passover lamb was still being sacrificed at this time.

The book of Jubilees also makes note of the passage in Deuteronomy 16:2 that states that once the Temple was established, the Passover sacrifice could only be offered there, as opposed to in individual homes:

> You shall sacrifice the Passover to the LORD your God from the flock and the herd, in the place where the LORD chooses to establish His name. (Deut. 16:2)

Jubilees highlights the changed nature of the Passover celebration:

> And they may not celebrate the passover in their cities, nor in any place save before the tabernacle of the Lord, or before His house where His name hath dwelt; and they will not go astray from the Lord." (Jubilees 49:21)[13]

Jewish people living far from the Temple would participate by sending their half-shekel Temple tax to Jerusalem by "sacred envoys" that represented their community, and celebrating Passover as a social occasion in the home or synagogue.[14] First-century Romano-Jewish historian Flavius Josephus writes:

> Accordingly, on the occasion of the feast called Passover, at which they sacrifice from the ninth to the eleventh hour, and a little fraternity, as it were, gathers round each sacrifice, of not fewer than ten persons (feasting alone not being permitted), while the companies often included as many as twenty . . . . (*Jewish War* 6.423 [Thackeray, Loeb Classical Library])

---

10. Jubilees is part of the Old Testament pseudepigrapha, an early extrabiblical source, and is dated at the latest as 100 B.C.E.

11. Jubilees is not considered part of the Bible by Protestant, Roman Catholic, or Eastern Orthodox Churches, but is considered canonical by the Ethiopian Orthodox Church as well as by Ethiopian Jews. For lists of the books in the Hebrew Bible and New Testament, see appendix 1, "The Jewish and Protestant Canons of the Bible." The Roman Catholic and Eastern Orthodox Churches include additional books in their editions of the Bible.

12. See R. H. Charles, trans., *The Book of Jubilees; or The Little Genesis*, Translations of Early Documents (1902; repr., London: SPCK; New York: Macmillan, 1917), 208. For another translation, see Joseph B. Lumpkin, trans., *The Book of Jubilees, [or], The Little Genesis, The Apocalypse of Moses* (Blountsville, AL: Fifth Estate, 2006).

13. Charles, *The Book of Jubilees; or The Little Genesis*, 211.

14. Bokser, *The Origins of the Seder*, 8.

The rabbis of the Mishnah (Tannaim) use similar language, referring to the observation of Passover as a fellowship, or in Hebrew, a *havurah*.[15] Many scholars believe the first-century Greek world influenced these early rabbis. These scholars view the first-century Passover Seder as an early rabbinic version of the Greek symposium, a dinner in the home in which people gathered to share sophisticated arguments over wine.[16] However, others argue that these meals occurred in the synagogue instead, basing this on a passage from a first-century inscription found by archaeologists that refers to the synagogue as a location where communal meals took place.[17] Still other scholars see the Mishnah as taking pains to differentiate the Seder from the Greek symposium.[18] Whether the Seder was influenced by Greek practice or not, it is clear that by the first century, the celebration of Passover took place among groups of family members or friends. Thus, Jesus's Last Supper, a celebration of the Passover with His disciples, is in line with what we know of Jewish customs of the time.[19]

Scholarly opinions differ, however, as to the degree to which the mishnaic description of the Passover represents the observance of the feast during the time of Jesus, and how much was added subsequently, after the Temple's destruction in 70 c.e. Once sacrifices could no longer be offered, the sacrificial lamb was omitted and the Passover celebration by necessity reverted back to one in the home and synagogue, as older traditions were assigned new meanings to make up for the inability to offer sacrifices. One scholar has argued that while the Mishnah depicts pre-70 c.e. observances of Passover, their portrayal is biased by the rabbis' desire to maintain continuity with the past as the rabbinic leadership learned to cope with the catastrophic loss of the Temple.[20]

THE FOUR CUPS

The first mention of the traditional four cups of wine to be taken during the Passover meal is found in the Mishnah. Because the Mishnah

---

15. See Aharon Oppenheimer, *The 'Am Ha-aretz: A Study in the Social History of the Jewish People in the Hellenistic-Roman Period*, trans. I. H. Levine, Arbeiten zur Literatur und Geschichte des hellenistischen Judentums 8 (Leiden: Brill, 1977), 118–56.

16. See, for example, Jordan D. Rosenblum, *Food and Identity in Early Rabbinic Judaism* (New York: Cambridge University Press, 2010), 167–69. See also Siegfried Stein, "The Influence of Symposia Literature on the Literary Form of the Pesaḥ Haggadah," *Journal of Jewish Studies* 8, no. 1–2 (1957): 15.

17. See discussion on the Theodotos inscription in M. Martin, "Communal Meals in the Late Antique Synagogue," *Byzantina Australiensa* 15 (2004): 55, http://www.aabs.org.au/byzaust/byzaus15/, reprinted in M. Martin, "Communal Meals in the Late Antique Synagogue," in *Feast, Fast or Famine: Food and Drink in Byzantium*, edited by W. Mayer and S. Trzcionka, Byzantina Australiensia 15 (Brisbane: Australian Associate for Byzantine Studies, 2005), 135–46; see also Lee I. Levine, *The Ancient Synagogue: The First Thousand Years* (New Haven; London: Yale University Press, 2005), 54–56, 129.

18. Bokser, *The Origins of the Seder*, xiv.

19. For a discussion of Jesus's Last Supper with His disciples related to the celebration of Passover in the Gospel of Luke, see chapter 4, "Passover in the Gospel of Luke," by Darrell L. Bock. For a related discussion of the same in the Gospel of John, see chapter 5, "Passover in the Gospel of John," by Mitch Glaser.

20. Bokser, *The Origins of the Seder*, xiii.

was written over many years, scholars have looked carefully at the various passages, trying to reconstruct the oldest depiction of the Seder. One talmudic scholar, Joseph Tabory, looking for the earliest core of the tradition, believes that the oldest passages are those that state a practice in the past tense, immediately followed by the present tense. Thus, he focuses on these passages and builds a detailed depiction of the oldest layer of the ceremony surrounding the eating of the Paschal lamb. Using those criteria, the passages listed below would be among the earliest passages describing the celebration of a Passover meal in the home or synagogue and can perhaps give us an insight into how Passover was celebrated in the time of Jesus. According to Tabory, the earliest sources show that the ceremony was originally organized around four cups of wine, and each cup had a text to be spoken along with it (emphasis added to verbs to show past versus present tense):

> They *poured* him [the leader of the Seder] the first cup . . . he *recites* the blessing for the day (v. 2).

> They *brought* him unleavened bread, lettuce, and haroset (fruit purée or relish) . . . they *bring* him the Paschal lamb (v. 3).

> They *poured* him the second cup, he *begins* with the disgrace (or: lowly status) [of our ancestors], and *concludes* with glory and he *expounds* the biblical passage "my father was a fugitive Aramean" until the end of the section (v. 4).

> They *poured* him the third cup; he *recites* the grace after meals (v. 5).

> The fourth [cup], he *recites* the *Hallel*,[21] and *says* over it the blessing of the song (v. 8).[22]

The blessings over the first and third cups were also recited on non-festival days, such as weekdays and the Sabbath. We know this is an early practice because in the Mishnah we see disagreements between Hillel and Shammai (two very famous and influential rabbis in the first century B.C.E.) about these weekday prayers, showing that they were in existence before the destruction of the Temple (see, e.g., m. Pesahim 10:2). However, the blessing

---

21.   Psalms 113–118 are known as the *Hallel*. Some scholars have speculated that Psalms 77, 78, 105, and 106 may also have been recited during very early Passover celebrations. For example, see Judith Hauptman, "How Old Is the Haggadah?," *Judaism* 51, pt. 1 (2002): 9, http://www.globethics.net/gel/9770555.

22.   These verses are taken from m. Pesahim 10, quoted in Joseph Tabory, *JPS Commentary on the Haggadah: Historical Introduction, Translation, and Commentary* (Philadelphia: Jewish Publication Society, 2008), 6. For a discussion on the different methods of discerning dating in early Jewish exegesis, see David Instone Brewer, *Techniques and Assumptions in Jewish Exegesis before 70 CE*, Texte und Studien zum antiken Judentum 30 (Tübingen: J. C. B. Mohr [P. Siebeck], 1992).

over the second cup, after which the leader relates the story of Passover, and the fourth cup, the *Hallel* (or praise), are not part of the daily blessings, and were specifically added for the Passover.[23]

It was customary in mishnaic times, in the period before 220 C.E., to precede a festive meal with the serving of hors d'oeuvres, or what we practice today as the different dippings during the Seder (these are possibly the "dippings" referred to in Matthew 26:23 and John 13:26–30). This would explain the statement by Rabbi Nachman[24] in which he says that reclining was only necessary for two of the four cups of wine. The first two cups would be taken in an anteroom before the meal, and cups three and four would be taken after the meal, which was eaten in a reclining position. The majority of rabbis disagreed with Rabbi Nachman, and decreed that all four cups should be taken while reclining to the left, as reclining was associated with the notion of freedom, because only free men could drink in such comfort while slaves would have to stand to serve them (b. Pesahim 108a).

Baruch Bokser, who taught Talmud and rabbinical studies at the Jewish Theological Seminary in New York City, points out that the tradition of the four cups was given several additional meanings in the Talmud, citing these talmudic passages:

1. Drawing on the example of Egypt: the four cups correspond to the four terms and dimensions of redemption used in Exodus 6:6–7.

2. Drawing on the example of Joseph, an individual redeemed from prison: the four cups correspond to four instances that the cup is mentioned in conjunction with the cupbearer's dream.

3. Drawing on the Daniel motif of four successive world empires: the four cups correspond to the four world empires, after which the kingdom of God will come.

4. Drawing on the prophetic references to a cup: the four correspond to "four cups of retribution that the Holy One, praised be He, will give to the nations of the world to drink . . . and corresponding to them [i.e., the four cups of retribution], the Holy One, praised be He, will give Israel four cups of consolation to drink" (y. Pesahim 37b–c on Mishna 10:1).[25]

---

23. Tabory, *JPS Commentary on the Haggadah*, 7.
24. Rabbi Nachman bar Yaakov, usually known just as Rabbi Nachman, was one of the greatest sages of his time, part of the third generation of Amoraim, sages who wrote the Gemara in Babylon (b. Pesahim 108a).
25. Quoted in Baruch M. Bokser, "Ritualizing the Seder," *Journal of the American Academy of Religion* 56, no. 3 (1988): 456–57.

From these very early examples, we can see that the tradition of four cups taken at Passover can credibly be dated to the time of Jesus and could very well be the cups that Jesus mentioned at the Last Supper Passover celebration in Luke 22.

THE PASSOVER MEAL

After the destruction of the Temple, when sacrifices could no longer be offered, the lamb was replaced by an ordinary festive meal centered around the four cups described above, and the telling of the Passover story became the more central part of the celebration.

The festive meal itself consisted of lettuce, *charoset* (a sweet mixture), and "two cooked foods," as opposed to just one dish served in a regular meal (b. Pesahim 114b).[26] According to later tradition, after the writing of the Talmud, and following extensive rabbinic discussion, the "two cooked foods" became symbolic of the two sacrifices that could no longer be offered: the Paschal lamb, later represented by a shankbone, and the *hagigah* sacrifice,[27] later represented by a roasted egg. These two "dishes" were the minimum to be served at the Passover Seder; Rabbi Saadiah in the tenth century suggested four dishes, and today, many more are often served.[28]

The earliest mention of the requirements of the Passover meal were in a quote attributed to first-century Rabbi Gamaliel I,[29] who declared that whoever did not discuss *pesach* (the Passover sacrifice), *matzah* (the unleavened bread), and *maror* (the bitter herbs) during the meal did not fulfill his Passover duty (m. Pesahim 10:5). The Passover sacrifice was meant to remind the children of Israel of the "angel of death" passing over their homes in Egypt, the matzah reminded them of the hurry in which they left Egypt, and the maror of the bitterness of their lives as slaves.

Matzah

Bokser points out that whereas the Torah makes the *eating* of the Paschal lamb central, Rabbi Gamaliel elevates the matzah and maror to equal importance, so that the mere *mention* of them was deemed sufficient to fulfill the obligation, rather than the physical eating. The Gemara further increases the importance of the matzah and maror by specifying that these should be lifted

---

26. Babylonian Talmud Pesahim 114a does not specify the kind of vegetable to use for the "lettuce."

27. The *hagigah* was the additional festive offering that was to be brought by Jewish males to Jerusalem during the holidays of Passover, Shavuot, and Sukkot. See more on this under the subheading "Hagigah" that follows.

28. Tabory, *JPS Commentary on the Haggadah*, 12. For more on the foods prepared and dishes eaten during a traditional Passover Seder meal, see chapter 19, "Passover Foods and Recipes," by Mitch Forman.

29. Rabbi Gamaliel I (also spelled Gamliel), who is mentioned in the book of Acts, was a leading rabbi in the early first-century Sanhedrin, and grandson of the great Rabbi Hillel. He is known for advising his peers not to persecute the believers in Jesus, lest they possibly find themselves fighting against God (Acts 5:33–42).

up while they are being discussed, but forbidding the lifting of the representation of the sacrifice, lest a person appear to be eating a sacrifice outside of the Temple (b. Pesahim 116b).[30]

Bokser notes that in attempting to maintain the relevancy of the Passover meal in a post-Temple world, when a lamb could no longer be offered, the Mishnah elevates the significance of the matzah to a central place in the Passover observance. Thus, the rabbis portray the Passover sacrifice as important but not crucial, while the presence of matzah became essential. In other words, according to Bokser, the Mishnah's response to the Temple's destruction represents "resisting the trauma," or "working through the traumatic disruption to find a new basis for religious life."[31] Judaism, which had revolved around the Temple and its sacrifices, now needed another, more relevant focus.

As a side note, talmudic scholar Judith Hauptman has pointed out that women were actually given a crucial role in the talmudic observance of Passover, since they were entrusted with baking the Passover matzah, a process filled with very detailed and crucial regulations. Hauptman points out that in m. Pesahim 3:3–4, the careful instructions about baking matzah are stated in the feminine gender.[32] This is significant because if the matzah were not prepared correctly, both the men and women consuming it were liable to the punishment of *karet*, or being cut off from their people (m. Pesahim 3:5).

Maror

According to the *Tosefta*,[33] even the poorest person in Israel was required to recline during the Seder (m. Tosefta 10:1).[34] However, because *maror* was eaten as part of the hors d'oeuvres, the eating of these bitter herbs did not require one to recline. Rashi[35] explains this in the eleventh century by pointing out that since reclining was a symbol of freedom, the maror, as a symbol of the bitterness of slavery, was not to be eaten while reclining (b. Pesahim 108a, 116a).

The Gemara discusses how the commandment of eating matzah and maror was fulfilled in the days of the Temple. Rabbi Hillel advocated eating them together in the form of a sandwich, to fulfill the passage in Numbers 9:11, "They shall eat it with unleavened bread [matzah] and bitter herbs [maror]," where both items (matzah and maror) appear together with just

---

30. See also Bokser, "Ritualizing the Seder," 449–50.
31. Bokser, *The Origins of the Seder*, 2.
32. Judith Hauptman, "The Talmud's Women in Law and Narrative," *Nashim: A Journal of Jewish Women's Studies and Gender Issues*, no. 28, no. 1 (2015): 37, http://www.jstor.org/stable/10.2979/nashim.issue-28.
33. The *Tosefta*, meaning "supplement" or "addition," is a compilation of writings from the time of the Mishna (pre-220 C.E.) that are not included in the Mishna but appear as fragments in other rabbinic sources.
34. Joshua Kulp, "Mishnah Tosefta Pesahim," *Shiurim Online Beit Midrash*, accessed December 2, 2015, http://learn.conservativeyeshiva.org/haggadah-and-the-seder-0-mishnah-tosefta-pesahim, based on the Kaufman manuscript: http://jnul.huji.ac.il/dl/talmud/mishna/selectmi.asp.
35. Rashi is an abbreviation of Rabbi Shlomo Yitzchaki (1040–1105 C.E.), a medieval French rabbi who wrote extensive authoritative commentaries on the Bible and the Talmud.

one verb ("shall eat") (b. Pesahim 115a). Other rabbis advocated eating them separately, so the compromise was made to first eat them separately, and then again together (Shulchan Aruch 475:1).[36] According to Rashi (eleventh century) and Maimonides (twelfth century),[37] the Hillel "sandwich" also included the Passover lamb before the destruction of the Temple when a sacrifice could still be made. While we do not know exactly how this was done at the time of Jesus, the Hillel sandwich today consists of matzah, maror, and charoset eaten together.

Charoset

While there is no mention in the Bible of *charoset*, the sweet apple mixture that is eaten at Passover, it is included in the Mishnah as part of the Passover observance, which means it was possibly a practice dating back to the time of Jesus. Rabbi Eleazar ben Zadok, a first-century rabbi, claimed that eating charoset at Passover was a *mitzvah*, i.e., a commandment. Because the Mishnah records both sides of rabbinic discussions, we know that the other sages of his time disagreed that it was a commandment, but did agree that it ought to be part of the observance of the Passover (m. Pesahim 10:3).

What exactly was charoset? The Mishnah mentions it, so we know it was part of the Passover tradition at least by the third century, but it does not tell us exactly what charoset was. It is only later, in the Babylonian Talmud, that we learn that it was a dip for the lettuce, and consisted of an apple mixture that resembled mortar, a reminder of the building materials used by the Israelite slaves in Egypt (b. Pesahim 115b, 116a). The rabbis of the Talmud also found symbolism not only in the appearance of the charoset but in the apple itself—one of the many traditional explanations was that an apple was eaten in remembrance of the Israelite women in Egypt. This is from a story in the Talmud that the Israelite women used to give birth under apple trees in Egypt to protect their newborns, thus continuing to experience God's blessing in the midst of persecution (b. Sotah 116a).[38]

The Jerusalem Talmud describes the charoset differently, noting that its consistency was more liquid, and thus was symbolic of blood (y. Pesahim

---

36. Shulchan Aruch is known as the Code of Jewish Law. Joseph ben Ephraim Karo, *Code of Jewish Law* (קיצור שולחן ערוך): *A Compilation of Jewish Laws and Customs*, comp. Solomon ben Joseph Ganzfried, trans. Hyman E. Goldin, rev. ed., 4 vols. (New York: Hebrew Publishing Company, 1927).

37. Moses Maimonides (1135–1204) was a Sephardic rabbi, philosopher, physician, and astronomer, as well as a major influential Jewish scholar.

38. Rabbi Eliyahu Kitov says that giving birth under the apple trees removed them "far from the notice of the Egyptians, who had decreed death on all newborn Jewish males." The Jewish sages explain, says Kitov, that unlike other fruit trees, the apple tree first produces its fruit and then its protective leaves; likewise the Israelite women, who concealed their pregnancies and gave birth in the fields, under the apple trees, trusting God to reveal Himself and protect them and their newborn children. Eliyahu Kitov, הגדה של פסח; *The Heritage Haggadah: With Laws, Customs, Traditions, and Commentary for the Seder Night*, trans. Gershon Robinson (1961; Jerusalem: Feldheim Publishers, 1999), 62–63.

10:3, 37d.). Joseph Tabory, who authored the Jewish Publication Society commentary on the Haggadah, offers several other interpretations, suggesting that the reminder referred to the blood of Israelite children killed by Pharaoh; or the shed blood leading to divine deliverance, symbolizing either the first or last plague; or the redemption brought by the blood of the lamb that was smeared on the doorposts of Israelite homes. Tabory notes further that eminent sixteenth-century talmudic scholar Rabbi Moses Isserles (1520–1572), as a compromise, concluded that the charoset should be thick, but red wine should be added in memory of the blood.[39] Essentially, however, we do not know how early the tradition of the charoset was practiced, or how it was understood at different points in time.

Hagigah

The *hagigah* was the voluntary offering that was to be made on the three main Israelite festivals: Passover (*Pesach*), the Feast of Weeks or Pentecost (*Shavuot*) and the Feast of Booths (*Sukkot*). An entire tractate of the Talmud is devoted to the laws of the hagigah.

While the Temple stood, the hagigah was originally a separate sacrifice, at Passover eaten before the lamb, according to the rabbis, so that the Passover lamb would not be eaten in great hunger, lest a bone of the sacrifice be broken in the rush to satisfy one's hunger (y. Pesahim 6:4, 33c.). In a different passage, the rabbis suggest that the Passover sacrifice was to be eaten solely to obey the commandment of God, and must not be eaten to satisfy one's hunger at all (b. Pesahim 115a).

This posed a problem in that the Torah specified that none of the Passover lamb was to be left for the following day. In that case, the rabbis said, if the size of the group was small, there was to be no hagigah sacrifice, lest the Passover lamb not be entirely consumed because the people were already full.[40] We have no record in the New Testament of Jesus or His disciples specifically offering the hagigah sacrifice; however, Leviticus 23:8 does mention a daily "offering by fire" to be made on each day of the Feast of Unleavened Bread, and we can assume that this sacrifice was being offered at the time of Jesus. After the destruction of the Temple, the hagigah came to be symbolized at Passover by a roasted egg, and is still part of the modern-day Passover celebration.

THE "FOUR SONS" AND THE CHANGING RABBINIC VIEWS OF REDEMPTION

A fundamental change had to be made in Judaism after the destruction of the Temple and the loss of national independence, as the traditional concept of redemption in the Passover—liberation from Egyptian bondage to the freedom of an independent nation—contradicted the daily reality of the Jewish people after 70 C.E. In order to reconcile the original

---

39. Tabory, *JPS Commentary on the Haggadah*, 8–9.
40. Tabory, *JPS Commentary on the Haggadah*, 9–10.

meaning of Passover redemption with the reality of Jewish life once the Temple was destroyed, the rabbinic leadership chose to spiritualize the concept of divine redemption as potentially present in every Israelite's daily life.

The concept of redemption evolved in many directions among the three main branches of Judaism. Orthodox Judaism believes in a personal Messiah who will redeem humankind and usher in a Messianic era of peace, which will include an eventual resurrection of the dead.[41] Conservative Judaism generally believes more in a Messianic era (although some Conservative Jews still believe in a personal Messiah) in which humankind will be redeemed from the evils of this world. In this view, each individual has the responsibility to bring about the Messianic age through good deeds in this present life.[42] Reform Judaism, the more liberal of the branches, believes that a personal Messiah is not needed, but rather that human beings will be redeemed by their own intellect, and will through their efforts bring about a Messianic era in which humanity will live in peace.[43]

The various rabbinic views of redemption evolved from a single event in history, the Exodus, to an experience affecting every Jewish person in every age, as well as something that would conceivably come in the distant future. The early transformation of the concept of redemption can be seen in the evolution of rabbinic interpretation regarding the "four sons."[44]

During the Passover Seder, four symbolic sons ask four different questions,[45] and the answers to those questions provide the structure for the retelling of the Passover story.

The *wise son* asks the meaning of the statutes that the Lord commanded Israel. The response is the telling of the story of the Exodus, the signs and wonders wrought by God, and the culmination in the commandments given by God to His people (Deut. 6:20–25).

The *simple son* merely asks, "What is this?" In response, he is told the story of the slaying of the firstborn of the Egyptians, and the redemption of

41. See Moses Maimonides, "Thirteen Principles of the Jewish Faith." The twelfth principle asserts belief in the coming of the Messiah and the thirteenth speaks of the belief in the resurrection of the dead. For more on these principles, see Aryeh Kaplan, *Maimonides' Principles: The Fundamentals of Jewish Faith;* י״ג עקרים של הרמב״ם, 2nd ed. (New York: National Conference of Synagogue Youth; Union of Orthodox Jewish Congregations of America, 1984).

42. The Jewish Theological Seminary of America, The Rabbinical Assembly, and United Synagogue of America, *Emet Ve'emunah* (אמת ואמונה): *Statement of Principles of Conservative Judaism* (New York: Jewish Theological Seminary of America, 1988), 28–32.

43. See Union of American Hebrew Congregations, *Reform-Liberal-Progressive Judaism: Its Ideals and Concepts, as Set Forth in the Guiding Principles of Reform Judaism* (New York: Union of American Hebrew Congregations, 1937).

44. See also the discussion on the Four Nights in Targum Neofiti in Clemens Leonhard, *The Jewish Pesach and the Origins of the Christian Easter: Open Questions in Current Research*, Studia Judaica 35 (Berlin: Walter de Gruyter, 2006).

45. These were originally three questions, based on three Torah passages: Exodus 12:26–27; 13:14–15; and Deuteronomy 6:20–23.

the firstborn among the Israelites (Exod. 13:11–16). There is also a *son who does not know how to ask*, and who is given a similar answer (Exod. 13:8).

The *wicked son*, however, asks, "What does this mean to *you*?" (Exod. 12:21–28; esp. v. 26). It is the (later) talmudic mention of the wicked son's question that displays a small but significant change in interpretation. An early commentary, the *Mekhilta*,[46] says:

> Because he excludes himself from the group, you also should exclude him from the group, and say unto him: "It is because of that which the Lord did for me" (v. 8)—for me but not for you. Had you been there, you would not have been redeemed. (Mekhilta on Exod. 12:26)[47]

The Jerusalem Talmud adds an interesting nuance:

> The wicked son, what does he say? "What mean you by this service?" (Exod. 12:26) What is this bother that you have troubled us with each and every year? Because he excludes himself from the group, you also should say to him: "It is because of that which the Lord did for me" (v. 8)—for me but He did not do for "that man" (the wicked son). Had "that man" been in Egypt, he would not have been fit to be redeemed from there ever. (y. Pesahim 10, 37)[48]

The Jerusalem Talmud declares that by asking in this way, this wicked son has removed himself from the community, thereby excluding himself from Israel's redemption as well. A *beraita*[49] in the Jerusalem Talmud says, "If that person had been in Egypt, he would never have been worthy to be redeemed from there."[50] In saying this, the Jerusalem Talmud differs from other rabbinic writings, making the redemption from Egypt conditional upon the worthiness of the recipient. This is key, because in doing so it then empowers every single Israelite with the ability to choose to become worthy of redemption if they are careful to obey the commandments.

This *beraita*, although not grounded in Scripture, reflected the common rabbinic perception of life. Faced with the absence of the Temple and the

---

46. The *Mekhilta de Rabbi Ishmael* is a rabbinic commentary to the book of Exodus; the identity of its author, "Rabbi Ishmael," is a subject of debate among scholars. Its date, also difficult to establish, is estimated to be some time in the third or fourth centuries. For more on the Mekhilta, see Jacob Z. Lauterbach, trans., *Mekilta de-Rabbi Ishmael: A Critical Edition on the Basis of the Manuscripts and Early Editions with an English Translation, Introduction and Notes*, 2nd ed., 2 vols., JPS Classic Reissues (1933–35; repr., Philadelphia: Jewish Publication Society of America, 2004).

47. Quoted from Mordechai Silverstein, trans., "The Four Sons of the Haggadah—Introduction to Rabbinic Midrash," *Shiurim Online Beit Midrash*, accessed December 2, 2015, http://learn.conservativeyeshiva.org/introduction-to-rabbinic-midrash-10-lesson-10-the-four-sons-of-the-haggadah.

48. Quoted from Silverstein, "The Four Sons of the Haggadah."

49. A *beraita* is a rabbinic quote from the mishnaic period that was not included in the Mishna but was quoted by later sources.

50. See Fred O. Francis, "The Baraita of the Four Sons," *Journal of the American Academy of Religion* 42, no. 2 (1974): 280–97.

reality of life under Roman rule, the rabbis of the Jerusalem Talmud provided a way for each individual to merit spiritual, and not political, redemption.[51]

After all four sons ask their questions, the Mishnah states that the father is to begin his answer with the humiliation faced by the wandering Aramean, and to finish with the redemption from Egypt (m. Pesahim 10:4; b. Pesahim 116a). In its reference to Joshua 24:2–4, where Joshua refers to God taking Abraham from idolatry to belief in Himself, the Jerusalem Talmud is continuing to reinterpret redemption in a spiritual manner, as meaning to go from idolatry to belief in the one true God. Thus once again the Jerusalem Talmud spiritualizes the concept of redemption, to make it relevant to every person in every generation as part of Judaism's reinvention of itself following the destruction of the Temple.

In addition, in closing with the *Hallel* praise psalms, the participants in the Passover meal give praise to God for bringing them as individuals from idolatry into true worship, thus making the concept of redemption relevant no matter what the physical reality of the Jewish people might have been.[52]

After the loss of the Temple and the sacrificial system, Passover in rabbinic teachings was transformed from a celebration centered on the sacrifice of the Lamb, to a home celebration. This shift recreated the holiday as a teaching tool reminding individual Jewish people and families of the importance of being faithful to the one true God and rejecting idolatry, that one might merit a future redemption of a more spiritual nature. Thus, the Jerusalem Talmud and other early rabbinic writings, through their reinterpretation of the Passover, recast redemption from merely a historic experience to a more spiritual reality available to those within the Jewish community who were loyal to the God of Abraham, Isaac, and Jacob.

This background could well have created the atmosphere within first-century Judaism enabling the Jewish faithful standing on the banks of the Jordan River to grasp the truth of John's testimony, that a greater redemption had now come through Jesus, the Lamb of God and Messiah who had come to take away the sin of the world (John 1:29).

Passover, both in Scripture and rabbinic tradition, from the first century onward pointed the Jewish community towards a greater Messianic hope. The question the Jewish people needed to answer both then and now is whether or not Jesus embodies this hope.

---

51. See Francis, "The Baraita of the Four Sons."
52. Baruch M. Bokser, "Changing Views of Passover and the Meaning of Redemption According to the Palestinian Talmud," *AJS Review* 10, no. 1 (1985): 11–12.

11
PASSOVER AND THE AFIKOMAN

DANIEL NESSIM

A mysterious tradition takes place every Passover in a ritual called the *Yachatz*, which means "he will divide." It is the breaking of a piece of matzah (unleavened bread) that has been placed inside a special matzah cover for the ceremonial part of Passover. The matzah cover has three pockets, with one piece of matzah inside each of three pockets. The middle piece of the three is broken in this ritual and is known as the *afikoman*. This piece is carefully set aside in an afikoman bag and hidden in order to be eaten later.

Shortly after the afikoman is broken, the Haggadah introduces us to four sons. The Haggadah describes the sons in this way:

> The Torah refers to four sons: One wise, one wicked, one simple and one who does not know how to ask a question. What does the wise son say? "What are the testimonies, decrees and ordinances the Lord our God commanded you?" You should tell him about the laws of Pesach, that one may not eat the Afikoman after eating the Pesach offering.[1]

This is the very wording found in the Mishnah, which tells us, "They must not call for more food [the afikoman] after the Passover offering" (m. Pesahim 10.8).[2] Later in the Seder, this afikoman will be the last taste

---

1. Another Haggadah describes the four sons as follows: "Concerning four sons does the Torah speak—a wise one, a wicked one, a simple one, and one who is unable to ask. The wise son—what does he say? 'What are the testimonies, decrees, and ordinances which Hashem, our God, has commanded you?'" Nosson Scherman and Meir Zlotowitz, eds. *The Family Haggadah: With Translation and Instructions*, trans. Nosson Scherman, 2nd ed., ArtScroll Mesorah Series (New York: Mesorah Publications, 2008), 29.

2. The Hebrew of Pesahim 10.8 reads, אֵין מַפְטִירִין אַחַר הַפֶּסַח אֲפִיקוֹמָן, *'en maftirin 'ahar hapesach 'afiqoman. Mishnayoth: Pointed Hebrew Text, English Translation, Introductions, Notes, Supplement, Appendix, Indexes, Addenda, Corrigenda*, trans. Philip Blackman, 2nd ed., 7 vols. (Gateshead, UK: Judaica Press, 1963–64), 2:221. See also Tosefta Pisha 10.11 and Mekhilta Pisha on Exodus 13:14.

of food the participants will eat. But what is this afikoman, and why is it forbidden to eat it after the Pesach offering?[3] The Haggadah itself does not give us a specific interpretation. The origins and meaning of the afikoman are shrouded by the mists of time. Few people give it any thought, so some deeper investigation is required.

WHAT IS THE AFIKOMAN?

The word *afikoman* (אֲפִיקוֹמָן, *'afiqoman*) is itself shrouded in mystery. One possibility is that the term is a loan word from the Greek ἐπί Κομός, *epi komos*, which means "that which is to come after."[4] Although the etymology is uncertain, this in any case raises the questions of what it exactly comes after, and why it is forbidden. The answer likely lies in the customs of ancient pagan society. Jewish people were living throughout the Roman world. A good example is the city of Antioch where, according to Josephus, the Jewish population was large and had dwelt in "undisturbed tranquility" since the days of Antiochus Epiphanes (reigned ca. 175–164 B.C.E.). Jews were not only "particularly numerous" but were very much intermingled with the general population (*Jewish War* 7.43). In an indication of their general integration with the social fabric of the region, Josephus claims that the Jews were "perpetually" active in proselytizing, thereby "in some measure" incorporating the general populace with themselves (*Jewish War* 7.45).

It should be no surprise, then, that over time the Jewish people also picked up customs from the Gentiles where they lived. One of these was the custom of the *symposium*, a Greek dinner party, where participants reclined, and at night went from party to party revelling. An illustration of this type of party is found in Plato's *Symposium* where first Alcibiades and then later a "great crowd of revellers" impose themselves upon a more sedate dinner party (223B [Lamb, Loeb Classical Library]).[5] This gives rise to the most common explanation for the command of the rabbis, and one that is accepted by the majority of scholars, namely, that in ancient times some Jewish people were liable to go partying after the Seder according to the custom of the Greeks. This was the view of the sixteenth-century Hebrew grammarian Elijah Levita, who has been credited with being the first person to discern the Greek origin of the term *afikoman*, leading to the connection with songs, dances, and games that followed banquets in the Greek manner.[6]

---

3. This is the same in both the Ashkenazic (generally European) and Sephardic (generally Spanish or Arabic) traditions. Marc D. Angel, הגדה של פסח כמנהג הספרדים; *A Sephardic Passover Haggadah: Translated with Commentary by Rabbi Marc D. Angel* (Hoboken, NJ: KTAV, 1988), 29; op. cit., Scherman and Zlotowitz, *The Family Haggadah*, 29.

4. Blackman, *Mishnayoth*, 2:221; Philip Goodman, ed., *The Passover Anthology*, JPS Holiday (Philadelphia: Jewish Publication Society of America, 1961), 378.

5. See also Plato, *Symposium*, 212C–E, 23B (Lamb, Loeb Classical Library).

6. Hayyim Schauss, *The Jewish Festivals: A Guide to Their Observance*, trans. Samuel Jaffe (New York: Schocken Books, 1938), 82.

Confirmation that this was a pagan activity frowned upon by the rabbis is seen in the interpretation found in the Babylonian Talmud.[7] It is in the Gemara, the later compilation of comments on the foundational mishnaic text, that a revealing discussion is portrayed in the tractate Pesahim section 119b. Rav interprets the meaning of afikoman to be that celebrants should not go from one group to another, saying "they must not move from one eating party to another." Additional figures in the Gemara, Hanina ben Shila and Rabbi Yochanan, contended that "you must not conclude after the Seder with dates, parched grains and nuts," seemingly also prohibiting after-parties.

While the Passover was a meal with a set structure, and therefore was in some ways similar to a symposium, the rabbis did not want there to be any confusion or merging of customs lest its significance be lost. It was therefore their instruction that celebrants should not go about eating elsewhere after the Seder, and by extension not be getting drunk or behaving licentiously either.[8] Rather, they taught that the Seder was an important rite commanded in the Torah that had to be celebrated respectfully and with due attention to all the commands given concerning it. It was important that people take the Seder seriously and not treat it like a party.

There is, however, more to be learned in relation to the question regarding the "dates, parched grains and nuts," which had caught the attention of the rabbis. The rabbis' comment on this might seem to be random, but it is not. Their instruction opens the door to another explanation of the word afikoman found in an ancient Yemenite Haggadah and echoed in the Talmud. The Hebrew word אֲפִיקוֹמָן, 'afiqoman, is comprised of two words: אָפִיק, afik, and מִין, min, which are taken to mean that one should not taste any kind of fruit or anything else after the matzah.[9]

The same ancient Haggadah also suggests that the word אֲפִיקוֹמָן, 'afiqoman, is an acronym for the Hebrew words for nuts, fruits, wine, roasted things, meat, water, and spikenard (see list below).[10] From the perspective of certain rabbis, these are clearly all things to be avoided after the Passover meal, which represent a more extended list of foods than that mentioned in the Babylonian Talmud Pesahim 119b, and avoiding them would preclude going partying after the Seder.

7. Bokser, *The Origins of the Seder*, 65.
8. "Mishnah," 2:221; Goodman, *Passover Anthology*, 378.
9. William H. Greenburg, trans., *The Haggadah According to the Rite of Yemen, Together with the Arabic-Hebrew Commentary* (London: David Nutt, 1896), 14.
10. Greenburg, *The Haggadah*, 16. Note that both of the *a* vowels as well as the *i* and *o* vowels in the proposed acronym for the word *afikoman* come from the vowel pointing of the Hebrew word אֲפִיקוֹמָן, 'afiqoman.

The Afikoman Acronym			
nuts	A	א	אֱגוֹזִים, *'egozim*
fruits	F	פ	פֵּירוֹת, *perot*
wine	I	י	יַיִן, *yayin*
roasted things	K	ק	קְלוּיִים, *keluyim*
meat	O	ו	וּבָשָׂר, *uvasar*
water	M	מ	מַיִם, *mayim*
spikenard	N	נ	נֵרְד, *nered*

The two ways of understanding the word *afikoman* can now be harmonized and seen in relation to one another. In one sense it refers to "that which comes after," that is, the final part of the meal. In another sense it may be an acronym for the various kinds of food eaten after a meal. All of this kind of eating could be connected to licentious behavior after meals, which would be completely inappropriate for such a spiritual occasion.

In light of this, the rabbis' prohibition makes perfect sense. In fact, the attitude of the rabbis is further explained in the Tosefta, which preserves traditions not included in the Mishnah. There we have the ideal practice: to "study the laws of Pesach all night" even if only with a son, student, or even by oneself (t. Pesahim 10:11).

CUSTOMS SURROUNDING THE AFIKOMAN

The afikoman has had something of a mysterious and mystifying significance within the host of Passover traditions observed throughout the centuries in Jewish communities around the world and has become a special part of the Seder.

One of the most interesting customs was preserved by the Jewish community of Baghdad. This was a community that survived for more than 2,500 years, from the Babylonian exile until Operation Ezra and Nehemiah (popularly called Operation Ali-Baba) evacuated by airlift almost all of this persecuted Jewish community from Iraq to Israel in 1950 and 1951.[11] Professor of Jewish folklore Dov Noy relates that in Baghdad "someone with the *afikoman* used to leave the *seder* and return disguised as a traveler. The leader would ask him, 'Where are you from?' to which he would answer, 'Egypt,'

---

11.   Joseph B. Schechtman, "The Repatriation of Iraq Jewry," *Jewish Social Studies* 15, no. 2 (1953): 151–72, http://www.jstor.org/stable/4465156.

and 'Where are you going?' to which he would reply, 'Jerusalem.'"[12] It is a charming tradition related to the longing of the Jewish people to celebrate the feast in the Holy City even after millennia of exile.

Even more interesting in terms of the Messianic significance of the afikoman is the custom of Djerba, a North African city on the southern coast of the Mediterranean, off the coast of Tunisia. There, "the person conducting the *seder* used to give the *afikoman* to one of the family, who tied it on his shoulder and went to visit relatives and neighbors to forecast the coming of the Messiah."[13]

Sometimes these ancient traditions have been carried over into modern Jewish practices. Richard Glaser found that Greek Jews in Baltimore would follow a custom of theirs from their ancient community in Greece whereby a piece of the afikoman would be kept from one year to the next to "stress the continual cyclical nature of the Jewish year." Some others in the Greek community recounted "a belief that was held by a few in Greece," and in this account, Greek Jews sometimes saved a piece of afikoman to take along when going on a sea voyage. "If a storm arose and threatened the safety of the vessel, one could throw the *afikoman* overboard and the waves would subside."[14] Another tradition carried over from the past into modern Jewish practice is referred to by Vanessa Ochs in her observation that in some Jewish homes the afikoman is "hung over doors as amulets to increase one's blessing."[15]

The most popular tradition related to the afikoman is a game played by the children, which gives them something to look forward to during the Seder. This elaborate game is common mostly in Western countries and particularly among European (Ashkenazic) Jews. It is not just the game but the sequence of events that lead up to it that continues to make it intriguing and suggests a possible deeper significance to it. As mentioned at the beginning of this chapter, early in the Seder the second of three matzot in a special matzah cover with three pockets is broken, and the larger part is set aside for eating later. This piece of matzah is now called the afikoman. After the meal, because it is essential to eat this matzah in order to conclude, the leader will look for it, but it will rarely be found. That is because if there are children present, someone will have hidden the matzah to keep it safe. Perhaps this is because of the command in Exodus 12:17, "You shall also observe the Feast of Unleavened Bread," which can literally be read as "You shall guard the matzot" (וּשְׁמַרְתֶּם אֶת־הַמַּצּוֹת, *ushemarttem 'et-hammatsot*). When a child finally does find the afikoman, a great fuss will be made over her or him and the child can ask for a reward before handing it over. This part of the Seder is fun for everyone and a highlight of the whole event.

---

12.   Dov Noy and Joseph Tabory, "Afikoman," in *EncJud*, 1:434.

13.   Noy and Tabory, "Afikoman," 1:434.

14.   Richard Glaser, "The Greek Jews in Baltimore," *Jewish Social Studies* 38, no. 3/4 (1976): 332, http://www.jstor.org/stable/4466941.

15.   Vanessa L. Ochs, "What Makes a Jewish Home Jewish?," *CrossCurrents* 49, no. 4 (1999/2000): 506, http://www.crosscurrents.org/ochsv.htm.

MYSTIFYING ECHOES

Intriguing echoes whispered discreetly throughout history suggest that the afikoman may have even more significance than is generally recognized. In particular, due to the connection between the Last Supper, the traditions surrounding the matzah, and Yeshua's sacrifice, the earliest believers may have had a role in the development of the afikoman tradition, as practiced historically during the Passover Seder.

It is worth remembering that among those who were part of the early Jerusalem Church were Jews from every nation (Acts 2:4; 4:4) who were held in high esteem by the rest of the Jewish population (5:13). Some of them were Pharisees (15:5) and part of the mix that led James to tell Paul, "You see, brother, how many thousands there are among the Jews of those who have believed, and they are all zealous for the Law" (21:20). There had been no "parting of the ways" between Jewish believers in Yeshua and the rest of the Jewish community in these early days. The Messianic Jews were still viewed as part of the mainstream Jewish community at that time, just as having chosen the "wrong" Messiah.

This opens the possibility that the traditions of the early Jewish believers in Yeshua, specifically those that identify Jesus with the afikoman, might well have found their way into a broader swath of Jewish homes, and from there perhaps into Jewish tradition—even after the early Messianic Jewish significance was forgotten by the general Jewish population.

These early believers broke bread together regularly, house to house (Acts 2:42, 46), and the Didache, a book quite possibly composed while the Apostles were still living, records how believers usually remembered the Lord as they ate together.[16] This book, called *The Teaching of the Lord through the Twelve Apostles for the Gentiles*, includes a difficult term for the bread that has perplexed scholars. The term "concerning the fragment" (περί δὲ τοῦ κλάσματος, *peri de tou klasmatos*) is different from the term for bread (ἄρτος, *artos*) as found in Luke 22:19 and is more closely related to the verb "to break" (κλάω, *klaō*). Later the passage (Didache 9.2–4) refers to "this fragment of bread" which "was scattered upon the mountains" (author's translation). This might link this later tradition with Yeshua "breaking" the bread, identifying it with His body to be sacrificed. Of course, we understand that this was not bread in the usual sense, but specifically unleavened bread, which was a particularly brittle bread

16. The Didache has been dated as early as 50 C.E., as is the case with Aaron Milavec, *The Didache: Text, Translation, Analysis, and Commentary* (Collegeville, MN: Liturgical Press, 2003), ix. The views of other scholars who have dated the Didache as late as the second century have largely fallen by the wayside after the discovery of the Dead Sea Scrolls and the demonstration of the close affinities between the Didache's Two Ways material and the Manual of Discipline as published by Jean-Paul Audet, "Affinités littéraire et doctrinales du 'Manuel de discipline,'" *Revue Biblique* 59 (1952): 219–38; English translation: Jean-Paul Audet, "Literary and Doctrinal Affinities of the 'Manual of Discipline,'" in *The* Didache *in Modern Research*, ed. and trans. Jonathan A. Draper (Leiden: Brill, 1996), 129–47.

easily broken into small fragments.[17] The bread used by these early Jewish believers was no fluffy loaf of bread, or even pita bread; it was crunchy, crumbly matzah.

MELITO OF SARDIS

Less than a century ago, "[t]he writings of an Early Church Bishop from Sardis were rediscovered . . . and republished for the first time in 1940."[18] The bishop's name was Melito of Sardis and he was also a Jewish believer in Jesus.[19] Melito wrote in the second century, in Greek, about the significance of the Passover with many comments based on Jewish traditions which he apparently knew well. All of this and more is found in his homily on the Passion (*Peri Pascha*). Melito saw a connection between the afikoman and Yeshua, and seemingly taking advantage of the literal meaning of the word *afikoman*, "that which is to come after," included a cryptic reference to it and its relationship to Yeshua. Melito took the afikoman as a foreshadowing of Yeshua's return as the one who comes "after" His sacrificial work of redemption in His second coming. This tradition is nothing short of remarkable.

Some in the world of Jewish academia have recognized this link between the afikoman and the breaking of the matzah at the Last Supper as well. Jewish scholar Eric Werner claims that Melito used the expression *afikoman* in an apparent attempt to mimic the enigmatic reference to afikoman in the Haggadah.[20]

> It is he who, coming [ἀφικόμενον, *aphikomenon*] from heaven to the earth because of the suffering one, and clothing himself in that same one through a virgin's womb, and coming forth [προελθὼν, *proelthōn*] a man, accepted the passions of the suffering one, through the body which was able to suffer. (*Peri Pascha* 66)[21]

This statement by Melito, made a century and a half after Messiah, stands as substantive evidence in support of the position that an ancient Messianic Jewish view of the afikoman somehow entered into the mainstream Jewish Seder. Melito's *Peri Pascha* presents a viewpoint which had become more

---

17. Kurt Niederwimmer, *The Didache: A Commentary*, trans. Linda M. Maloney, ed. Harold W. Attridge, Hermeneia (Minneapolis: Fortress Press, 1998), 148.
18. John Behr, in Melito of Sardis, *On Pascha: With the Fragments of Melito and Other Material Related to the Quartodecimans*, ed. John Behr, trans. Alistair Stewart-Sykes, Popular Patristics Series 20 (Crestwood, NY: St Vladimir's Seminary Press, 2001), 9. For more on Melito of Sardis and the afikoman tradition, see chapter 7, "Passover, the Temple, and the Early Church," by Scott P. Nassau.
19. See the letter of Polycrates of Ephesus in Eusebius, *Ecclesiastical History* 5.24.
20. Eric Werner, "Melito of Sardes, the First Poet of Deicide," *Hebrew Union College Annual* 37 (1966): 205, http://www.jstor.org/stable/23503121.
21. Melito of Sardis, *On Pascha and Fragments*, ed. Stuart G. Hall, Oxford Early Christian Texts (Oxford: Clarendon, 1979), 35.

developed by the second century, so much so that Melito used the term *afikoman* in his Haggadah[22] to refer to Messiah (*Peri Pascha* 65–66).[23]

As the Church became more anti-Jewish in its theology and rhetoric, the Jewish community minimized any connection between Yeshua and the Seder, including the afikoman, so the observance fell out of favor. In light of this, Israel Yuval, professor of Jewish history at Hebrew University, is of the opinion that by the compilation of the Mishnah in the third century C.E., the phrase "'One may not conclude . . . with *afikoman*'" (m. Pesahim 10.8) "was meant to undermine the Christian interpretation" of the afikoman's meaning. Thus, in Yuval's view, this question served to exclude the "Jewish-Christian." [24]

DID YESHUA USE THE AFIKOMAN?

In Yeshua's day, the Haggadah was primitive and had yet to be committed to writing.[25] This means that we need to ask specifically whether the rituals of the afikoman were known or practiced in the first century, particularly in the region where Yeshua lived. Further, was it actually the afikoman that Yeshua took and identified with His body, or was it some other piece of matzah during the Seder?[26] Some scholars question the idea that the tradition of the afikoman was practiced in Yeshua's day and that the Haggadah was not even committed to writing until after the destruction of the Temple in 70 C.E.[27] However, there has now been enough evidence offered to suggest that the Haggadah as we have it is the process of a centuries-long development that began in the intertestamental period and continued after the destruction of the Temple.[28]

---

22. Later in the sentence Melito uses a different word for "coming forth," suggesting that he used the word *afikoman* specifically in order to make a point that his readers would have understood. The word was uncommon and in the context of his writing on the Haggadah is a purposeful reference to that word in the Haggadah itself. In addition, this term comes right after Melito's preceding reference to "the mystery of the Pascha, which is Christ" (*Peri Pascha* 65) and his following reference to Messiah's "body which was able to suffer" (66). Both these themes are related to the theme of the afikoman.
23. See Melito of Sardis, *On Pascha and Fragments*, 35.
24. Yuval, "Easter and Passover as Early Jewish-Christian Dialogue," 107.
25. For more on the kind of Passover Seder meal Jesus celebrated with His disciples, see chapter 4, "Passover in the Gospel of Luke," by Darrell L. Bock, and chapter 5, "Passover in the Gospel of John," by Mitch Glaser.
26. While Luke 22:20 makes it clear that the cup after the meal was the one to refer to the new covenant in Jesus's blood, verse 19 does not indicate that the bread He broke was at the end of the meal. Matthew 26:26 indicates that Jesus took bread as the disciples were eating, thus during the meal. However, the afikoman clearly symbolizes the entire meal, including the bread that was broken.
27. A skeptical view is taken by Jonathan Klawans, "Was Jesus's Last Supper a Seder?," *Bible Review* 17 (2001): 24–33, http://www.biblicalarchaeology.org/daily/people-cultures-in-the-bible/jesus-historical-jesus/was-jesus-last-supper-a-seder/. On the other hand, a good number of the issues raised by Klawans have been addressed in a much more nuanced picture of the development of the Haggadah by Joel Marcus, "Passover and Last Supper Revisited," *New Testament Studies* 59, no. 3 (2013): 303–24.
28. The oldest surviving Haggadah, which is from the tenth or eleventh century, does not contain the tradition of the afikoman. This is not proof, however, that the tradition was unknown; rather, it indicates only that the afikoman was not universally included in the Haggadah. As we have already

Nevertheless, in Matthew 26:26[29] Yeshua says, "Take, eat; this is My body." This is an invitation to His disciples to eat at the Seder and partake of the matzah. Thus Yuval may well be right to suggest that this is an echo of the invitation of the Haggadah. This invitation is right after the afikoman has been broken off and just before the *Maggid,* the telling of the story of redemption. At that point the head of the household lifts up the remaining matzah and says, "This is the bread of affliction which our ancestors ate in the land of Egypt; let those who are hungry, enter and eat."[30] It is quite possible that Yeshua made the connection between the matzah and His body at this point.

The New Testament shows that the early believers were well aware of the connection between the matzah and Yeshua's body. When Paul wrote, "Clean out the old leaven," which was a reference to the preparations before baking unleavened bread (matzah), he linked it directly to the fact that "Christ our Passover also has been sacrificed" (1 Cor 5:7). That leaven is often a picture of corruption can be seen in other Scriptures as well. This is, for example, how the Lord used it in referring to the "leaven of the Pharisees and Sadducees" in Matthew 16:6. Paul did not want this kind of leaven to characterize the Corinthian church. He did not directly specify that he was referring to the afikoman, but was clearly making a connection between the perfect, sinless, and thus "unleavened" body of Messiah and the unleavened bread eaten at Passover, "as you are in fact unleavened" (1 Cor. 5:7b). This is the same connection that Yeshua made. He may not have identified His body with the afikoman in particular, but there is more than enough reason to conclude that He intentionally identified it with the unleavened bread, or matzah.

Significantly, the Mishnah designates the afikoman as the last thing to be eaten as part of the Seder meal. In the Talmud, b. Pesahim 119b makes it clear that this should be "as much as an olive of unleavened bread at the end." In other words, this olive-size piece of matzah is not an inconsequential amount. The rabbis do not say what the significance of this is, but it seems reasonable to consider it as part of the entire Passover meal prescribed in Exodus 12:8: "They shall eat the flesh that same night, roasted with fire, and they shall eat it with unleavened bread and bitter herbs." In this case the unleavened bread is somewhat symbolic of the meal as a whole. Thus, when Yeshua took the bread and identified it with His body, He identified His body with the whole Paschal sacrifice. We cannot say with full certainty that it was the afikoman that Yeshua took to distribute among His disciples, but it is certain that the afikoman is the epitome of all that the matzah symbolizes during the Passover meal, and therefore the possibility certainly exists that Yeshua identified with the afikoman.

---

seen, the much earlier Mishnah and Talmud refer to the tradition of the afikoman. This lack of mention in the oldest copies of the Haggadah simply highlights the question as to whether Yeshua referred to the afikoman, since this may not have been a universally practiced custom.

29. For parallels of Jesus's words in Matthew 26:26, see Mark 14:22, Luke 22:19, and 1 Corinthians 11:24.

30. Harold A. Sevener, ed., *Messianic Passover Haggadah* (New York: Chosen People Ministries, 1994), 14.

MESSIANIC ANALOGIES

There is no doubt that there is something special about the afikoman. It is a tradition that enters the Seder liturgy quite early as the Yachatz—or breaking of the matzah—and reappears after the meal, when all has been eaten. As Jewish scholar of ancient and biblical law David Daube notes, it is a "telling sign" that at neither occasion is a blessing said over the bread, a sign that the rabbinic establishment may have wanted to downplay the significance of the afikoman.[31] This would be a natural defensive response if they found that it gave Jewish believers in Yeshua an opportunity to use the tradition to point to Yeshua.

In Daube's theory, this downplaying is compounded by the fact that *any* reference to a human redeemer has been virtually expunged from the Haggadah. Thus despite telling the whole story of the Exodus and the redemption from Egypt, the central character, Moses, is only once mentioned. This puts the focus on God as the redeemer, but directs one's attention away from any one person whom God might use.[32]

David Daube was not the only scholar to see startling Messianic symbology in the Passover Seder. The Austrian Jewish art historian and biblical scholar Robert Eisler also wrote on the topic of the afikomen, referring to the Didache and other ancient Jewish texts.[33] Maybe partly because of the pointers provided by Daube, Messianic Jews have long seen an uncanny series of parallels and significance in the role of the afikoman within the Passover. Its initial appearance in a special matzah cover is particularly intriguing. The *matzah tash*, as it is sometimes called, has three pockets (*taschen*, in Yiddish), and one piece of matzah is placed in each of the three pockets of the one matzah tash. There seems to be no authoritative tradition as to why there are three pieces of matzah in three separate compartments, and why it is the second one from which the afikoman is broken off. In what is a natural development, this has given those who celebrate Yeshua in the Passover tradition an opportunity to elaborate with a striking analogy. Just as there are three distinct pieces of matzah in three distinct pockets of the matzah tash, so God identifies Himself as three persons: Father, Son, and Spirit. Further, just as it is always the middle, or second, matzah that is broken for the afikoman, so it was the Second Person of the Three, the Son, who gave His body to be broken for the redemption of His people. The Sephardic tradition is quite instructive in this regard. In Rabbi Marc Angel's words, "The three matsot symbolize three things: the top one symbolizes thought; the middle one symbolizes speech; and the bottom one symbolizes action."[34] From a New Testament perspective, an analogy can be drawn, particularly with the

---

31. Cited in Deborah Bleicher Carmichael, "David Daube on the Eucharist and the Passover Seder," *Journal for the Study of the New Testament* 13, no. 42 (1991): 50, https://doi.org/10.1177/0142064X9101304203.

32. Carmichael, "David Daube on the Eucharist and the Passover Seder," 54.

33. Robert Eisler, "Das Letzte Abendmahl," *Zeitschrift für die neutestamentliche Wissenschaft* 24 (1925): 161–92.

34. Angel, הגדה של פסח כמנהג הספרדים; *A Sephardic Passover Haggadah*, 21.

middle piece symbolizing words, for Yeshua is described as "the Word" (John 1:1) and is the one through whom God has "spoken" to us (Heb. 1:2).

Yet more analogies have been adopted by those of us who see Yeshua in the Passover Seder. Later traditions of breaking the matzah, hiding it, and returning it at the end of the meal are reminders to believers of Jesus's death, burial, and resurrection. The symbolic link between matzah as unleavened bread and Jesus's sinless nature is also apparent to Messianic Jews today. We cannot demonstrate that these traditions all existed at the time of the Last Supper. However, they do exist today and the parallels are hard to avoid. Even so, what Yeshua and His disciples observed and knew at the time remains difficult to discern.

Early on, Jewish believers in Yeshua were very clear on the connection between the Father, the Son, and the Holy Spirit (Matt. 28:19; Didache 7.1, 3). It is always the Son (Yeshua) who is the Second Person mentioned, and it is always the second piece of matzah that is broken in half. When Yeshua said, "This is My body" (Luke 22:19), He took matzah from the meal, and from the context in Luke 22, it seems that He did so at or towards the end of the meal, just before the cup "after they had eaten" (v. 20).

The Messianic significance of the afikoman may very well have been commonly known during the Last Supper, or else why would Jesus identify the breaking of the bread with His death for sin and the cup with His shed blood? We cannot "prove" that every parallel so obvious to Messianic Jews today was present during Jesus's celebration of the Passover. Yet we have reason to believe that the afikoman and its Messianic implications were understood by Yeshua and His disciples. Is it just a coincidence that the afikoman, the last piece of the meal, has found its way into the Passover tradition in the way it has?

CONCLUSION

We began by telling the story of the four types of sons, and in particular the "wise" son who is given the command not to eat of the afikoman after the eating of the Pesach offering. We can now see that the afikoman is laden with significance in Jewish history, pointing to the importance of the Pesach feast. Even more so, Melito of Sardis leads us on in our belief that this tradition was one used by early believers to point to the body of our Messiah, Yeshua, as our Passover offering. We finally are able to see an amazing analogy in the way the afikoman is broken during the Seder, and the identity of our Messiah as the Second Person of Three, the Word of God. Is it just coincidence? We doubt it.

PART 4
COMMUNICATING THE GOSPEL
THROUGH THE PASSOVER

12
PASSOVER AND THE ATONEMENT

MICHAEL COHEN

I grew up in a Jewish home. Every year that I can remember we celebrated the Passover. As a young boy, our family usually attended my *bubbe's*[1] Seder. Throughout the evening, we often made jokes and looked forward to a fast conclusion to the ceremony so that we could get to the matzah ball soup. As I grew older, the Passover of my youth became more of an obligation and not the fun family dinner I enjoyed as a child. In fact, I lost interest in religion in general, including Judaism.

This all changed dramatically when, at the age of twenty-three, I came to faith in Jesus the Messiah. God opened my eyes in so many ways, including a rekindling of my love for my Jewish identity and heritage. I was especially fascinated to find out that Passover points to the work and ministry of the Messiah of Israel, Jesus of Nazareth.

WHY PASSOVER?

This new relationship with God through Jesus the Messiah gave me a greater interest in the Bible and especially the Jewish holidays. As I started to study the Passover in greater depth, I began to have more and more questions, since I now took these matters seriously. I was hungry for the truth and eager to discover the ways in which the Hebrew Scriptures found fulfillment in Jesus. I also came to know Jesus as Yeshua, the Hebrew way to say "Jesus," which means "salvation."

For example, I wondered why God required the blood of an unblemished male lamb (Exod. 12:5–7) as His means of delivering the firstborn males from death and my people from Egyptian bondage. Why did God require that the blood be applied to the lintel and doorposts of the homes where the Israelite people lived (vv. 7, 21–23)? It seemed that God could easily have destroyed Egypt's firstborn and freed the Israelites without the blood of the lamb. Yet God required the blood of an unblemished lamb to

---

1. The word *bubbe* is Yiddish for grandmother.

be smeared on the entryway of the Israelite homes as the means by which He would protect His chosen people from destruction (vv. 11–13, 29). I also wondered why God gave such intricate details regarding the handling of the sacrifice and eating of the meal (vv. 7–13).

I was especially amazed that God chose Passover as the day for Yeshua's death.[2] In my mind this transforms the holiday from a national event, celebrating the universal ideal of freedom from slavery, to one having profound spiritual and eternal significance. I began viewing these passages in Exodus as a narrative filled with types, symbols, and prophetic portraits of greater things to come. This is easy to see when you are looking back to the first Passover through the lens of Yeshua's sacrifice for the sins of the world when He died on the cross, was buried, and rose from the dead on the third day (1 Cor. 15:3–4). For example, the Passover lamb now points to the Lamb of God, Yeshua our Messiah. Redemption goes beyond national freedom to spiritual freedom, forgiveness of sin, and new life and identity. The death of the Messiah on Passover completely changes the way I now view the first Passover and even the way I view the many Passover Seders we celebrated at my bubbe's house.

Ironically, Moses never mentions sin or atonement in Exodus 12. The first time atonement is explicitly linked to sacrifice in Scripture is in reference to the sin offering used in the service to consecrate the priesthood after the Law is given to the nation of Israel: "Thus they shall eat those things by which atonement was made at their ordination and consecration; but a layman shall not eat them, because they are holy" (Exod. 29:33).

And what's more, God has chosen Passover as a backdrop to help us understand the New Covenant for the "forgiveness of sins" (Matt. 26:28). Even though atonement is not specifically linked to the sacrifice of the lamb in Exodus 12, the Passover helps form the foundation for the entire sacrificial system, which God revealed at Sinai and is mentioned in Exodus and detailed in Leviticus and Numbers. The sacrificial system enables us to understand the way God reconciles sinful human beings to Himself, through the shedding of blood. The sacrifice of the lamb in Exodus 12 forms the background that enables us to grasp the truth of atonement in Scripture, leading to the once-for-all atonement made by Yeshua the Messiah (Heb. 9:11–12; 1 Peter 3:18). Passover provides the canvas upon which the portrait of atonement may be illustrated and understood in beautiful and dynamic colors.

ATONEMENT: THE DEFINITION

In the Torah the Lord says to Moses, "For the life of the flesh is in the blood, and I have given it to you on the altar to make atonement for your souls; for it is the blood by reason of the life that makes atonement" (Lev. 17:11). The divine work of atonement to bring humanity back to a right

---

2. For more on the timing of Messiah's death in relation to the Festival of Passover, see chapter 4, "Passover in the Gospel of Luke," by Darrell L. Bock, and chapter 5, "Passover in the Gospel of John," by Mitch Glaser.

relationship with the God of creation is "the great central fact" of the biblical faith.[3] It is the means by which God reconciles His creation back to Himself.[4] Moreover, it is the way that God "raises human life to its highest functioning efficiency."[5] According to Leviticus 17:11, blood is the primary requirement to make atonement for human sin. Blood is an essential part of how God delivered the children of Israel out of Egypt.

A basic dictionary definition of atonement is "satisfaction or reparation for a wrong or injury."[6] In terms of the biblical and theological sense of the word, the Hebrew verb כָּפַר, *kaphar*, means "make an atonement, make reconciliation, purge."[7] From this word the Hebrew noun כִּפֻּר, *kippur*, is derived (used in the plural כִּפֻּרִים, *kippurim*) and means "atonement"; it is used especially in the expression "Day of Atonement,"[8] or Yom Kippur, a national day of observance in Israel. The range of meaning for this Hebrew word can include such actions as "to cover over," "to forgive," "to expiate," "to wipe away," or "to reconcile."[9] Atonement enables differing parties to get along with one another.[10] In Christianity there are multiple theories of atonement such as Christ as victor, satisfaction, penal substitution and exchange, etc.[11] All of the various theories for how God makes atonement for us can be summarized by the following: sin separates humanity from God, and an appropriate payment or action is required to restore and reunite the fellowship with God that was lost in the Garden of Eden when human sin allowed death to enter into the world (Gen. 2:16–17; 3:17–19; 5:5; Rom. 5:12).

In this chapter, we will outline atonement in the following manner. First, atonement recognizes a "broken relationship" between two parties and the desire of both parties to initiate a restoration.[12] Second, an adequate payment is necessary to "cover the breach."[13] Third, the atonement stipulates an appropriate response by the recipient that produces efficacious results for both parties.[14] Fourth, upon completion of the payment and the appropriate

3. John J. Martin, "The Nature of the Atonement," *American Journal of Theology* 14, no. 3 (1910): 385.

4. Martin, "The Nature of the Atonement," 387.

5. Martin, "The Nature of the Atonement," 391.

6. *Dictionary.com Unabridged*, s.v. "atonement," accessed February 2, 2016, http://www.dictionary.com/browse/atonement.

7. R. Laird Harris, "כָּפַר," *Theological Wordbook of the Old Testament*, ed. R. Laird Harris, Gleason L. Archer Jr., and Bruce K. Waltke (Chicago: Moody Press, 1999), 1:452.

8. Harris, *Theological Wordbook of the Old Testament*, 1:452.

9. James Strong, *Strong's Exhaustive Concordance of the Bible* (1890; Peabody, MA: Hendrickson Publishers, 2007), s.v. "3722 כָּפַר."

10. Strong, *Strong's Exhaustive Concordance of the Bible*, s.v. "3722 כָּפַר."

11. Ted Peters, "Models of Atonement," *Theological Brief for PLTS/ITE*, December 10, 2005, PDF file, 19, http://www.plts.edu/faculty-staff/documents/ite_models_atonement.pdf.

12. Vincent Brümmer, "Atonement and Reconciliation," *Religious Studies* 28, no. 4 (1992): 439, 441.

13. H. Wheeler Robinson, "Hebrew Sacrifice and Prophetic Symbolism," *Journal of Theological Studies* 43, no. 171/172 (1942): 129–39, http://www.jstor.org/stable/23957190.

14. Robinson, "Hebrew Sacrifice and Prophetic Symbolism," 129–39; Brümmer, "Atonement and Reconciliation, 450.

response, both sides are now reconciled and there is a transfer or exchange of benefits,[15] which includes the future destiny of the relationship and the responsibility conferred upon both parties. These four stages form a general outline for understanding God's process of atonement.

Throughout the remainder of this chapter we will show how these four stages of God's atonement in relation to the Passover are presented as a way to understand the deeper links between the saving work of Yeshua on the cross and the first Passover in Egypt. Please note that it is simply a tool to help us better understand Scripture, and therefore not every parallel will work perfectly. We hope you find this approach helpful and that it will be a blessing to you. Below is a brief outline of the four stages of the atonement in relation to the first Passover.

The first stage of atonement suggests that there is separation between God and the one to be redeemed, leading to that person's recognition of the need for deliverance. In Egypt, the Israelites are separated from God, His promises, and His Land; therefore the Jewish people "cried out" for deliverance (Exod. 1–4). Second, God secures their deliverance through the offering of an unblemished lamb (Exod. 12:3–6). Third, God requires a faith response through the application of the blood of that lamb to the door (12:7). Finally, there is a transfer of benefits: God establishes new identity, privileges, and obligations for the people He delivers from Egypt (12:8, 24–25; 19:4–6) and fulfills the divine destiny of His people—bringing them through the wilderness to the land of Canaan known as the Promised Land. The Egyptian Passover provides a template for atonement that aligns with Israel's sacrificial system and Yeshua's death on a Roman cross.

We will now look at these stages in more depth.

ATONEMENT STAGE ONE: THE PASSOVER SEPARATION

In the first stage of atonement God recognizes the problem of separation.[16] As early as the Garden of Eden, God notices when we are absent from Him (Gen. 3:8). God provides atonement as a solution to the problem of our separation from Him due to our sin. This is how God restores our relationship with Him.

In the book of Genesis, God had promised that through Abraham's seed, "all the families of the earth will be blessed" (Gen. 12:3). God's promise to Abraham passes through his son Isaac (22:14–18) and then his grandson Jacob (28:13–15) whose name changes to Israel ("he strives with God," 32:28). Jacob's son Joseph is a special child who, through a series of events, saves Jacob's entire family as well as the Egyptians from a harsh, prolonged famine (Gen. 37–44). During the famine, Jacob's entire family, the Hebrews as they were then called, move to Egypt to live under Joseph's care. In this way all of Jacob's offspring came to live in Egypt,

---

15. George Smeaton, *The Doctrine of the Atonement: As Taught by the Apostles; or, The Sayings of the Apostles Exegetically Expounded; with Historical Appendix* (Edinburgh: T&T Clark, 1870), 393.

16. Peters, "Models of Atonement," 11.

and after about four hundred years grew to become a great vast multitude of people. After the death of Joseph, a Pharaoh emerges who does not know this son of Jacob and sets out to persecute the children of Israel. Pharaoh persecutes the Israelites with bitter bondage by requiring them to build storehouses and live their lives in hard labor (Exod. 1:11–14). Pharaoh seeks to decrease the burgeoning population through the murder of their infant male babies, prompting Israel to cry out to the God of their forefathers because of the bondage (2:23). God hears the cry of His people (vv. 24–25) and then initiates deliverance for His people from slavery through His appointed deliverer, Moses (3:10).

The Israelites, as they were later called, were thus separated from their homeland and unable to enter into God's promises to Abraham, which include the land (Gen. 12:7). There may have been many reasons why the people of Israel found themselves separated from the plan and purposes of God at this time. Although sin (other than Pharaoh's) is not mentioned within the Exodus narrative (Exod. 1–15), there could have been specific moral failures that contributed to the broken relationship between God and His people.[17] The sons of Jacob acknowledge their personal sin in Genesis 50, when collectively the brothers beg Joseph, "Please forgive the transgression of the servants of the God of your father" (v. 17). Earlier, God had revealed to Abraham that his offspring will return to the Promised Land, a critical part of the Abrahamic blessing, after the sins of the Amorites were complete (15:7, 13–16). So the transgression of Jacob's sons, the iniquity of the Amorites, as well as the sins of Egypt and Pharaoh's cruelty and control over the Israelites by inflicting bitter bondage (Exod. 1:11–14) and even murdering the male infants (vv. 15–21) all illustrate the impact of sin on the situation of the people of Israel, which in all post-Sinai instances will require atonement.

The God of Israel recognizes Israel's separation as well as Pharaoh's separation and sets out to establish a prescription that will include all people. Prior to their cry for deliverance (Exod. 2:23), God has already initiated a process of deliverance through a special Israelite child named Moses (2:2, 10). This child will grow into a man who receives specific revelation from God to bring the children of Israel out of Egypt (3:10). God commissions Moses along with his brother Aaron (4:27) to be His ambassadors to Pharaoh and instruments to reveal God's power to Pharaoh and Egypt. Thus, the separation of the Israelites and their recognition of their need for deliverance begins the process of atonement.

ATONEMENT STAGE TWO: THE PASSOVER PAYMENT

The second stage of atonement is God's provision to people of an unblemished animal for an offering, which requires shedding that animal's blood. According to Leviticus 17:11, this action will satisfy the payment

---

17. For discussion of an earlier instance of sin that Joseph's brothers commit against him and their father that eventually leads Jacob and his family to reside in Egypt outside the Land of Promise, see chapter 1, "Passover in the Torah," by Robert Walter.

required to atone for "your souls." This instruction will deliver His people from the bondage of slavery in Egypt as well as reconcile them to God and reorient them toward God's promises to Abraham.

The Offering

As mentioned earlier, atonement requires a reparation, payment, or ransom to the offended party. This is why God directs Moses to instruct each family "to take a lamb" on the tenth day of the first month (Exod. 12:3). Each lamb represents a household in Israel, and God requires each household to pay the price for their deliverance. If the household is small, two Israelite families will share a lamb as long as this provides enough for each family member to eat the Passover meal (v. 4).

The specifications for the lamb require it be "an unblemished male a year old," and they can "take it from the sheep or from the goats" (v. 5). The term "unblemished" comes from the Hebrew word תָּמִים, *tamim*, which can also mean "full, whole, upright, perfect," or "blameless" as used of Noah in contrast to the wickedness of humanity in his time (Gen. 6:9).[18] Since the tenth plague is a judgment upon the firstborn of Egypt, God requires a perfect male animal to die in the place of the firstborn sons of Israel.

In order to ensure that the lamb meets the Mosaic criteria, the animal has to live in the Israelite household from the tenth to the fourteenth of the month (Exod. 12:3, 6). The family is to make sure that the animal is perfect, without spot or defect, with no illnesses or inadequacies of any kind. Then, on the fourteenth, "the whole assembly of the congregation of Israel is to kill it at twilight" (v. 6). The purity of the animal, without defect, later becomes a regular requirement for the animal sacrifices according to the Torah given on Mount Sinai (Exod. 24:1–8; Lev. 1:3; 3:1; 4:3; 6:6; 9:3–7; 14:10–18; Num. 6:11–14). When the ritual sacrifices for Passover are reintroduced in the book of Numbers, seven lambs are to be offered daily during the Feast of Unleavened Bread and one goat offered on the first day as a sin offering. Each lamb and the goat are to be offered without blemish as part of the Burnt Offering, which is always performed in the context of atonement (Num. 28:16–22). Thus, atonement will become part of the Passover festival as early as the Israelite journey in the wilderness.

Many years later when Jesus of Nazareth comes to the waters of immersion, John the Baptist announces, "Behold, the Lamb of God who takes away the sin of the world!" (John 1:29). Just as the Passover lamb becomes the necessary means to deliver Israel from Egypt and "take away" Israel's slavery and separation from God, Jesus the Lamb of God, without blemish, comes to deliver all creation from sin and remove its alienation from God (v. 29).

Finally, in reflecting on the life of Messiah, Peter the Apostle describes Jesus Himself as "a lamb unblemished and spotless," the One who came to

---

18. J. Barton Payne, "תָּמַם," *Theological Wordbook of the Old Testament*, ed. R. Laird Harris, Gleason L. Archer, and Bruce K. Waltke (Chicago: Moody Press, 1980), 2:973–74.

ransom all of us who believe in Him from our futile ways and purify our souls (1 Peter 1:17–23).

The Blood

We also understand from Scripture that to make atonement, God requires the shedding of blood in order to justify us and save us from His wrath against sinners (Rom. 5:9–11). The Scripture first reveals the importance of blood after the flood when God blesses Noah and instructs him to be fruitful and multiply and tells him that every moving thing that is alive will be food for him and his family (Gen. 9:1–3). Then, He commands Noah not to eat flesh with blood in it. He tells him that the blood is the life of the animal.

> Only you shall not eat flesh with its life, that is, its blood. (Gen. 9:4)

In Exodus 12:13, the Lord states,

> The blood shall be a sign for you on the houses where you live; and when I see the blood I will pass over you, and no plague will befall you to destroy you when I strike the land of Egypt.

When the destroyer sees the sign, the blood upon the doorposts and lintel, he passes over that home (Exod. 12:23).[19] The lamb's blood provides the basis for saving the firstborn's life (v. 29).[20] In this way the household that offers the lamb's blood makes the necessary payment to redeem the life of the firstborn. The shedding of sacrificial blood thus takes on a central role in the process of atonement. The Torah teaches the following:

> For the life of the flesh is in the blood, and I have given it to you on the altar to make atonement for your souls; for it is the blood by reason of the life that makes atonement. (Lev. 17:11)

> For as for the life of all flesh, its blood is identified with its life. Therefore I said to the sons of Israel, "You are not to eat the blood of any flesh, for the life of all flesh is its blood; whoever eats it shall be cut off." (Lev. 17:14)

In these passages, God is helping the Israelites understand that failure to fulfill the blood requirement in their worship will cause them to be destroyed (Deut. 12:23–30).

Jesus, at His last Passover, states that His blood will be "poured out for many for forgiveness of sins," and will thus inaugurate the New Covenant

---

19. For an alternate interpretative possibility regarding the destroyer, see same discussion in chapter 1 text and note 15.
20. J. H. Roberts, "The Lamb of God," *Neotestamentica* 2 (1968): 43, http://www.jstor.org/stable/43047704.

(Matt. 26:28). Peter, in the passage quoted earlier, says that it is the precious blood of the Lamb without blemish that redeems humanity from its futile ways (1 Peter 1:18–19).

The blood of the Passover lambs shed by the Israelites was the sacrificial means through which God redeemed the Israelites and took them as His people (Exod. 6:7–8). Through Jesus's blood, God redeems both Jews and Gentiles (Gal. 4:4–5; Titus 2:11–14) and propels them forward as His ambassadors and ministers of reconciliation (Acts 20:17–27; 2 Cor. 5:17–21). One of those ministering ambassadors, the Apostle Paul, seems to allude to the Passover when he states that by the blood of Jesus, the people's sins will be "passed over" (Rom. 3:25). Once again we see how the Passover is both a paradigm of atonement and a type or pictorial prophecy of what is to be manifested through the Messiah.

ATONEMENT STAGE THREE: THE PASSOVER CONFESSION OF FAITH

For the third stage of atonement, we recognize that God gave clear instructions to the Israelites regarding what they must do to save the life of their firstborn sons. They would still have died unless the household exercised faith and obeyed God's instructions. On the night of the first Passover, it is not enough to be a descendant of Abraham. God requires an obedient response to His instructions for deliverance. Each Israelite family needs to follow God's requirements in order to save their firstborn male and be set free from Egypt.

Thus, God provides atonement, but we are responsible for exercising faith. And faith leads to obedience and action. In the same manner, the Israelites acknowledge God's instructions and do them.

In the Exodus story, the Lord instructs each household to "take some of the [lamb's] blood and put it on the two doorposts and on the lintel of the houses in which they eat it" (Exod. 12:7). The father or head of the household offers the lamb as a sacrifice and then applies its blood by dipping a bunch of an herbaceous plant called hyssop into the basin containing the lamb's blood and then sprinkling the blood on the doorframe in the specific places God designates. And by these efforts, the Israelites demonstrate faith in His Word.

Faith is an essential component of God's plan of redemption, as atonement must always be personally or nationally embraced by faith in the God who provides. By his obedience and actions our forefather Abraham demonstrated this kind of faith when "he believed in the LORD; and He reckoned it to him as righteousness" (Gen. 15:6). The Israelites had a choice to make on that dreadful night; they could either obey God or fail to exercise faith. Nine prior plagues had provided ample evidence that God was speaking through Moses and what He said came true, so disobedience would have been the height of foolishness.

Speaking of Moses and the Exodus, the author of the book of Hebrews says, "By faith he kept the Passover and the sprinkling of the blood, so that he who destroyed the firstborn would not touch them" (Heb. 11:28). Faith is the necessary response to God's payment for humanity's sin.

The Apostle Paul writes, "For by grace you have been saved through faith; and that not of yourselves, it is the gift of God" (Eph. 2:8). By faith, believers acknowledge their inability to obtain their own freedom. We are called to place our faith in the Lamb of God, Jesus the Messiah, in order to receive forgiveness of sins, much like the children of Israel trusted in God's provision for redemption on that long-ago first Passover.

ATONEMENT STAGE FOUR: THE PASSOVER TRANSFER

The fourth stage of atonement involves an amazing transfer of benefits. If we apply our faith to God's revelation, then we will experience a joyous transfer that includes a new identity, new purposes, and future promises. In the manner of the first Exodus and later on through faith in Jesus, this transfer of benefits is experienced through a celebratory meal and secured by a covenant.

The Gathering Together

The greatest benefit for the Israelites is the deliverance of the firstborn males from "judgment" during the tenth plague (Exod. 12:12–13; 28–30). However, when we think of a transfer of benefits, we recognize God's desire not just to deliver people but to remake them into something new. God tells Moses:

> Speak to all the congregation of Israel, saying, "On the tenth of this month they are each one to take a lamb for themselves, according to their fathers' households, a lamb for each household. Now if the household is too small for a lamb, then he and his neighbor nearest to his house are to take one according to the number of persons in them; according to what each man should eat, you are to divide the lamb." (Exod. 12:3–4).

When the Israelites leave Egypt, they journey not as a nation of slaves, but in households as part of a greater community brought together as one nation united by the commands of God (Exod. 12:11). Eventually, the Lord who saved and delivered them gives them their new identity as a holy people (19:3–6). The sacrifice of the lamb and the smearing of its blood on the door frames begins the process of Israel's transformation from a slave nation into a treasured covenant nation, set apart by God to be in a special relationship with Him (Gen. 12, 15, 17, 22).

As a result of the Passover, God sets Israel on the path to becoming the nation He called them to be. The sacrifices of Leviticus that begin with the Passover offering are stepping stones guiding the Israelites along a path leading to the ultimate, once-for-all sacrifice made by Jesus on the greatest of all Passovers!

The Meal

The next benefit reflects God's desire to be in relationship with His people as revealed in the ceremonial meal. God confirms His relationship with Israel through the peace established at the Passover sacrifice's celebratory meal. On the night of the Passover, the Israelites are brought near to God through a sacrifice (Exod. 12:28), and the meal that followed serves to solemnize the reality of their freedom from bondage (Gen. 12, 15, 17, 22, 28, 35; Exod. 6:6–7).

On Passover, Jesus similarly invites His disciples to eat the unleavened bread, "My body which is given for you," and to drink the cup, "the new covenant in My blood" (Luke 22:19–20), the payment for their deliverance from sin and death. And through His disciples He invites all of us to join Him at the Table for a great celebration leading to our transformation and a personal relationship with God.

The Covenant

A further benefit reveals God's desire to give us a new purpose as reflected in the covenants He provides. God chooses Israel, the descendants of Abram, to be His covenant people (Gen. 12:1–3). He instructs Moses to say to Pharaoh, "Let My people go, that they may serve Me" (Exod. 9:1). Consequently, God calls Israel out of slavery on "eagles' wings" to obey Him and keep His covenant (19:4). The redeemed sons of Jacob will be God's "own possession," a "holy nation," and a "kingdom of priests" (vv. 5–6).[21] The Israelites begin a slow march to Mount Sinai where they will receive the Law and instructions on how to construct the Tabernacle (Exod. 25–40), enabling them to worship God. Atonement will play an important and daily role in their national life, which includes the daily, special, monthly, festival, and most significantly the once-a-year national Day of Atonement (Yom Kippur) sacrifices.

When celebrated, Passover presses an important reset button for the Jewish people, reminding Israel to return to God and live as His covenant people. For example, when the Israelites cross over the Jordan and enter into Canaan, the Promised Land, they commemorate the event by celebrating the Passover (Josh. 5:10). Hundreds of years later during the Assyrians' invasion of the kingdoms of Israel and Judah, Hezekiah initiates a national repentance through the celebration of the Passover (2 Chron. 30:8). When Hilkiah the priest discovers the book of the Law, one of the first actions King Josiah takes is to observe the Passover (2 Chron. 34:14; 35:1–19). Upon their return from exile in Babylon, Ezra reinitiates the observance and celebration of the Passover (Ezra 6:19–22).

Most important, on the night He was betrayed, Yeshua gives new significance to the Passover when He takes the unleavened bread, or matzah, and says, "'This is My body which is given for you; do this in remembrance of Me.' And in the same way He took the cup after they had eaten, saying, 'This cup which is poured out for you is the new covenant in My blood'" (Luke 22:19–20). This New Covenant is the same one God declares through Jeremiah the prophet, in which God promises to write the Torah on our hearts and on our minds and

---

21.   In quoting Exodus 19:5–6, the Apostle Peter in 1 Peter 2:9 calls the redeemed sons of Jacob a "chosen people, a royal priesthood, a holy nation, God's special possession" (NIV), or for the last item a "peculiar people" (KJV).

says He will be our God, and we shall be His people (Jer. 31:31–34). Fifty days after Yeshua's atoning death on the cross for the world's sins, the New Covenant comes into effect and the Torah is written on the hearts of those first believers on the day of Pentecost (*Shavuot*) by the power and life of the Holy Spirit (Acts 2). The same Spirit who raised Yeshua from the dead is now alive in our hearts and in the hearts of all those who are in Messiah (Rom. 8:11)!

The Future Promise

One further benefit involves the destiny of God's people. When the Israelites left Egypt, they received God's promise of a future land. In Exodus 6:8, the Lord says to Moses after the Exodus, "I will bring you to the land which I swore to give to Abraham, Isaac, and Jacob, and I will give it to you for a possession; I am the LORD.'" After forty years of wilderness wanderings, the Israelites receive the promise, enter the Promised Land, and celebrate the Passover (Josh. 5:10). Passover points forward to a greater day of redemption. That day will come when the Lord returns to establish the new heavens and the new earth (2 Peter 3:13; Rev. 21:1–5; cf. Isa. 65:17; 66:22). We look back now to remember that life begins with atonement, but that atonement also provides not only eternal life, but an eternity of benefits to the people of God. Like the Passover, faith in Yeshua's sacrifice is a one-time event that transforms us forever.

CONCLUSION

I remember as a young seeker learning for the first time that Jesus was Jewish. Not only that, but His disciples were Jewish and celebrated the Passover with Him. Further, Jesus fulfills the prophecies about Messiah found in the Hebrew Scriptures. This includes both explicit prophecies such as Isaiah 53 as well as types, symbols, and the beautiful prophetic portraits painted by the authors of Scripture, which I believe includes the Passover to help us recognize Him once He came.

Explicitly, the Passover narrative tells how God delivered the Israelites from Egypt, creating a backdrop for understanding the great biblical themes of salvation, deliverance, and even atonement. Although atonement is never mentioned during the original Passover, everything about the event serves as a template and sets the stage for the sacrificial system's atoning function, pointing towards the ultimate atoning work of Yeshua. This is accomplished in various stages.

First, we have the Israelites living in Egypt under the tyranny of Pharaoh and the Egyptians. Next, there is the payment of an unblemished lamb with its blood shed, which payment frees and ushers in a new reality. Third, there is a faith response reflected in the Israelites' obedience and the application of the blood of the lamb on the doorposts and on the lintel of the houses. Finally, there is the transfer of benefits that provided the Israelites with a new identity, relationship, purpose, and promise as revealed in the corporate worship and celebration of a community meal and journey. Their journey takes God's people through the wilderness to receive a covenant that details a new lifestyle and into the Promised Land as a new nation.

God fulfilled His promise to deliver the children of Abraham, Isaac, and Jacob from their bondage in Egypt (Gen. 15:13–16). God ended their separation and slavery and provided them a new life as His people. He accomplished this task through the Passover lamb, which foreshadowed the sacrificial system and the eventual once-for-all atonement made by Messiah Jesus who died for our sins and rose from the grave, crushing death for all who believe (Acts 13:16–41).

Not only does this first Passover reveal to us God's method of reconciliation through the work of the atonement, but it also gives us confidence that Yeshua of Nazareth is the Jewish Messiah for the Jewish people as well as all the nations on the earth. We can proclaim individually as well as together that he is "the Lamb of God who takes away the sin of the world!" (John 1:29). He has removed the separation between humanity and God by his unblemished life. When we respond in faith to the shedding of His blood applied to the doorposts and lintel of our heart, we enter into a new covenant with Him that provides us with a new identity, relationship, purpose, and an eternal destiny in heaven with Him.

Further, the Exodus propelled the Israelites forward to begin a new life as His holy people (Exod. 19:6). We who believe in Jesus have experienced something similar in that by faith the blood of Yeshua has been applied to the door of our hearts and we have "passed out of death into life" (John 5:24). As God's New Covenant children we have had our sins atoned for. We also have received the gift of eternal life that begins now and lasts forever (John 3:16). This is why we cry out with Paul,

> Clean out the old leaven so that you may be a new lump, just as you are in fact unleavened. For [Messiah] our Passover also has been sacrificed. Therefore let us celebrate the feast, not with old leaven, nor with the leaven of malice and wickedness, but with the unleavened bread of sincerity and truth. (1 Cor. 5:7–8)

The Bible teaches us through prophecy and patterns that the great themes of Scripture revealed at the first Passover culminate in the death of our Messiah Jesus for our sins because He is the Lamb of God who takes away the sin of the world. By acknowledging or even celebrating the Passover, we are able look back and reflect upon this progression of truth revealed at the Exodus—the first Passover—declared fulfilled by Jesus at the Last Supper and by His atoning death, and received through faith by all who know the Lord as their Savior.

13

THE GOSPEL IN THE PASSOVER SEDER

LARRY FELDMAN

*P*assover is the story of redemption. It reveals how God redeemed our people, the Israelites, from the bondage of slavery in Egypt and also delivered "a mixed multitude," perhaps including some Egyptians who chose to identify with the God of Abraham, Isaac, and Jacob (Exod. 12:38). Any and all who acted in faith and obeyed God's instructions given through Moses experienced God's deliverance from His judgment on Egypt.

It is likely that those who offered the lamb originally did not fully comprehend the significance of sacrificing an animal, shedding its blood, and then placing that lamb's blood on the two doorposts and lintel of the house in which they were to eat it (Exod. 12:7). From our vantage point, we recognize that this sacrifice foreshadows the death of the Messiah, Yeshua (Jesus), the Lamb of God who takes away the sin of the world for both Jewish and Gentile people. For everyone who believes and receives Yeshua as their atonement, it is as if, by faith in His atoning sacrifice, they personally put His blood over the doorposts and lintel of their lives and are redeemed from the bondage of sin and death.

The Passover *Seder*, a Hebrew word that means "order" or "service," refers to the ancient ceremonial meal that has become the primary means of celebrating the Passover today.. The Passover Seder proclaims the message of salvation for all people, and each aspect of the ceremonial meal can be used to proclaim the good news of Messiah Yeshua. It makes sense, therefore, that we examine in this chapter the many elements of the Seder, some directly from Scripture and some introduced by Jewish tradition over the years, which point to redemption through Messiah Yeshua's death and resurrection. We will focus on how various aspects and elements of the Passover Seder can be explained to your Jewish friends and family that by faith they might see with hearts unveiled the glory of Messiah in the Passover (2 Cor. 3:12–18).[1]

---

1.   For more on how the Passover Seder can be used to explain the truths of the Gospel to Jewish as

SHARING THE GOOD NEWS THROUGH THE *KARPAS* (DIPPING OF THE PARSLEY)

The Passover ceremony revolves around a plate (called a "Seder plate") with various elements placed on it to remind us of the key aspects of Passover. One such element is green parsley. After initiating the Passover Seder by drinking the first cup of the fruit of the vine, the ceremony continues with the dipping of the parsley (Hebrew, *karpas*). The leader of the Seder, generally the father in the home, asks everyone to take a sprig of the herb and hold it up as he explains its significance. He begins by stating the obvious, that the *karpas* is green. The color is supposed to remind everyone that in springtime, during the first months of the Hebrew calendar, God's mighty arm brought the people of Israel forth from slavery in Egypt to freedom (see appendix 2).

He then goes on to explain that the karpas is dipped twice in salt water. The first time is to remind us that we were redeemed from the bitterness of slavery and many tears. The second time reminds us that we were brought forth through the Red Sea, which God parted for us but closed over the Egyptians. The Red Sea is also salty and so this second dipping once more reminds us of God's deliverance.

The most significant part of this ceremony is understanding the reason why we dip at all. The explanation is found in the Bible, in the book of Exodus:

> Then Moses called for all the elders of Israel and said to them, "Go and take for yourselves lambs according to your families, and slay the Passover lamb. You shall take a bunch of hyssop and dip it in the blood which is in the basin, and apply some of the blood that is in the basin to the lintel and the two doorposts; and none of you shall go outside the door of his house until morning. For the LORD will pass through to smite the Egyptians; and when He sees the blood on the lintel and on the two doorposts, the LORD will pass over the door and will not allow the destroyer to come in to your houses to smite you. (Exod. 12:21–23)

The karpas, or parsley, is symbolic of the hyssop that the Israelites dipped into the blood and placed on their doors, demonstrating their faith and trust that God would fulfill the promise He had made concerning the slaying of the firstborn. Because of the blood, they were "passed over," and their first-born sons were spared the tenth plague.

In hindsight we recognize that this is a picture of our deliverance from the consequences of sin, which includes not just physical death, but spiritual death or separation from God. Viewing the Seder in light of its fulfillment in Yeshua the Messiah, we see the dipping of the parsley in salt water as a declaration that one day all our tears will be wiped away (Rev. 21:4), and until then our sorrows are made sweet through knowing the Lord. When we put our faith in Him, His blood is placed over the doorposts and lintel

---

well as non-Jewish friends, see chapter 16, "Passover in Your Home," by Cathy Wilson, and chapter 18, "A Messianic Family Haggadah," by the staff of Chosen People Ministries.

of our hearts and lives. God sees that the blood of the Lamb covers our sin, His judgment passes over us, and we pass from death to life (John 5:24). The Lamb took our punishment upon Himself and we have been set free from the bondage of sin and death.

As the Apostle Paul writes to the Roman believers,

> But now having been freed from sin and enslaved to God, you derive your benefit, resulting in sanctification, and the outcome, eternal life. For the wages of sin is death, but the free gift of God is eternal life in Christ Jesus our Lord. (Rom. 6:22–23)

During Passover we look back at the biblical text through the lens of the modern Seder and see these beautiful parallels of redemption that help us explain the truths of the Gospel to our Jewish friends and even to our Gentile friends as well. We view the dipping of the parsley into salt water as a reminder of God's cure for the bitterness of life caused by sin. By linking the redemption found in Jesus to the Passover tradition, it will help your Jewish friends better understand what God has done for us through the Messiah.

SHARING THE GOOD NEWS THROUGH THE *YACHATZ* (BREAKING OF THE MIDDLE MATZAH)

The next Passover ceremony helping us share the Gospel with our Jewish friends is the *Yachatz* (lit., "divide"), the breaking of the middle *matzah* (unleavened bread). We set the Seder table with an item known as a *matzah tash*—often a nicely embroidered pouch containing three compartments, each holding a piece of matzah. Early in the Seder, the leader picks up the matzah tash and explains the significance of the three different pieces of matzah. There are two traditional explanations. One view is that the three compartments represent the Patriarchs: Abraham, Isaac, and Jacob. A second interpretation is that they represent the three categories of Jewish people: priests, Levites, and laymen. Having identified the matzah tash, the leader removes the middle piece of matzah, breaks it in half, wraps one half in a linen cloth, and hides it, so it can be brought back at a later time in the ceremony.

Throughout the centuries, Jewish people have added varying traditions to the Seder. But the source of this tradition of the Yachatz, the breaking the middle matzah, is unknown. Some Jewish scholars maintain that early Jewish followers of Yeshua added it to their Seder and it was adopted by traditional Judaism at a later date. There are volumes of material written on the topic, and we have included a chapter by Daniel Nessim that will enable you to further explore this mysterious tradition (see chapter 11, "Passover and the Afikoman").

As Messianic Jews, we see the Passover ceremony through three lenses: the Hebrew Scriptures, Jewish tradition, and the New Testament, or New Covenant Scriptures. We are not sure to what degree the Jewish traditions surrounding the Yachatz had been developed during the time of Jesus. Nonetheless, we can use this symbol to help explain the Gospel to those we love.

Based upon what is recorded in Luke 22, it seems possible that the ceremony involving the three pieces of matzah may have already been known by the time of the Last Supper. We do know that Yeshua identified with the broken matzah: "When He had taken some bread and given thanks, He broke it and gave it to them, saying, 'This is My body which is given for you; do this in remembrance of Me'" (Luke 22:19). Therefore we find a good basis for explaining the Gospel in light of the Yachatz to our Jewish friends. It is wise to use known symbols and work our way forward, from the known to the unknown, in explaining the Gospel to those we love.

Most people raised in a Jewish home, celebrating the Passover every year, know what Yachatz is and understand the tradition of breaking the middle piece of matzah, wrapping it, hiding it, and bringing it back. This is why, when we present the Gospel through the Yachatz tradition, we are beginning with what is already well understood by our Jewish friends and linking this symbol to Jesus.

As Messianic Jews we see a third option for the symbolism of the matzah tash and its three compartments in that they represent the unity of God: Father, Son, and Holy Spirit, three in one, and one in three. We also see the breaking of the middle matzah as symbolic of our Messiah's death, the wrapping of the middle piece of matzah as speaking of His burial, and the bringing back of the hidden matzah as pointing to His resurrection. We are not dogmatically asserting that the modern Messianic view is exactly the same as the Passover ceremony celebrated by Jesus and His disciples. But we do know that during a Passover meal right before His arrest and crucifixion, Jesus broke a matzah and used it to represent His body, given for us (Luke 22:19). By using these traditional symbols you will be able to engage with your Jewish friends at a whole new level of familiarity. We pray this link between symbol and reality will help your friends better understand that the Gospel is not as foreign as most Jewish people are raised to believe.

SHARING THE GOOD NEWS THROUGH "*DAYENU*" ("IT WOULD HAVE BEEN ENOUGH")

During the Seder, the participants give thanks to God for all His benefits to us by singing a special song called "*Dayenu*" ("it would have been enough").[2] The song expresses the idea that if God had limited His gifts to Israel—it would have been enough and we would have been satisfied. Yet God, acting in His rich mercy, love, and faithfulness, did far more for us than we could ever imagine, and therefore we celebrate His great kindness.

Each verse of the song recounts an aspect of the Passover event, and after each verse we joyfully sing the chorus "*Dayenu*." For instance, one verse declares, "If He had merely rescued us from Egypt, but had not punished the Egyptians, it would have been enough." Other verses continue the celebration

---

2. For more on "*Dayenu*," see discussion in chapter 7, "Passover, the Temple, and the Early Church," by Scott P. Nassau.

of all God did for us: He punished the Egyptians, destroyed their gods, slew their firstborn, gave us their property, split the Red Sea, gave us dry land on which to cross, drowned our enemies, sustained us in the desert for forty years, fed us manna, gave us the Torah, gave us the Shabbat, brought us to Mount Sinai, led us into the Promised Land, and built us a Temple. If He had not done any of these, it would have been enough and we would still have been satisfied.

As followers of Yeshua, we can add one more verse that is not especially traditional! If God had only given us Messiah Yeshua and provided for our redemption through His death and resurrection, it would have been enough. Nevertheless, God gave us far more than the immediate gift of salvation. As Yeshua Himself said, "I came that they may have life, and have it abundantly" (John 10:10). It is true, and we are satisfied that through believing the good news, the message about the death and resurrection of the Messiah Yeshua, we have been granted forgiveness of sin and the gift of eternal life. Yet He gives us so much more. He generously provides us with an abundant life filled with love, joy, peace, fulfillment, and purpose.

The *"Dayenu"* song reminds us that by believing the good news of Yeshua we will be satisfied for all eternity. The moment of salvation is just the beginning of the abundant life we will enjoy forever. This is why one of the best ways to communicate the Gospel to your Jewish friends is to share your personal testimony. Do not stop at the point where you embraced Yeshua as your Lord and Savior—continue on to tell your friends about the great blessings, answers to prayer, and joy you have received because you know and serve Him. Your testimony is the most powerful tool you have to demonstrate the truth of the Gospel. You can also encourage your friends to go online and watch the video testimonies posted on the I Found Shalom site (www.ifoundshalom.com). It will be a great blessing to them and will help them understand why you are shouting *Dayenu*!

SHARING THE GOOD NEWS THROUGH THE *ZEROAH* (SHANKBONE)

Rabban Gamaliel said that in order for one to discharge his Passover duty, he must discuss three elements: the shankbone of a lamb, the matzah, and the bitter herb.[3] Therefore, after the *"Dayenu"* song, the Seder leader picks up a lamb shankbone to discuss this essential part of the Seder. The Seder plate includes a place for the *zeroah*, or shankbone of a lamb, in order

---

3. See Mishnah Pesahim 10:5. Some have conjectured that the reason for Gamaliel's inclusion of these three Passover essentials is as a response to early followers of Yeshua. From an early date, followers of Yeshua identified the lamb with Yeshua, the Lamb of God who takes away the sin of the world; the matzah with the body of Yeshua, given as a sacrificial atonement as expressed in the Eucharist (Lord's Supper or Communion); and the bitter herbs, descriptive of the suffering of Yeshua for sin. Hence, Gamaliel called for a discussion of these elements to counter those interpretations, since they so clearly depict Yeshua. Professor of Jewish History Israel J. Yuval states, "Rabban Gamaliel is demanding a declaration of loyalty to the Jewish interpretations and, therefore, an implicit denial of the Christian alternative" ("Easter and Passover as Early Jewish-Christian Dialogue," 107).

to recall the sacrificial lambs of the first Passover. Regarding that Egyptian Passover, God commands Moses,

> Speak to all the congregation of Israel, saying, "On the tenth of this month they are each one to take a lamb for themselves, according to their fathers' households, a lamb for each household. . . . Your lamb shall be an unblemished male a year old; you may take it from the sheep or from the goats. You shall keep it until the fourteenth day of the same month, then the whole assembly of the congregation of Israel is to kill it at twilight. . . . They shall eat the flesh that same night, roasted with fire, and they shall eat it with unleavened bread and bitter herbs." (Exod. 12:3, 5–6, 8)

A change does occur later in the unfolding of the Torah. Moses tells the people of Israel,

> You are not allowed to sacrifice the Passover in any of your towns which the LORD your God is giving you; but at the place where the LORD your God chooses to establish His name, you shall sacrifice the Passover in the evening at sunset, at the time that you came out of Egypt. (Deut. 16:5–6)

So, in time, the sacrifice of the lambs became attached to the Temple.

However, after the Temple was destroyed in 70 C.E., there was no longer a place to perform this sacrifice, and eating lamb as part of the Seder became a point of disagreement within the wider Jewish community. As the years went by, the raising of the shankbone of a lamb became a symbol of the destruction of the Temple and the sacrifices of previous days. Presently, due to differences in rabbinic rulings, Sephardic Jews eat lamb as part of their Passover tradition, but for Ashkenazic Jews lamb too closely resembles the Pascal lamb sacrifice, so they eat chicken, beef or turkey instead.

In the book of Leviticus, God gives the Jewish people instructions through Moses regarding the full range of sacrifices. There are many different types of offerings, including those sacrificed on behalf of the Israelites as atonement for their sin. The offerings of the Passover are not specifically identified in that way, but when viewed through the lens of the original Passover sacrifice and linked to the Last Supper of Jesus, it is easy to see the Passover sacrifice as another substitutionary offering that serves as a type of the ultimate sacrifice God will effect through the work of His Son. This gives new and deeper meaning to the heart cry of John the Baptist:

> The next day he saw Jesus coming to him and said, "Behold, the Lamb of God who takes away the sin of the world!" (John 1:29)

The New Covenant Scriptures declare that the offerings of sheep and goats could never take away sin, but they were prophetic shadows and types of the once-for-all offering of our Messiah Yeshua (Heb. 10:4). The Prophet Isaiah speaks of the Servant of the Lord who will function as the true Lamb that is to come for all Israel and the world.

> But He was pierced through for our transgressions,
> He was crushed for our iniquities;
> The chastening for our well-being fell upon Him,
> And by His scourging we are healed.
> All of us like sheep have gone astray,
> Each of us has turned to his own way;
> But the LORD has caused the iniquity of us all to fall on Him.
>
> He was oppressed and He was afflicted,
> Yet He did not open His mouth;
> Like a lamb that is led to slaughter,
> And like a sheep that is silent before its shearers,
> So He did not open His mouth. (Isa. 53:5–7)

Although the shankbone is a "stand-in" for the lamb no longer offered, we also recognize that the Passover sacrifice was itself a type or "stand-in" for the future Messiah who would take away the sin of the world. When the Israelites in Egypt placed the blood of their sacrificial Passover lambs on the doorposts of their houses, God "passed over" them and judged Egypt by slaying their firstborn males.

In the same way, when anyone today applies the blood of Messiah Yeshua to the doorposts of their heart by faith, God promises that His holy judgment will "pass over." All who put their trust in Messiah's death as their Passover Lamb will experience the promise of salvation and deliverance from the bondage of sin and death. The Gospel can clearly be seen in lifting up the shankbone of the lamb during the Seder meal.

It is our hope and prayer that your Jewish friends will see this connection between the Exodus story, the Passover Seder, and Yeshua. May God give you wisdom in explaining these profound truths to your Jewish friends.

SHARING THE GOOD NEWS THROUGH THE *MATZAH*

Rabban Gamaliel's second Passover essential, after the lamb shankbone, is to include a discussion of the *matzah* (unleavened bread). The leader of the Seder raises a piece of the matzah and tells the story of how the people of Israel were forced to flee Egypt in great haste. They had no time to bake their bread and could not wait for the dough to rise. The sun then beat down on the dough as they carried it along and baked it into unleavened bread called matzah. According to the Torah, "They baked the dough which they had brought out of Egypt into cakes of unleavened bread. For it had not become leavened, since they were driven out of Egypt and could not delay, nor had they prepared any provisions for themselves" (Exod. 12:39).

Messianic believers in Yeshua include reflections on intriguing parallels between matzah and the Messiah. After all, He is not only the Lamb of God, but also the bread of life. Matzah is unleavened, is made striped, and has holes or pierce marks. Each of these illustrates truths about Yeshua the Messiah.

Leaven in Scripture is frequently a symbol of sin (cf. 1 Cor. 5:6–8; Matt. 16:6). Therefore, the bread without leaven reminds us of Messiah's purity as He lived life on earth without sin (Heb. 4:15). This was predicted by the prophet Isaiah, when speaking of Messiah's brutal death, indicated that "He had done no violence, nor was there any deceit in His mouth" (Isa. 53:9; cf. 1 Peter 2:22).

The matzah is striped as Yeshua was striped by a Roman whip. This reminds us of Isaiah's prediction that "by His scourging we are healed" (Isa. 53:5).

Additionally, the matzah is pierced.[4] It was foretold that the Servant of the Lord would be pierced for our sins. The prophet Isaiah wrote:

> Surely our griefs He Himself bore,
> And our sorrows He carried;
> Yet we ourselves esteemed Him stricken,
> Smitten of God, and afflicted.
> But He was pierced through for our transgressions,
> He was crushed for our iniquities;
> The chastening for our well-being fell upon Him. (Isa. 53:4–5)

This is also what David predicted one thousand years before Yeshua's crucifixion,

> For dogs have surrounded me;
> A band of evildoers has encompassed me;
> They pierced my hands and my feet.
> I can count all my bones.
> They look, they stare at me;
> They divide my garments among them,
> And for my clothing they cast lots. (Ps. 22:16–18)

The great prophet Zechariah foretold the day when the Jewish people would recognize Yeshua as Israel's Messiah.

> I will pour out on the house of David and on the inhabitants of Jerusalem, the Spirit of grace and of supplication, so that they will look on Me whom they have pierced; and they will mourn for Him, as one mourns for an only son, and they will weep bitterly over Him like the bitter weeping over a firstborn. (Zech. 12:10)

---

4. Perforating matzah has always been the tradition in order to slow down the fermentation process (cf. Ari Greenspan, Ari Z. Zivotofsky, and Elli Wohlgelernter, "Matzah" in *EncJud*, 13:689–70).

The matzah is essential both to the story of the Exodus and to the life and witness of Yeshua and His suffering. It reveals a crucial element of the good news: a sinless Messiah will be striped with a Roman whip and pierced by a Roman spear and cruel nails, all to redeem us from slavery to sin.

SHARING THE GOOD NEWS THROUGH THE *BEITZAH* (EGG)

Another element on the Passover Seder plate is the *beitzah* (egg), which is either hard-boiled or roasted. Although the egg is a traditional element on the Seder plate, it is notable that nothing in the Passover liturgy discusses it. Traditionally, the egg is peeled and dipped in salt water before it is eaten.

It reminds us of a second type of offering, the Festival Offering, the *hagigah* in Hebrew, which was brought to the Temple on each of the *Shalosh Regalim* (lit., "three feet," meaning the three pilgrimage holidays): Passover (*Pesach*), Pentecost (*Shavuot*), and Tabernacles (*Sukkot*).

> Three times in a year all your males shall appear before the LORD your God in the place which He chooses, at the Feast of Unleavened Bread and at the Feast of Weeks and at the Feast of Booths, and they shall not appear before the LORD empty-handed. Every man shall give as he is able, according to the blessing of the LORD your God which He has given you. (Deut. 16:16–17)

Traditionally, this represented an additional festival sacrifice. Since the Holy Temple was destroyed in 70 C.E. by the Romans, it is no longer possible to offer the sacrifice. Therefore, the egg is used to commemorate this annual *hagigah* sacrifice. We show our sorrow over the Temple's destruction by dipping the egg in salt water (symbolic of tears) and eating it.

Followers of Messiah Yeshua have good news—Messiah came and offered Himself as a final sacrifice, making salvation available for all who trust in Him. The writer of Hebrews says that "not through the blood of goats and calves, but through His own blood, He [Messiah Yeshua] entered the holy place *once for all*, having obtained eternal redemption" (Heb. 9:12, emphasis added). He goes on to say that Messiah was "offered once to bear the sins of many" (v. 28).

There is no need to lament the lack of availability of the festival sacrifice. So why would a Messianic believer still eat the egg in salt water? The answer is to express sorrow for all those who do not yet know and believe in the good news of Messiah Yeshua's ultimate and eternal sacrifice.

SHARING THE GOOD NEWS THROUGH THE *AFIKOMAN* (BROKEN MATZAH)

After the actual Passover meal and just prior to partaking of the third cup (the cup of redemption), it is traditional to search for the matzah that was broken and hidden earlier in the Seder (see discussion above on the Yachatz). Remember, the middle piece of matzah was removed from the matzah tash, broken, wrapped in a linen cloth, and then hidden. After the meal, the children search for this hidden matzah. Once it is found, the leader purchases it back from the finder and distributes olive-size pieces of the matzah for all participants to eat.

The origin of this tradition and of its name, the *afikoman*, is unclear.[5] Traditionally, Judaism defines the word *afikoman* as "dessert," and thus it is the last food to be eaten after the meal. Even the cakes and other Passover desserts must be consumed before the afikoman. While the Temple still stood, participants in a Seder would save a piece of the sacrificial Passover lamb as the final food consumed. Thus, the last taste on a person's palate would be the lamb, so central to the celebration and commemoration of Passover (cf. m. Pesahim 10:8; b. Pesahim 119b–120a).

One explanation for the afikoman is that it harks back to a custom begun by early Jewish followers of the Messiah Yeshua, which involved eating a small piece of matzah instead of lamb at the close of the Passover meal. Some Jewish scholars suggest that after the destruction of the Temple, traditional Judaism adopted this substitution of matzah for lamb without recognizing its symbolic significance for early Jewish followers of Yeshua.[6] As for the word *afikoman* itself, although traditionally defined as "dessert," its derivation is from Greek and actually means "the one who has come," a clear Messianic title.[7]

With this in mind, the significance of eating the afikoman becomes apparent. As all participants prepare to partake of the third cup, the middle matzah that was previously broken, wrapped in linen, and hidden is now returned to complete the memorial meal. This piece of matzah now represents the body of Yeshua, offered as a sacrifice.

Two thousand years ago, Yeshua took the matzah and told His followers, "Take, eat; this is my body," "which is given for you" (Matt. 26:26; Luke 22:19; cf. 1 Cor. 11:24). Just as the Passover lamb pointed to the Messiah, so the bread points back to our Messiah Yeshua. The breaking of the middle matzah is a picture of the death of the Messiah. When we add the search for the afikoman and its return, or Yeshua's resurrection, to the Seder table,

---

5. For more on the afikoman tradition, see chapter 11, "Passover and the Afikoman," by Daniel Nessim.

6. This was first proposed in a two-part article appearing in a German language journal by Austrian Jewish scholar Robert Eisler, "Das Letzte Abendmahl" (Part 1), *Zeitschrift für die neutestamentliche Wissenschaft und die Kunde der älteren Kirche* 24 (1925): 161–92; Robert Eisler, "Das Letzte Abendmahl" (Part 2), *Zeitschrift für die neutestamentliche Wissenschaft und die Kunde der älteren Kirche* 25 (1926): 5–37.

7. The twentieth century's preeminent Jewish scholar of ancient and biblical law, David Daube, supports Eisler's view that the afikoman came from the Seders of ancient Jewish followers of Yeshua and is derived from the Greek Messianic title, meaning "the one who has come" (cf. David Daube, *He That Cometh* [London: Council for Christian-Jewish Understanding, 1966], 6–14; reprinted in David Daube, *New Testament Judaism*, vol. 2 of *Collected Works of David Daube*, ed. Calum M. Carmichael, Studies in Comparative Legal History [Berkeley: Robbins Collection Publications / University of California at Berkeley, 2000], 429–40). His views on the origins of the Eucharist and its connection to the Seder are also discussed in his article, "The Earliest Structure of the Gospels," *New Testament Studies* 5, no. 3 (1959), 174–87.

there is a powerful picture of the Gospel, namely, the death and resurrection of Messiah Yeshua.

While especially meaningful to believers in Yeshua, these symbols also enable you to share the story of the Gospel with nonbelievers in a very picturesque way. This is a wonderful tool to tell your Jewish friends the very Jewish story of Passover's ultimate fulfillment in Yeshua.

SHARING THE GOOD NEWS THROUGH THE THIRD CUP (THE CUP OF REDEMPTION)

After the eating of the afikoman, the Seder participants turn their attention to the third cup, called the Cup of Redemption. This cup represents the price of redemption for the deliverance of the people of Israel from Egyptian bondage. Through Moses, God told the Israelites to sacrifice a lamb and smear its blood upon the doorposts and lintels of their houses. On that first Passover, at midnight, when the Lord passed through Egypt, He struck down the firstborn in the land. All the people who placed the blood on their houses were spared the death of their firstborn, as God had promised:

> For I will go through the land of Egypt on that night, and will strike down all the firstborn in the land of Egypt, both man and beast; and against all the gods of Egypt I will execute judgments—I am the LORD. The blood shall be a sign for you on the houses where you live; and when I see the blood I will pass over you, and no plague will befall you to destroy you when I strike the land of Egypt. (Exod. 12:12–13)

The cup of redemption symbolizes the purchase price paid for the release of the people of Israel from Egypt. It also speaks of a greater purchase price, for our redemption from sin and death through the shed blood of Yeshua.

Yeshua took the cup after the meal and said, "This cup which is poured out for you is the new covenant in my blood" (Luke 22:20). The blood of the Passover lamb pointed to this greater story of redemption: that Yeshua would die, pour out His blood, and redeem all those who would believe by faith and put their trust in Him. The Apostle Peter writes,

> You were not redeemed with perishable things like silver or gold from your futile way of life inherited from your forefathers, but with precious blood, as of a lamb unblemished and spotless, the blood of Christ. (1 Peter 1:18–19)

The good news of the Gospel flows from the cup each time our lips touch the sweet fruit of the vine proclaiming the magnificent truth of Yeshua's sacrificial death for all. As Paul again writes to the mostly Gentile Corinthian believers,

> In the same way He took the cup also after supper, saying, "This cup is the new covenant in My blood; do this, as often as you drink it, in remembrance

of Me." For as often as you eat this bread and drink the cup, you proclaim the Lord's death until He comes. (1 Cor. 11:25–26)

Remember, your Jewish friends are not familiar with the Christian tradition of the Lord's Supper or Communion. However, with some patient explanation, you can help them understand how important the Passover is to you and that it is the very basis for your salvation. They will be astonished to learn that a Jewish tradition fulfilled by Jesus means so much to you personally. This is a great way to build common ground between yourself and the Jewish people you are praying will become followers of the Lamb of God.

SHARING THE GOOD NEWS THROUGH ELIYAHU (THE CUP OF ELIJAH)

Near the conclusion of the Passover Seder, there is a significant ceremony related to the prophet Elijah. In fact, Elijah is the invited guest to every Seder. Therefore, there is always an extra place setting for Elijah at each Seder. If 20 people will be attending the Seder, the table must be set for 21. If 100 attend, there must be 101 place settings.

According to the prophet Malachi, God's messenger must come before the Messiah to usher in the times of the Lord. He writes,

> "Behold, I am going to send My messenger, and he will clear the way before Me. And the Lord, whom you seek, will suddenly come to His temple; and the messenger of the covenant, in whom you delight, behold, He is coming," says the LORD of hosts. (Mal. 3:1)

Furthermore, the prophet declares,

> Behold, I am going to send you Elijah the prophet before the coming of the great and terrible day of the LORD. (Mal. 4:5)

According to Jewish tradition, Elijah will announce the coming of the Messiah during the Passover Seder. So at the end of the meal, the leader will have someone go to the door to see if Elijah is there. When the door is opened, the leader will ask if Elijah has come tonight. When told that he has not, the leader states that Elijah is not here tonight and that maybe next year he will come, in which case we would all celebrate Passover in Jerusalem with the Messiah for whom we wait.

According to the New Covenant Scriptures, someone did come who was like Elijah. He wore a similar garment, belt, ate a similar diet, and preached a message of repentance in the desert. His message was to turn back to God and prepare for the coming of the Messiah.

When the disciples asked Yeshua why Elijah must come first, He replied that Elijah is still coming and will restore all things. But Yeshua added that in a sense, Elijah already came (Matt. 17:12). To explain what He meant, He declared that if they cared to accept it, John the Baptist is the Elijah who was to come. Certainly, he was not stating that John was literally Elijah, but that John had come in the power and spirit of Elijah. Jesus goes on to say that they (the Jewish leaders) did not recognize John, but did to him whatever they wished. Yeshua compared this rejection of John to the Jewish leaders' rejection of Him; Yeshua had come, but Israel's leaders did not recognize Him as their Messiah and would do to Him as they wished also.

How sad that during Passover, Jewish people all over the world say that Elijah is not here and do not realize that he did indeed come. We missed John the Baptizer who had come in the power and spirit of Elijah, and also missed that Yeshua, the Messiah had come soon thereafter.

It is during the cup of Elijah that Messianic Jewish celebrants declare that Elijah has already come and introduced the Messiah, Yeshua, to the world. It is John who said, "'I am not the Christ,' but, 'I have been sent ahead of Him'" (John 3:28).

At the conclusion of the Seder, the long wait begins again. The cup of Elijah is poured into the sink and the Jewish people sing the poignant song "Next Year in Jerusalem." How heartbreaking it is to realize that John indeed was an Elijah-like prophet who had prepared the way for the Lord. And the Lord Himself had come—Jesus the Messiah—though not exactly as expected. He came in humility to fulfill the mandate of His first coming—to suffer and die for the sins of both Jews and Gentiles. His second coming will be quite different. At that point, He will come to judge the living and the dead and to establish His kingdom in Jerusalem as promised. We look forward to that great day and with the Jewish community sing, "Next Year in Jerusalem," hoping that He will return soon.

Until then, we rejoice in the holy obligation given to us to share the good news with our Jewish friends and neighbors, proclaiming that the Messiah has come.

CONCLUSION

In so many ways, the Passover Seder makes the Good News Jewish-friendly and profoundly clear. If people are open to God and His message, the elements of the Seder will speak to their hearts and reveal the truth that Yeshua is the Messiah of Israel, the Passover Lamb (Rom.10:1; 1 Cor. 5:7).

Yeshua's death, burial, and resurrection are observed from the very beginning of the dipping of the parsley to the last cup at the table, the cup of Elijah. It is these elements that make it possible to use the Passover Seder to explain the Gospel to your Jewish friends and relatives.

He is the One who came, the Bread of Life, the Lamb of God, and He provides the cup of salvation to all who drink. This is the glorious message He has given us to share with our friends; to the Jew first and also to the Gentiles. May the Lord empower and bless you as you show how the Passover points to Jesus the Messiah.

14

SERMON: "JESUS, THE LAMB OF GOD"

RICHARD E. FREEMAN

*H*ave you ever noticed how often lambs or sheep are mentioned in the Bible? The title "Lamb of God" has become an important part of our common understanding of the person and work of Jesus the Messiah. John the Baptist sees Jesus approaching the Jordan River and cries out, "Behold, the Lamb of God who takes away the sin of the world!" (John 1:29).

The fifty-third chapter of Isaiah, a passage sometimes called the Gospel in the Old Testament, describes Jesus the Servant of the Lord in this way, "Like a lamb that is led to slaughter, and like a sheep that is silent before its shearers, so He did not open His mouth" (Isa. 53:7). This is the passage the Ethiopian eunuch is reading when Philip preaches Jesus to him (Acts 8:32–35). The book of Revelation uses the term "Lamb" to describe Jesus more than thirty times. Jesus and the term "Lamb" are intrinsically related, and the connection point is Passover. There is also an amazing prophetic parallel between the last week of Jesus and the story of the first Passover as found in Exodus 12.

A LAMB FOR EACH HOUSEHOLD

The story of the Passover begins with careful instructions given to the Israelites regarding a lamb. Moses writes,

> Speak to all the congregation of Israel, saying, "On the tenth of this month they are each one to take a lamb for themselves, according to their fathers' households, a lamb for each household." (Exod. 12:3)

The children of Israel are told here to choose a lamb and bring it into the household on the tenth day of the first month, which is the Hebrew month of Nisan. There is a difference of opinion among commentators as to whether there was a day on which a lamb was selected prior to it being brought into the household. Some say a lamb was selected on the ninth of Nisan and then brought into the household on the tenth day; others say a lamb was selected on the same day it was brought into the household, both occurring on the tenth of Nisan.

The next set of instructions involved the community. Moses continues,

> Now if the household is too small for a lamb, then he and his neighbor nearest to his house are to take one according to the number of persons in them; according to what each man should eat, you are to divide the lamb. (Exod. 12:4)

Family units are commanded here to come together and feast upon the lamb. But if a family unit does not exist and there are perhaps only two single people, who probably cannot eat an entire lamb, then the family units are allowed to include others and this newly combined community will share it. The lamb belongs to this newly combined community. Moses adds a qualification regarding the health and age of the lamb,

> Your lamb shall be an unblemished male a year old; you may take it from the sheep or from the goats. You shall keep it until the fourteenth day of the same month, then the whole assembly of the congregation of Israel is to kill it at twilight. (vv. 5–6)

This is all very personal as indicated by the change in pronoun. The instructions begin with selecting "a lamb." Then with the combining of smaller households to make one community, "a lamb" becomes identifiably, "the lamb." Finally, "the lamb" becomes "your lamb," marking the animal as part of the particular community. The Passover is intended to be very personal and yet also an event and experience shared by the entire community.

THE FIRST PASSOVER

Imagine what this first Passover might have looked like more than three thousand years ago. The Exodus from Egypt is finally at hand after four hundred years of slavery. Nine horrific plagues have all but devastated the land of Egypt, and the people of Israel hold their breath with great anticipation, wondering what God will do next. Word comes to the people that a tenth plague will be the last and they should be prepared to leave.

Imagine now that it is the tenth day of Nisan and the family is gathered together in their dwelling: Mom, the children, and Dad. Then Papa, the head of that family and of the little community, brings the little lamb that was selected into the house. The children are excited about their new pet! Papa on the other hand is somber. He knows what is in store for this newest member of the family and community. For Moses has told the people, "You shall keep [the lamb] until the fourteenth day of the same month, then the whole assembly of the congregation of Israel is to kill it at twilight" (Exod. 12:6).

The lamb is to be unblemished, with no imperfections whatsoever. In order to determine that this lamb is unblemished and without imperfections, the fathers, the heads of those little communities, have to watch their lambs interact within the community. They have to be sure that the lamb is perfect in order for it to be the sacrifice that will save them from the last plague. Imagine how hard it must have been for the children (and adults) to care for this animal, treat it like a pet, and then watch it die and eat it. But that is exactly what will happen, and ultimately the fathers and the leaders of various households will have to acknowledge that the lambs are worthy to be slain. The whole assembly of the congregation of Israel will kill the lambs all at the same time, at twilight, as though all the lambs are killed as one.

The time for redemption is at hand. The destroyer, the one who will kill each and every firstborn in Egypt, is on his way. The only way for the firstborn males to be saved from this last deadly plague is through obeying God and smearing the blood on the door so that the destroyer will see the blood of the lamb and pass over the home, saving the inhabitants from this plague. Passover paints a prophetic picture pointing to the day Jesus the Messiah will die as the Passover Lamb, the One who takes away the sin of the world.

The instructions God gives Moses for the Israelites regarding the placement of the blood requires a certain plant:

> You shall take a bunch of hyssop and dip it in the blood which is in the basin, and apply some of the blood that is in the basin to the lintel and the two doorposts; and none of you shall go outside the door of his house until morning. (Exod. 12:22)

The hyssop plant functions like a natural paintbrush. It has a long stem with a brushlike ending. It was used to sprinkle the blood in ordinary purifications (Lev. 14:51; Num. 19:18). In Psalm 51, David's psalm of repentance, David writes, "Purify me with hyssop, and I shall be clean" (v. 7). Here in Exodus 12:22 the instructions are to "dip it in the blood [of the lamb] which is in the basin." There are two thoughts as to what the basin is.

One, according to Targum Jonathan, is that the basin is an earthen vessel, into which the blood of the lamb is received when slain, and therefore is placed at the bottom of the door, and the precious blood of the lamb is not trampled upon (Targum Pseudo-Jonathan 12:22).

Two, the Hebrew word for "basin," בַּסַּף, *bassaph,* can also be translated "threshold." Therefore, the blood of the slain lamb runs into the threshold by the bottom of the door and pools in this natural basin. Either way the picture is similar. The hyssop plant is dipped in a pool of blood at the bottom of the doorframe. The brush of hyssop, now covered with blood, is applied by the Israelite to the lintel and doorposts per Moses' instructions to "apply some of the blood that is in the basin to the lintel and the two doorposts" (Exod. 12:22).

Some interpreters through the years have envisioned this act as tracing a bloody cross on the door of the home. Whereas we cannot demonstrate this from the text in Exodus, we do believe that in light of (1) Leviticus 17:11, which notes that "the life of the flesh is in the blood," and (2) the foreshadowed death of Jesus as the Lamb of God who takes away the sin of the world, the image created by the blood on the door of the home points in a beautiful way to the future redemption available to all by faith in the shed blood of the Messiah Jesus. When by faith we accept Him as our Savior, then the blood of the Lamb covers our hearts as the blood of that little lamb in Exodus covered the homes of the Israelites acting in faith and obedience to what God commanded.

JESUS CAME TO BETHANY

John 12 parallels Exodus 12 and begins with this temporal note, establishing a time frame for the events that follow:

> Jesus, therefore, six days before the Passover, came to Bethany where Lazarus was, whom Jesus had raised from the dead. (John 12:1)

Jesus enters Bethany and the home of Lazarus, Martha, and Mary, his friends. It is late in the day on Friday, the eighth of Nisan, six days before Passover, but before sunset when the Sabbath begins.

Lazarus is an anomaly to the crowds gathered in Bethany. He is the one Jesus raised from the dead after four days. According to a midrash, an ancient rabbinical commentary written long before the first century, it was a Jewish belief that the soul stays near the body for three days after a person's death: "For three days the soul hovers over the grave, contemplating a return to the body, but once it sees that the facial color has faded, it goes away, never to return" (Genesis Rabbah 50:10). So probably the Jewish community in Bethany viewed Lazarus as having been dead long enough for his spirit to have returned to God. And now Jesus is coming over to his house to have a Sabbath dinner with him and his family!

As usual, Martha is serving and Mary is sitting at the feet of Jesus. The Jewish religious leaders in opposition to Jesus come to see both Jesus and Lazarus, who simply by being alive is a walking testimony of Jesus's Messianic authority. The dinner ends and the Jewish religious leaders decide to treat both Jesus and Lazarus as threats and begin plotting against them.

The action slows on the next day, which is the Sabbath (Saturday), the ninth day of Nisan. It picks up again on the tenth of Nisan, sunset Saturday to sunset Sunday. This is the day the Passover lambs are selected and brought into the households. We believe this is the very day Jesus enters Jerusalem, presenting Himself as Messiah and King and ultimately as the Lamb of God. John describes the scene in and around the bustling city that day:

> On the next day the large crowd who had come to the feast, when they heard that Jesus was coming to Jerusalem, took the branches of the palm trees and went out to meet Him, and began to shout, "Hosanna! Blessed is He who comes in the name of the Lord, even the King of Israel." Jesus, finding a young

donkey, sat on it; as it is written, "Fear not, daughter of Zion; behold, your King is coming, seated on a donkey's colt." (John 12:12–15)

Why the palm branches? The palm branches are actually part of the celebration of the Feast of Tabernacles, which takes place in the seventh month. This celebration is described for us in the Torah:

> On exactly the fifteenth day of the seventh month, when you have gathered in the crops of the land, you shall celebrate the feast of the LORD for seven days, with a rest on the first day and a rest on the eighth day. Now on the first day you shall take for yourselves the foliage of beautiful trees, palm branches and boughs of leafy trees and willows of the brook, and you shall rejoice before the LORD your God for seven days. (Lev. 23:39–40)

Why did the Jewish people link the Feast of Tabernacles and the coming of the Messianic King? Writing about the end of days when the King of Kings will be reigning on earth, the Prophet Zechariah says,

> And the LORD will be king over all the earth; in that day the LORD will be the only one, and His name the only one.

> Then it will come about that any who are left of all the nations that went against Jerusalem will go up from year to year to worship the King, the LORD of hosts, and to celebrate the Feast of Booths. (Zech. 14:9, 16)

Jewish tradition in the first century had already joined the Feast of Booths or Tabernacles with the coming of the Messiah and His ascending the throne of David in Jerusalem. As Jesus rides on the colt of the donkey, the people recognize the picture from Zechariah's prophecy,

> Rejoice greatly, O daughter of Zion!
> Shout in triumph, O daughter of Jerusalem!
> Behold, your king is coming to you;
> He is just and endowed with salvation,
> Humble, and mounted on a donkey,
> Even on a colt, the foal of a donkey. (Zech. 9:9)

The crowds are shouting, "Hosanna to the Son of David" (Matt. 21: 9, 15), thereby acknowledging their belief that Jesus is the coming King described by the Prophet Zechariah. And though this is a few days away from the start of Passover, the waving of the palm branches, usually associated with the Feast of Tabernacles, is done to underscore their belief that Jesus is the Messiah and true King of Israel.

However, the people's response to His entry into Jerusalem shows they do not understand that His kingdom will come in a very different way than expected. His subsequent weeping over Jerusalem will cut to the heart of His purpose for coming this first time. The Savior mourns over the spiritual state of His chosen people,

> O Jerusalem, Jerusalem, the city that kills the prophets and stones those sent to her! How often I wanted to gather your children together, just as a hen gathers her brood under her wings, and you would not have it! Behold, your house is left to you desolate; and I say to you, you will not see Me until the time comes when you say, "Blessed is He who comes in the name of the Lord!" (Luke 13:34–35)

The Jewish people think they are getting a king who will vanquish the Romans the way the Maccabees vanquished the Seleucid king Antiochus IV (reigned 175–164 B.C.E.). Instead, Jesus enters Jerusalem on the day the lamb is selected and presents Himself as the perfect, spotless Lamb of God.

TEMPTED IN ALL THINGS . . . YET WITHOUT SIN

Just as the first Passover lamb is brought into each household, each community, to be examined to make sure it is perfect and without blemish, Jesus enters the household of Israel and allows Himself to be examined for four days to show that He is a spotless and unblemished lamb. The religious leaders question the authority of His teaching. The chief priests and elders of the people come to him and ask,

> By what authority are You doing these things, and who gave You this authority? (Matt. 21:23)

His response stuns the Jewish leaders:

> I will also ask you one thing, which if you tell Me, I will also tell you by what authority I do these things. The baptism of John was from what source, from heaven or from men? (vv. 24–25)

The leaders do not answer the question as they are afraid of how the people will react if they do. And as He promised, Jesus does not answer their question about the nature of His authority.

The next question, asked by the Pharisees and the Herodians, involves the role of government. The Pharisees are the purists and separatists, not wanting Rome to be involved in Jewish religious questions. The Herodians are supportive of Herod and Roman rule and thereby are hated by most Jews. Yet these strange bedfellows approach Jesus together and ask a question:

> Tell us then, what do You think? Is it lawful to give a poll-tax to Caesar, or not? (Matt. 22:17)

They test Jesus to see if He will acknowledge Roman authority or encourage rebellion. Again, His answer disarms them.

> But Jesus perceived their malice, and said, "Why are you testing Me, you hypocrites? Show Me the coin used for the poll-tax." And they brought Him a denarius. And He said to them, "Whose likeness and inscription is this?" They said to Him, "Caesar's." Then He said to them, "Then render to Caesar the things that are Caesar's; and to God the things that are God's." And hearing this, they were amazed, and leaving Him, they went away. (vv. 18–22)

The Sadducees, the high priestly caste who do not believe in the resurrection, ask a third question. Their question seems to be designed to show that Jesus's knowledge of Scripture is inferior to theirs. They ask about a possible Levirate marriage that suddenly ends when the man dies, and so his name and property rights continue on through his brother, who dutifully marries the widow and becomes a father to his dead brother's children. However, in this unusual case concocted by the Sadducees, there are seven brothers, none of whom father any children, and they and finally the widow all eventually die. The question they then ask is designed to stump even Jesus:

> In the resurrection, therefore, whose wife of the seven will she be? For they all had married her. (Matt. 22:28)

The question drips with sarcasm, and they are sure that Jesus will stumble and be unable to answer, proving He is not the Messiah. Jesus's response overwhelms them. He says,

> "You are mistaken, not understanding the Scriptures nor the power of God. For in the resurrection they neither marry nor are given in marriage, but are like angels in heaven. But regarding the resurrection of the dead, have you not read what was spoken to you by God: 'I am the God of Abraham, and the God of Isaac, and the God of Jacob'? He is not the God of the dead but of the living." When the crowds heard this, they were astonished at His teaching. (vv. 29–33)

Jesus passes all the tests and shows Himself to be pure, spotless, and without sin.

Later, even the pagan Pontius Pilate, the Roman governor and political head of the community, will declare that Jesus is without blemish. After examining him, he will say, "I find no guilt in this man" (Luke 23:4). The Lamb is indeed worthy to be slain.

After completing this period of testing during the first four days of the week, the time for Yeshua's final Passover meal with His disciples has come. This is the apex of His ministry and the beginning of what many think will be the end of His ministry. At last it is Thursday, the fourteenth of Nisan, and Yeshua and the Twelve recline at the table and celebrate Passover. During the meal Jesus tells His disciples that there is a betrayer among them. He warns them with an announcement: "Truly, truly, I say to you, that one of you will betray Me" (John 13:21). The disciples are shocked and cannot believe this is possible. Prompted by Peter, John asks Jesus who it is, and Jesus responds, "That is the one for whom I shall dip the morsel and give it to him" (v. 26). Jesus then dips the matzah in what some have suggested was the bitter herbs placed on the Passover table and offers it to Judas, who takes it from Jesus, acknowledging he will indeed be the betrayer. Satan then takes possession of Judas and the betrayal process begins that will lead to Jesus's brutal death foreshadowed in the death of the perfect lamb at that first Passover in Egypt.

WORTHY IS THE LAMB THAT WAS SLAIN

Jesus is the Lamb of God who takes away the sin of the world. He is the fulfillment of Passover. Like the first Passover lambs sacrificed to redeem Israel from slavery in Egypt, Jesus's death on the cross redeems us from slavery to sin. Reflecting on all of this, the Apostle Paul says, "Christ our Passover also has been sacrificed" (1 Cor. 5:7), and just as the first Passover was very personal and the Israelites personally applied the blood of the lambs to the doors of their houses, we too, by faith, need to personally apply the blood of Jesus, the Lamb of God, to the doors of our hearts. Have you made Passover personal? If you haven't, I pray that you will—perhaps this Passover.

15

SERMON: "THE THIRD CUP"

DAVID SEDACA

*G*rowing up in a Messianic Jewish home, the traditional Jewish holidays were special times for our family. My fondest memories are of Passover. We always observed this festival at home, and the entire family was involved.

In addition to celebrating the biblical holiday, my mother cooked special meals for a whole week! In our family we measured how good Passover was by comparing the matzah balls my mother cooked this year to those she made last year. It goes without saying that she never used boxed mixes from the supermarket; her matzah balls were made from scratch! During the week we also visited other family members and had similar but smaller meals—and of course compared matzah ball soups! Another fun Passover activity was competing with my siblings to find the *afikoman*, the broken middle *matzah* (unleavened bread) hidden early in the Seder and searched for by the children after the meal. Regrettably it was my sister, Alice, who for some unknown reason was always able to beat my brother and me to the afikoman and get the resulting reward.

When I formed my own family, we joyfully carried on these same wonderful traditions. These days it is my wife, Julia, who makes the best matzah ball soup in the world, and I leave the task of asking "the four questions" to my grandchildren. When it comes to the afikoman, I am simply the one who pays the children for finding it!

In the midst of all the joyful noise around the Passover table, my father was always able to remind us of the spiritual lessons we should learn from Passover. As a teenager I used to go along with my father when he was invited to give "Messiah in the Passover" presentations at various churches. From the change in the tone of his voice, I learned how important the meaning of the third cup of Passover was and that something deeply personal happens when we drink it.

Every element of the Passover celebration—the bitter herbs, the unleavened bread, the dipping of the parsley, and the roasted lamb shankbone—not only speak of God's salvation but are a powerful picture of the redemption brought to us by Jesus the Messiah. Yet not one of these elements speaks more directly to us as individuals than the third cup of Passover. The third cup reminds us that today we are given the opportunity to enjoy a far greater salvation than my Jewish ancestors' deliverance from Egypt. As Messianic Jews, we understand that God, through Jesus the Messiah, has fulfilled His Passover promise and granted us freedom from the slavery of sin and the dire consequences of living life separated from God.

The purpose of celebrating Passover then and now is to remind the children of Israel and their descendants how God, without human intervention or effort, made good on the promise to rescue them from the bondage of slavery. This event, which marks the birth of Israel as a nation, is of such importance that throughout the pages of the Bible, the Lord reminds His chosen people again and again of His sovereign plan by saying, "I am the LORD your God, who brought you out of the land of Egypt to give you the land of Canaan and to be your God." This phrase from Leviticus 25:38 is repeated in similar ways forty-eight times in Scripture!

Passover lasts eight days and is observed simultaneously with the Feast of Unleavened Bread (Lev. 23:5–8). On the first night of the festival, Jewish families gather together to celebrate the Passover Seder, though it is observed again on the second night in the Diaspora (wherever Jews live outside modern Israel). The word *Seder* refers to the Passover meal, and simply means "order," speaking of the Passover ceremony conducted in Jewish homes.

Passover is not usually celebrated in the synagogue as Jewish families enjoy the Seder in their homes. In order to observe the ceremony, all participants—children and adults, members of the family, or guests—read from a booklet called the *Haggadah*, which includes the prayers, biblical passages, and explanations that developed over centuries within Jewish tradition to help us tell the story throughout the evening.

Three aspects of the meal always stood out for me when my father led our family in celebrating Passover. The first is that the Lord fulfilled His promises given in Exodus 6:6–8. The second is a reminder that God did it Himself, without our help. The third is that although we weren't actually there in Egypt, we are encouraged by our rabbis to celebrate the Seder as if we were, to personalize the story so deeply that it burns within our hearts and souls and those of our children. It is this profoundly personal nature of the Passover that I want to share with you in this chapter.

We believe that Jesus and His disciples followed the Jewish traditions of the day in the way they celebrated Passover. This is at least indicated in the Gospels when Jesus tells His disciples, "Go and prepare the Passover for us that we may eat it" (Luke 22:7; cf. Matt. 26:17–19; Mark 14:12–16). They must have had some idea of what to prepare! It is during the celebration of this Passover, known later among Christians as the Lord's Supper or Communion, that Jesus introduces a new element that will change the tone and message of this celebration for succeeding generations of His followers.

Up to this point in history the main purpose of the Passover meal was to remind the Jewish people of how God redeemed and delivered the children of Israel from slavery in Egypt through the shed blood of the Passover lamb. But when Jesus takes the third cup, what He says introduces a new and radical principle of life for His disciples, along with hopefully all Jews and Gentiles—the Gospel of redemption through His shed blood.

The previous elements of the Seder spoke about what God did for the children of Israel, but now Jesus, in a sense, tells the Twelve, "This is what I will do *for you.*" With these few words, Yeshua, by establishing a new covenant with His disciples and with all who believe that He is the Messiah and Savior of the world, transforms the Passover from a national celebration to something much more personal.

JEWISH TRADITIONS REGARDING THE CUP OF WINE

Although the celebration of Passover has changed over time, especially since the destruction of the Temple in 70 C.E., there is very little explanation in the Hebrew Bible as to how to celebrate this holiday. New generations have developed a more comprehensive narrative that found its way into the Passover Haggadah. It wasn't until the first and second centuries of the present era that Jewish religious laws and traditions began to be recorded. These oral traditions were compiled and edited by the end of the second century C.E. and are known as the *Mishnah*. An additional commentary to the Mishnah, the *Gemara*, was completed by the fifth century, and the Mishnah and Gemara make up what we know as the *Talmud*.

The Talmud is divided into six "orders," and the Second Order, *Mo'ed*, contains the teachings regarding the sacred Jewish Holy Days. Although rabbinic tradition was developed and written down after the destruction of the Second Temple, the Talmud contains many explanations as to how the Passover lamb was to be sacrificed during Temple times. However, it says very little about the significance of the cups of wine. One of the few references to the cups of wine in the Talmud is found in Mishnah Pesahim 10:1, where it says that the officiant must give the participant "no fewer than four cups of wine." That same chapter in verse 7 says, "They mix a third cup; he blesses his meal."[1]

Other rabbinic traditions have also found their way into additional commentaries, such as the *midrash*. These are explanations of biblical texts along with homiletic stories as taught by rabbis that give us additional analysis of passages in the Hebrew Bible. Some of these add clarity to the Passover Seder,[2] but little information is found about the four cups of wine that are such a vital part of today's Seder. When we search for traditions in the Targumim (pl.), we come up almost empty-handed as well.[3] The Targumim were

1. Quoted from *Open Mishnah, Sefaria Community Translation*, Sefaria, http://www.sefaria.org/Mishnah_Pesachim.10.

2. For more on rabbinic traditions and texts, see Susie Kisber, "Midrashim and Prayer for Passover," Ritualwell, http://www.ritualwell.org/ritual/midrashim-and-prayer-passover.

3. Joseph Tabory, review of *Passover in Targum Pseudo-Jonathan Genesis: The Connection of Early Biblical Events with Passover in Targum Pseudo-Jonathan in a Synagogue Setting*, by Per Å. Bengtsson, *Jewish Quarterly Review* 93, no. 1 (2002): 317–19, http://muse.jhu.edu/article/390121/pdf.

spoken paraphrases, explanations, and expansions of the Hebrew Scriptures that the rabbis gave in the common language of the listeners.

Therefore, other than the talmudic explanation in Pesahim 10, verses 1 and 7, there is little explanation in rabbinic or related literature on the significance of the four cups of wine poured during the Passover Seder.

JESUS AND THE THIRD CUP

The tradition of pouring four cups of wine at the Passover Seder goes back to at least the first century c.e. In the Jerusalem Talmud (compiled from about 200 to 500 c.e.) we read:

> Why do we have four cups of wine? R. Yochanan said in the name of Rabbi Benayah, this refers to four stages in the redemption . . . "I will bring you out from under the burdens of Egypt." Even if He had left us in Egypt to be slaves, He would have ceased the burdensome yoke. For this alone we would have been grateful to Him and therefore we drink the first cup. "I will deliver you from their slavery." We drink the cup of salvation for he delivered us completely from serving them. "I will redeem you with an outstretched arm. . . ." Because he confused them and crushed them on our behalf so that they could no longer afflict us, we drink the third cup. "I will take you. . . ." The greatest aspect of the redemption is that He brought us near to Him and granted us also spiritual redemption. For this we raise the fourth cup.[4]

Judaism has given a different name to each one of the four cups poured during the celebration of Passover. The Hebrew name for the first cup is *Kiddush*, literally meaning "to sanctify," and this is the Cup of Blessing, also called the Cup of Sanctification. The second cup is called the Cup of Judgment. When we drink it we remember the plagues by which God brought judgment upon the Egyptians. The Hebrew word for the third cup is *Ha-Geulah*, since the term *geulah* means "redemption or deliverance . . . . [and] also refers to the ransoming or redeeming of property that used to be yours."[5] Thus the third cup is called the Cup of Redemption. The fourth cup is the final one to be poured during the Passover celebration and is the called the Cup of Rejoicing.

The Gospel of Luke mentions Jesus drinking at least two of the four cups, and as we said before, there is no reason to doubt that Jesus observed the Passover in the same way as His fellow Jews did at that time. In Luke 22:17, Jesus takes one cup before the meal, and later takes another cup. Having celebrated Passover in my own home and served the Lord's Supper many

---

4. Quoted from Eliyahu Kitov, *The Book of Our Heritage: The Jewish Year and Its Days of Significance*, trans. Nachman Bulman, rev. ed., 3 vols. (1968; Jerusalem: Feldheim Publishers, 1988), 2:269.
5. Julian Sinclair, "Geulah," *The Jewish Chronicle*, March 6, 2009, https://www.thejc.com/judaism/jewish-words/geulah-1.8102. See next section for further discussion of the term *geulah*.

times, I believe that Jesus takes the other cup *after* the meal (Luke 22:20), which we believe is the third cup, the Cup of Redemption.

Moreover, Paul's letter to the Corinthian church affirms the same when he writes of Jesus that "He took the cup also *after* supper, saying . . ." (1 Cor. 11:25, emphasis added). It makes sense to me that the cup of wine mentioned by Paul in this instance is the same cup taken by Jesus after the meal—the Cup of Redemption. It is in this moment, when He takes the Cup of Redemption, that Jesus gives new meaning to this cup. He transforms the Passover into a very personal matter. And today He offers you and me the same Cup of Redemption, inviting us to accept His New Covenant with us and to receive forgiveness of sin, spiritual rebirth, and a new personal and dynamic relationship with the God of Abraham, Isaac, and Jacob.

THE THIRD CUP: THE PRICE FOR OUR SALVATION

Perhaps because we as believers have taken the Lord's Supper so many times, we tend to overlook the deep personal significance of what Jesus says after He takes the Cup of Redemption in His hand. So please pay careful attention to what follows, because the Savior is addressing you and me.

The word often translated "redemption" is the Hebrew term גְּאֻלָּה, *geulah*,[6] and the word usually refers to the payment made for the recovery of property, animals, or persons. In nearly every instance, redemption referred to a payment made allowing the individual who had caused an offense to become free of obligation, bondage, or danger. And further, redemption conveys two basic principles: (1) something was lost and is no longer in our possession, and (2) to recover what was lost or taken a price must be paid.

Jesus reaffirms the nature of redemption by telling His disciples that the third cup represents the price paid for our redemption. Let me explain. Jesus says of this cup, "Drink from it, all of you; for this is My blood of the covenant, which is poured out for many for forgiveness of sins" (Matt. 26:27–29). The red color of the fruit of the vine represents the blood of the Passover lamb. Jesus, as the ultimate Lamb of God sacrificed for our redemption, now compares the shedding of His blood to that of the little lamb in Exodus. The earlier lamb was a mere foreshadowing of the Lamb of God to come. Jesus declares that the time of fulfillment has come and He is the One, the Lamb of God, for whom the Jewish people had been waiting.

This is the heart of the mission given by the Father who sent His Son to die for our sins. John the Baptist knew this when he saw Jesus coming to him

6. "OT:1353 *geullah* (gheh-ool-law'); feminine passive participle of OT:1350; redemption (including the right and the object); by implication, relationship." *Biblesoft's New Exhaustive Strong's Numbers and Concordance with Expanded Greek-Hebrew Dictionary*, (Seattle, WA: Biblesoft and International Bible Translators, 2006).

to be baptized and said, "Behold, the Lamb of God who takes away the sin of the world!" (John 1:29).

We may ask ourselves, why such a dear price? This is because a holy God considers our sin so grave that the perpetrators are worthy of death. This is why our sins can only be forgiven through the offering of another in our stead. The shedding of blood reminds us of the price God demands for sin. This principle is clearly indicated in the Torah when the Lord says, "For the life of the flesh is in the blood, and I have given it to you on the altar to make atonement for your souls; for it is the blood by reason of the life that makes atonement" (Lev. 17:11). If God had not provided a substitute, neither you nor I would be saved!

In order for God to maintain this biblical principle and yet spare our lives through payment for our own sins, He introduced a system of gracious substitutionary sacrifices, a reflection of His mercy and grace towards us. This is best seen in the way the children of Israel observe Yom Kippur, the Day of Atonement. The Lord says of this day that "it is the Day of Atonement, when atonement *is made for you*" (Lev. 23:28–29 NIV, emphasis added). None of us can afford the price that needs to be paid! Jesus paid the price for our redemption because we all have sinned and would be perpetually enslaved to sin and death if God had not taken the initiative to send His Son to be our substitute. Because Yeshua died—we live!

The Apostle Paul makes this very clear when he says of this new life of everyone who believes,

> There is no difference between Jew and Gentile, for all have sinned and fall short of the glory of God, and all are justified freely by his grace through the redemption that came by Christ Jesus. God presented Christ as a sacrifice of atonement, through the shedding of his blood—to be received by faith. (Rom. 3:22–25 NIV)

In the same way, extolling the glory of the Lamb, the redeemed sing a new song about their Redeemer,

> Worthy are You to take the book and to break its seals; for You were slain, and purchased for God with Your blood men from every tribe and tongue and people and nation. (Rev. 5:9)

And the Apostle Peter adds,

> [You know] that you were not redeemed with perishable things like silver or gold from your futile way of life inherited from your forefathers, but with precious blood, as of a lamb unblemished and spotless, the blood of Christ. (1 Peter 1:18–19)

THE CUP OF REDEMPTION: THE BASIS FOR A NEW COVENANT

When taking the third cup, Jesus says, "This cup is the new covenant in My blood; do this, as often as you drink it, in remembrance of Me" (1 Cor. 11:25).

In many churches these words of Jesus are repeated every time we take Communion or celebrate the Lord's Supper.

The Savior speaks of a New Covenant "*in my blood.*" The New Covenant enjoyed by both Jewish and Gentile believers in Jesus focuses on the personal aspects of the New Covenant, that our sins are forgiven and the law is now written on our hearts by the Holy Spirit. The fullness of the New Covenant predicted by the prophet Jeremiah is more extensive than the Old Covenant; it will be fulfilled at a date yet future, and it also describes the future national salvation of Israel (Jer. 31:31–37; Rom. 11:11–29). On this great future day God will take the Law from stone tablets and write it on the hearts and minds of the children of Israel. The New Covenant that Jesus is offering to you and me now is not *national* but *personal* and is available to both Jews and Gentiles.

We also need to understand that a "covenant" is a pact, a contract, an agreement between two parties.[7] To paraphrase what Jesus says, "This cup represents the price I'm willing to pay to buy you back from a life of slavery to sin to a life of joyous personal fellowship with God." I frequently hear people say that salvation is free. Actually the opposite is true. No one but our sinless Messiah could have paid the price of our redemption. Only the blood of Jesus's sacrifice, represented by the third Seder cup, is sufficient and able to restore us to a loving and eternal relationship with God.

I said at the beginning that the third cup makes Passover personal. Here is the bottom line: Jesus is willing to enact the New Covenant with each one of us, and by this covenant He is willing to apply the price He personally paid in His own blood.

Knowing that Jesus shed His blood for our salvation *does not* mean we are saved. He is proposing that we choose to enter this "new covenant," since this covenant can only go into effect when affirmed by both parties. Jesus fulfilled His part of the covenant when He shed His blood on the cross, but His sacrifice does not make the covenant effectual. The covenant is only valid when both parties fulfill their obligations. Jesus's sacrifice has no benefit to you unless you embrace it by repentance and faith!

We need to ask ourselves if the covenant offered in the third cup of Passover has taken effect in our lives. Have you signed the contract by giving your life back to the One who created and redeemed you? A contract is invalid with only one signature, so we need to sign it as well. You of course understand that I am speaking figuratively and there is no literal contract to be signed. However, we "sign on the dotted line" when we receive Jesus into our hearts and acknowledge that we are unable to pay the price for our salvation. The covenant is fulfilled and comes into effect when we recognize that He paid the price for us, through His shed blood. He fulfilled

---

7.   "Covenant—An agreement between two people or two groups that involves promises on the part of each to the other." Ronald F. Youngblood, ed., *Nelson's Illustrated Bible Dictionary*, rev. ed. (Nashville: Thomas Nelson, 2014), 274.

His part and we need to fulfill ours. The third cup of redemption is freely offered to you, but you must accept this gift by faith and drink deeply of His grace. He has done it all. Now it is your turn to turn to the Lord and receive the salvation He has graciously offered to us by saying yes to Yeshua. Now is the time of salvation (2 Cor. 6:2), according to the Scriptures. Are you ready to take the next step?

PART 5
CELEBRATING MESSIAH
IN THE PASSOVER

16

PASSOVER IN YOUR HOME

CATHY WILSON

*W*hen I first joined the staff of Chosen People Ministries, I didn't see why I should have to give "Messiah in the Passover" presentations in various churches and Bible study settings as a part of my ministry. "Maybe they would make an exception for me," I thought. "After all, I'm a Gentile! I never celebrated Passover. Why would I begin to commemorate this feast or teach others the ways in which Jesus fulfills the Passover?" But, my questions faded quickly once I began to understand the importance of Passover and the ways in which Jesus is present in the celebration of this holiday.

I am a Gentile believer in Jesus, but I have been grafted into the blessings of the Abrahamic Covenant (Gen. 12:1–3; Eph. 2:11–22). God tells Abraham that all the families of the earth will be blessed through the Messiah who will come through Jewish lineage. I have been personally blessed through the Promised One of Israel, the Jewish Messiah Jesus. The Jewish festivals are an important part of the Old Testament, and though Gentile believers are not required by covenant to observe them, I have chosen to better understand these holidays by celebrating them with my family—especially the Passover. This has already brought incredible enrichment to my life, and I am hoping that you will engage with these great festivals and find the same spiritual blessings I have enjoyed.

As I began to journey through the Scriptures, I asked the Lord, "What is the importance of the Passover festival in relation to Your plan for the world?" After months of intensive Bible study, the Lord began to answer my question. I began to understand the weighty implications of Passover in God's plan of redemption! And my family has been celebrating the Passover as fulfilled in Jesus the Messiah every year since my journey began. May I give you a few steps to take to begin your pilgrimage with the Passover?

PRAYER

How does a Gentile go about understanding and even hosting a Passover Seder? These questions can only be answered through prayer. Ask God to give you direction and an increased burden to begin the adventure of taking hold of your Jewish roots in Jesus. The Apostle Paul, who was Jewish, uses the illustration of an olive tree to explain this magnificent truth to the Gentile Christians in Rome, who were unaware of how deeply rooted their faith was in the Old Testament and that they were now grafted into covenants and promises God gave to the children of Israel.

> But if some of the branches were broken off, and you, being a wild olive, were grafted in among them and became partaker with them of the rich root of the olive tree, do not be arrogant toward the branches; but if you are arrogant, remember that it is not you who supports the root, but the root supports you. (Rom. 11:17–18)

This does not mean that Gentile (non-Jewish) believers have replaced the Jewish people, which is a false notion the Apostle warns us against by encouraging Gentile Christians to have a humble attitude. But what a joy it is to realize that in the Messiah, both Jewish and Gentile followers of Jesus share a rich faith heritage, of which Passover is a vital part.

LOOKING BACK BUT MOVING FORWARD

In the Hebrew Scriptures and especially through the great festivals of Israel, God calls upon the children of Israel to remember what He has done on their behalf. He instructs them to rejoice in His power to deliver and to thank Him for His provision. He teaches His chosen people through the words of His prophets to anticipate a glorious future as well as the coming of the Promised One, the Messiah. Repeatedly, God tells His people to remember the day when He took them out of Egypt, as looking back provides strength to go forward as His chosen beacon of redeeming light to the nations.

I began to research the Passover with a view towards celebrating the Feast as a follower of Yeshua. Since the Jewish people celebrate Passover, I decided to begin my search with the experts! I began by reading several different versions of the *Haggadah*—the Passover Seder guidebook containing prayers, songs, and the account of the first Passover in Egypt read by Jewish families during the observance of the Festival. I pored over traditional Jewish Haggadahs; I also perused Messianic Haggadahs that were developed by Jewish believers in Jesus, which showed the fulfillment of the Passover in Jesus the Messiah and emphasized the link between the Passover, the Last Supper, and Communion.

The staff of Chosen People Ministries has put together "A Messianic Family Haggadah" (see chapter 18). This chapter provides many insights and suggestions for using the Haggadah when celebrating Passover in your home. You are permitted to make copies of the Haggadah from this book for use with your family, home group, or church to celebrate a Jesus-centered Passover Seder, or you can go to www.messiahinthepassover.com and download a printable copy for those attending your Seder. We trust you will find our Haggadah's blend of traditional elements with its biblical and Messianic aspects especially fitting for all believers and friends and family who are not yet believers in Yeshua our Messiah.

When planning your menu for Passover, please note the chapters within this book that to one degree or another address the Passover Seder plate and its ingredients (chapters 10–15) as well as provide recipes for the Passover meal (chapter 19). Consider joining together with those with whom you fellowship who might help you in the preparation of your Passover Seder.

INVITING FAMILY: INCLUDING JEWISH PEOPLE WHO ARE NOT YET JESUS FOLLOWERS

A key Hebrew word for "feast" is מוֹעֵד, *mo'ed*, which in passages such as Leviticus 23 means "appointed feast" or "appointed time" (vv. 2, 4, 37, 44). It also designates an "appointed place" or "place of assembly" such as the tent of "meeting" (Exod. 33:7).[1] What a beautiful picture of God's heart! God is a personal God whose desire is to meet with us for communion and fellowship. Celebrating the Passover and the other great festivals of Israel draws us closer to the Lord. Far from being a series of cold unfamiliar rituals, the Passover leads us to delight in His presence and understand His plan and purpose for our lives. After all, life begins with redemption—that's the day we were set free by the blood of the Lamb, our Savior and Messiah Jesus. Our lives are built upon the foundation of redemption.

You can share this truth as you extend to Jewish and Gentile friends an invitation to gather with you at your Passover Seder. The event is more than a religious ceremony and is designed have a deep and personal meaning for all who participate.

AN OVERVIEW OF THE PASSOVER

Should the Lord lead you to present a Passover Seder at your church or in your Bible study or home group, it is wise to consider including an introduction about the significance of the Passover. You might even suggest that your fellowship invite a Chosen People Ministries staff person to instruct the group (chosenpeople.com/church). Our Church Ministries staff would be happy to speak with you, your group leader, or your pastor.

Allow me then to share some of what I tell those who are interested in but unfamiliar with Passover to engage them in learning more and even celebrating a Seder. You will help your believing friends by introducing them to this great opportunity to better appreciate redemption!

The Lamb: Center Stage

The Body of Christ, the Church, is in existence today because of Passover. Paul, the Apostle to the Gentiles, writes, "Christ our Passover also has been sacrificed" (1 Cor. 5:7). Passover, the first feast God gave to the children of

---

1. Jack P. Lewis, "יָעַד [see under מוֹעֵד]," *Theological Wordbook of the Old Testament*, ed. R. Laird Harris, Gleason L. Archer, and Bruce K. Waltke (Chicago: Moody Press, 1980), 1:388–389.

Israel, focuses on redemption through the shed blood of the Passover Lamb. If you are a follower of Jesus, you know that the death and resurrection of Jesus is the very foundation of our faith.

At the first Passover in Egypt, lambs enter the lives of the family members and are scrutinized from the tenth until the fourteenth of the month of Nisan (Exod. 12:1–7). An attachment to the lamb, now part of the Jewish household, naturally develops. To help His people understand the cost and value of redemption, it may be that God's intention was for the lambs to be cherished and then later mourned.

Can you imagine what the children of Israel really thought about God's instructions? "We're to do—what? Why?" The children of Israel may not have remembered what God had so graphically conveyed about a lamb years ago when He called Abram to offer his *only* son as a burnt offering. The father and son climbed one of the mountains in the land of Moriah and Isaac asked about the whereabouts of the burnt offering. His father plainly stated, "God will provide for Himself the lamb for the burnt offering, my son" (Gen. 22:8).

But, what happened on that day? Where was the lamb that God promised? The Lord provided a ram caught in the thicket by his horns as a substitute for Isaac (v. 13). This may well have been the first substitutionary sacrifice in the Bible. If not, it nevertheless dramatically displayed the biblical theme of substitutionary sacrifice.

We see this pattern emerge again in the Exodus when the time came for the first Passover, as God requires another lamb to be slain and its blood smeared upon the lintel and doorposts of each Israelite home as a substitute for the death of the firstborn sons of Israel. If the Israelites obey, their firstborn sons will not need to die. For the Lord will go through the land of Egypt to smite all the firstborn sons of the Egyptians, but when He sees the blood on the lintel and on the two doorposts, the Lord will pass over the door and will not allow the destroyer to come into the Israelites' houses to smite them (Exod. 12:7, 12–13, 21–23).

The lamb of the Egyptian Passover presents a foreshadowing of the Lamb mentioned in the fifty-third chapter of Isaiah, where Isaiah speaks of a lamb to come as a substitute for His people, Israel:

> But He was pierced through for our transgressions,
> He was crushed for our iniquities;
> The chastening for our well-being fell upon Him,
> And by His scourging we are healed.
> All of us like sheep have gone astray,
> Each of us has turned to his own way;
> But the Lord has caused the iniquity of us all
> To fall on Him.
>
> He was oppressed and He was afflicted,
> Yet He did not open His mouth;

like a lamb that is led to slaughter,
and like a sheep that is silent before its shearers,
so He did not open His mouth. (Isa. 53:5–7)

The theme of the sacrificial lamb continues through Scripture, but can only be fully appreciated by first understanding the original Passover. By retelling the Passover story during the Seder, we deepen our connection to both the people and God of Israel as we understand that the ultimate sacrificial lamb is Jesus Himself.

A Mixed Multitude

Scripture tells us that there were other people who were delivered from Egypt along with the children of Israel. The Hebrews did not leave Egypt alone; there were some people from other nations who came along with them.

A mixed multitude also went up with them, along with flocks and herds, a very large number of livestock. (Exod. 12:38)

"Mixed" simply means "not Israelite"! Egypt had conquered other lands and took captives as slaves. This mixed multitude was most likely comprised of people captured from other nations and enslaved by Egypt.

God chose the children of Israel to bless the world. God's plan is not limited to the descendants of Abraham, Isaac, and Jacob but includes "all the families of the earth" (Gen. 12:3). Both Israelites and some non-Israelites were redeemed that night through the blood of the Passover lamb! The first Passover was not limited to the Hebrews but also was enjoyed by non-Hebrews as well. This is all the more true of the redemption purchased at Calvary by the shed blood of the Lamb of God. This message is so beautifully summarized in the well-known verse John 3:16—perhaps a New Testament version of Genesis 12:3.

For God so loved the world, that He gave His only begotten Son, that whoever believes in Him shall not perish, but have eternal life.

The Church—God's Current Redemptive Tool

Passover reveals God's heart for the world. The Lord's charge to the people of Israel to keep Passover as a memorial forever demonstrates His desire to make sure that His people continue to tell His story of redemption to future generations. God is currently using the Church comprised of Jewish and Gentile believers in Jesus, "one new man" (Eph. 2:15), to tell this same story. The Church is called to proclaim the message of redemption through Jesus, the Passover Lamb, to the entire world. We know from Scripture that the Lord does not want "any to perish but for all to come to repentance" (2 Peter 3:9).

The story of *the* Lamb, from Genesis 22 to Exodus 12 to Isaiah 53 and on through the inspired pens of the New Testament writers, contributes greatly to our understanding of God's plan of redemption outlined in Scripture.

Remembering through an Annual Reenactment

God commands the children of Israel to observe Passover as an everlasting memorial (Exod. 12:14). "You shall observe this event as an ordinance for you and your children forever" (v. 24; cf. 17). The Hebrew word for "observe" is שָׁמַר, *shamar*, a root with the basic idea of "to exercise great care over."[2] Whereas elsewhere in the Bible this word literally means to keep, guard, or protect, here "it expresses the careful attention to be paid to the obligations of a covenant, to laws, statutes, etc."[3] Yet the literal sense informs the ceremonial sense. As God guards the homes marked by the blood of the lamb, so He calls His people to keep vigilant watch over the message of His redemption by remembering the Passover each year. The message of the Passover needs to be indelibly stamped on the minds and hearts of our future generations by an annual reenactment of the Exodus event through the Passover ceremony that engages the hearts, minds, and souls of participants.

Both Jewish and Gentile believers in Jesus can glean so much from celebrating this feast. It is a glorious way to remember the story of redemption and to share these eternal truths with others.

Passover is a beautiful home-based holiday and provides an ideal way to be spiritually enriched and to share your faith with your Jewish friends and others who do not know the Lord. We should especially encourage Jewish people we know to attend the Seder in our home. Try asking your Jewish friends if they will be celebrating the Passover meal. If they are planning to, talk with them about what you are learning about the Passover. If they are not planning to attend a Seder, then invite them to your home to celebrate! One rationale for inviting Jewish friends is to ask them to join your family Seder to help make sure you properly explain the Jewish traditions of the Passover. This will make them feel more comfortable in coming.

God desires that the world may know Him (John 17:23; cf. Isa. 43:9–10). In addition to using the Messianic Haggadah mentioned earlier (see chapter 18), you might speak to your guests some of the words in the narrative section that follows, starting with "The Telling." Partake together of the Passover Seder plate and explain what each element represents. Remember, your Jewish friends can help with this. Rejoice with each other "that Christ has become a servant to the circumcision on behalf of the truth of God to confirm the promises given to the fathers, and for the Gentiles to glorify God for His mercy" (Rom. 15:8–9).

The Apostle John, who was given a unique and extended revelation of Jesus much like the prophets Daniel and Ezekiel, writes,

> Then he showed me a river of the water of life, clear as crystal, coming from the throne of God and of the Lamb . . . There will no longer be any curse; and

---

2. John E. Hartley, "שָׁמַר," *Theological Wordbook of the Old Testament*, ed. R. Laird Harris, Gleason L. Archer, and Bruce K. Waltke (Chicago: Moody Press, 1980), 2:939.

3. Hartley, *Theological Wordbook of the Old Testament*, 2:939.

the throne of God and of the Lamb will be in it, and His bond-servants will serve Him. (Rev. 22:1, 3)

As redeemed Jews and Gentiles, we will rejoice before the risen Lamb forever! The Lamb is not only for a person, a family, a nation, and the world; the Lamb is for eternity. What a delight to meet with God and honor Him during the feast of Passover in our homes today in preparation for the great day coming!

The following narrative may help you explain the Passover Seder and the grand story of redemption beginning with the Exodus and first Passover and incorporating the Jewish traditions surrounding Passover viewed in light of Jesus the Lamb of God. I hope this will help you tell this wonderful story to your family and all who are willing to learn more about the Jewish Messiah.

You may simply adapt this narrative as a Bible study to be used with the traditional Seder symbols as object lessons, or you may use parts of this narrative as a backdrop to help you present a Seder, especially if you have not done this previously. If you provide participants with a copy of "A Messianic Family Haggadah" for reference during the Seder (see chapter 18), you do not need to read all of this, but you (and they) may find the information in the narrative helpful as you fill in the gaps of the story presented in the Haggadah.

We hope you will find creative ways to use this narrative with both young and old!

THE TELLING (HAGGADAH)

It's Passover! Welcome to God's Passover table. God told the Jewish people to keep Passover as a memorial—forever! He told them to remember His mighty deeds on their behalf—His deliverance of them from the bondage in Egypt. Passover is central to God's plan of redemption for the world!

Unleavened Bread

At Passover in Jewish homes, elaborate spring cleaning begins before the Feast. Foods containing *chametz* (leaven) are not allowed. The house must be cleaned and all leaven removed. Leaven is a symbol of sin in the *Tanakh*, the Hebrew Scriptures. When God commanded the children of Israel to leave Egypt, they had to do so in haste. The dough was made without yeast as they did not have time to prepare loaves for baking and rising.

The unleavened bread points to our Messiah, Jesus, and reminds us of His sinless purity and complete innocence as described by the prophet in Isaiah 53:5–6,

> But He was pierced through for our transgressions,
> He was crushed for our iniquities;
> The chastening for our well-being fell upon Him,
> And by His scourging we are healed.
> All of us like sheep have gone astray,

each of us has turned to his own way;
but the LORD has caused the iniquity of us all
to fall on Him.

At Passover, the Papa, according to Jewish tradition, personally inspects each room to make sure that all *chametz* is removed. He gathers the family together and they walk from room to room; and by the light of a wax candle they search for the leaven. Light exposes sin. Who is the Light of the world? Jesus! (See John 8:12.) Traditionally, the Papa is equipped with a large feather and a wooden spoon to collect any crumbs. Crumbs of leaven, a symbol of sin in the Hebrew Scriptures, are collected on a wooden spoon to make sure it does not touch the collector who would then be defiled by the leaven.

The Mama will sometimes leave a little leaven on the kitchen windowsill and will always act surprised when the Papa finds it. It makes him feel important and it makes the children laugh. It's good to begin the feast of Passover with merriment and joy!

With all the crumbs of leaven collected on the wooden spoon, the Papa will then take the leaven and the spoon, wrap them in a linen cloth, and join the other Jewish men in the community in burning the leaven. The fire speaks of purging and purity, as the home must be leaven-free for the Feast of Unleavened Bread.

Lighting the Candles

Once the leaven has been removed, the Passover Feast can begin. Mama kindles the Passover candles on the Seder table and recites a blessing in Hebrew welcoming the festival to her home. Light is a symbol of God's presence (Exod. 3:2; 24:17). Lighting candles during Jewish holidays is a constant reminder that God is light.

The beautiful prayer in Hebrew, with a phonetic English transliteration for pronunciation, is as follows,

בָּרוּךְ אַתָּה אֲדֹנָי אֱלֹהֵינוּ מֶלֶךְ הָעוֹלָם אֲשֶׁר קִדְּשָׁנוּ בְּמִצְוֹתָיו וְצִוָּנוּ לְהַדְלִיק
נֵר שֶׁל יוֹם טוֹב.

Baruch atah Ado-nai Elo-hei-nu me-lech ha-Olam, asher kid-sha-nu bemits-vo-tav vetsi-va-nu lehad-lik ner shel yom tov.

Translated into English, the words above mean

Blessed art Thou, O Lord our God, King of the universe, who has sanctified us with Thy commandments and commanded us to kindle the festival lights.

Some have asked, "Why does the woman light the Passover candles?" The Jewish woman has a very significant role in the religious Jewish home. The request to light the candles honors her. As Messianic Jews, we see something more! As the woman begins the Seder and gives light to the Passover table, so it was from the seed of a woman that the Messiah came to perform His redemptive ministry and bring light to the world (Gen. 3:15; Isa. 7:14; John 8:12).

The lighting of the candles initiates the Seder.

The Story of Passover

The term *Seder* means "order" and refers to the ensuing order of service for the Passover ceremony. The minimum requirement for observing the Passover is noted in God's instructions to the children of Israel found in Exodus 12:8,

> They shall eat the flesh that same night, roasted with fire, and they shall eat it with unleavened bread and bitter herbs.

The rabbis added additional elements including green vegetables, a roasted egg, *charoset*, and the four cups of wine. (The Seder plate and its elements will be discussed further below.)

On this night we will enjoy the best meal of the Jewish year. Passover, like most of the biblical holidays, features special, meaningful foods. This reminds us that, from a Jewish perspective, theology is not only taught, it is also eaten!

During the Seder, the Papa reads from the Haggadah. The Hebrew term *Haggadah* means "the telling," and the Hebrew word *Pesach* means "Passover," which comes from the verb *pasach*, "to pass over." During Passover we will retell the story of the way God passed over the firstborn sons of the children of Israel with the tenth plague and then delivered His chosen people from Egyptian bondage.

The Papa continues to share with his family from the Haggadah. He reads,

> Passover is an account of miraculous transitions from slavery to freedom, from despair to hope, from darkness to light. God's efforts to redeem Israel began that first night of Passover in Egypt. He instructed the children of Israel that on the tenth day of the month of Nisan a lamb was to be taken.

We read from Exodus 12:3–5 that the children of Israel were commanded to take a lamb from the flock and set it apart. The rest of the instructions regarding the lamb are found in Exodus 12:1–13. We will simply summarize the instructions given to the Israelites by God.

The lamb was to be an unblemished and perfect male and it was to become part of the family. What happens when you take an animal into your home? It's no longer just an animal. It becomes a pet. Can you imagine how the people felt when they brought the lamb into their home? It was *their* lamb! The next four days were a time to scrutinize the lamb and make sure it was without blemish. And then, if the lamb was spotless, they were commanded to kill it on the fourteenth day of the same month, as God instructed. Not a bone was to be broken and its blood was to be applied to the two doorposts and to the lintel of the house in which the Passover would be observed.

Further details are given in the remainder of Exodus chapter 12. God instructed the children of Israel to take a bunch of hyssop, which is an herb, a shrub used for purification rites. They were to dip that hyssop in the blood that was in the basin. The basin was probably the threshold or ditch that was dug in front of the doorways of the houses in Egypt to help prevent flooding. It appears that the children of Israel killed their Passover lambs by the door of their homes, outside the house. The blood from the slaughter ran into the depression and was smeared on each doorpost and lintel and then, with the blood already in the basin, the door was sealed on all sides.

What a prophetic portrait of redemption! On that first Passover night, the children of Israel blood-sealed their doors and found safety. The next morning they left Egypt and began their journey toward the land promised to them by God (Gen. 15:17–21).

Papa then reads from Exodus 12,

> For I will go through the land of Egypt on that night, and will strike down all the firstborn in the land of Egypt, both man and beast; and against all the gods of Egypt I will execute judgments—I am the LORD. The blood shall be a sign for you on the houses where you live; and when I see the blood I will pass over you, and no plague will befall you to destroy you when I strike the land of Egypt. (vv. 12–13)

> For the LORD will pass through to smite the Egyptians; and when He sees the blood on the lintel and on the two doorposts, the LORD will pass over the door and will not allow the destroyer to come in to your houses to smite you. (v. 23)

The Papa exclaims, "This was our deliverance! This was our redemption!"

The First Cup: The Cup of Sanctification

Jewish people drink four cups of wine during the Passover Seder to commemorate the four aspects of redemption found in Exodus 6:6–7:

> Say, therefore, to the sons of Israel, "I am the LORD, and I will bring you out from under the burdens of the Egyptians, and I will deliver you from their bondage. I will also redeem you with an outstretched arm and with great judgments. Then I will take you for My people, and I will be your God; and you shall know that I am the LORD your God, who brought you out from under the burdens of the Egyptians."

We do not know when this tradition of the four cups was added to the Passover dinner, although we do find two cups delineated in the New Testament account of the Last Supper.

Papa pours the first cup and lifts it. This is the Cup of Sanctification, also called the Cup of Blessing. Sanctification means holiness or being set apart for an intended purpose. The first cup sets apart this meal to accomplish God's plans and purposes. Papa recites the blessing,

בָּרוּךְ אַתָּה אֲדֹנָי אֱלֹהֵינוּ מֶלֶךְ הָעוֹלָם בּוֹרֵא פְּרִי הַגָּפֶן.

Baruch atah Ado-nai Elo-hei-nu me-lech ha-Olam, bo-ray pri ha-gah-fen.

The English translation is,

> Blessed art Thou, O Lord our God, King of the universe, Creator of the fruit
> of the vine.

On a night nearly two thousand years ago, a Passover Seder was conducted by a Rabbi among His followers in an upper room in Jerusalem. His
name was Yeshua in Hebrew. Yeshua celebrated Passover at that Last Supper
with His disciples. He lifted the first cup at the Passover that evening and
recited the blessing in Hebrew. He then said, "Take this and share it among
yourselves." And Jesus and His disciples drank (see Luke 22:14–18).

The Washings

In Jesus's day and at the Passover Seder in Jewish homes today there
are a number of washings. At the first hand washing, only Papa washes his
hands. This sets him apart from the rest of the family. It shows that he has a
significant role as the spiritual leader of the family. It was an ancient custom
in that part of the world to wash one's hands before eating.

It was customary for a servant to perform this task of washing the hands.
But Yeshua did something completely different by washing the feet of His
disciples. This was an act of servanthood, performed to teach servanthood by
example to His disciples. Yeshua even washed the feet of Judas Iscariot, the
disciple whom He knew would betray Him later that evening!

The Seder Plate

Papa turns his attention to the Passover plate upon which the various
elements are situated: parsley, horseradish, lettuce, roasted egg, *charoset*
(chopped apple mixture), and the shankbone of a lamb.

Papa lifts a sprig or two of parsley and reads from the Haggadah,

> This parsley which is green represents life, a renewed life. Life in Egypt during
> the time of the first Passover was a life of pain, suffering, and tears. The tears
> are represented by this salt water.

Yes, there was the hardship and the suffering in Egypt. Scripture tells us that
Pharaoh made it difficult for the Jewish people. But there was also the renewal of
life when God delivered the children of Israel from Egypt. Passover is observed in
the spring when the earth is green with life after the deadness of winter. We see
a resurrection in this celebration of Passover. Jesus rose from the dead on a day
during the week of Passover! Passover is all about a renewed life and resurrection!

The family dips the parsley into a bowl of salt water and eats.

The Second Cup: The Cup of Plagues

Papa pours the second cup of wine, the Cup of Plagues or Judgment. Everyone at the table dips their little finger into the wine ten times, reciting each of the ten plagues and dropping the wine on their plate: Blood! Frogs! Gnats! Flies! Pestilence! Boils! Hail! Locusts! Darkness! Death of the First-born!

This is very meaningful for a variety of reasons. Our action brings to life the holiness and judgment of God. It also reminds us that the wine that previously symbolized joy is reduced by a drop for every plague and thereby speaks of God's compassion for the Egyptians and our mercy as well toward those who suffer—even when they suffer as a result of what they have done to us.

The actual taking of the cup comes a bit later in the Passover Seder, and as far as we know this cup is not specifically mentioned in the New Testament accounts.

At this time in the Seder, the family sings a joyful song entitled "*Dayenu*," which means "it is enough," or "we would have been satisfied." At the Passover Seder in Jewish homes, many verses of "*Dayenu*" are sung:

> If He had merely rescued us from Egypt,
>   but had not punished the Egyptians—*Dayenu!*
> If He had merely punished the Egyptians,
>   but had not destroyed their gods—*Dayenu!*
> If He had merely destroyed their gods,
>   but had not slain their firstborn—*Dayenu!*
> If He had merely fed us with manna,
>   but had not given us the Sabbath—*Dayenu!*
> If He had merely given us the Sabbath,
>   but had not brought us to Mount Sinai—*Dayenu!*
> If He had merely brought us to Mount Sinai,
>   but had not given us the Torah—*Dayenu!*
> If He had merely given us the Torah,
>   but had not brought us to the land of Israel—*Dayenu!*
> If He had merely brought us to the land of Israel,
>   but had not built us the Temple—*Dayenu!*
>   *We would have been satisfied!*

Those of us who are Messianic believers, and recognize that Jesus is the Messiah, can add a further *Dayenu*, knowing that if God had only provided salvation through the death and resurrection of our Messiah, it would have been enough! But we know that He did much more. As Jesus says, "I came that they may have life, and have it abundantly" (John 10:10). He satisfies us and gives us a joy in living which can only come from trusting in Him.

On the tenth day of Nisan when all the lambs to be sacrificed were led into Jerusalem, Jesus, the perfect Passover Lamb, rode into Jerusalem on a colt of a donkey. For four days He lived with the community, and they scrutinized Him and found Him blameless, without blemish. Likewise, Pontius Pilate, Herod, the Sanhedrin, and the thief on the cross found no fault in Jesus.

And so, because Jesus was found to be perfect, on the fourteenth day of the month of Nisan, in accordance with Exodus 12, on the day of Passover, at nine o'clock in the morning, when the Passover lambs were tied to the altar in the Temple, Jesus, the sinless Son of God, was nailed to the cross. At three o'clock, when the priest slaughtered the last Passover lamb in the Temple, Jesus, our perfect Passover Lamb, the ultimate sacrifice for sin, cried from the cross, "It is finished!" and gave up His life for us. The debt was paid. Jesus fully satisfied God's righteous demands.

Was that the end? *No!* Three days later Jesus rose from the dead and conquered sin and death. And, it is because of Him that we can understand Passover, and it is enough! *Dayenu!*

The Matzah Tash

Papa then lifts the matzah tash, or the "Unity" as it is often called. The Unity holds three pieces of matzah. It seems strange that it should be called Unity and yet have three sections. Papa removes the matzah in the middle, raises it, breaks it in half, and says,

> This is the bread of affliction our fathers ate in Egypt. Let all who are hungry come and eat. Let all who are in need come and celebrate Passover.

Today in Jewish homes, the Papa takes one half of the middle piece of matzah, wraps it in a linen napkin, and hides it. After dinner the children search for it, find it, and raise it from its hiding place. This buried and raised middle piece of matzah is called the *afikoman.*

Jewish tradition tells us that the three pieces of matzah represent Abraham, Isaac, and Jacob, or perhaps the three classes of Jewish people: the priests, the Levites, and the common people of Israel. However, some Messianic Jews also suggest that the three pieces of matzah placed in one pouch remind us of the unity of God who reveals Himself in three persons: Father, Son, and Holy Spirit.

Admittedly, this reads meaning into the ceremony, as Judaism does not teach that God is triune in nature, and so we hold this interpretation with great humility. However, it is true that there is tremendous discussion among the rabbis as to why there are three pieces of matzah, what the names of these pieces are, what they represent, and why the middle piece of matzah is broken, wrapped, hidden, and brought back at the end of the Passover Seder.

In following through with the idea that the three pieces of matzah reflect the triune nature of God, and the middle piece represents the Son of God, then the meaning of the breaking of the middle piece of matzah is even more significant. Once again, this is not taught within Judaism but is an interpretation that has developed among Messianic Jews over the years.

There is more to come regarding the afikoman at the conclusion of the Seder.[4]

The Four Questions

The youngest child asks the *four questions* that need to be asked at the Passover table. Prior to the first question, an opening question is asked, which in Hebrew is,

מַה נִשְׁתַּנָה הַלַּיְלָה הַזֶּה מִכָּל הַלֵּילוֹת?

Mah nish-ta-nah ha-lai-lah ha-zeh mi-kohl ha-lay-lot?

In English, "Why is this night so different from all other nights?" Papa then answers from the Haggadah, "On this night we celebrate the going forth of the children of Israel from slavery into freedom."

Child: "On all other nights we eat bread with leaven. On this night why do we eat only matzah?"

Papa: "When Pharaoh let our forefathers go from Egypt, they were forced to flee in great haste. As the children of Israel fled from Egypt, they did not have time for their dough to rise. The sun, which beat down on the dough as they carried it along, baked it into unleavened bread called matzah."

Child: "On all other nights we eat all kinds of vegetables; on this night why do we eat only bitter herbs?"

Papa: "On Passover we eat only bitter herbs because our forefathers were slaves in Egypt and their lives were made very bitter."

Child: "On all other nights we never think of dipping herbs in water or in anything else; why on this night do we dip the parsley in salt water?"

Papa: "We dip the parsley in salt water because it reminds us of a renewed life that we longed for following a life of pain, suffering, and tears."

Child: "On all other nights we eat either sitting or reclining; on this night why do we eat only reclining?"

Papa: "Reclining was a sign of a free man long ago, and since our forefathers were freed on this night, we recline at the table."

---

4. For more on the afikoman tradition, including its origin and role in the Passover, see chapter 11, "Passover and the Afikoman," by Daniel Nessim.

In response to the four questions, the leader of the Seder will continue to tell the story of redemption—with both brief answers and lengthy readings from the Bible and Jewish tradition—all part of the service detailed in the Haggadah.

The Horseradish: Maror
Papa, lifting the horseradish, the *maror*, reads the following,

> As sweet as our lives are today, let us remember how bitter life was for the children of Israel in the land of Egypt. As we dip the matzah into the bitter herbs, the maror, let us allow the bitter taste to cause us to shed tears of compassion for the sorrow that our ancestors knew.

Papa then reads,

> The children of Israel made bricks for Pharaoh's cities. We remember this task with a mixture of apples, cinnamon, nuts, and wine called *charoset*. Let us dip the matzah into the charoset and remember the hardships the Israelites endured under the whips of Pharaoh's taskmasters. But its sweetness will remind us of the freedom that was ours through God's deliverance.

The family dips their matzah into the apple mixture. As followers of the Jewish Messiah Jesus, we are reminded that even in the midst of bitter times, our lives are kept sweet through our relationship with the Lord.

The Beitzah: Roasted Egg
Papa turns his attention to the roasted egg on the Seder plate and reads,

> On the Seder plate there is a *beitzah*, a roasted egg. The egg speaks of a Festival (*hagigah*) sacrifice which can no longer be made because the Temple was destroyed.

Strange, you might think, that an egg is used to represent this sacrifice. An egg usually represents life, but there is more to it. According to tradition, the egg reminds us of the daily sacrifices offered in the Temple. It is roasted brown because the sacrifices were roasted. The rabbis added the egg to the Seder plate after the destruction of the Temple in 70 C.E. The egg is an annual reminder of that future day when the Messiah will establish His throne in Jerusalem, rebuild the Temple, and reintroduce the Temple sacrifices. We believe that this great day is coming, but we also understand that the once-for-all sacrifice for sin through Jesus the Messiah has already been made, and the future Temple will honor His sacrifice.

The Shankbone of a Lamb: The Zeroah
Papa next turns his attention to the shankbone of the lamb on the Seder plate and reads,

On the Seder plate there is a shankbone of a lamb. This roasted shankbone represents the lambs whose blood marked the houses of the children of Israel. Since the Temple in Jerusalem no longer stands, lamb is not eaten at Passover by Ashkenazic Jews, though lamb is eaten by Sephardic Jews—from Spain, North Africa, etc. This shankbone reminds us of the sacrificial lambs.

The Hebrew name for the shankbone is *zeroah*, which literally means "arm." The zeroah speaks of the outstretched arm of the Lord by which He redeemed His people from Egypt (Deut. 26:8). Messianic Jews link the term *zeroah* with the Lamb who comes to save us from sin and death as the word is used in the Servant Song of Isaiah beginning in Isaiah 52:7 and concluding in Isaiah 53:12. We believe this great passage speaks of the coming Messiah, so we view the saving arm of God as fulfilled in the Lamb of God—Jesus.

> The LORD has bared His holy *arm*
> In the sight of all the nations,
> That all the ends of the earth may see
> The salvation of our God. (Isa. 52:10, emphasis added)

> Who has believed our message?
> And to whom has the *arm* of the LORD been revealed? (Isa. 53:1, emphasis added)

There is no Temple in Jerusalem today, no altar, and no sacrifice for sin as God commanded. How then can sins be forgiven? We find in Leviticus 17:11 that God tells the children of Israel,

> For the life of the flesh is in the blood, and I have given it to you on the altar to make atonement for your souls; for it is the blood by reason of the life that makes atonement.

God still requires the shedding of blood for the forgiveness of sin. It is the blood that makes atonement for the soul. Atonement means a covering for sin. This is God's provision.

The blood of the Passover lamb on the doorposts physically saved Israelites that first Passover night and allowed them to begin their journey to the Promised Land. The blood of the perfect Passover Lamb, Jesus, saves us internally. He changes our hearts. When we trust in Messiah Yeshua, we receive God's gift of salvation, which includes forgiveness of sins as well as eternal life.

Again, remember that the first Passover in Egypt included not only the children of Israel but Gentiles as well (Exod. 12:38). What a glorious picture of God's plan of redemption for the world!

The Third Cup: The Cup of Redemption
After the third cup is poured, Papa reads,

God promised that He would return His people from slavery, that He would redeem His people with an outstretched arm.

It is this cup that Jesus raised and drank after supper in the upper room, that the Gospel writer describes in Luke 22:20:

> And in the same way He [Yeshua] took the cup after they had eaten, saying, "This cup which is poured out for you is the new covenant in My blood."

Our Messiah came. He died, shedding His blood to make atonement for sins. He is the perfect Passover Lamb. Through His outstretched arms on the cross, He provides redemption from sin and death forever, for any and all—Jew or Gentile—who place their faith and trust in Him.

We are not sure how much of the Passover tradition was developed at the time of Jesus, but we do know that He used this cup (which according to ancient tradition would have been the third cup) to join together the backdrop of the Passover with the promise of the New Covenant spoken of by the prophet Jeremiah in Jeremiah 31:31–34.

The Hidden Matzah: Afikoman

After dinner, the children look for the *afikoman*. The wrapped matzah is taken from its hiding place and a prize is given to the child who finds it.

Prior to the Temple's destruction in 70 C.E., Jewish people ate the Passover lamb during the Passover Seder. No other solid food was to be eaten after eating the Passover lamb. Today Jewish people partake of the afikoman as the last solid food of the Seder.

After taking the cup with His disciples, Jesus institutes a further memorial using the afikoman to represent His own body. In Luke 22:19, the Gospel writer says,

> When He had taken some bread and given thanks, He broke it and gave it to them, saying, "This is My body which is given for you; do this in remembrance of Me."

If you accept the actions of Yeshua during this Passover meal to be prophetic of His death and resurrection, then the parallels between His passion and the Passover are quite apparent. However, we cannot read the modern-day Seder into the Passover meal Jesus celebrated with His disciples. Nor can we expect that the Passover meal as it developed a few hundred years later in the Mishnah was known and practiced detail for detail by Jesus and His disciples at the Last Supper. However, in that this was oral tradition, to be written down later on, it is possible that some or even many of the traditions that were written down in the mishnaic tractate Pesahim were already known at this time. Let's take these parallels into consideration in reflecting upon the Last Supper of our Messiah.

Matzah is both striped and pierced. According to Isaiah 53, the Messiah will be both striped and pierced (v. 5). The Gospels tell us that Jesus's body was scourged for us; His body was pierced for us. Additionally, matzah is a food without leaven. Remember, leaven is a symbol for sin in the Scriptures. The matzah speaks of the sinless, perfect life of the Messiah who came to fulfill all righteousness. At His death, Jesus's body was wrapped in a linen cloth as is the afikoman. Jesus's body was buried in a tomb, just as the afikoman is hidden by the Papa during the Seder. Jesus's body was raised as the afikoman is found and raised from its hiding place by the children after dinner. Papa then breaks the afikoman in small pieces and distributes the pieces for each person to eat.

The Fourth Cup: The Cup of Praise

The fourth cup is called the Cup of Praise, or the Cup of Rejoicing, and the same prayer that has been sung over the first three cups is once again chanted by the Papa. We believe Jesus and His disciples also took the fourth cup as they left the upper room, singing a song from Psalm 118! Verse 24 of this psalm says, "This is the day which the LORD has made, let us rejoice and be glad in it." This may have been what Jesus sang as He made His way with the disciples to the Garden of Gethsemane and ultimately to the cross.

Papa reads as he takes the fourth cup,

> With this cup God is saying, "I will take you to Me for a people." This speaks of the time when the Lord will gather Israel.

The family then drinks the fourth cup.

The Fifth Cup: The Cup of Elijah

In Jewish homes today, the Papa continues to read from the Haggadah and notes the fifth cup of wine,

> We have a place setting that has not been touched. This is the place setting for Elijah. This cup is for Elijah. Where is Elijah? He is not here.

Each year in Jewish homes during the Passover, the door is opened to look for Elijah and invite him to join the Seder. When he is not there, Papa reads,

> Each year we pray that Elijah would come to the Seder, bringing a time of peace and freedom, bringing the time of the Messiah.

This coming of Elijah was predicted by the Prophet Malachi (see chapters 3 and 4 of the book of Malachi) and reaffirmed by Jesus when He told His disciples that John the Baptist came performing the ministry of Elijah, turning "the hearts of the fathers to their children and the hearts of the children to their fathers" (Mal. 4:5–6).

There is actually a charming tradition whereby Papa sends the children to the front door of the house, which is open wide, and the children are to invite the prophet to sit down at the table and drink the wine and share the sumptuous feast. The participants at the Seder also sing a mournful and soulful song entitled "Elijah the Prophet," asking the prophet to come and bring the One Israel has been waiting for—the Messiah, the Son of David.

So far, however, there has only been disappointment, and the Cup of Elijah has been poured out into the sink. Yet, there is always hope expressed in the concluding song of the Seder, !לְשָׁנָה הַבָּאָה בִּרוּשָׁלָיִם, *L'shanah HaBa'ah B'Yerushalayim!* "Next Year in Jerusalem!"

The Conclusion of the Seder

The Passover Seder is now complete, even as our salvation and redemption are complete because the Messiah Jesus has fulfilled the Passover. He is our Passover who has been sacrificed for us (1 Cor. 5:7)!

Jewish people are still waiting for their Messiah. How important it is for us to tell our Jewish friends and neighbors that the Messiah has already come and that through Yeshua we can experience the fullness of personal redemption.

Celebrating Passover is a wonderful way to demonstrate the unity of Scripture and to give us a deeper understanding of the history of redemption culminating in the death and resurrection of our Messiah Jesus. We look back to look forward, and because of what God has done we are assured that He will accomplish what He promised. This includes the return of the Messiah Jesus and even the restoration of His chosen people by turning their hearts to His Son. Paul attests to this in Romans 11:25–27, that one day God's chosen people will recognize that Jesus is "the Lamb of God who takes away the sin of the world!" (John 1:29).

Now you are better equipped to tell this glorious story and to share the Good News of Passover with both Jews and Gentiles!

17
PASSOVER LESSONS FOR YOUR CHILDREN

RACHEL GOLDSTEIN-DAVIS

The children are the most important observers of the Passover Seder! We hope you will find this chapter useful in engaging the children to celebrate the Seder and to understand the Gospel truths woven throughout this great celebration.

WHY TEACH CHILDREN ABOUT THE PASSOVER?

It is important to teach the Bible to our children, as it says in Deuteronomy 6:6, "You shall teach them [the commandments] diligently to your children, and shall talk of them when you sit in your house, and when you walk by the way, and when you lie down, and when you rise" (ESV). We spend a lot of time praying for our children and helping them draw close to Jesus, whose Hebrew name is Yeshua. We want them to walk closely with their Messiah and we know that their spiritual lives are best shaped when they are young.

We teach them stories from the Old and New Testaments, but many times we might not fully understand some of the backgrounds of the stories ourselves. That's because both the Old and New Testaments were written by people whose cultures were far different from ours today. There is great value in teaching our children God's truth from the Old Testament, as it is especially picturesque and filled with physical illustrations of spiritual truths. But to teach the Old Testament we first need to put ourselves in that ancient culture's "sandals," and then create lessons that can be understood in our modern age.

One Old Testament story that's especially important to teach is the Passover. This magnificent story paints a portrait of redemption that became a reference point for all future stories of national and spiritual liberation in the Scriptures and points beautifully to the ultimate story of salvation in Jesus, "the Lamb of God who takes away the sin of the world!" (John 1:29).

Every year Jewish people across the globe gather in homes to celebrate the Passover Seder and remember how the Lord won their ancestors' freedom from bondage; miraculously sustained them in the desert with food, water, and shelter; and taught them to rely utterly on Him. They celebrate how He brought their forefathers back to the Promised Land of Israel. There are so many wonderful lessons embedded in the Passover that enable us to impact the young lives God has called us to mold and develop.

Most importantly, we can use the Passover to teach our children about the glorious salvation we have received through Jesus the Messiah. There are so many parallels between the Gospel story and the ancient Passover as well as the way the holiday has been observed by Jewish people throughout the centuries.

For example, in the story of the Exodus from Egypt the Lord, passed over the homes of the Israelites whose doors were smeared with the blood of the perfect and innocent sacrificial lamb and did not slay the firstborn males in those homes. We understand that this was a prophetic type of what was to come as God has also forgiven and passed over all whose hearts are covered by the blood of Yeshua, the Lamb of God, and have received Him as their Savior and Lord. And just as the Israelites of old were freed from bondage, those who have trusted in Yeshua are freed from bondage to sin.

We do not need to wander in the wilderness of this life and in a world that is passing away. The Lord through His Word and His Spirit has given us redemption, hope, and direction to live for Him. We are not simply wandering through this life, but instead are becoming more and more like our Messiah each day until He comes again. We have a purpose in life that goes beyond our everyday concern for survival. He is our joy and salvation and provides for all of our needs. We understand that redeemed people still struggle, but the Lord is faithful. These are lessons our children need to understand, and the Passover story provides us with excellent teaching tools. But, of course, there is much more! The Passover helps our kids understand that the Lord, who is great and mighty, cares for even the smallest details in our lives.

Through interacting with the items on the Seder table, our children are able to handle, see, and experience the message of redemption Jewish people have been retelling for centuries. We are also able to introduce our children to the story of the Last Supper observed by Jesus and His disciples, which was most likely an earlier version of the Passover Seder that has developed to the modern version since the destruction of the Temple in 70 c.e. By understanding the parallels between the traditions of the Jewish Passover Seder and the Last Supper, our children will gain a perspective on their own salvation that is richer and deeper and more understandable because the Seder is so very visual and tactile.

Passover in Israel and in Jewish communities throughout the world is a major undertaking and requires a great deal of work and preparation. All foods must be bought days ahead as the family usually gathers from all over for what is by far the largest family get-together of the year. Although many Jewish homes are secular, Passover is still celebrated by more than 80 percent of Jewish households, and in Israel that number is probably closer to 100 percent! Jewish people know the Passover story, and it is one of the experiences that draws Jewish people together across countries, nationalities, and languages.

The Passover provides a perfect point of commonality between Jewish people and Christians. Jewish people simply do not understand the ultimate fulfillment of the holiday through Jesus the Messiah. It is our responsibility as believers in Yeshua to share this story with our Jewish loved ones and friends. It is also an opportunity for our children to speak to their young friends about their faith in Jesus.

Your children probably have Jewish friends in school, extended families, the playground, etc. They can wish their Jewish friends a "Happy Passover!" and speak with them about their upcoming Seder, if they know something about Passover and how the Jewish festival ties in to their own faith in Jesus. These simple conversations about the Lord can be used by God as a small seed planted in the lives of Jewish children when they are young. We believe it is not appropriate for adults to take these initiatives in talking with children without the Jewish parents' permission. But we believe it is appropriate for your children to swap stories about their culture and faith.

GOALS FOR THESE LESSONS

The goals for the following three lessons are (1) to teach your children about Passover and its fulfillment in Jesus through the retelling of the Bible's story of Passover, (2) to show your children how Jewish people celebrate Passover, and (3) to educate your children about Jewish people through playing games, learning Hebrew words, doing crafts, and eating some of the Passover elements. Depending on your time, you might decide to do the complete lesson or pick and choose parts. At least the option is available. You will find a helpful summary of the story at the beginning of every lesson.

We hope and pray you will find the lessons to be helpful and that your children will be blessed through understanding the Jewish backgrounds of the Last Supper and will gain a better understanding of our salvation through Jesus, the Lamb of God.

LESSON 1: PREPARING FOR PASSOVER

Retelling: The Story of Moses and the Israelites in Egypt

More than 2,500 years ago, Joseph and his family moved to Egypt to escape a famine in the land of Canaan, which was later called Israel. They survived, and the generations of their family grew until they became a very large group of people. Pharaoh, the ruler of Egypt, became afraid of all the Hebrews, as the Jewish people at that time were called, living in his country, so he made them slaves. He even made a law that when Hebrew babies were born, the boys should be killed.

A baby boy named Moses was born and his mother wanted to save him, so she put him in a waterproof basket and put the basket in the Nile River. Pharaoh's daughter found the baby and adopted him, and he was raised in Pharaoh's palace.

When Moses grew up, he became very upset about how his people, the Israelites, were being treated. When he saw a Hebrew slave being beaten by an Egyptian taskmaster, Moses killed the Egyptian. This was a horrible thing, and Moses fled to the desert in fear. While Moses was in the desert, in the land of Midian, God spoke to him from a burning bush that would not burn up. God told him to go back to Egypt and tell Pharaoh, "Let my people go." (Exod. 9:1)

Moses asked Pharaoh many times to let the people of Israel go free, but even after nine plagues fell on Egypt, Pharaoh's heart was still hard and he would not agree. The final plague was the scariest—the destroyer, sometimes referred to as the "angel of death," was going to kill all the firstborn males in Egypt.

The Lord told Moses to warn his people to carefully listen and obey in order to save their lives. They had to clean their houses and get rid of all *chametz* (KHUH-mitz). Chametz is yeast, or leaven. So the Hebrews had to throw out all their bread and cookies. They had to bake *matzah* (MAHTZ-uh), which is bread made without yeast, and it's more like crackers than bread. And God also said that the people had to kill a little lamb. The lamb was to be perfect, with no spots or bruises and no broken bones. The people had to take some blood from the lamb and put it on the doorposts and lintels (doorframes) of their houses so that the destroyer would "pass over" their home. The lamb was to be roasted and eaten with bitter herbs and matzah, and the people had no time to relax. They had to be packed and ready to leave—with their shoes and jackets on.

That night, the destroyer came and killed all the firstborn sons in Egypt—except those in families that had obeyed God's instructions to put the lamb's blood on their doors. There was much crying in Egypt that night, and Pharaoh's own son died. Finally, after this horrible thing, Pharaoh told the Jewish people they were free to go.

Main Points

1. The Israelites were slaves in Egypt, and they wanted to be free so they could go and live in the Promised Land.

2. Moses kept asking Pharaoh to let the people go and Pharaoh said no, even after nine plagues.

3. The people prepared for the Passover night by getting rid of *chametz* (leaven or yeast). The New Testament says that leaven, or yeast, represents sin in our lives. Yeast is the ingredient that makes bread puffy. We don't want to be "puffed up" with pride, making fun of other people and thinking we are better than them (read 1 Corinthians 5:7–8).

4. Just like the lamb that was sacrificed had to be perfect, Jesus (who is called the Lamb of God) was also perfect and sinless. The blood of the Passover lamb saved the people from death in Egypt, and Jesus's blood saves us from eternal death and gives us eternal life!

Craft

Make two batches of dough, one with leaven (yeast) and one without, so that the children can see the difference between risen dough and flat dough. You can make flat dough right in front of the children, getting their help too, but you might need to make risen dough at home so that it has hours to rise. You can also bring in a box of store-bought matzah for the kids to eat.

Hebrew Words

Seder (SAY-der).[1] The Jewish ceremonial dinner on the first night of Passover, with lots of Bible reading and eating traditional foods.

matzah (MAHTZ-uh). A hard cracker-like bread made from only flour and water (taste it).

chametz (KHUH-mitz). Leaven or yeast, or all food that has this ingredient.

Bible Passage

1 Corinthians 5:7–8

Game: Search for the Chametz

Hide bagels, muffins, bread, cereal, or cookies all over the room for the kids to find. These could be plastic food items (like toys or magnets) or the real thing (which they will be quite happy about). If the food is real, make sure to seal the items in plastic bags to prevent a crumbly mess and in case some are not found.

LESSON 2: THE PLAGUES OF PASSOVER

Retelling: *The Story of Pharaoh and the Ten Plagues*

Pharaoh was the ruler of his country; he was boss over everyone in Egypt. Suddenly, Moses came and demanded that the Israelites—Pharaoh's slaves—all leave Egypt. Pharaoh had gotten used to having this free labor. He was building a huge kingdom and needed workers to make himself great, so when Moses delivered God's message, "Let my people go!" Pharaoh would

---

1. For a helpful reference work that also includes phonetic pronunciation, see Joyce Eisenberg and Ellen Scolnic, *Dictionary of Jewish Words*, rev. ed. (Philadelphia: Jewish Publication Society, 2006).

not listen to Moses. God sent plague after plague on Egypt, but Pharaoh was stubborn and would not change his mind.

Each plague that fell on Egypt represented a battle between our God and the Egyptian gods. The Egyptians had "gods" for everything—water, crops, livestock, health—so each plague was directed towards these areas on purpose to show that the Egyptian gods were false gods. Our God is mighty and powerful, and the plagues that fell on Egypt are an example of His strength.

During the first nine plagues, Pharaoh would not listen and did not want to admit that he had lost against the Most High God. The tenth plague—the death of all the firstborn males in Egypt—was the harshest. Finally, Pharaoh agreed to let the Israelites go, but not before his people and the land of Egypt had suffered dire consequences.

Main Point

God wants us to pay close attention to Him. How many times does God try to get our attention and we are stubborn or we think our ideas are better than His? Still, He keeps trying to get us to listen and obey Him. He gives us chances and is patient with us. How many times will it take?

Theme Words / Bible Passages / Object Lessons

This lesson can be as interactive as you wish. Start by asking the children to list the plagues; chances are that they will forget one or two. Give them the word for each plague (blood, frogs, gnats, etc.). Ask them what they think it was like to live through the plagues. Maybe they have experienced something similar (hail, tornados, hurricanes, heavy floods). How did they react? You could also reenact the plagues—this will take some props and preparation on your part.

1. *The Plague of Blood* (Exod. 7:14–24). All the water in Egypt was turned to blood. It was disgusting; it stank and the fish died. In a hot, desert country, the people needed fresh water to drink and water their crops!
   OBJECT LESSON: If you want to be creative, have a clear pitcher in place with inconspicuous red dye on the bottom (maybe place the pitcher on a dark table mat or piece of paper to hide the dye). Fill the pitcher with clear water and let the children watch it turn to "blood."[2]

2. *The Plague of Frogs* (Exod. 7:25–8:15). There were frogs everywhere! Have the children imagine all the places where the frogs would be!

---

2. This can also be done using an inexpensive kit that turns water into "wine" or "blood" using a pH indicator (phenolphthalein solution) and an alkaline chemical to change pH from neutral to basic (sodium carbonate powder). Turn Water into Wine Kit, The Science Company, https://www.sci-encecompany.com/Turn-Water-Into-Wine-Kit-P16807.aspx. When the two glasses of water, each treated with one of the chemicals, are mixed, the solution will immediately turn red. You should *not* drink these chemicals.

Once the plague was over, all the frogs died and stank—pretty gross. OBJECT LESSON: If the children want to be silly—have them hop around like frogs!

3. *The Plague of Gnats* (Exod. 8:16–19). These tiny bugs were every-where: on the ground, in the homes, even on people's skin! OBJECT LESSON: Suddenly throw some store-bought plastic bugs on the kids next to you. It should get a reaction!

4. *The Plague of Flies* (Exod. 8:20–32). Do you know the song "Shoo fly, don't bother me"? Imagine swarms and swarms of flies hover-ing everywhere, touching you, covering the ground, in your food, on your pets—so annoying and disgusting. However, there were no insects bothering the Israelites where they were living. OBJECT LESSON: Pretend to gulp the imaginary flies around you. "Oops, I think I swallowed a fly!"

5. *Plague of Pestilence* (Exod. 9:1–7). In those days, they didn't have cars or tractors to pull heavy things around; instead they had horses, camels, and strong cattle. All these animals died. How were they to get milk and meat? How were they going to eat, to work . . . and what happened if you had a favorite goat? The Isra-elites' livestock did not die. Pharaoh knew this, but it only made him more stubborn.

6. *The Plague of Boils* (Exod. 9:8–12). Have you ever had the chicken pox, or better yet, a really big red zit? That is kind of what boils are. The Egyptians and their animals had them everywhere on their bod-ies and it hurt to touch, to sleep, to move. OBJECT LESSON: Have the children pretend to scratch like they have the worst chicken pox in the world!

7. *The Plague of Hail* (Exod. 9:13–35). The Lord sent the worst hail-storm ever; Egypt had never seen a storm like this! Remember that in a desert climate like Egypt's, they might never have seen ice or snow! The hailstones were so big that they destroyed everything, and anyone who was left outside died—both people and animals. The hail destroyed most of the crops, too. But God was merciful and gave the message to Pharaoh with enough time to tell the people to bring everything under shelter. There was thunder and hail and fire that ran down to the earth. But where the children of Israel were living there was no hail. Pharaoh almost listened to God and let the people go, but after the terrifying storm was over, he changed his mind. OBJECT LESSON: In the middle of your explanation, throw cotton balls, ping pong balls, or marshmallows on the kids.

8. *The Plague of Locusts* (Exod. 10:1–20). Pharaoh tried to make a deal with God by allowing the men to leave Egypt but making the women and children stay. This was not acceptable, and God sent another devastating plague to teach Pharaoh to listen. There had already been frogs, gnats/lice, and flies to swarm around everything, and then hail to destroy the crops. Now locusts came to eat up the last bits of grass, leaves, and fruit. They were so numerous that the ground was completely covered by them!

9. *The Plague of Darkness* (Exod. 10:21–29). The Lord then sent complete darkness on Egypt for three days. But the children of Israel had light in their homes. Pharaoh sent for Moses and tried to make another deal with God, saying that the people could leave, but their cattle had to stay. Moses reminded Pharaoh that everything must leave Egypt—even all the Israelites' possessions. It was all or nothing! Pharaoh got angry and told Moses never to come before him again. OBJECT LESSON: Have you ever been in a dark cave where you can't even see your hand in front of you? In darkness, you get disoriented, you can't get anything done; it's boring and scary! If you can, turn off the lights and sit in darkness for a few minutes. Maybe retell this part of the story in darkness (or with the kids' eyes closed).

10. *Death of the Firstborn* (Exod. 11:1–10). (Don't worry, we won't reenact this one!) It would have been better if the Egyptians had recognized God's power over the natural and spiritual elements of the world.

   Instead, the destroyer passed through Egypt and wherever the blood of the spotless lamb was not seen on the doors of the homes, the firstborn males died—both human and animal. During this horrible night, the Israelites had very important instructions from God that would save their lives and prepare them for leaving Egypt. They obeyed God and were ready to go with everything packed, and as they ate their Passover dinner they knew they were saved from the destroyer as he passed over them. That night, even Pharaoh's own son died.

   After these ten plagues, Pharaoh at last let the Israelites leave Egypt. It took ten plagues for Pharaoh to finally obey God. How many times does it take for us to listen to God and do what He says? It's best if it's just one time!

Craft
Ask the kids which of the first nine plagues would have bothered them the most. Invite them to draw a picture about one of the plagues.

LESSON 3: PARTICIPATING IN THE PASSOVER SEDER
This lesson focuses on the actual Passover Seder. There is some preparation you can do beforehand, and some you can do with the children. The

Seder elements are listed below, and after the kids have decorated their Seder plates, you can eat together and discuss their meanings.

If you would like to see if a Chosen People Ministries staff person is available to present the Passover Seder to your Sunday school class, home school group, or your church family, contact our Church Ministries staff (chosenpeople.com/church) would be happy to speak with you or your pastor.

Main Point

It is God who saves us. He wants us to remember what He has done for us so we will trust in Him.

Bible Passage

Exodus 12

Retelling / Craft / Hebrew Words

Let's have a Seder!

Buy some large throwaway paper plates and child-safe markers. Each child can draw five circles on his or her plate and write the names of the items (given below) in transliterated Hebrew and/or English.

Now you get to participate in your own Seder! We will go through each Seder item and explain what it means, so you can see, smell, and taste them and learn more about God and His Messiah in the Passover meal. Some of these items are biblical and some are traditional. The biblical items that Moses and the Israelites used are found in Exodus 12 and are the most important—matzah (unleavened bread), maror (bitter herbs) and zeroah (lamb shankbone)—while the other items have been added over the years by Jewish rabbis from around the world for families to use to help them celebrate the Passover.

You will want to try to find some matzah, the unleavened bread representing a life without sin. The Jewish people had to bake this bread quickly, without allowing the dough time to rise, because they ate their dinner with their jackets and shoes on—ready to leave Egypt at any moment as soon as Moses said, "Go!" How different it is now. As we participate in your Seder so many years after the first Passover, we use the best dishes, take our time, and eat like kings and queens in freedom!

The Cup of Blessing (or *The Cup of Sanctification*). Take a sip of grape juice. We begin the Seder by saying "Blessed are You, Lord our God, King of the Universe, who created the fruit of the vine."

Passover Items on the Seder Plate

Using the Seder plates that the kids have made, put all the items on the plates in their correct positions before starting the Seder.

1. *Zeroah* (zeh-ROH-ah). Lamb shankbone. The bone reminds us of the Passover lamb sacrificed for the first Passover. Jesus is our

Passover Lamb who died to give us eternal life! Jewish people don't understand that Jesus is the Lamb of God, so let's take a moment to pray for them. Put this item in the top right-hand circle on your plate—at the 2:00 position on a clock.

2. *Charoset* (khah-ROH-set). A mixture of apples (finely chopped and allowed to turn brown), honey, nuts (do not include if there are allergies), cinnamon, and a dash of grape juice—*very tasty*! This mixture looks like mortar for bricks. When the Israelites were slaves, they had to mix straw, dirt, and water to make their own mortar for building. The charoset reminds us of the hard slave work in Egypt. But why does a reminder of something so bitter taste so sweet? Because we remember that even in hard work and suffering, we can have redemption. The Israelites were freed and were able to go to the Promised Land! We can remember that our lives can be sweet and wonderful with Jesus! Put this item in the bottom right circle on the plate—at the 4:00 position on a clock. Enjoy eating some charoset spread on pieces of matzah crackers.

3. *Maror* (mah-ROAR). Horseradish root (from a jar—the red kind is not as spicy as the white kind. It is wise to taste only a dip first, as it might be too spicy for some!). This bitter herb represents the harsh suffering and bitter times the Jewish people endured when they were slaves in Egypt. Put this item in the circle in the middle of the plate. Spread a little on pieces of matzah and eat.

4. *Karpas* (CAR-pahs). Parsley (just a sprig or two). The parsley is a symbol of spring and new life—just as new leaves grow on trees in the spring! It reminds us of the rebirth of the Jewish nation and of freedom. Put this item in the bottom left circle on the plate—at the 8:00 position on a clock. Break off a sprig, dip it in salt water, and eat it. Life was hard for the Israelites and even though there was the season of spring and new life, there were also many salty tears.

   Cups of salt water are meant for dipping the parsley and egg pieces. Salt water represents tears. As the Israelites yearned to be freed from slavery and go to live in the Promised Land, they shed tears of sorrow. Thankfully, we can rejoice as believers in Jesus, because we have been given the ultimate gift anyone could receive—eternal life with Him! (This is not placed on the seder plate but is available on the table.)

5. *Beitzah* (bay-TZAH). Hard-boiled or roasted egg (this can be cut up and each child can be given a half or a quarter). This reminds us of the ceremonial offering that was brought to the Temple each Passover. Also, since Passover always falls in the spring, the egg reminds

us of life—new life in Jesus. Put this item in the 10:00 position on a clock. Also, take a piece of your egg and dip it into the salt water. New life was immersed in tears when the Israelites were slaves.

Charoset and Maror Sandwich. Put a bit of the horseradish and the sweet apple mixture between two pieces of matzah and eat the "sandwich." These two ingredients together stand for the joy and sorrow that was found in the Israelites' lives when they were in Egypt: they were slaves (which was bitter) and then were granted freedom (which was sweet). Even though bad things sometimes happen in our lives, we have the sweetness of knowing that Jesus set us free from being slaves to sin.

The Cup of Plagues (or ***The Cup of Judgment***). Have the children dip a finger in their cup and make a dot of grape juice on their plate for each of the ten plagues (they can make designs like smiley faces or rainbows on their plate). Recite the plagues together while doing so.

Matzah Tash (MAHTZ-uh TAHSH). A matzah bag with three compartments. If you don't have one, you can take a large white napkin or a large white cloth and fold it into three sections. Place a piece of matzah in each section. Then remove the middle matzah, break it in two, and put half back. The remaining piece is now named the ***afikoman*** (ah-fee-KO-men), a Greek word meaning "that which is to come after." The afikoman is wrapped in white linen and hidden. Have all the kids close their eyes for a minute. Hide the afikoman and ask the kids to get up and look for it. Tell them the child who finds it should bring it back. When this happens, unwrap the afikoman, break it in pieces and distribute to all the participants.

You might pause for a moment and ask, "Does anyone know why the matzah tash and the hidden matzah are important?" Then explain that some rabbis described the three compartments as representing the Patriarchs: Abraham, Isaac, and Jacob; and others said they stood for the divisions of the people of Israel: the priests, the Levites, and the Jewish people in general. As believers in the Messiah, we might look at the three pieces as representing the triune nature of God: the Father, the Son, and the Holy Spirit, although we realize that Jewish people traditionally do not believe in the Trinity.

Did you notice that the middle piece of matzah was broken, and the afikoman part was wrapped in a napkin and hidden? The rabbis aren't sure why this custom started. We believe this might represent the piece of matzah Jesus broke and handed to His disciples at the Last Supper. We read in the Gospel of Luke,

> And when He had taken some bread and given thanks, He
> broke it and gave it to them, saying, "This is My body which
> is given for you; do this in remembrance of Me." (Luke 22:19)

Understanding the traditions of the afikoman gives us a better understanding of the Lord's Supper, since on the very next day Jesus would be crucified, wrapped for burial (hidden), and three days later raised from the dead (1 Cor. 15:3–4). We now understand that Jesus may have intended the breaking of the matzah at the Last Supper as a prophecy of His death, burial, and resurrection. We are sure the disciples did not fully understand this until after these events happened, but as followers of Jesus and upon reflection, we can see it. *Eat your piece of afikoman matzah.*

The Cup of Redemption. Jesus next took the cup that is sipped after the meal. This is associated with the third cup of the Passover, the cup called Redemption. It reminds us of the shed blood of the little lamb slain for the redemption of the firstborn male of the Israelite homes in Egypt. This event, of course, led to the Exodus. In the Gospel of Luke we read,

> And in the same way He took the cup after they had eaten, say-
> ing, "This cup which is poured out for you is the new covenant
> in My blood." (Luke 22:20)

Once again we see that Jesus was speaking about Himself, since the next day His blood would be shed for the forgiveness of sin. The cup Jewish people sipped for centuries pointed to the death of the Lamb of God who was sacrificed for the sins of us all. We celebrate the fulfillment of this salvation when we take the cup of juice at the Lord's Table for Communion or the Lord's Supper. *Drink a little cup of grape juice.*

The Cup of Praise (or *The Cup of Rejoicing*). We drink the fourth cup to express the joy we have as a people because of God's glorious act of redemption on our behalf. He saved our sons through the shed blood of the lamb in the original Exodus. As followers of Yeshua, we understand that the third cup was fulfilled at the Lord's Supper with the cup Jesus used to remind us that ultimate redemption comes through His blood shed for our sins. This gives us a greater reason to rejoice, and we drink the fourth cup and praise God for the salvation available to both Jews and Gentiles through the Lamb of God who takes away the sin of the world.

A *song* is sung at the end of every Seder: *L'shana Haba'ah B'Yerushalayim!* "Next Year in Jerusalem!" This wonderful and lively song speaks of the future day of Messianic redemption when the Messiah will come and bring the Jewish people back to the Land of Israel to celebrate the Passover. Of course, as believers in Jesus, we believe He has come once and is coming again. What a wonderful opportunity we have now to tell our Jewish friends that the Messiah has come and His name is Yeshua—"the Lamb of God who takes away the sin of the world!" (John 1:29).

PASSOVER AROUND THE WORLD

Games and Songs

Every child loves the Passover Seder. It is meant for kids and has many object lessons and hands-on experiences. The parents involve the kids, as it is a long meal and they might get restless. Songs, games, and great memories can be had by all. One game, just mentioned, is the hiding and finding of the afikoman. Although hidden for part of the meal, the afikoman is still integral to the Seder and it helps to communicate a powerful message. Usually, the child who finds it can barter for its return, knowing how important it is to the Seder. Money, tickets to fun events, and special meals are all great rewards for the one who finds the afikoman.

At the start of the Seder, a final, thorough search for chametz is traditionally made in the home. Often, the father hides some crumbs in a corner for a child to find. The crumbs are scooped up in a dust pan or newspaper. In some places and/or eras, these last crumbs of leaven were taken outside to a communal bonfire and thrown in, burning the last "sin" found in the home.

It's the job of the youngest child at the Seder who is able to do this, to recite special questions (traditionally in Hebrew), including "Why is this night different than all other nights?" and "Why do we eat all these different foods?" It's a rite of passage for the youngest and takes many days and weeks to practice (and to get over the nerves and embarrassment of public speaking), but it's well worth the effort..

The point of the Seder is to keep the kids engaged, asking questions, learning, and interacting. You can even play Passover Bingo, Questions and Answers in a Moses Basket, and Eye Spy, as well as make clay models of Passover items. Suggestions for such games and family activities can readily be found online. Getting ready for Passover can be a stressful time, but playing some games or doing special activities can make it fun for everyone!

Every Seder has many songs that can be sung to many different tunes and melodies. It seems like each country and culture has its own way to sing these traditional songs. Many are in Hebrew and take a while to learn, but some notable ones are *L'Shanah HaBa'ah, Dayenu, Echad Mi Yodeah*, and *Eliyahu HaNavi*.[3]

---

3. For these and other Passover songs (titles spelled in various ways), see our website for additional Passover-themed resources: www.messiahinthepassover.com. There are also Passover karaoke apps that will play songs on your phone or mobile device.

Everyone remembers Mom's brisket on Passover, but not everyone might want to eat the bitter herbs. Jewish children will remember the double-daring done to see who would eat the biggest bite of horseradish (maror) and subsequently turn red, choke a little, and have tears streaming down their faces after the flush simmered down a little. Each country prepares the *gefilte* fish (traditional appetizer) a little differently, and most children will poke it with their fork to see if it wiggles back. Everyone loves the charoset (be mindful of the nuts in the recipe if anyone has food allergies), the grape juice, and the special Passover desserts. This is what Passover fun is all about—the feasting on food!

TO REMEMBER ESPECIALLY

Passover is a wonderful holiday that helps bond us with our Jewish brothers and sisters who are celebrating the feast around the world. It will break down walls of suspicion when you, too, understand this festival and can genuinely wish your Jewish friends "Happy Passover!" It helps us more fully comprehend the message of redemption in both the Old and New Testaments and especially gives us new insight into the words of Jesus. The Passover will help the children appreciate the Lord's Supper or Communion in a new and deeper way.

Teaching kids about celebrating Passover takes some preparation and study, but the rewards are immense. Each element is an object lesson of redemption, joy, tears, offerings, life, freedom, prophecy, faithfulness, and conquering death! We could dwell on these words for weeks!

It is fun to teach the kids some Hebrew words and Jewish customs and to introduce them to new foods. It will help them better understand their physical and/or spiritual Jewish heritage (Rom. 11:17–21) and even create opportunities for them to witness to their friends. Making a fun and interactive Seder will be well worth the effort—for kids and adults, too!

PRAYING WITH CHILDREN TO ACCEPT JESUS THROUGH THE PASSOVER

During these lessons and especially during the Seder, there will be opportunities to ask the children how they feel about what they are learning and if they have questions. As you prepare to discuss salvation with a child, here are a few things to keep in mind. First, spend time in prayer asking:

- that the Holy Spirit would prepare your child.
- that He would help you present the information clearly.
- that He would give your child understanding.
- that He would convince your child of the truth of your words.

We recommend that you talk with each child alone and don't rush through it. Use simple words your child will understand and explain phrases that might confuse him or her (like "invite Jesus into your heart"). At the end, ask questions to make sure your child understands all that you have said.

Don't push your children to make a decision. Your children's salvation is a matter between them and the Holy Spirit. The Holy Spirit must be the one who convinces them of their sin and need for salvation. As a result, you may need to revisit the conversation with your children several times. At the right time the Holy Spirit will speak to them.

You can ask the children what part of the Passover lesson really impacted them. It might be the matzah—how it represents purity and is not puffed up. It might be how God protects and cares for us and provides for all our needs. It might be the afikoman—how it is wrapped in linen, hidden, and brought back—just as Jesus died, was buried, and raised from the dead. It might be how the Passover lamb had to be perfect, without blemish, and its blood was put on the people's doors—just as Jesus, the Lamb of God, was perfect and sinless and His blood is put on the doors of our hearts when we give our hearts to Him. It might simply be the dipping of the parsley (life) in salt water (tears). You never know what might touch a child's heart and understanding.

You can spend time with your children and discuss these amazing points about the Lord and our salvation, and pray together. Take some time to pray, confess sin, acknowledge that Jesus is our Messiah and that He died to give us the gift of eternal life. He died willingly for us, and will take on all our sin and shame. We can have joy forever, knowing that if we belong to Him, we will live with Him for eternity. In the meantime, we are on earth to share His joy and glory and love with others, to proclaim His message and tell others of their Messiah.

For additional information you might review any number of Jewish websites on the topic of Passover.[4] And of course, this entire volume will provide you with all the background you need to teach the children about this glorious festival.

---

4. For additional resources, see the series of brief Passover-themed articles at "Passover," BBC, last updated July 9, 2009, http://www.bbc.co.uk/religion/religions/judaism/holydays/passover_1.shtml. Also see this book's website for additional Passover-themed resources: www.messiahinthepassover.com.

18
A MESSIANIC FAMILY HAGGADAH

CHOSEN PEOPLE MINISTRIES

The following Messianic Family Haggadah is designed for use with your family, home group, or church to celebrate a Jesus-centered Passover Seder. You are permitted to make copies of the Haggadah from this book for this purpose or go to www.messiahinthepassover.com and download a printable copy for those attending your Seder. Additional Passover-themed resources such as song suggestions for the Seder are also available on this website.

For many centuries, Passover has been celebrated with the help of a Haggadah, a book or booklet that includes liturgy, stories, participatory readings, and biblical references to guide Jewish families in their celebration of this holy festival. The Haggadah, which means "the telling," was compiled by Jewish sages over hundreds and perhaps thousands of years. You will find many versions of the Haggadah from Jewish cultures around the world that tell the story of God's redemption of the people of Israel from bondage in Egypt.

This particular Haggadah, based upon the traditional order of service of the Passover, is adapted for use by both Jewish and Gentile followers of Yeshua (Jesus). Along with the usual elements of the Seder, we highlight the links between the traditional Seder and the Last Supper. It is our prayer that you will set aside time during Passover week and enjoy a Seder together with family and friends, so that your faith in the Lamb of God who takes away the sin of the world will be deepened, or even perhaps awakened for the first time if you have not yet committed your life to God's Messiah.

The word *Seder* simply means "order" and refers to an order of service designed to tell the story of the Passover. This telling (Haggadah) reminds the children of Israel each year of what God did by the hand of Moses in delivering them from Egyptian bondage. This is a great way to enhance your understanding of Scripture. The Feast of Passover is especially for the children, as they can personally participate in the Seder. By touching, tasting, and smelling the elements on the Seder table, participants are brought back to the great events of the original Exodus and become better able to identify with the Exodus and the redemption of the children of Israel.

Yet, for followers of the Messiah, the story of redemption reminds us of far more than the deliverance from Egypt. It brings our minds to the redemption and deliverance from sin that God has provided through His Son. We believe that Yeshua celebrated an early form of the Passover Seder with His disciples. This Haggadah, especially created for you and your family, will wed these two great stories of redemption together as we join the Savior on that night when He celebrated His last Seder with His disciples on this earth.

ORDER OF SERVICE (SEDER)

Birkat HaNer, Lighting of the Candles

Kiddush, First Cup: The Cup of Sanctification

Urchatz, First Washing of the Hands

Karpas, Dipping of the Parsley

Yachatz, Breaking of the Middle Matzah

Maggid, The Story of the Passover

Ma-Nishtanah, The Four Questions

Makkot, Second Cup: The Cup of Plagues

Zeroah, or *Pesach*, The Lamb Shankbone

Rachtzah, Second Washing of the Hands

Maror, Eating of the Bitter Herbs

Korech, Eating of the Bitter Herbs with Charoset

Beitzah, The Roasted Egg

Shulchan Orech, The Passover Supper

Tzafun, Eating of the Afikoman

HaGeulah, Third Cup: The Cup of Redemption

Eliyahu, Elijah's Cup

Hallel, Fourth Cup: The Cup of Praise

Birkat HaNer, *Lighting of the Candles*

Traditionally, Passover is celebrated at home with family after all leaven has been removed from the household. Once the house and the participants are ceremonially clean, the Passover Seder can begin. The woman of the house says a blessing and lights the Passover candles. It is appropriate that the woman brings light into the home, because it was through the woman that the light of the world, Messiah Jesus, came into the world (Gen. 3:15; Luke 2:7).

The woman of the house recites the following Hebrew prayer:

בָּרוּךְ אַתָּה אֲדֹנָי אֱלֹהֵינוּ מֶלֶךְ הָעוֹלָם אֲשֶׁר קִדְּשָׁנוּ בְּמִצְוֹתָיו וְצִוָּנוּ לְהַדְלִיק
נֵר שֶׁל יוֹם טוֹב.

Baruch atah Ado-nai Elo-hei-nu Me-lech ha-Olam, asher kid-sha-nu bemits-vo-tav vetsi-va-nu lehad-lik ner shel yom tov.

Blessed art Thou, O Lord our God, King of the universe, who has sanctified us with Thy commandments and commanded us to kindle the festival lights.

THE FOUR CUPS OF THE FRUIT OF THE VINE

The Passover Seder is structured around four cups of the fruit of the vine, which serve as the foundation for the experience. Each cup is named after one of the four specific promises that God made to Israel in Exodus 6:6–7. Each cup is thematically connected to a different stage in the progression of the Seder.

1. The Cup of Sanctification

2. The Cup of Plagues

3. The Cup of Redemption

4. The Cup of Praise

Kiddush, *First Cup: The Cup of Sanctification*

The Seder begins with a blessing recited over the first cup, the Cup of Sanctification (also called the Cup of Blessing). This first cup is meant to sanctify—to set apart—the rest of the evening as a holy occasion. We fill the cup until it overflows, as in Jewish tradition a full cup is a symbol of joy. Passover moves us to rejoice and celebrate God's goodness to His people. As a symbol of freedom, we drink comfortably leaning to the left.

All fill the cup. The leader recites the blessing and all drink leaning to the left:

בָּרוּךְ אַתָּה אֲדֹנָי אֱלֹהֵינוּ מֶלֶךְ הָעוֹלָם בּוֹרֵא פְּרִי הַגָּפֶן.

Baruch atah Ado-nai Elo-hei-nu Me-lech ha-Olam, bo-ray pri ha-gah-fen.

Blessed art Thou, O Lord our God, King of the universe, Creator of the fruit of the vine.

Urchatz, *Washing of the Hands (John 13:1–11)*

This first washing of the hands is a symbolic gesture of personal sanctification as we enter into the holy celebration of the Passover. Traditionally, two children carry a pitcher, a basin, and a towel and go around the table pouring a little water on the guests' hands, starting with the leader of the Seder.

Karpas, *Dipping of the Parsley (Exodus 12:21–22)*

The parsley symbolizes the hyssop used to place the blood of the Passover lamb upon the doorposts and lintels of the homes of the children of Israel during the tenth and most terrible plague that the Lord visited upon Egypt—the slaying of the firstborn. The salt water represents the tears of the children of Israel and the Red Sea. We are therefore reminded of the tears shed by those not yet redeemed and still in slavery. This is a good time to mention those around the world who are hurting and enslaved.

All dip a sprig of parsley in the salted water, the leader recites the blessing, all eat the parsley.

בָּרוּךְ אַתָּה אֲדֹנָי אֱלֹהֵינוּ מֶלֶךְ הָעוֹלָם בּוֹרֵא פְּרִי הָאֲדָמָה.

Ba-ruch Atah Adonai Elo-hei-nu Me-lech ha-Olam, boh-ray pri ha-adamah.

Blessed art Thou, O Lord our God, King of the universe, Creator of the fruit of the earth.

Yachatz, *Breaking of the Middle Matzah*

One of the central elements of the Passover is *matzah* (unleavened bread). For the Passover Seder, three separate sheets of matzah are inserted into a bag with three compartments, known as the *matzah tash.*

In Jewish tradition, this three-in-one bag has many interpretations. It is said to represent the three Patriarchs: Abraham, Isaac, and Jacob; or the three kinds of people of Israel: the priests, the Levites, and the masses. Believers in Yeshua suggest that this could be a representation of the triune nature of God: the Father, the Son, and the Holy Spirit.

The leader takes the middle matzah, breaks it in two and puts one half back in the middle of the matzah tash. He then wraps the other half, now known as the *afikoman,* in a white napkin and hides it. This hidden matzah will reappear at the conclusion of the Passover meal.

Maggid, *The Story of the Passover (Read Exodus 12:1–15)*

It is tradition to read the story of the Passover every year at the Seder, to ensure that every generation keeps the memory of Israel's deliverance from slavery alive.

Ma-Nishtanah, *The Four Questions*

As the retelling of the Exodus story begins, the youngest child (who can read!) asks the Four Questions to the leader of the Seder. You might choose to have all the children read together, have one child ask each question, or ask a different child to read them all.

מַה נִּשְׁתַּנָה הַלַּיְלָה הַזֶּה מִכָּל הַלֵּילוֹת?

Mah nish-ta-nah ha-lai-lah ha-zeh mi-kohl ha-lay-lot?

"Why is this night so different from all other nights?"

1. "On all other nights we eat bread with leaven. On this night why do we eat only matzah?"

2. "On all other nights we eat all kinds of vegetables; on this night why do we eat only bitter herbs?"

3. "On all other nights we never think of dipping herbs in water or in anything else; why on this night do we dip the parsley in salt water?"

4. "On all other nights we eat either sitting or reclining; on this night why do we eat only reclining?"

The leader of the Seder responds to the questions with the traditional answer:

> We were slaves to Pharaoh in Egypt, and God brought us out with a strong hand and an outstretched arm. And if God had not brought our ancestors out of Egypt, we and our children and our children's children would still be subjugated to Pharaoh in Egypt. Even if we were all old and wise and learned in Torah, we would still be commanded to tell the story of the Exodus from Egypt.

THE TEN PLAGUES

Each Passover cup is a symbolic full cup of joy except for the second cup—the Cup of Plagues—because God teaches us never to rejoice over the fate of our enemies. For this reason, the contents of the second cup must be reduced.

The second cup is filled. The leader of the Seder leads the group in a recitation of the ten plagues that the Lord poured out upon the Egyptians.

To reduce the second cup, each participant dips their little finger into the cup, removing one drop and placing it onto a plate in front of them, once for each plague. The names of the plagues are recited in unison as the drops are removed.

Blood! Frogs! Gnats! Flies! Pestilence! Boils! Hail! Locusts! Darkness! Slaying of the Firstborn!

"DAYENU," IT WOULD HAVE BEEN ENOUGH

Just as we do not rejoice over the fate of our enemies, we also recognize the magnitude of God's salvation and His gracious actions toward us. With a grateful heart and a healthy fear of the Lord, we sing *"Dayenu"* ("it would have satisfied us") together, remembering the many great acts that God has done on behalf of His people.

> *Ilu hotzi, hotzianu, hotzianu miMitzrayim, hotzianu miMitzrayim, dayenu!*
> *Dai-dai-yenu, dai-dai-yenu, dai-dai-yenu, dayenu, dayenu!*
> Had God done nothing but save us from the land of Egypt, for that alone we would have been satisfied!

> *Ilu natan natan lanu, natan lanu et haTorah, natan lanu et haTorah, dayenu!*
> *Dai-dai-yenu, dai-dai-yenu, dai-dai-yenu, dayenu, dayenu!*
> Had God given us nothing more than the Torah, for that alone we would have been satisfied!

> *Ilu natan natan lanu, natan lanu et Yeshua, natan lanu et Yeshua, dayenu!*
> *Dai-dai-yenu, dai-dai-yenu, dai-dai-yenu, dayenu, dayenu!*
> Had God given us nothing more than Yeshua, for that alone we would have been satisfied (yet He continues to give us so much more)!

Makkot, *Second Cup: The Cup of Plagues*

The reduced second cup, the Cup of Plagues (also called the Cup of Judgment), is raised and all recite the following:

> Truly, we can say Hallelujah for the great redemption that God has wrought on our behalf, redemption at a terrible price: in Egypt, the death of the first-born; for us, redemption from sin, the death of God's Son. "For God so loved the world, that He gave His only Son, that whoever believes in Him should not perish but have eternal life." (John 3:16)

This is also a good time to sing a chorus or two about God's love and Yeshua's sacrifice for our sins.

The leader recites the blessing, all drink leaning to the left:

בָּרוּךְ אַתָּה אֲדֹנָי אֱלֹהֵינוּ מֶלֶךְ הָעוֹלָם בּוֹרֵא פְּרִי הַגָּפֶן.

Baruch Atah Adonai Elo-hei-nu Me-lech ha-Olam, bo-ray pri ha-gah-fen.

Blessed art Thou, O Lord our God, King of the universe, Creator of the fruit of the vine.

Zeroah or Pesach, *The Lamb Shankbone*

The lamb shankbone is a symbol of the Temple sacrifice. It sits on the Passover plate as a reminder of the first Passover lamb sacrificed for the children of Israel. The lamb's blood was applied to the lintel and doorposts of the homes. We raise the shankbone of the lamb and again remind ourselves of the lamb slain on behalf of the firstborn males among the Jewish people. We also take this moment to reflect upon the death of Jesus for our sins, as He was the Lamb of God who takes away the sin of the world (John 1:29). We explain to our children the nature of redemption and the need for the shedding of blood for all of us to experience forgiveness of sin (Lev. 17:11; Heb. 9:22).

It might be appropriate to read all or part of Isaiah 52:13–53:12 at this time as a way to remember the work of Jesus the Messiah on our behalf.

Rachtzah, *Second Washing of the Hands*

The second symbolic washing of the hands reinforces personal sanctification as we continue the celebration of the Passover. Yeshua appears to have taken *Rachtzah* one step further by washing the feet of His disciples, providing us with an unparalleled lesson in servanthood and humility (John 13:2–17). This second washing is followed by a blessing:

בָּרוּךְ אַתָּה אָדֹנָי אֱלֹהֵינוּ מֶלֶךְ הָעוֹלָם אֲשֶׁר קִדְּשָׁנוּ בְּמִצְוֹתָיו וְצִוָּנוּ עַל נְטִלַת יָדָיִם.

Ba-ruch Atah Adonai Elo-hei-nu Me-lech ha-Olam, ash-er kid-sha-nu b'mits-vo-tav v'tsi-va-nu al ne-ti-lat ya-dayim.

Blessed art Thou, O Lord our God, King of the universe, who sanctified us with His commandments, and commanded us concerning the washing of hands.

Matzot

As the first portion of the Seder draws to a close, the family partakes of several of the remaining elements on the Seder plate. These elements are intended to involve our senses in the remembrance of the Passover story. Each one helps us connect with a different step in the process of Israel's deliverance from slavery. For believers in Yeshua, these elements remind us of the process of deliverance from our slavery to sin to our freedom in Messiah.

The matzah tash is raised and the following blessing is recited.

בָּרוּךְ אַתָּה אָדֹנָי אֱלֹהֵינוּ מֶלֶךְ הָעוֹלָם הַמּוֹצִיא לֶחֶם מִן הָאָרֶץ.

Ba-ruch Atah Adonai Elo-hei-nu Me-lech ha-Olam, ha-mo-tzi le-chem min hah-ah-retz.

Blessed art Thou, O Lord our God, King of the universe, who brings forth bread from the earth.

Each person now breaks off a small piece of matzah and all recite the following blessing:

בָּרוּךְ אַתָּה אֲדֹנָי אֱלֹהֵינוּ מֶלֶךְ הָעוֹלָם אֲשֶׁר קִדְּשָׁנוּ בְּמִצְוֹתָיו וְצִוָּנוּ עַל אֲכִלַת מַצָּה.

Ba-ruch Atah Adonai Elo-hei-nu Me-lech ha-Olam, ash-er kid-sha-nu b'mits-vo-tav v'tsi-va-nu al a-chi-lat ma-tzah.

Blessed art Thou, O Lord our God, King of the universe, who sanctified us with His commandments, and commanded us concerning the eating of unleavened bread.

All eat together of the matzah.

Maror, *Eating of the Bitter Herbs*

The *maror* (bitter herbs) reminds us of the bitterness of Israel's slavery in Egypt and the bitterness of humankind's slavery to sin. It is tradition to dip one's matzah and take a heaping portion of the bitter herb, enough to make one shed a tear.

Each person breaks an olive-sized piece of matzah and dips it in the bitter herbs. The following blessing is recited:

בָּרוּךְ אַתָּה אֲדֹנָי אֱלֹהֵינוּ מֶלֶךְ הָעוֹלָם אֲשֶׁר קִדְּשָׁנוּ בְּמִצְוֹתָיו וְצִוָּנוּ עַל אֲכִלַת מָרוֹר.

Ba-ruch Atah Adonai Elo-hei-nu Me-lech ha-Olam, ash-er kid-sha-nu b'mits-vo-tav v'tsi-va-nu al a-chi-lat mah-ror.

Blessed art Thou O Lord our God, King of the universe, who sanctified us with His commandments, and commanded us concerning the eating of the bitter herbs.

All eat together of the maror.

Korech, *Eating of the Bitter Herbs and Charoset*

The *charoset* (sweet mixture) symbolizes the mortar the children of Israel used to make the bricks as they toiled under Pharaoh's harsh taskmasters. It is eaten with matzah.

In order to settle a controversy about how the Passover is to be eaten, Rabbi Hillel, a famous sage, began the tradition of the "Hillel sandwich," which is made by eating the maror and the charoset together between two pieces of matzah. It is also said that this combination of bitter and sweet reminds us that God's promise can bring joy in the midst of sorrow.

Each person takes two small pieces of matzah and places some charoset and maror in the middle. All eat together.

Beitzah, *The Roasted Egg*

The roasted egg on the Seder plate brings to mind the roasted daily Temple sacrifice that no longer can be offered because the Temple no longer stands. In the very midst of the Passover Seder, Jewish people are reminded that there is no sacrifice to bring righteousness before God. We take a piece of the egg and dip it in salt water, a symbol of tears, and all eat.

THIS CONCLUDES THE FIRST PORTION OF THE SEDER

Shulchan Orech, *The Set Table*

The Passover meal can now be served. Eat, tell stories, and enjoy! Be sure to use the recipes included in this book (see chapter 19, "Passover Foods and Recipes," by Mitch Forman).

Tzafun , *Finding and Eating the Afikoman*

After the meal is finished, the leader of the Seder sends the children to find the afikoman, which is the middle piece of matzah that was broken, wrapped in a napkin and hidden before the meal. The child who finds it brings it to the leader of the Seder, who redeems the afikoman with a symbolic reward, usually some money or chocolate.

According to tradition, the leader of the Seder then unwraps the afikoman, blesses it, and breaks it up into small olive-sized pieces. He then distributes a small piece to everyone seated around the table and all eat the afikoman together.

For believers in Yeshua, there is great significance in this tradition. We believe that it was at this point in the Passover Seder when Yeshua seized the moment to reveal to His disciples His identity and the pending suffering and death that He would soon endure. The Gospel of Luke records Messiah's words on this occasion: "And when He had taken some bread and given thanks, He broke it and gave it to them, saying, 'This is My body which is given for you; do this in remembrance of Me'" (Luke 22:19).

We believe that Yeshua Himself was the middle piece of matzah, the piece representing the priest or mediator between God and the people. He was broken in death, wrapped for burial, and resurrected from the dead. The matzah represents His sin-free (unleavened) sacrifice for our redemption from sin and death.

When the leader of the Seder unwraps the afikoman and distributes a piece to everyone seated at the table, it reminds us that Yeshua the Messiah distributed His life to all who believe.

We might also reflect upon the appearance of traditional matzah, which is made both striped and pierced, as His body was striped and pierced (Isa. 53:5). This middle piece of matzah, the afikoman, is the "Bread of Life" (John 6:35) we share in the Lord's Supper or Communion as believers.

Having explained this to the participants, now the leader breaks the afikoman into olive-sized pieces and gives one to each person to hold briefly as together they reflect on the sacrifice that Yeshua endured in His body. Then all partake in unison after the following prayer is said:

בָּרוּךְ אַתָּה אֲדֹנָי אֱלֹהֵינוּ מֶלֶךְ הָעוֹלָם הַמּוֹצִיא לֶחֶם מִן הָאָרֶץ.

Ba-ruch Atah Adonai Elo-hei-nu Me-lech ha-Olam, ha-mo-tzi le-chem min ha-ah-retz.

Blessed art Thou, O Lord our God, King of the universe, who brings forth bread from the earth.

HaGeulah, *Third Cup: The Cup of Redemption*

The Cup of Redemption is based on God's promise in Exodus 6:6, "I will also redeem you with an outstretched arm and with great judgments." It is a reminder of the lamb's blood, the price paid for Israel's promised redemption. In the same way, Yeshua likely took this cup and spoke the words in Luke 22:20, "This cup which is poured out for you is the new covenant in My blood." In so doing, He spoke of a greater redemption than the Israelites experienced in Egypt. Yeshua had in mind the redemption and deliverance of humankind, forgiven of sin through the shed blood of the Lamb of God. Yeshua is quoting from the great New Covenant prophecy given by the prophet Jeremiah in Jeremiah 31:31–34.

The cup is filled and the following blessing is recited:

בָּרוּךְ אַתָּה אֲדֹנָי אֱלֹהֵינוּ מֶלֶךְ הָעוֹלָם בּוֹרֵא פְּרִי הַגָּפֶן.

Baruch Atah Adonai Elo-hei-nu Me-lech ha-Olam, bo-ray pri ha-gah-fen.

Blessed art Thou, O Lord our God, King of the universe, Creator of the fruit of the vine.

All drink leaning to the left.

Eliyahu, *Elijah's Cup (Luke 1:17; Malachi 4:5–6)*

The Bible tells us in Malachi 4:5 that Elijah will appear to herald the coming of the Messianic King:

Behold, I am going to send you Elijah the prophet before the coming of the great and terrible day of the Lord.

It is tradition to have an additional place setting, complete with a cup of the fruit of the vine, for Elijah at Passover. The leader of the Seder usually sends a child to the front door to look outside and see if Elijah is coming. Thus far, he has never attended a Seder!

But has he? The Bible tells us in Luke 1:17, speaking of John the Baptist, "It is he who will go as a forerunner before Him in the spirit and power of Elijah." John did indeed come to fulfill Elijah's role as herald to announce the first coming of the Messiah, fulfilled in the coming of Yeshua.

Hallel, *Fourth Cup: The Cup of Praise*

What is the proper response to redemption? Joy, of course! We rejoice, knowing that the Jewish people were delivered from Egyptian bondage and that both Jewish and Gentile followers of the Messiah were redeemed from the bondage of sin and death. The fourth and final cup of the Passover Seder is the Cup of Praise—a cup of rejoicing, joy, and consummation. It is the first taste of freedom beyond redemption. It is a reminder of Israel's promised future beyond slavery in Egypt—dwelling instead in freedom in the Promised Land. In many ways, this cup also foreshadows the glorious future for Israel and the world to come in the age of the Messianic kingdom.

The cup is filled, all lift it and the following blessing is recited:

בָּרוּךְ אַתָּה אֲדֹנָי אֱלֹהֵינוּ מֶלֶךְ הָעוֹלָם בּוֹרֵא פְּרִי הַגָּפֶן.

Baruch Atah Adonai Elo-hei-nu Me-lech ha-Olam, bo-ray pri ha-gah-fen.

Blessed art Thou, O Lord our God, King of the universe, Creator of the fruit of the vine.

All drink leaning to the left.

Hallel *Psalms (Psalms 113–118)*

In the spirit of joy and celebration, we rejoice together for all that God has done for us! He has set us apart to be His people, He has brought us out of slavery, He has redeemed us, and He has brought us to Himself. For all of this we praise Him! As the Seder comes to a close, we go out singing the Hallel Psalms (Pss. 113–118). It is incredible to realize that in Yeshua's last moments of freedom and fellowship on earth, He and His disciples also sang as they finished their Seder and went out to the Mount of Olives (Matt. 26:30; Mark 14:26).

This is a wonderful opportunity to read and reflect on these psalms together, and consider the strong Messianic undertones of each. There are traditional tunes for these songs, but we also encourage you to find some traditional hymns or contemporary worship songs that are based on these Psalms.

Next Year in Jerusalem!

It is tradition to conclude the Seder with a joyous proclamation of hope and faith by reciting in unison:

לְשָׁנָה הַבָּאָה בִּרוּשָׁלָיִם!

L'shana HaBa'ah B'Yerushalayim!

"Next Year in Jerusalem!"

This has great meaning to followers of Jesus the Messiah because we expect Him to return! We do not know the day of His second coming, but we wait in hope, knowing that as surely as the Messiah came once to redeem us from sin, so He will come again as judge to establish His kingdom. As God promises through the prophet Isaiah,

> For a child will be born to us, a son will be given to us;
> And the government will rest on His shoulders;
> And His name will be called Wonderful Counselor, Mighty God,
> Eternal Father, Prince of Peace.
> There will be no end to the increase of His government or of peace,
> On the throne of David and over his kingdom,
> To establish it and to uphold it with justice and righteousness
> From then on and forevermore.
> The zeal of the LORD of hosts will accomplish this. (Isa. 9:6–7)

And as the Apostle Paul writes, in light of our expectation of Messiah's return,

> Therefore, my beloved brethren, be steadfast, immovable, always abounding in the work of the Lord, knowing that your toil is not in vain in the Lord. (1 Cor. 15:58)

Happy Passover!

19

PASSOVER FOODS AND RECIPES

MITCH FORMAN

*T*he special foods we eat are a major part of the way we celebrate the Jewish holidays. In fact every feast has something to do with food except one, the Day of Atonement, in which Jewish people eat nothing at all. Passover is the culinary epitome of the entire year.

So why the connection between food and feasts? As a chef I can only answer this from my own experience. Everyone has to eat to sustain life. However, on occasion, people will eat out at a special restaurant to celebrate a major event. Everyone remembers the one or two exceptional meals they have especially enjoyed, and often what they ate commemorating that day.

By connecting food to the feasts, we enter into a greater experience of the holy days as the ceremonies engage our sense of smell and taste, and the foods we eat help to create memories for a lifetime. In fact, there are three foods biblically mandated for Jewish people to eat on Passover. These are lamb, bitter herbs, and unleavened bread.

> Your lamb shall be an unblemished male a year old; you may take it from the sheep or from the goats. You shall keep it until the fourteenth day of the same month, then the whole assembly of the congregation of Israel is to kill it at twilight. Moreover, they shall take some of the blood and put it on the two doorposts and on the lintel of the houses in which they eat it. They shall eat the flesh that same night, roasted with fire, and they shall eat it with unleavened bread and bitter herbs. (Exod. 12:5–8)

Jewish people still eat unleavened bread (matzah) and bitter herbs during the Passover Seder. However, certain groups of Jewish people no longer eat lamb at Passover in remembrance of the destruction of the Temple.

Before we continue on with various recipes, we need to distinguish between the two major groups of Jewish people in the world. Jewish people are often defined religiously as Orthodox, Conservative, or Reform. But the greater distinction has to do with where these groups of Jewish people come from and the traditions that have developed as a result of their differing backgrounds from where they live. The first major group is the Ashkenazic Jews, who trace their roots back to Germany and Eastern Europe. The second major group is the Sephardic Jews, who were originally from Spain, and today are mostly from Spain, Portugal, North Africa, and other parts of the Middle East.

Curiously, Sephardic Jews will eat lamb at Passover, but Ashkenazic Jews will not. Jewish people from Sephardic backgrounds also eat rice at Passover, which Ashkenazic Jews view as leavened. Rice and lamb are a more significant part of the overall diet for Jews from the Middle East and North Africa than for Jewish people from either Eastern or Western Europe, which may be one reason for these differences.

As you can easily see, Jewish people are not demographically monolithic, and therefore the foods attached to the various holidays differ quite a bit depending on where Jewish people have their roots. In Israel it is quite remarkable in that there is almost a 50/50 mix between Ashkenazic and Sephardic Jews and considerable intermarriage between them. Therefore, the eating of lamb might be even more common in Israel than it is in North America or Europe.

Some of my fondest memories of celebrating Passover were spent at my grandparents' homes. Both grandmothers would cook up a feast. As is no doubt true for most Jewish families, on Passover we eat foods that are both biblical and traditional, and over time these foods have become synonymous with the Passover Seder.

So now to those recipes! This chapter is divided into three sections. The first section will provide instructions and recipes for setting your Passover table using traditional Passover foods. The next section will describe a traditional Passover dinner and show you how to prepare it. The final section will suggest some foods and recipes made without leavened foods that you can enjoy with your family during the eight days of the festival; and if you are not Jewish, then you might want to try the discipline of abstaining from foods made with leaven or yeast and see what your Jewish friends experience!

A TRADITIONAL SEDER MEAL

The Seder Plate

The Seder plate is where the foods used during the Passover Seder are placed. This includes the *karpas* (parsley), *hazeret* (lettuce), *charoset* (apple mixture), *maror* (bitter herbs), *beitzah* (roasted egg), and *zeroah* (lamb shankbone). Note pronunciations of key terms below and throughout this chapter.

Preparing the Seder plate requires precision. The foods we eat on Passover are there by design and used during the meal to enhance and embellish the story of God's redemption of the children of Israel from Egypt.

Although every home has its own traditions, most families follow the same basic pattern for the Seder. Passover, which includes the Festival of Unleavened Bread, is observed for eight days. The Seder is celebrated on the first night of the Feast, and, outside of Israel, on the second night as well. The second Seder traditionally has allowed for families outside Israel to hold their Seder on the right night based on the lunar calendar and timing detailed in Scripture,

> In the first month, on the fourteenth day of the month at twilight is the LORD's Passover. (Lev. 23:5)

The foods placed on the Seder plate are listed below, and we have explained the reason why each is included, the means of preparing it, and the role the food plays in the Passover Seder. Ordinarily, each person will have a Seder plate with the following foods.

Karpas (CAR-pahs). A green vegetable, usually parsley, signifying springtime. It also reminds us of the hyssop (herbaceous plant) that was used by the Israelites to apply the blood to the doors of their homes.
   Preparation: Clean a bunch of parsley, rinse and dry. Set out one sprig for each person present.
   Role in the Seder: This is the first item eaten in the Seder. We dip the parsley into salt water, which symbolizes tears, to remind us that life in bondage produces tears.

Maror (mah-ROAR). The bitter herb, usually horseradish, again represents the bitterness of life for slaves in Egypt.
   Preparation: Freshly grated horseradish can be used, or you may choose to buy a jar of prepared horseradish. Provide one tablespoon for every eight persons at the Seder. (Note: Simply be aware that this amount of horseradish is strong enough to make most people tear up, especially children.)
   Role in the Seder: We eat bitter herbs as commanded in Scripture. It causes us to cry (or at least shed tears) as we remember that our people cried out to God because of the bitterness of their lives as slaves in Egypt.

Charoset (khah-ROH-set). A sweet apple mixture made with dates, nuts, and honey that is left standing out for a time to turn brown. This symbolizes the mortar used in Egypt by Jewish slaves for making bricks.
   Preparation:

   Ingredients:
      4 red apples
      1 cup chopped walnuts
      ½ cup chopped dates
      ¼ cup of honey
      ½ cup sweet red wine (or grape juice)
      ½ teaspoon cinnamon
      ¼ teaspoon nutmeg

Instructions:
1. Peel and grate the apples.
2. Mix in the nuts, dates, honey and spices.
3. Add the wine and mix well.
4. Refrigerate until serving. The mixture will turn brown.

Yield: 12 portions

Role in the Seder: The charoset represents our labor in Egypt and the sweetness of the mixture gives us hope for the promise of redemption.

Beitzah (bay-TZAH). A roasted egg symbolizing the annual sacrifices (called the *hagigah*) that can no longer be offered in the Temple.

Preparation: Roast one egg for the Seder plate and roast additional eggs, one per every four people. This should take about 1 hour at 350°F in the oven to roast. Many Jewish people simply use a brown egg or actually boil it in coffee to give the egg a roasted appearance.

Role in the Seder: Place one roasted egg on the Seder plate. The additional eggs are peeled and sliced and will be eaten right before the meal. This browned appearance is important as the egg is supposed to remind us of the missing sacrifices that were roasted on the altar at the Temple.

Zeroah (zeh-ROH-ah). The shankbone of a lamb reminds us of the Passover lamb. The first Passover lambs were sacrificed at twilight, and their blood was smeared on the doorposts and lintel of the Israelite homes.

Preparation: The shankbone of a leg of lamb is roasted on high heat until browned.

Role in the Seder: The shankbone reminds us of the lamb that was sacrificed at the first Passover in Egypt and in ensuing days in the Temple.

Salt water. Used to symbolize the tears of life. Serves as a dip for both the *karpas* and the *beitzah*.

The Matzah Tash

Matzah. This is the unleavened bread described as the bread of affliction. During Passover we do not eat foods that contain leaven. It is one of the most important symbols on the Passover table. We have a special pouch called a *matzah tash* (MAHTZ-uh TAHSH) in which we place three pieces of matzah.

Our Jewish tradition allows for variety of opinion on the meaning of the three sections, but one pouch. Some say it represents the priesthood of Judaism: the priests, the Levites, and the people of Israel. Others say it represents the three Patriarchs: Abraham, Isaac, and Jacob. Still others say it represents the three cakes Abraham served to the angels who visited him. Some Messianic Jews take this a step further and view the three pieces, yet one pouch of the matzah tash as representing the triunity of God: the Father, the Son, and the Holy Spirit.

The Fruit of the Vine

The wine at Passover is always red, representing the blood of the lamb. Jewish people usually use a sweet red kosher wine made by companies such as Manischewitz, Mogen David, and Kedem. Kosher grape juice for children and adults who do not drink wine is always acceptable. Everyone drinks four cups of the fruit of the vine at the Seder. Traditionally, the four cups represent the four statements on redemption found in Exodus 6:6–7:

> Say, therefore, to the sons of Israel, "I am the LORD, and I will bring you out from under the burdens of the Egyptians, and I will deliver you from their bondage. I will also redeem you with an outstretched arm and with great judgments. Then I will take you for My people, and I will be your God; and you shall know that I am the LORD your God, who brought you out from under the burdens of the Egyptians."

The four cups representing these four statements on redemption are named as follows:

1. The Cup of Sanctification (or Blessing): "I will bring you out from under the burdens of the Egyptians" (v. 6).

2. The Cup of Plagues (or Judgment): "I will deliver you from their bondage" (v. 6).

3. The Cup of Redemption: "I will also redeem you with an outstretched arm" (v. 6).

4. The Cup of Praise (or Rejoicing): "I will take you for My people" (v. 7).

The Passover Seder Dinner

Matzah Ball Soup

This soup, favored by the Ashkenazic Jews, is made from a mixture of matzah meal and chicken fat and is the traditional soup served on Passover. We all know that it was our grandmother who made the best matzah ball soup, so no two recipes are the same, except that the standard soup includes chicken soup and matzah balls. In some Jewish homes, soft noodles will be added to the soup, along with carrots and sometimes celery, etc.

Ingredients:

For the matzah balls:

> 4 eggs
>
> 2 tablespoons chicken fat (substitute oil if you can't find fat)
>
> 2 tablespoons soup stock or water
>
> 1 cup matzah meal (buy it at the store)
>
> ½ teaspoon salt

Instructions:

1. Beat eggs slightly with fork in a bowl.
2. Add chicken fat, salt, and water.
3. Add matzah meal gradually until it thickens.
4. Refrigerate for 20 minutes in a covered bowl. This will allow the matzah to absorb the liquid and make it easier to use.
5. Scoop out portions of the matzah ball mixture with a standard ice cream scoop; and with wet hands, form into balls.
6. Fill a medium-sized stockpot halfway with water and bring to simmer on medium heat.
7. Cook for 30 minutes.
8. Drain and set aside.

Yield: 16 matzah balls

Ingredients:

For the chicken soup:

> 1 chicken (5 pounds), quartered
>
> 2 medium size onions, diced
>
> 6 carrots, diced
>
> 1 stalk celery, diced
>
> water
>
> 2 tablespoons salt

Instructions:

1. Peel onions and carrots and wash celery and cut all vegetables into ½-inch cubes.
2. Place chicken and vegetables in large stockpot.
3. Add salt and water to cover.
4. Bring to boil and then lower the flame and simmer for 2 hours.
5. Remove chicken parts and let cool. Remove the chicken meat from the bones and shred.
6. Strain the soup of all the vegetables pieces and bring stock back to a simmer.
7. Add the shredded chicken to soup and keep on a low simmer.

8. About 30 minutes before serving, add the matzah balls to the soup and simmer.
9. Dish out soup with 1 matzah ball per serving.

Yield: 14 to 16 servings

Gefilte Fish

Gefilte fish is a prized delicacy for Jewish people from Eastern Europe, where using every part of the fish was necessary for life when one had very little to eat. The term *gefilte* (guh-FILL-teh) is Yiddish for "stuffed fish." It bears a resemblance to fish pâté that is eaten cold. Jewish people love eating this for Shabbat dinners and festival meals.

Since gefilte fish is an acquired taste, we recommend that you buy a jar of gefilte fish in the Jewish section of the supermarket to try it first. It is traditionally served with horseradish. However, for those of you who are more adventurous, you may try to make your own. This recipe comes from a friend's mom who, legend has it, made gefilte fish that was out of this world!

For the gefilte fish balls:
   3 pounds whitefish*
   3 pounds carp*
   3 medium onions
   2 medium carrots
   1 stalk celery
   3 large eggs
   2 teaspoons sugar
   1 teaspoons salt
   ½ teaspoon pepper
   ¾ cup corn oil
   ½ cup matzah meal
   ½ cup cold water
   1 jar of red or white prepared horseradish

*Go to your local fish market and ask for these fish to be skinned and filleted. Ask the fish dealer to give you the heads and bones as well for the stock. Note that you may need to order ahead for whole fish.

Instructions:

1. In a food processor, grind the fish until very smooth. (You may also put the fish in an electric mixer and macerate with a dough hook. However, the onions and carrots will still need to be ground in a food processor before adding to the fish mixture.)

2. Then add 2 onions and 1 carrot and grind until smooth. (You may have to make this in two batches if your food processor cannot hold all the ingredients.)
3. Take the fish mixture and in a large bowl add the water a little at a time until all the water is incorporated into the mixture.
4. Then add the eggs, sugar, salt, and pepper, and mix very well with a wooden spoon.
5. Stir in the matzah meal, and mix until everything is incorporated.
6. Refrigerate overnight in a covered container.
7. The next day, place the fish bones and heads in a stock pot with 1 onion, 1 carrot, and celery stalk, all diced. Fill the stock pot halfway with water and bring to a boil and then lower to simmer for 1½ hours.
8. Next remove the fish mixture from the refrigerator to make fish patties. (To make patties take some of the fish mixture and place in a big metal spoon and then slowly drop the fish ball in the simmering fish stock).
9. Cook the fish patties for 1½ hours.
10. Remove fish patties, onions, and carrots from the stock pot and place on a paper towel to dry and cool.
11. Place the fish patties with the onions and carrots in a closed container and place in the refrigerator overnight.
12. Place 2 pieces of gefilte fish with some onions and carrots pieces on a plate and eat with red or white horseradish.

Yield: 12 patties (4-ounce portions)

Chopped Liver
Chopped liver is part of most Jewish people's upbringing. My two grandmothers made their chopped liver a little differently from each other, but both were tasty. This recipe combines the best of each. Chopped liver is a developed taste, but to get the full Jewish experience at Passover, we recommend you at least try a little bit on a piece of matzah.

Ingredients:
1½ pounds chicken livers, trimmed
3 eggs
1 large onion, sliced
2 tablespoons chicken schmaltz* (or 2 tablespoons olive oil)
2 tablespoons sweet red wine or chicken stock
salt and freshly ground black pepper to taste
*Chicken schmaltz (SHMALTZ) is rendered chicken fat.

Instructions:
1. Hard-boil the eggs for 10 minutes, drain, and set aside.
2. In a sauté pan, cook the onion on low heat until a nice golden brown color appears. Remove from the pan and let cool on a paper towel.
3. Add wine and chicken schmaltz to the sauté pan and bring to simmer on medium heat.
4. Add the livers and cook for 5 minutes or until the livers are firm to the touch.
5. Pour mixture into a food processor and mix until the ingredients come together, but not too smooth.
6. Scrape mixture into a bowl.
7. Grate the eggs and add to the bowl. Then add the onions and mix together.
8. Salt and pepper to taste.
9. Refrigerate overnight and serve the next day.

To make chicken schmaltz:
1. Take the spare fat from a raw chicken. This can be done by removing the skin and fat from chicken thighs and cutting into strips.
2. Cook on low heat in a sauté pan with 2 sticks (8 ounces) of butter for 60 to 90 minutes until all fat has been rendered gently out of the chicken skin.
3. Remove skin from pan and drain on paper towels to form *gribenes* (Yiddish for "cracklings").
4. Pour the fat (schmaltz[†]) into a bowl and refrigerate until needed.

[†]The schmaltz (fat) will keep for up to 3 to 4 weeks in the fridge if stored correctly with a lid.

Tzimmes

Tzimmes (TSIM-ess) is one of those Jewish dishes that doesn't sound good when reading the ingredients, but one taste of this gooey, sticky, roasted vegetable dish will have you wanting more! The sweetness of this dish reminds us of the sweetness of redemption.

Ingredients:
8 carrots, chopped
2 yellow onions, chopped
2 turnips, chopped
4 sweet potatoes, peeled and diced
8 ounces dried apricots, chopped
8 ounces apple juice
1 cup honey

2 teaspoons salt
1 teaspoon pepper
2 teaspoons tarragon

Instructions:
1. Preheat oven to 350°F.
2. Heat the apple juice, honey, salt, pepper, and tarragon and simmer in a small pot.
3. Place the vegetables and apricots in a 4-inch deep casserole dish.
4. Pour the honey and juice mixture over the vegetable/apricot mixture.
5. Cover and cook in oven at 350°F for 90 minutes.
6. Remove cover and cook for 30 minutes more, and serve.

Yield: 10 to 12 servings

Egg Noodle Kugel

Noodle kugel (COO-gull) is a casserole of noodles drenched in an egg mixture. It is made with egg noodles, so it is kosher for Passover. When it is done, you will be introduced to a savory meal that has sweetness to it as well.

Ingredients:
1 package (16-ounce) wide egg noodles
6 large eggs
1 pound sour cream
8 ounces cottage cheese
8 ounces cream cheese, softened
8 ounces raisins
½ cup sugar
1 stick (8 ounces) unsalted butter, melted
¼ teaspoon salt
4 tablespoons cinnamon
4 tablespoons nutmeg

Instructions:
1. Preheat oven to 350°F.
2. Add the noodles to a pot of boiling water and cook for 5 minutes, or until soft.
3. In a food processor combine the eggs, sour cream, cottage cheese, and cream cheese and mix until smooth.
4. Add sugar, melted butter, and salt and blend well.
5. Place noodles mixed with raisins in a 9 x 13-inch glass baking dish and pour egg mixture over noodles.

6. Sprinkle mixture with cinnamon and nutmeg.
7. Cover dish with aluminum foil and bake for 60 minutes.
8. Remove from oven and let sit for 15 minutes.
9. Cut into squares and serve warm.

Yield: 10 to 12 servings

Roast Brisket

Brisket is always a favorite at Passover season. In fact my family would always prepare a roast brisket for the Passover Seder. Here is the recipe my grandma used, my mom used, and now I use.

Ingredients:
  1 whole beef brisket (8 pounds)
  10 cloves garlic, peeled and smashed
  2 yellow onions, sliced
  6 carrots, sliced
  32 ounces tomato puree
  2 cups beef stock
  salt and pepper to taste

Instructions:
  1. Preheat oven to 350°F.
  2. Heat a sauté pan on high for 2 minutes and sear the brisket on each side for 3 minutes.
  3. Place sliced onions and carrots on the bottom of a large roasting pan and set the brisket on top with the fat side up.
  4. Coat the brisket with the smashed garlic, tomato puree, and salt and pepper to taste. Then add the beef stock.
  5. Cover pan and cook the brisket for 3 hours at 350°F.
  6. When meat is done, remove from pan and let sit for 30 minutes.
  7. Slice the meat against the grain in ¼-inch slices and serve with the onions and carrots.
  8. Reduce remaining tomato broth till thick and pour over the meat, and serve.

Yield: 12 to 16 servings

Macaroons

Macaroons are made every Passover season. They are unleavened and the egg whites mixed with the coconut binds the cookie together. This recipe allows the sugar to spread to the edges and caramelize. These cookies are so easy to make, yet they taste so good. For a variation, add the cocoa powder to the mixture and make chocolate macaroons.

Ingredients:

  1 package (14-ounce) sweetened shredded coconut
  4 large egg whites, beaten
  ½ cup sugar
  1 tablespoon grated orange zest
  1 tablespoon grated lemon zest
  ¼ teaspoon salt
  ½ cup cocoa powder (optional)

Instructions:

  1. Preheat oven to 340°F.
  2. Line a baking sheet with parchment paper.
  3. Combine the coconut, sugar, orange and lemon zest, and salt.
  4. Add the beaten egg whites to the coconut mixture.
  5. Place heaping tablespoons of the mixture on the parchment-lined baking sheet, spacing the spoonfuls 3 wide by 4 long for 12 macaroons per sheet.
  6. Cook the macaroons for about 20 minutes or until the edges start turning brown.
  7. Cool on a wire rack for 30 minutes and serve.

Yield: 12 macaroons (2-ounce cookies)

PASSOVER FOODS SERVED DURING THE EIGHT DAYS OF THE PASSOVER FEAST

Matzah Dishes

It requires great inventiveness to substitute matzah (unleavened bread) for regular bread made with yeast in our meals during Passover. Below are some of the better-known recipes utilizing matzah.

Matzah Brei

This is a breakfast item that replaces French toast. The key is to soak the matzah enough to get it soft but not too mushy. My mom liked to top the matzah brei with grape jelly, but you may use banana slices, chocolate syrup, or honey.

Ingredients:

  4 matzahs, broken into pieces
  4 large eggs
  ¼ cup milk
  ¼ cup pure maple syrup
  ¼ cup grape jelly
  ¼ cup olive oil

Instructions:

1. Soak matzah pieces in cold water for 1 minute and drain.
2. Mix eggs and milk.
3. Pour olive oil in skillet and heat.
4. Add matzah and egg mixture and cook for 3 minutes on medium heat.
5. Flip matzah brei, and cook for 5 more minutes or until golden brown.
6. Transfer matzah brei to a plate spread with grape or your favorite jelly, or top with banana slices or drizzle with chocolate syrup or honey, and serve.

Yield: 4 servings

Mushroom/Matzah Flan

This is a variation on quiche. Since we can't make a flour crust, we use matzah in this delicious brunch item. The recipe calls for mushrooms, but you can add any kind of vegetables to make it your own.

Ingredients:

8 plain matzahs
¼ cup olive oil
½ cup milk
1 bunch green onions, chopped fine
12 ounces mushrooms, sliced
½ bunch fresh thyme, chopped fine
8 large eggs, lightly beaten
½ cup crumbled soft goat cheese or feta
salt and pepper to taste

Instructions:

1. Preheat oven to 350°F.
2. Break matzahs into pieces, soak for one minute under cold water, drain, and place in a bowl.
3. In a large skillet, cook the green onions and mushrooms with half the olive oil until soft.
4. Add matzahs and cook for 1 more minute.
5. Mix the eggs, cheese, and thyme in a bowl and whisk until smooth.
6. Place the mushroom and matzah mixture in the bowl with the eggs, cheese, and thyme and mix together with a spoon.
7. Season with salt and pepper.
8. Transfer mixture to a 9 x 13-inch glass baking dish and cook in the oven for 40 minutes at 350°F.

9. Remove from oven and let cool for 5 minutes.
10. Cut into 12 pieces and serve.

Yield: 12 servings

Matzah and Strawberry Napoleon

This is a variation on the classical Napoleon dessert. Instead of using puff pastry, we will be using matzahs for the three layers.

Ingredients:

6 pieces of matzah, cut into 4 squares per piece
12 ounces strawberries
1 cup heavy cream
1 cup sour cream
½ cup sugar
½ cup lime juice
¼ cup lime zest
4 ounces powdered sugar

Instructions:

1. Slice strawberries and marinate in the lime juice for 30 min.
2. Combine the heavy cream and sugar and whip until stiff.
3. Add the sour cream to the whipped cream and mix together.
4. Add the lime zest.
5. Place one piece of matzah on a plate.
6. Spread some strawberries on the matzah and top with the whipped cream mixture.
7. Place a second piece of matzah on top and repeat step 6.
8. Top with one more matzah piece, sprinkle with powdered sugar and serve.

Yield: 8 Napoleons

Additional Soups

Nana's Sweet and Sour Cabbage Soup

This was my Nana's favorite soup to make. It reflects the influence of her Polish background on the classical Russian borscht. My favorite part of eating the soup is having a second bowl.

Ingredients:

1 large head of green cabbage, diced
1 bag (8-ounce) julienned carrots
2 yellow onions, diced
2 turnips, diced
8 cloves garlic, peeled and minced

4 quarts chicken stock or water
32 ounces tomato puree
32 ounces diced tomatoes
2 pounds brisket of beef or short ribs
2 tablespoons dark brown sugar
juice of 2 fresh lemons
salt and pepper to taste

Instructions:
1. Place the chicken stock, tomato puree, and diced tomatoes in an 8-quart pot and bring to a simmer.
2. Add the cabbage, carrots, onions, turnips, and garlic and simmer 30 minutes.
3. Place the meat in the stockpot and simmer for another 2 hours covered.
4. When the meat is tender, add lemon juice, brown sugar, and salt and pepper to taste and serve.

Yield: 12 servings (6-ounce portions)

Cream of Carrot Soup

This soup I have made many times. I add extra onions because when cooked with the carrots, they make the soup very sweet. The heavy cream adds an extra richness that should be pleasing for everyone.

Ingredients:
4 quarts chicken stock
4 large yellow onions, diced
12 carrots, diced
4 sweet potatoes, diced
¼ cup garlic, peeled and chopped
1 teaspoon salt
1 quart heavy cream
1 bunch dill, chopped

Instructions:
1. Simmer the chicken stock in a large stockpot.
2. Add the onions, carrots, potatoes, garlic, and salt and simmer for 2 hours covered
3. Place the ingredients in a food processor and puree.
4. Pour the puree back into the stockpot, add the heavy cream, and simmer for 30 minutes.
5. Serve in individuals bowls and sprinkle with fresh dill.

Yield: 12 servings (4-ounce portions)

Additional Main Courses, Including Sephardic Versions
Lemon Garlic Chicken

Chicken is a great dish to serve at Passover. It is quick and easy to make and this recipe gives it a Mediterranean flavor.

Ingredients:
- 8 chicken breasts, with skin on
- 4 ounces olive oil
- ¼ cup chicken stock
- ¼ cup juice from fresh lemons
- 12 garlic cloves, peeled
- ¼ cup grated lemon peel
- ¼ cup chopped fresh thyme
- salt and pepper to taste

Instructions:
1. Preheat oven to 385°F.
2. Heat a sauté pan with the olive oil on high heat for 1 minute.
3. Season chicken breasts with salt and pepper, add to the pan and sauté on both sides for 2 minutes each, then transfer to a 9 x 13-inch glass baking dish.
4. Add the chicken stock, lemon juice, and garlic and cook the chicken in the oven for 30 minutes.
5. Remove the chicken from oven and let sit.
6. Simmer the juices and garlic in a small sauce pan on the stove until the garlic is soft.
7. Place the chicken on a platter and pour some of the garlic/lemon sauce over the chicken.
8. Sprinkle chicken with lemon zest and fresh thyme and serve.

Yield: 8 chicken breasts, one per person

Moroccan Roast Chicken (Sephardic)

Since Ashkenazic Jews don't eat lamb on Passover, homes will serve some kind of roast chicken instead. This is actually a Sephardic-inspired recipe taken from recipes from Jews who live in the Middle East.

Ingredients:
- 2 chickens (5 pounds each), cut into 8 pieces per chicken
- 1 cup dried apricots
- 1 cup golden raisins
- ½ cup pecans, chopped
- 4 teaspoons cumin
- 4 teaspoons cinnamon
- 4 teaspoons paprika

2 teaspoons curry powder
2 teaspoons turmeric
1 cup honey
¼ cup olive oil
¼ cup garlic, peeled and chopped

Instructions:

1. Preheat oven to 375°F.
2. Place the chicken parts, apricots, raisins, and pecans in a large bowl.
3. Mix in a separate bowl the spices, honey, olive oil, and garlic.
4. Pour spice mixture over the chicken and rub thoroughly.
5. Cook the chicken with remainder of rub mixture in two 9 x 13-inch glass baking dishes for 50 minutes or until the chicken is cooked through.
6. Transfer to platter and serve.

Yield: 8 servings of 2 pieces of chicken

Tabikha Bil Karrate (Sephardic)

This is a traditional Middle Eastern lamb dish served at Passover. The addition of leeks reminds one of when the children of Israel ate this member of the onion family when they were slaves in Egypt prior to the Exodus. Sephardic Jews, unlike Ashkenazic Jews, will eat lamb at Passover, as long as it is not a whole roasted lamb, which would resemble the sacrifice in the Temple.

Ingredients:

4 lamb shanks
3 medium leeks
1 large onion, diced
¼ cup olive oil
4 ounces tomato paste
½ teaspoon red pepper flakes
3 cups beef stock
16 ounces crushed tomato
4 cinnamon sticks
4 potatoes, quartered
1 bag (16-ounce) frozen peas
1 bunch dill, chopped
salt and pepper to taste

Instructions:

1. Cut the leeks lengthwise and then slice thin. Place in a colander and rinse all the dirt out.

2. Heat the olive oil in a large skillet (big enough to hold the 4 lamb shanks).

3. Over medium heat, cook the leeks and onions for 5 minutes, until they appear translucent.

4. Add the tomato paste and red pepper flakes and cook 5 more minutes.

5. Add the beef stock, crushed tomato, and cinnamon sticks and bring to a simmer. Salt and pepper to taste.

6. Add the lamb shanks and cover with a lid and simmer for 2 hours.

7. Add the potatoes and simmer for 30 more minutes.

8. Add the frozen peas and simmer 15 more minutes.

9. Remove the lamb shanks from the skillet and remove the meat from the bone and cut into bite-size pieces.

10. Put a heaping amount of the vegetables on each plate, arrange the lamb pieces on top, and sprinkle with fresh dill and serve.

Yield: 8 to 10 servings

Additional Vegetable Dishes, Including Sephardic Versions
Roast Beets, Turnips and Parsnips with Fresh Olives, Parsley and Orange Marmalade

This is a quick-roasted vegetable dish that can be served with any of the meat dishes.

Ingredients:
    4 beets
    4 turnips
    12 parsnips
    ¼ cup pitted black olives
    ½ bunch fresh Italian (flat) parsley, chopped
    ¼ cup olive oil
    1 jar (8-ounce) orange marmalade

Instructions:
1. Place the beets in one baking pan and the turnips and parsnips in another baking pan and roast in the oven for 60 minutes.

2. Allow the vegetables to cool, then peel and dice into large pieces (like quartered potatoes).

3. Combine the pitted olives, parsley, and olive oil and bring to a coarse grind in a food processor. Add marmalade.

4. Combine the roasted vegetables and the olive/marmalade mixture and serve.

Yield: 10 to 12 servings

Sautéed Eggplant Pieces with Roast Garlic, Capers, and Oregano
This recipe again reflects a Middle Eastern and Mediterranean foundation. The roast garlic balances out the bitterness of the eggplant, all balanced with the sweetness of the balsamic vinegar.

Ingredients:
> 2 medium eggplants, peeled and diced into ½-inch thick pieces
> 2 garlic heads, peeled
> ¼ cup olive oil
> 1 small jar capers
> 1 bunch oregano, chopped fine
> ½ cup balsamic vinegar
> salt and pepper to taste

Instructions:
1. Preheat oven to 350°F.
2. Place the peeled garlic pieces in a baking pan and roast in the oven for 30 minutes.
3. Heat a large sauté pan and cook the eggplant on medium heat in the olive oil for 5-6 minutes or until the eggplant is semisoft to the touch.
4. Combine the eggplant in a bowl with the garlic, capers, oregano, balsamic vinegar, and salt and pepper to taste, and serve warm.

Yield: 8 to 10 servings

Stuffed Eggplant Slices (Sephardic)

Ingredients:
> 1 large eggplant, sliced into ½-inch-thick pieces (thin enough to roll and toothpick)
> 1 small onion, chopped fine
> 1 cup walnuts, chopped fine
> 1 ounce dill
> 1 ounce parsley
> 1 cup dried pomegranate seeds
> 2 ounces red wine vinegar
> 2 ounces orange juice
> salt and pepper to taste

Instructions:
1. Season eggplant slices with salt and pepper.
2. Heat the olive oil in a large skillet.

3. Cook the eggplant slices 3 minutes on one side and then flip over and cook for 1 more minute or until the eggplant is soft to the touch.
4. Place eggplant on a paper towel for 5 minutes.
5. Take the onions and chop fine in a food processer and place in a bowl.
6. Take the walnuts with the dill and parsley and chop fine in a food processor and then add to the onions.
7. Add the dried pomegranates, red wine vinegar, and orange juice to the mixture and mix well.
8. Place a tablespoon of mixture on each eggplant slice and roll the eggplant slice and then put a toothpick through the slice to hold in place.
9. Place the slices arranged in rows in a 9 x 13-inch glass baking dish and cover with aluminum foil.
10. Refrigerate overnight.
11. Serve the slices cold.

Yield: 8 to 10 servings

Additional Desserts

Individual Flourless Chocolate Lava Cake

Making desserts can be a challenge because no flour is used during the Passover holidays. This leads us to be creative with desserts that are flourless. A flourless chocolate cake is a staple during the Passover season.

Ingredients:

1 stick (8 ounces) unsalted butter, with half the stick cut into pieces
1 cup heavy cream
12 ounces bittersweet chocolate, chopped
5 large eggs
1 cup granulated sugar
½ cup unsweetened cocoa powder
½ cup sour cream
¼ cup powdered sugar, sifted

Instructions:

1. Preheat oven to 350°F.
2. Using the first ½ stick (4 ounces) of butter pieces, rub the insides and bottoms of 12 ramekins* with the butter and dust with the cocoa powder making sure you cover the insides and bottoms of the ramekins.
3. In a sauce pan, heat the remaining ½ stick (4 ounces) of butter with half of the heavy cream.

4. Add the chocolate, melt all the way through, and remove from the heat.
5. In another bowl beat the eggs, sugar, and cocoa powder until there are no lumps.
6. Add the melted chocolate and mix well.
7. Place the ramekins in a baking pan with water halfway up the ramekin.
8. Scoop the mixture into each ramekin, filling them three-quarters of the way to the top.
9. Bake for 30 to 40 minutes, or until the cakes are cooked all the way through.
10. Remove from the oven and let cool.
11. Combine the sour cream, powdered sugar, and the remainder of the heavy cream and whip until stiff.
12. Serve one ramekin per person with a dollop of whipped cream on top.

*A ramekin is a small, fluted ceramic dish that is used to cook individual-size portions (6-ounces).

Yield: 12 servings

Chocolate Almond Sponge Cake

Sponge cake is a very popular dessert during Passover because it does not need any leavening agent other than the steam that comes from the eggs that are in the cake. This is a chocolate sponge cake that can be served with various fruits like strawberries, raspberries, etc.

Ingredients:
    12 eggs
    1 cup sugar
    ¼ cup cocoa powder
    3 teaspoons potato starch
    6 ounces almond slices

Instructions:
1. Preheat the oven to 375°F.
2. Separate the eggs and set yolks aside in a bowl.
3. Using an electric mixer, whip the whites until they make a soft peak (medium stiff). Add half of the sugar very slowly as you continue to whip.
4. In another bowl whip the egg yolks with an electric mixer until they are stiff. Then add the remaining sugar slowly until all the sugar is incorporated.
5. Fold the egg whites very carefully into the egg yolk mixture, being careful not to let the volume of the batter come down.

6. Sift the cocoa powder and potato starch together and very carefully blend into egg mixture using a rubber spatula, taking care not to mix too long. Add the almonds and fold very carefully into the mixture.
7. Pour the batter into a very clean 12-inch Bundt cake pan and bake in the oven for 50 minutes or until a knife comes out clean.
8. Let the cake cool on a wire rack, then flip over.
9. Slice and serve with whipped cream.

Yield: 10 to 12 servings

Enjoy!!

CONCLUSION
IN HONOR OF THE LAMB

DARRELL L. BOCK AND MITCH GLASER

*W*hereas it is our hope that both Jewish and Gentile seekers will read this book, *Messiah in the Passover*, we understand that the majority of readers will already be followers of Jesus the Messiah. Knowing this, the book is designed to deepen the Bible knowledge and discipleship of those who have come to know the glorious truths of salvation through the Lamb of God—Jesus the Messiah—while also making the book accessible to others.

Also, as you now understand, although our authors are in general agreement with the essential truths related to the Passover, they may differ about some of the particulars. It is the hope of the editors that these differences will enrich and not confuse you. Diversity of opinion is a treasured aspect of Jewish life as articulated in the old Jewish joke, "Where there are two Jewish people, there are three opinions." This is true in many different ways. Jewish people tend to learn through disagreement and debate regarding truths about God, the Bible, Jewish life, and interpretation. However, I hope you have sensed the great unity of understanding and purpose among our authors throughout the course of this book. We would like to highlight these points of unity as we conclude our journey through the pages and chapters of *Messiah in the Passover*.

We have come to some common conclusions as authors about the Messiah in the Passover. Allow me to list a few:

1. We are certain that Jesus observed the Passover!

2. We believe Jesus celebrated some type of Passover meal with His disciples and that it was probably Thursday night—the evening before the first day of Passover.

3. We believe that the Passover reinforces lessons about salvation and redemption that permeate Scripture and Jewish life.

4. We believe the Lord's Supper, or as it is also called, the Eucharist or Communion, originated in the Passover meal that Jesus celebrated with His disciples. Through it, Jesus took the message of redemption beyond the nation of Israel to the world in a personal and far deeper way than His disciples expected.

5. We believe the Savior based some of His teachings at the Last Supper on already-existing Jewish Passover traditions.

6. We believe that the Passover traditions, rich in themes of redemption and salvation, provide a bridge from Judaism to the truths of the Gospel message and are a good starting point for Christians to speak to their Jewish friends about Jesus.

7. We believe that the Passover has unfortunately been maligned by misinformed Christians throughout the centuries and used as a platform for antisemitic attacks against the Jewish community.

8. We believe that there have been Messianic Jews throughout history who continued to observe the Passover as followers of Messiah.

9. We believe that Christians should tell their children the story of Passover from Scripture and should even utilize Jewish traditions as a way to help their families understand the unity of Scripture and the greater story of redemption found in the entire Bible.

10. We believe that Christians will enjoy celebrating the Passover, using the modern Passover Seder, which is enriching for believers today when properly linked to Jesus Messiah and the Last Supper.

11. We believe that when John the Baptist described Jesus as "the Lamb of God who takes away the sin of the world," he was referring to the great themes of the sacrificial lamb found in Scripture linked to the observance of the Passover.

12. We believe that the events of the Exodus and of the first Passover in Egypt are prophetic types of the greater Lamb and greater redemption manifested in the sacrificial death of Jesus the Messiah.

Our many authors hope our readers will be both blessed and changed in the following ways:

1. That we will have a better understanding of the Jewish context of the New Testament.

2. That we will have a better understanding of the Jewish context of the Messiah himself.

3. That we will have a better understanding of the Passover throughout Scripture.

4. That we will have a better understanding of how Jewish people observe the Passover.

5. That we will have a better understanding of the Jewish roots of our faith in Yeshua the Messiah.

6. That we will have a better understanding of the links between the Last Supper and the Lord's Supper.

7. That we will be equipped to share the Gospel with Jewish people through the Passover in a more knowledgeable and sensitive manner.

8. That we will have a better understanding of how Jewish people interpret the Bible.

9. That we will deepen our understanding of redemption and the shadow of salvation which the Exodus and Passover events cast upon all of Scripture and Jewish life.

10. That we will have a deeper love for the God of Israel, the people of Israel, and the Messiah of Israel.

11. That we will experience the joy of celebrating Messiah in the Passover in our own homes and churches.

12. That we will have a deeper and more profound understanding of what it means for Jesus to be the Lamb of God who takes away the sin of the world.

We speak on behalf of our authors as to how meaningful this pilgrimage through Scripture, church history, and Jewish tradition has been for all of us. Thank you for taking the time to read this book. We pray it will continue to impact your life for many years and many Passovers to come. Most of all, we hope that by joining us in this pilgrimage you will now have a better understanding of our glorious Jewish Messiah and Savior—Jesus, *Yeshua*—the Lamb of God who not only takes away the sins of the world, but because of His mercy and grace has removed our sins "as far as the east is from the west" (Ps. 103:12).

We hope you enjoy this salvation each day as you look forward to the return of the Lamb.

APPENDIX 1
THE JEWISH AND PROTESTANT
CANONS OF THE BIBLE

THE JEWISH CANON (*TANAKH*)

The Hebrew canon, the list of books included in Jewish Bibles, is based on the Masoretic tradition of Hebrew manuscripts. There are twenty-four books in the Jewish canon, since 1–2 Samuel, 1–2 Kings and 1–2 Chronicles are considered to be single books, as are the Twelve Prophets. The Hebrew Bible is called the *Tanakh*, which is a Hebrew acronym for the three major divisions: *Torah* (Law, or Instruction), *Nevi'im* (Prophets), and *Ketuvim* (Writings).

The Hebrew Bible (*Tanakh*)

The Law (*Torah*)
    Genesis (*Bereshit*)
    Exodus (*Shemot*)
    Leviticus (*Vayikra*)
    Numbers (*Bamidbar*)
    Deuteronomy (*Devarim*)

The Prophets (*Nevi'im*)
    Former (or Early) Prophets (*Nevi'im Rishonim*)
        Joshua (*Yehoshu'a*)
        Judges (*Shofetim*)
        1–2 Samuel (*Shemu'el 'aleph* and *bet*)
        1–2 Kings (*Melakhim 'aleph* and *bet*)
    Latter Prophets (*Nevi'im 'Aharonim*)
        Isaiah (*Yesha'yahu*)
        Jeremiah (*Yirmeyahu*)
        Ezekiel (*Yehezqe'l*)
    The Book of the Twelve (*Tere 'Asar*)
        Hosea (*Hoshe'a*)

Joel (*Yo'el*)
Amos (*'Amos*)
Obadiah (*'Ovadyah*)
Jonah (*Yonah*)
Micah (*Mikhah*)
Nahum (*Nahum*)
Habakkuk (*Havakkuk*)
Zephaniah (*Tsefanyah*)
Haggai (*Haggay*)
Zechariah (*Zekharyah*)
Malachi (*Mal'akhi*)

The Writings (*Ketuvim*)
Psalms (*Tehillim*)
Proverbs (*Mishlei*)
Job (*'Iyyob*)
Song of Songs (*Shir Hashirim*)
Ruth (*Ruth*)
Lamentations (*'Ekhah*)
Ecclesiastes (*Qoheleth*)
Esther (*'Ester*)
Daniel (*Daniyye'l*)
Ezra–Nehemiah (*'Ezra'–Nehemyah*)
1–2 Chronicles (*Divrei Hayyamim 'aleph* and *bet*)

THE PROTESTANT CANON

The Protestant Old Testament canon is the same as the Hebrew canon, only numbered and ordered differently. There are thirty-nine books in the Protestant canon, since each book is treated individually. The order of the books derives from the Greek Septuagint (LXX), which was a commonly used version of the Bible in first-century Judaism. Just like the Hebrew canon, the Protestant canon leaves out the additional books found in the Septuagint, which are called the Apocrypha.

The Old Testament in the Protestant Canon

Pentateuch
Genesis
Exodus
Leviticus
Numbers
Deuteronomy

Historical Books
    Joshua
    Judges
    Ruth
    1–2 Samuel
    1–2 Kings
    1–2 Chronicles
    Ezra
    Nehemiah
    Esther

Wisdom and Poetry Books
    Job
    Psalms
    Proverbs
    Ecclesiastes
    Song of Songs

Prophetic Books
    Former (Major) Prophets
        Isaiah
        Jeremiah
        Lamentations
        Ezekiel
        Daniel
    Twelve Latter (Minor) Prophets
        Hosea
        Joel
        Amos
        Obadiah
        Jonah
        Micah
        Nahum
        Habakkuk
        Zephaniah
        Haggai
        Zechariah
        Malachi

The New Testament

Gospels
    Matthew

Mark
Luke
John

Apostolic History
Acts

Pauline Epistles
Romans
1–2 Corinthians
Galatians
Ephesians
Philippians
Colossians
1–2 Thessalonians
1–2 Timothy
Titus
Philemon

General Epistles
Hebrews
James
1–2 Peter
1–3 John
Jude

Apocalypse
Revelation

APPENDIX 2
HEBREW MONTHS OF THE YEAR

Month	Hebrew Calendar	Western Equivalent
1	Nisan (Aviv in Ex. 13:4	March–April
2	Iyyar (Ziv in 1 Kings 6:1)	April–May
3	Sivan	May–June
4	Tammuz	June–July
5	Av	July–August
6	Elul	August–September
7	Tishri (Ethanim in 1 Kings 8:2)	September–October
8	Cheshvan (Bul in 1 Kings 6:38)	October–November
9	Kislev	November–December
10	Tevet	December–January
11	Shevat	January–February
12 (leap years)	Adar I (leap years only)	February–March
12 (13 in leap years)	Adar (Adar II in leap years)	February–March March–April (leap years)

The Hebrew calendar is a lunar calendar, whereas the Western Gregorian calendar is a solar calendar. Consequently, the calendars are not synced with each other, which cause the months to begin and end at different times in the Western year.

The "Western Equivalent" months in the table reflect a regular (non-leap) year. On a leap year, an extra month is added to the Hebrew calendar (Adar II), so the equivalent Western months are shifted up one month. For example, in 2016 (a leap year), Adar II ended on April 8, which means that Nisan started on April 9 and continued until May 8. Instead of Nisan falling in the March–April range (as shown on the chart), on the leap-year, it falls one month later, in the April–May range.

APPENDIX 3
PASSOVER OBSERVANCES IN
BIBLICAL HISTORY

Hebrew Bible References		
Passage	**Date**	**Description**
Exod. 12	ca. 1400 B.C.E.	Directions for the original Passover in Egypt
Exod. 13:3–10	ca. 1400 B.C.E.	Directions for the original Feast of Unleavened Bread while leaving Egypt
Exod. 23:15	ca. 1400 B.C.E.	Commandment to keep the Feast of Unleavened Bread on a yearly basis
Exod. 34:18–25; Num. 28:16–25; Deut. 16:1–8	ca. 1400 B.C.E.	Instructions for the yearly observance of both Passover and the Feast of Unleavened Bread
Lev. 23:4–8	ca. 1400 B.C.E.	Commandments to keep both feasts on a yearly basis
Num. 9:1–14	ca. 1400 B.C.E.	Laws regarding Passover observance and cleanliness. Institution of the second month observance.
Num. 33:3–4	ca. 1400 B.C.E.	Recounting the events of the Egyptian Passover
Joshua 5:10–12	14th century B.C.E.	Israel's Passover and Unleavened Bread observance on the plains of Jericho
2 Kings 23:21–23	7th century B.C.E.	Josiah's restoration of Passover observance

Hebrew Bible References		
Passage	Date	Description
2 Chron. 8:13	10th century B.C.E.	Solomon's observance of the Feast of Unleavened Bread
2 Chron. 30	7th century B.C.E.	Hezekiah's celebration of Passover and Unleavened Bread
2 Chron. 35:1–19	7th century B.C.E.	Josiah's celebration of Passover and Unleavened Bread
Ezra 6:19–22	5th century B.C.E.	Post-exilic celebration of Passover and Unleavened Bread in the Land
Ezek. 45:21–24	6th century B.C.E.	Eschatological Passover and Unleavened Bread observance in Ezekiel's Temple

Selected Intertestamental References		
Passage	Date	Description
Aramaic Papyri of the Fifth Century 21	5th century B.C.E.	A personal letter to a Jewish garrison in Egypt about the proper observance of Passover and Unleavened Bread
Jubilees 49	2nd century B.C.E.	Retelling of the Exodus story and the laws relating to Passover and Unleavened Bread
Exagoge by Ezekiel the Tragedian	2nd century B.C.E.	Retelling of the Exodus story in the style of Greek drama
Dead Sea Scroll Temple Scrolla 17:6–16	pre-70 C.E.	Dead Sea Scroll describing the laws for Passover and Unleavened Bread
Wisdom of Solomon 18:1–19	ca. 1 C.E.	Poetic retelling of the victories granted Israel over the Egyptians at the Passover
Philo, On the Special Laws 2 145–175	1st century	Historical retelling of Egyptian Passover and an allegorical interpretation of its meaning; includes Unleavened Bread and First Fruits

Selected Intertestamental References		
Passage	**Date**	**Description**
Pseudo-Philo 13.4	1st century	Laws requiring the celebration of Passover and Unleavened Bread
Philo, *On the Life of Moses 2* 224–233	1st century	Restatement of the laws of Passover and Unleavened Bread
Josephus, *Jewish War* 6.290–296	late 1st century C.E.	Miraculous and ominous events that took place during Passover and Unleavened Bread before the Roman attack in 70 C.E.
Josephus, *Jewish War* 6.420–428	late 1st century C.E.	The numbers of Jewish people trapped in Jerusalem due to the Feast of Unleavened Bread in 70 C.E.
Josephus, *Antiquities of the Jews* 11.109–111	late 1st century C.E.	Celebration of the feasts during the post-exilic Persian period
Josephus, *Antiquities of the Jews* 20.106–112	late 1st century C.E.	Description of a deadly Passover uprising during the time of Cumanus (48–52 C.E.)

New Testament References		
Passage	**Date**	**Description**
Luke 2:41–43	ca. 10 C.E.	Yeshua attends Passover in Jerusalem with his family
John 2:13–23	ca. 30 C.E.	Yeshua attends Passover. The first Passover in Yeshua's three-year public ministry.
John 6:4	ca. 31 C.E.	Mentions that Passover was approaching. The second Passover in Yeshua's three-year ministry.
Matt. 26:17ff., Mark 14:1ff., Luke 22:1ff., John 11:55ff.	ca. 32 C.E.	Yeshua is crucified at Passover and is resurrected during the Feast of Unleavened Bread. The third Passover in Yeshua's three-year ministry.

New Testament References		
Passage	Date	Description
Acts 12:1–4	mid-30s C.E.	Mentions that Peter was arrested during the Feast
1 Cor. 5:7–8	ca. 54 C.E.	Describes Yeshua as the Passover who was sacrificed for believers
Acts 20:6	ca. 55 C.E.	Reference to Paul waiting to sail away from Philippi until he had celebrated the Feast of Unleavened Bread

APPENDIX 4
FIVE PASSOVER MEALS COMPARED

Below is a comparison of five meals that derive their meaning from the original Passover observance in Egypt.

Category	Exodus Passover	The Last Supper	The Lord's Supper	Mishnaic Seder	Modern Seder
Primary Text	Exodus 12	Luke 22:14–21 and parallels	1 Cor. 11:23–26	Tractate Pesahim	Modern Haggadah
Date of Origin	ca. 1400 B.C.E.	ca.32 C.E.	ca.54 C.E. (earliest mention of a liturgy) until today	2nd century C.E. and earlier	Today
Occasion for Celebration	The escape from Egypt	Commandment to celebrate the looming Passover sacrifice of the Lamb of God	The accomplished Passover sacrifice of the Lamb of God	Commandment to celebrate on 14 Nisan	Commandment to celebrate on 14 Nisan
Historical (one time) or Liturgical (repeated)	Historical	Historical	Liturgical, frequency varies	Liturgical, yearly	Liturgical, yearly
People Celebrating	Enslaved Israelites	Yeshua and His disciples	Jews and Gentiles united in the Corinthian church	Jewish people	Jewish people
Location of Celebration	Egypt	Jerusalem	Corinth and beyond	Diaspora, primarily	Diaspora, primarily, until return of Jews to Israel in 19th century

Category	Exodus Passover	The Last Supper	The Lord's Supper	Mishnaic Seder	Modern Seder
Purpose for Celebration	To escape judgment, to anticipate redemption	For Yeshua to explain His crucifixion through the Passover elements	For believers to remember, thank, and worship Yeshua	To regard oneself as personally redeemed from Egypt and to praise the Lord for it	To regard oneself as personally redeemed from Egypt and to praise the Lord for it. To anticipate the future Passover in Jerusalem.
Essential Elements	Sacrificed lamb, lamb's blood on doorposts, unleavened bread, bitter herbs	Sacrificed lamb, unleavened bread, wine	Unleavened bread, wine	Removal of leaven, unleavened bread, four cups of wine, bitter herbs, Hallel Psalms	Reading the Haggadah, removal of leaven, unleavened bread, four cups of wine, bitter herbs, Hallel Psalms
Posture of Hope	Forward to redemption from Egypt	Forward to redemption from sin; fulfillment of Scriptures	Backward to accomplished redemption from sin; forward to Yeshua's return	Backward to redemption from Egypt; forward to restoration	Backward to redemption from Egypt; forward to restoration

APPENDIX 5
LAST SUPPER SAYINGS COMPARED

Below is a table that compares the accounts of the Last Supper on a phrase-by-phrase basis, using Luke 22 as the base text and aligning all others to it.

Passage	Luke 22:14	Matt. 26:20	Mark 14:17–18a	John 13:12a	1 Cor. 11:23
Reclining at the Table in the Evening	When the hour had come, He reclined at the table, and the apostles with Him.	Now, when evening came, Jesus was reclining at the table with the twelve disciples.	When it was evening He came with the twelve. As they were reclining at the table and eating,	So when He had washed their feet, and taken His garments and reclined at the table again,	...the Lord Jesus in the night in which He was betrayed...
Passage	Luke 22:15				
Yeshua's Desire to Eat the Passover	And He said to them, "I have earnestly desired to eat this Passover with you before I suffer;				
Passage	Luke 22:16				1 Cor. 11:26
No Passover for Yeshua until the Future Kingdom	for I say to you, I shall never again eat it until it is fulfilled in the kingdom of God."				For as often as you eat this bread and drink the cup, you proclaim the Lord's death until He comes.

Passage	Luke 22:17				
The First Cup	And when He had taken a cup and given thanks, He said, "Take this and share it among yourselves;				

Passage	Luke 22:18	Matt. 26:29	Mark 14:25		1 Cor. 11:26
No Passover Wine for Yeshua until the Future Kingdom	for I say to you, I will not drink of the fruit of the vine from now on until the kingdom of God comes."	"But I say to you, I will not drink of this fruit of the vine from now on until that day when I drink it new with you in My Father's kingdom."	"Truly I say to you, I will never again drink of the fruit of the vine until that day when I drink it new in the kingdom of God."		For as often as you eat this bread and drink the cup, you proclaim the Lord's death until He comes.

Passage	Luke 22:19	Matt. 26:26	Mark 14:22		1 Cor. 11:23b–24
The Bread Instituted	And when He had taken some bread and given thanks, He broke it and gave it to them, saying, "This is My body which is given for you; do this in remembrance of Me."	While they were eating, Jesus took some bread, and after a blessing, He broke it and gave it to the disciples, and said, "Take, eat; this is My body."	While they were eating, He took some bread, and after a blessing He broke it, and gave it to them, and said, "Take it; this is My body."		the Lord Jesus in the night in which He was betrayed took bread; and when He had given thanks, He broke it and said, "This is My body, which is for you; do this in remembrance of Me."

Passage	Luke 22:20	Matt. 26:27–28	Mark 14:23–24		1 Cor. 11:25
The Cup of Redemption	And in the same way He took the cup after they had eaten, saying, "This cup which is poured out for you is the new covenant in My blood.	And when He had taken a cup and given thanks, He gave it to them, saying, "Drink from it, all of you; for this is My blood of the covenant, which is poured out for many for forgiveness of sins.	And when He had taken a cup and given thanks, He gave it to them, and they all drank from it. And He said to them, "This is My blood of the covenant, which is poured out for many.		In the same way He took the cup also after supper, saying, "This cup is the new covenant in My blood; do this, as often as you drink it, in remembrance of Me."
Passage	Luke 22:21	Matt. 26:21	Mark 14:18b	John 13:21	1 Cor. 11:23
The Announcement of Betrayal	"But behold, the hand of the one betraying Me is with Mine on the table.	As they were eating, He said, "Truly I say to you that one of you will betray Me."	Jesus said, "Truly I say to you that one of you will betray Me—one who is eating with Me."	When Jesus had said this, He became troubled in spirit, and testified and said, "Truly, truly, I say to you, that one of you will betray Me."	...in the night in which He was betrayed...
Passage		Matt. 26:23	Mark 14:20	John 13:26	
The Identity of the Betrayer Revealed		And He answered, "He who dipped his hand with Me in the bowl is the one who will betray Me.	And He said to them, "It is one of the twelve, one who dips with Me in the bowl.	Jesus then answered, "That is the one for whom I shall dip the morsel and give it to him." So when He had dipped the morsel, He took and gave it to Judas, the son of Simon Iscariot.	

Passage	Luke 22:22	Matt. 26:24	Mark 14:21		
The Woe of Being Yeshua's Betrayer	"For indeed, the Son of Man is going as it has been determined; but woe to that man by whom He is betrayed!"	"The Son of Man is to go, just as it is written of Him; but woe to that man by whom the Son of Man is betrayed! It would have been good for that man if he had not been born."	"For the Son of Man is to go just as it is written of Him; but woe to that man by whom the Son of Man is betrayed! It would have been good for that man if he had not been born."		

Passage	Luke 22:23	Matt. 26:22	Mark 14:19	John 13:22–25	
The Disciples' Bewilderment at the Announcement	And they began to discuss among themselves which one of them it might be who was going to do this thing.	Being deeply grieved, they each one began to say to Him, "Surely not I, Lord?"	They began to be grieved and to say to Him one by one, "Surely not I?"	The disciples began looking at one another, at a loss to know of which one He was speaking. There was reclining on Jesus's bosom one of His disciples, whom Jesus loved. So Simon Peter gestured to him, and said to him, "Tell us who it is of whom He is speaking." He, leaning back thus on Jesus's bosom, said to Him, "Lord, who is it?"	

Passage		Matt. 26:30	Mark 14:26		
The Final Hymn		After singing a hymn, they went out to the Mount of Olives.	After singing a hymn, they went out to the Mount of Olives.		

APPENDIX 6
THE LAMB OF GOD IN THE
NEW TESTAMENT

As our Passover Lamb, Yeshua died to bring redemption to His people. The New Testament, particularly the Apostle John, often uses this motif to describe Jesus. Below is a table of verses that describe Yeshua as the Lamb of God.

Reference	Scripture Passage
John 1:29	The next day he saw Jesus coming to him and said, "Behold, *the Lamb of God* who takes away the sin of the world!"
John 1:36	He looked at Jesus as He walked, and said, "Behold, *the Lamb of God*!"
Acts 8:32–35	Now the passage of Scripture which he was reading was this: "He was led as *a sheep* to slaughter; And as *a lamb* before its shearer is silent, So He does not open His mouth. In humiliation His judgment was taken away; Who will relate His generation? For His life is removed from the earth." The eunuch answered Philip and said, "Please tell me, of whom does the prophet say this? Of himself or of someone else?" Then Philip opened his mouth, and beginning from this Scripture he preached Jesus to him.
1 Cor. 5:7	Clean out the old leaven so that you may be a new lump, just as you are in fact unleavened. For Christ our *Passover* also has been sacrificed.
1 Peter 1:19	But with precious blood, as of *a lamb* unblemished and spotless, the blood of Christ.
Rev. 5:8	When He had taken the book, the four living creatures and the twenty-four elders fell down before *the Lamb*, each one holding a harp and golden bowls full of incense, which are the prayers of the saints.

Rev. 5:12–13	Saying with a loud voice, "Worthy is *the Lamb* that was slain to receive power and riches and wisdom and might and honor and glory and blessing." And every created thing which is in heaven and on the earth and under the earth and on the sea, and all things in them, I heard saying, "To Him who sits on the throne, and to *the Lamb*, be blessing and honor and glory and dominion forever and ever."
Rev. 6:1	Then I saw when *the Lamb* broke one of the seven seals, and I heard one of the four living creatures saying as with a voice of thunder, "Come."
Rev. 6:16	And they said to the mountains and to the rocks, "Fall on us and hide us from the presence of Him who sits on the throne, and from the wrath of *the Lamb*."
Rev. 7:9–10	After these things I looked, and behold, a great multitude which no one could count, from every nation and all tribes and peoples and tongues, standing before the throne and before *the Lamb*, clothed in white robes, and palm branches were in their hands; and they cry out with a loud voice, saying, "Salvation to our God who sits on the throne, and to *the Lamb*."
Rev. 7:14	I said to him, "My lord, you know." And he said to me, "These are the ones who come out of the great tribulation, and they have washed their robes and made them white in the blood of *the Lamb*."
Rev. 7:17	For *the Lamb* in the center of the throne will be their shepherd, and will guide them to springs of the water of life; and God will wipe every tear from their eyes.
Rev. 12:11	And they overcame him because of the blood of *the Lamb* and because of the word of their testimony, and they did not love their life even when faced with death.
Rev. 13:8	All who dwell on the earth will worship him, everyone whose name has not been written from the foundation of the world in the book of life of *the Lamb* who has been slain.
Rev. 14:1	Then I looked, and behold, *the Lamb* was standing on Mount Zion, and with Him one hundred and forty-four thousand, having His name and the name of His Father written on their foreheads.
Rev. 14:4	These are the ones who have not been defiled with women, for they have kept themselves chaste. These are the ones who follow *the Lamb* wherever He goes. These have been purchased from among men as first fruits to God and to *the Lamb*.

Rev. 14:10	He also will drink of the wine of the wrath of God, which is mixed in full strength in the cup of His anger; and he will be tormented with fire and brimstone in the presence of the holy angels and in the presence of *the Lamb*.
Rev. 15:3	And they sang the song of Moses, the bond-servant of God, and the song of *the Lamb*, saying, "Great and marvelous are Your works, O Lord God, the Almighty; Righteous and true are Your ways, King of the nations!"
Rev. 17:14	These will wage war against *the Lamb*, and *the Lamb* will overcome them, because He is Lord of lords and King of kings, and those who are with Him are the called and chosen and faithful.
Rev. 19:7	Let us rejoice and be glad and give the glory to Him, for the marriage of *the Lamb* has come and His bride has made herself ready.
Rev. 19:9	Then he said to me, "Write, 'Blessed are those who are invited to the marriage supper of *the Lamb*.'" And he said to me, "These are true words of God."
Rev. 21:9	Then one of the seven angels who had the seven bowls full of the seven last plagues came and spoke with me, saying, "Come here, I will show you the bride, the wife of *the Lamb*."
Rev. 21:14	And the wall of the city had twelve foundation stones, and on them were the twelve names of the twelve apostles of *the Lamb*.
Rev. 21:22–23	I saw no temple in it, for the Lord God the Almighty and *the Lamb* are its temple. And the city has no need of the sun or of the moon to shine on it, for the glory of God has illumined it, and its lamp is *the Lamb*.
Rev. 21:27	And nothing unclean, and no one who practices abomination and lying, shall ever come into it, but only those whose names are written in *the Lamb's* book of life.
Rev. 22:1	Then he showed me a river of the water of life, clear as crystal, coming from the throne of God and of *the Lamb*.
Rev. 22:3	There will no longer be any curse; and the throne of God and of *the Lamb* will be in it, and His bond-servants will serve Him.

APPENDIX 7
MAP OF THE
EXODUS

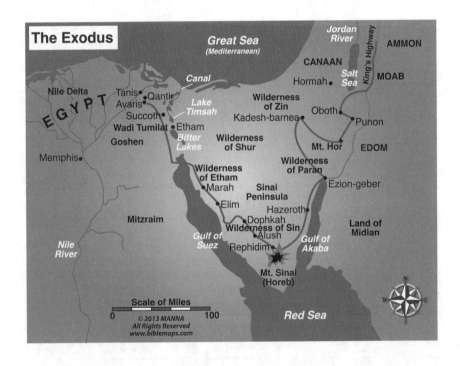

APPENDIX 8
MAP OF JERUSALEM DURING
MESSIAH'S FINAL DAYS (PART 1)

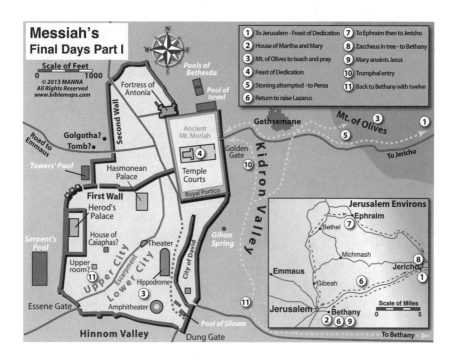

APPENDIX 9
MAP OF JERUSALEM DURING
MESSIAH'S FINAL DAYS (PART 2)

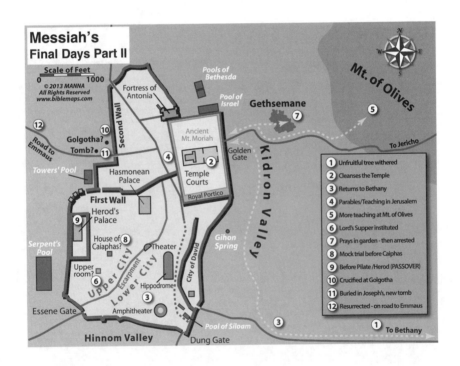

ABBREVIATIONS

GENERAL AND BIBLIOGRAPHIC

B.C.E.	before Common Era
ca.	circa (about, approximately)
C.E.	Common Era
EncJud	*Encyclopaedia Judaica*. Edited by Fred Skolnik and Michael Berenbaum. 2nd ed. 22 vols. Detroit: Macmillan Reference USA, 2007
ESV	English Standard Version
HCSB	Holman Christian Standard Bible
KJV	King James Version
lit.	literally
LXX	Septuagint
MSG	The Message
NASB	New American Standard Bible
NET	NET Bible
s.v.	*sub verbo*, under the word

HEBREW BIBLE / OLD TESTAMENT (INCLUDING SEPTUAGINT)

Gen.	Genesis
Exod.	Exodus
Lev.	Leviticus
Num.	Numbers
Deut.	Deuteronomy
Josh.	Joshua
1 Kings	1 Kings
2 Kings	2 Kings
2 Chron.	2 Chronicles
Ezra	Ezra
Ps./Pss.	Psalm(s)
Isa.	Isaiah

Jer.	Jeremiah
Ezek.	Ezekiel
Zech.	Zechariah
Mal.	Malachi

NEW TESTAMENT

Matt.	Matthew
Mark	Mark
Luke	Luke
John	John
Acts	Acts
Rom.	Romans
1 Cor.	1 Corinthians
2 Cor.	2 Corinthians
Gal.	Galatians
Eph.	Ephesians
Col.	Colossians
2 Tim.	2 Timothy
Titus	Titus
Heb.	Hebrews
1 Peter	1 Peter
2 Peter	2 Peter
Rev.	Revelation

MISHNAH, TALMUD, AND RELATED LITERATURE

b.	Babylonian Talmud (tractate)
m.	Mishnah (tractate)
t.	Tosefta (tractate)
y.	Jerusalem (or Palestinian) Talmud (tractate)

OTHER ANCIENT SOURCES

| Josephus | Josephus |
| *Ant.* | *Antiquities of the Jews* |

GLOSSARY

adoptionism. The belief that Jesus was adopted as a son by God at His baptism, resurrection or ascension. A heretical understanding of Yeshua's identity, since He is the preexistent Son.

afikoman (ah-fee-KO-men). Etymology unclear, but probably from the Greek meaning "that which comes after," or "dessert." In the Passover Seder, the half piece of matzah that is broken, hidden, brought back and distributed to the participants after the meal. Many believers see parallels between this practice and Yeshua's last Seder.

aliyah (ah-lee-YAH). Literally, "going up." (1) Generic name for the three biblical feasts that Israelites were required to go up to Jerusalem to celebrate. (2) The act of immigrating to the Land of Israel. (3) The honor of being called up to the Reading of the Scriptures in synagogue.

Amora (ah-moe-RAH; pl. *Amoraim*, ah-moe-rah-EEM). Literally, "one who says." Jewish scholars who commented on the Mishnah in the third to sixth centuries. Their commentaries are known as the Gemara and became part of the Talmud.

antisemitism. The hatred of Jews or the Jewish people characterized by destructive thoughts, words, and/or actions against them, and further characterized by irrationality.

Ashkenazi (osh-keh-NAH-zee; pl. *Ashkenazim*, osh-keh-nah-ZEEM; adj. *Ashkenazic*, osh-keh-NAH-zic). Jewish people whose medieval ancestry is from Germany, Central or Western Europe.

atonement. In the Bible, the reconciling of humankind to God by the covering of sins.

bar mitzvah (bar MITZ-vah). The religious ceremony initiating a thirteen-year-old boy into manhood and declaring him to be responsible for his actions and able to participate in public worship.

baruch (bah-RUKH). Literally, "blessed be." Many Jewish blessings begin with "*Baruch atah Adonai*," meaning, "Blessed are you, O Lord."

beitzah (bay-TZAH). A roasted egg placed on the Seder plate. The beitzah is a reminder of the destruction of the Temple and our inability to offer sacrifices.

beraita (beh-RYE-tah). Literally, "external." An early rabbinic oral tradition that was not included in the Mishnah but is quoted in later rabbinic sources.

blood libel. Originating in Norwich, England in the twelfth century, the false accusation that Jews murdered Christian children in order to use their blood in Jewish rituals. Blood libels were common in Christendom in the Middle Ages and have resurfaced as sources of antisemitism as recently as the twenty-first century.

chag or *hag* (KHAG). Literally "festival" or "holiday."

chagigah. See *hagigah*.

chametz or *hametz* (KHUH-mitz). Literally, "leaven." Leaven and all foods made with leaven are forbidden during the celebration of Passover and the Feast of Unleavened Bread.

Chanukah. See *Hanukkah*.

charoset (khah-ROH-set) (meaning is of unknown origin). A mixture of sweet ingredients such as apples, nuts, and dates, chopped and combined into a paste resembling the mortar used by the Jewish slaves in Egypt.

chattat (kha-TAHT). Literally, "sin offering."

Conservative Judaism. Also known as *Masorti* (traditional) Judaism, it is a major branch in Judaism, particularly in the United States, that believes Jewish law is binding but subject to changes according to contemporary needs. Conservative Judaism traces its roots to the Positive-Historical school of thought led by Rabbi Zecharias Frankel in mid-nineteenth-century Europe in reaction to the liberal tendencies of Reform Judaism.

Communion. See *Eucharist.* The partaking of bread and wine in commemoration of Yeshua's body and blood given for us at the Last Supper.

Dayenu (dye-AY-noo). Literally, "It would have been enough for us." A Passover song, over 1,000 years old, that has many stanzas praising the Lord for each of His blessings, proclaiming "*Dayenu*" after each stanza.

Diaspora (di-AS-puh-rah). The "dispersion" of Jewish people living outside the Land of Israel.

Ebionites. An early sect of Jewish believers in Jesus as the Messiah. There is controversy over whether this group accepted the Messiah's divinity.

eschatology. The theological study of the doctrine of the end times.

etymology. The study of the historical origin and changing meaning of words.

Eucharist. Literally, "thanksgiving." Also known as Communion or the Lord's Supper.

Exodus. (1) The second book of the Bible; contains the story of God delivering Israel out of slavery in Egypt. (2) The act of God redeeming His people from Egypt.

First Fruits. The feast in which Israel is required to present the first sheaf of the harvest before the Lord (Lev. 23:9–14). Observed the day after the Sabbath in Passover Week.

gaon (gah-OWN; pl. *geonim*, geh-oh-NEEM). The head of a rabbinic academy, particularly in Babylonia in the sixth to eleventh centuries. Sometimes applied to very prominent later rabbis.

Gemara (guh-MAR-ah) (Aramaic). Literally, "completion." Rabbinic analysis and commentary on the Mishnah, now forming the larger part of the Babylonian and Palestinian Talmuds. The Jerusalem Gemara was completed in 340–400 C.E., and the Babylonian around 500 C.E.

Gentile. A non-Jewish person.

hag. See *chag.*

Haggadah (hah-GAH-dah). Literally, "the telling." A Jewish text that tells the story of the Passover and serves as a guide to the celebration of the Passover Seder in the home. The Haggadah includes prayers, songs, and rituals that bring the story to life.

hagigah (khah-GEE-gah). Literally "festival offering." The name of the voluntary sacrifices offered at Passover. Also a Mishnaic and Talmudic tractate dealing with the three pilgrimage festivals, including Passover.

halakhah (hah-lah-KHAH). Literally, "to go" or "to walk." Jewish religious law, including both the Oral (rabbinic) and Written (biblical) Law.

Hallel (hah-LAIL). Literally, "praise." A term applied to Psalms 113–118, the joyous psalms of praise sung during the Passover Seder.

hametz. See *chametz.*

Hanukkah (KHAH-noo-kah). Literally, "dedication." The Hebrew festival of lights, an eight-day holiday commemorating the rededication of the Temple after the victory of the Maccabees over Antiochus Epiphanes in 164 or 165 B.C.E. Celebrated by Yeshua in John 10:22–23.

haroset. See *charoset.*

Hashem (hah-SHEM). Literally, "the name." In Talmudic tradition and Jewish culture, it is forbidden to say the name of God written in Scripture (the Tetragrammaton) because God's name is something to be revered and not used casually. Hashem is a polite way to refer to God with traditional Jewish people.

Hebrew. (1) The language of the Hebrew Scriptures, also used in prayer books and scholarly works. (2) The term (often plural, *Hebrews*) used for descendants of Abraham, Isaac, and Jacob.

Hellenistic. Of or relating to Greek culture or use of language. The "Hellenistic period" of Jewish history refers to the period (323 B.C.E. to 31 B.C.E.) in which Greek influence was dominant in the Mediterranean and the Middle East.

Holocaust. The state-organized mass persecution and murder of European Jewry by the Nazis and their collaborators (1933–1945).

horseradish. Consumed at Passover to help recall the bitter pain the Israelites endured while enslaved in Egypt. Fulfills the command to eat "bitter herbs" in Exodus 12:8 and Numbers 9:11.

hyssop. A common herb in the mint family, used in biblical times for medicinal, cleaning, and cooking purposes. The Israelites were commanded to use hyssop branches to put the blood of lambs upon their doorposts and lintels during the first Passover (Exod. 12:22).

Israel. (1) The modern nation, also called the State of Israel, established in 1948. (2) In biblical times, the kingdom of David and Solomon. Following Solomon's reign, Israel referred solely to the ten tribes of the Northern Kingdom; the remaining tribes were known as Judah. (3) The new name given to Jacob after he wrestled with the angel in the book of Genesis.

Iyyar (EE-yar). Eighth month of the Jewish civil calendar and second of the religious calendar, usually falling around April or May.

Jew. (1) A descendant of Abraham, Isaac, and Jacob. (2) A person whose religion is Judaism.

Jewish calendar. A lunar calendar based on the biblical feasts and holy days, and calculating years from the creation of the world.

karet (CAR-ret). Literally, "cut." Separation from God or His people, a biblical punishment for certain kinds of disobedience.

karpas (CAR-pahs). (Greek) Literally, "fresh raw vegetable." The leafy green vegetable on the Passover Seder plate.

kashrut (kosh-ROOT). From *kosher*, literally "fit" or "proper." Jewish dietary laws, specifying what foods are allowable to eat and how they are to be prepared.

Ketuvim (keh-too-VEEM). Literally, "writings." The Hebrew Bible is comprised of three parts, the *Torah* (Law, or Instruction; the five books of Moses), the *Nevi'im* (the Prophets), and the *Ketuvim* (the Writings). Some of the books included in the Ketuvim include Esther, Psalms, and Proverbs.

kiddush (KID-ish or kid-OOSH). sanctification. A blessing recited over wine on the eve of the Sabbath and festivals.

kippur (kee-POOR). Literally, "covering" or "atonement." Yom Kippur is the day of atonement.

kosher (KOH-sher). Literally, "clean" or "pure." Used in relation to biblical kosher foods, specified in Leviticus 11 and later expanded in Jewish tradition.

Last Supper. The momentous last meal that Yeshua shared with His disciples before His crucifixion.

Lord's Supper. See *Last Supper.* See also *Communion.*

Mashiach (mah-SHEE-akh). Literally, "anointed." Often translated "Messiah," or the anointed one.

Masoretes (MA-zoh-reets). Jewish scholars who standardized the spelling and punctuation of the Hebrew Scriptures between the seventh and eleventh centuries C.E.

Masoretic (ma-zoh-REH-tik). Literally, "traditional." In accordance with tradition. The Masoretic Text is the authoritative text of the Hebrew Bible.

maror (mah-ROAR). Bitter. The bitter herbs on the Passover Seder plate.

matzah (MAHTZ-uh; pl. *matzot*, mah-TZOTE). Bread made without yeast. Matzah is flat and is striped and pierced to prevent rising during baking. Eating unleavened bread is a requirement during the Feast of Passover and Unleavened Bread.

matzah tash (MAHTZ-uh TAHSH). A bag with three compartments to hold Passover matzah at the Seder.

Messianic Jew. A Jewish person who believes Yeshua is the Messiah of Israel.

Messianic Age. A time in the future, in which there will be universal peace on earth. The term is subject to many interpretations in both Judaism and Christianity.

midrash (MID-rahsh; pl. *midrashim*, mid-rah-SHEEM). Literally, "inquire" or "seek." A genre or collection of rabbinic interpretation of Scripture that can be of a legal (*midrash halakhah*) or didactic (*midrash aggadah*) nature.

Mishnah (MISH-nah; pl. *mishnayot*, mish-nah-YOTE). From *shanah*, meaning "to repeat." (1) The oldest written record of the Jewish Oral Law, codified at the end of the second century C.E. by Judah haNasi. Together with the Gemara, it comprises the core of the Talmud. (2) Individual passages within the Mishnah.

mitzvah (MITZ-vah). Literally, "commandment." Biblical or rabbinic commandment; also used colloquially to refer to good deeds.

Nevi'im (neh-vee-EEM). Literally, "prophets." The name for the portion of the Hebrew Scriptures that contains the books of the prophets.

netzer (NEH-tzer). The Hebrew word for "branch" or "stem" in Isaiah 11:1. A common ancient name referring to the Messiah.

next year in Jerusalem. The traditional phrase said at the end of the Passover Seder, in hopes that Messiah would return and would gather Jewish people to Jerusalem.

Nicaea. The Council of Nicaea (325 C.E.) was the first church council held after Christianity was legalized under Constantine.

Nisan (NEE-san). Seventh month of the Jewish civil year and first month of the religious year, usually falling in March or April, also known in the Bible as Aviv. Passover takes place on the fourteenth of Nisan.

Notzrim (notz-REEM). Literally, "Nazarenes." (1) Used to describe early believers in Yeshua. (2) In modern Hebrew, word meaning "Christians."

Novellae (Latin). Literally, "new." Anti-Judaic edicts enacted by Justinian I (reigned 527–565 C.E.) that placed restrictions on Jewish people within the Roman Empire.

Orthodox. A word signifying having "correct belief" about a subject. Historically, believers in Yeshua have been defined as "orthodox" if they believe in the historic creeds of the church councils. However, [Eastern] Orthodox Christianity is a branch of Greek Christendom, and Orthodox Judaism is a sector of Judaism.

Orthodox Judaism. As a modern term, it refers to the traditional sector of Judaism that believes in the revelation of Scripture and strict observance of Jewish Law.

Passover. (1) Jewish festival commemorating the Exodus of the Israelites from Egypt. (2) The tenth and final plague in which all the firstborn males in Egypt were doomed to die. Moses, as directed by God, instructed the Israelites to sacrifice a lamb and place its blood over the doorway of their homes, thus causing the the destroyer, sometimes referred to traditionally as the "angel of death," to pass over them.

Pesach (PAY-sakh). See *Passover.*

Pesahim (pay-sa-KHEEM). A tractate in the Mishnah and Talmud by early rabbinic scholars outlining the observance of Passover and other festivals.

Pharisee (FAIR-uh-see). Literally, "separate one." A member of a Jewish sect from the time of the Second Temple. One Pharisaic distinctive among others was belief in the Oral Law as well as the Written Law. The Pharisees are considered the ideological ancestors of rabbinic Judaism.

plagues. See *Ten Plagues.*

pogrom (puh-GRUM) (Yiddish/Russian). Literally, "demolish violently." An organized, violent attack by non-Jews on a Jewish community, resulting in rape, murder, and the destruction of property. The term originated in the Russian Empire in 1821 but is used of similar incidents in other countries as well.

Quartodeciman (KWAR-to-DES-ah-man) (Latin). Literally "a fourteenther." A position in the early church that held that Easter should be celebrated on the fourteenth of Nisan, the date of Passover in the Jewish calendar. This position was decided against at the Council of Nicaea.

Rabban (rab-AN). Title given to heads of the Sanhedrin in mishnaic times; higher than rabbi.

rabbi (RAB-eye). Literally "my great one." Came to mean "teacher." Since the time of the Second Temple's destruction, rabbis have been the authoritative leaders of the Jewish community. Jewish people turned to rabbis for counsel, judgments, spiritual guidance, life-cycle events, and learning.

redemption. A biblical term referring to God freeing His followers from slavery, oppression, or sin.

Reform Judaism. Also known as Liberal or Progressive Judaism, this sector of modern Judaism believes in the evolving nature of the faith, modifying Jewish observance with the needs of the culture. Reform Judaism arose in mid-nineteenth-century Europe, and sought to make Judaism relevant to modern Jews in response to the breakdown of traditional Jewish beliefs and observance resulting from Enlightenment thought.

Sabbath. See *Shabbat.*

Sadducee (SAJ-uh-see). Literally, "righteous one." A member of a Second Temple-period Jewish sect that adhered to the strict interpretation of the Written Law and disregarded rabbinic tradition known as the Oral Law. The Sadducees, whose sect revolved around the priesthood and the Second Temple, ceased to exist shortly after the latter's destruction in 70 C.E.

Sanhedrin (san-HED-rin) (Greek). Literally, "sitting together." In the ancient Jewish judicial system, it was an assembly of twenty-three to seventy-one ordained rabbinic scholars who decided legal cases in each city of the Land of Israel. The Great Sanhedrin, based in Jerusalem, functioned as a supreme court in the first century C.E.

Seder (SAY-der). Literally, "order." The ceremonial meal observed in Jewish homes on the first night of Passover (celebrated on the first two nights outside Israel).

Seder plate (SAY-der plate). A special plate, placed on the dinner table at the Passover Seder, that contains foods symbolic of the holiday.

Sephardi (seh-FAR-dee; pl. *Sephardim*, seh-far-DEEM). Jewish people whose medieval origins were in Spain or Portugal. Today, Sephardic Jews are spread throughout the world after the expulsion of the Jews from Spain in 1492. Their tradition is a minority position in the midst of the larger numbers of Ashkenazic Jews.

Septuagint (SEP-too-uh-jint) from the Latin word for "seventy." Abbreviated as LXX, refers to the translation of the Hebrew Scriptures into Greek by "seventy" Jewish scholars in the third to second centuries B.C.E.

Shabbat (shah-BAHT). Literally, "rest." The Sabbath, or seventh day of the week in the Jewish calendar. A day of rest set apart for the Lord. Starts Friday at sundown and ends Saturday at sundown.

Shavuot (shah-voo-OTE). Literally, "weeks." The Feast of Weeks, or Pentecost. Occurring fifty days after the second day of Passover, this second of three annual pilgrim festivals celebrates the first fruits of the wheat harvest. According to tradition, God gave Israel the Torah on Shavuot.

soteriology. The theological study of the doctrine of salvation.

Sukkot (soo-COTE). Literally, "booths." Also known as the Feast of Tabernacles. Celebrated on the fifteenth of the Jewish month of Tishri, commemorating the forty years of Jewish life in the wilderness after the Exodus from Egypt.

synagogue (SIN-uh-gahg). From the Greek word for "house of assembly."

Synoptic Gospels. The Gospels of Matthew, Mark, and Luke in the New Testament, or New Covenant Scriptures.

Talmud (TAHL-muhd) teaching. A body of rabbinic conversation, argument, law, stories, and commentaries on the Hebrew Scriptures. Composed of the Mishnah and the Gemara, compiled over many centuries and codified by the sixth century C.E. The Talmud exists in two versions: the Jerusalem (or Palestinian) Talmud compiled in the Land of Israel, and the later Babylonian Talmud, reflecting the commentaries of the Babylonian academies.

Tanakh (tah-NAHKH). An acronym for the three sections that make up the Hebrew Bible: the *Torah* (Law, or Instruction; the five books of Moses), *Nevi'im* (the Prophets), and *Ketuvim* (the Writings). Contains the same books as the Christian Old Testament, but grouped differently.

Tanna (TAH-nah; pl. *Tannaim*, tah-nah-EEM) Literally, "teacher" or "repeater." Teachers of the Oral Law from 10 to 220 c.e., whose sayings were recorded in the Mishnah.

Targum (tar-GOOM; pl. Targumim, tar-goom-EEM). Literally, "translation." Aramaic paraphrased translations and interpretations of the Hebrew Scriptures. The two major Targumim are Targum Onkelos on the Torah and Targum Jonathan on the Prophets, although Targumim exist for other parts of the Scriptures as well. Originally transmitted orally, written Targumim were in use by the third century c.e.

Temple. From the Latin for "open or consecrated space." The First Temple, built by Solomon, was destroyed by the Babylonians in 587 b.c.e. The Second Temple, finished under Ezra and Nehemiah in 516 b.c.e., was reconstructed by Herod and stood through the time of Yeshua until its destruction by the Romans in 70 c.e. The Western Wall in Jerusalem is all that remains of the Second Temple, being a retaining wall from the time of Herod.

ten plagues. The punishments inflicted by God on Pharaoh and the Egyptians for enslaving the Israelites in ancient days.

Tishri (TISH-ree). First month of the Jewish civil year, and seventh month of the religious year; usually falls in September to October.

Torah (TOE-rah). Literally "teaching" or "instruction." The first five books of Moses, known as the Pentateuch (Genesis, Exodus, Leviticus, Numbers, and Deuteronomy). Can also refer to the entire body of Jewish tradition. The Hebrew Bible is comprised of three parts, the *Torah* (Law, or Instruction), the *Nevi'im* (the Prophets) and the *Ketuvim* (the Writings).

Tosefta (toe-SEF-tah). Literally "supplement" or "addition." Supplementary traditions of the Tannaim, not included in the Mishnah but quoted in other rabbinic writings.

tractate. One of the sixty-three sections of the Mishnah. Also used of sections of the Talmud.

transliteration The changing of characters from one language into similar-sounding characters of another language.

transubstantiation. The view, held in Catholicism, that bread and wine taken at communion are literally the body and blood of Christ. According to Catholic doctrine, through the service of a Catholic priest, the elements of communion are translated into a different substance, but retain their same appearance.

typology. The study of patterns and correspondences between New Testament people, events, or institutions with people, events, or institutions in the Hebrew Bible.

Yerushalayim (yeh-ROO-shah-LYE-eem). Literally, "city of peace." Hebrew name for the city of Jerusalem.

Yiddish (YID-ish) (Yiddish). From the German *juedisch*, meaning "Jewish." A language spoken by Ashkenazi Jews beginning in the ninth century c.e. A combination of High German, Hebrew, Russian, Slavic, and other languages, Yiddish is still spoken in some communities in Russia, Israel, and the United States.

Yisrael (yis-rah-ALE). The Hebrew word for Israel.

Yom Kippur (YOME key-POOR), *Yom haKippurim* (YOME ha-key-poor-REEM). Literally, "Day of Atonement." A solemn fast day and the holiest day of the Hebrew year; falls on the tenth day of the month of Tishri.

zeroah (zeh-ROH-ah). Shankbone of a lamb that is placed on the Passover Seder Plate.

RECOMMENDED READING

PRIMARY SOURCES

Masoretic Text
Biblia Hebraica Stuttgartensia. 5th ed. Stuttgart: Deutsch Bibelgesellschaft, 1997.

Greek New Testament
Nestle, Eberhard, and Erwin Nestle. *Nestle-Aland: Novum Testamentum Graece.* Edited by Barbara Aland, Kurt Aland, Johannes Karavidopoulos, Carlo M. Martini, and Bruce M. Metzger. 28th ed. Stuttgart: Deutsche Bibelgesellschaft, 2012.

Mishnah in English
Blackman, Philip. *Mishnayoth.* 6 vols. 2nd ed. Gatehead, NY: Judaica Press, 2000.

Babylonian Talmud (Bavli) in English
Epstein, Isidore, trans. *The Babylonian Talmud.* 18 vols. London: Soncino Press, 1978.

Jerusalem Talmud (Yerushalmi) in English
Neusner, Jacob. *The Jerusalem Talmud: A Translation and Commentary.* 28 vols. Peabody, MA: Hendrickson Publishers, 2008.

Church Fathers in English
The Ante-Nicene Fathers. Edited by Alexander Roberts and James Donaldson. 1885–1887. 10 vols. Peabody, MA: Hendrickson, 1994. Originally published by Christian Literature Company.

Brannan, Rick, trans. *The Apostolic Fathers in English.* Bellingham, WA: Lexham Press, 2012.

Schaff, Philip, ed. *A Select Library of the Nicene and Post-Nicene Fathers of the Christian Church*. 28 vols. Buffalo, NY: Christian Literature Company, 1887–1900.

Old Testament Pseudepigrapha
Charlesworth, James H., ed. *The Old Testament Pseudepigrapha*. 2 vols. Garden City, NY: Doubleday, 1983–1985.

Josephus
Josephus, Flavius, and William Whiston, trans. *The Works of Josephus: Complete and Unabridged*. Peabody: Hendrickson, 1987.

The Dead Sea Scrolls in English
Wise, Michael O., Martin G. Abegg Jr., and Edward M. Cook, trans. *The Dead Sea Scrolls: A New Translation*. Rev. ed. New York: HarperSanFrancisco, 2005.

PASSOVER WORKS

Bokser, Baruch M. *The Origins of the Seder: The Passover Rite and Early Rabbinic Judaism*. Berkeley: University of California Press, 1984.

Bradshaw, Paul F., and Lawrence A. Hoffman, eds. *Passover and Easter: Origin and History to Modern Times*. Two Liturgical Traditions 5. Notre Dame, IN: University of Notre Dame Press, 1999.

Goodman, Philip. *The Passover Anthology*. JPS Holiday Anthologies. Jewish Publication Society of America, 2003.

Jeremias, Joachim. *The Eucharistic Words of Jesus*. New York: Scribner, 1966.

Melito of Sardis. *On Pascha: With the Fragments of Melito and Other Material Related to the Quartodecimans*. Edited by John Behr. Translated by Alistair Stewart. 2nd ed. Popular Patristics 55. New York: St Vladimir's Seminary Press, 2017.

Tabory, Joseph. *JPS Commentary on the Haggadah: Historical Introduction, Translation, and Commentary*. Philadelphia: Jewish Publication Society, 2008.

HAGGADOT

Scherman, Nosson, and Avie Gold, eds. *The Family Haggadah*. Brooklyn, NY: Mesorah Publications, 1981.

Steinsaltz, Adin Even-Israel. *Passover Haggada*. Jerusalem: Koren Publishers, 2016.

SELECTED TOPICS

Antisemitism and the Church
Parkes, James. *The Conflict of the Church and the Synagogue*. New York: Atheneum, 1977. Originally published by Soncino Press in 1934.

Simon, Marcel. *Verus Israel: A Study of the Relations Between Christians and Jews in the Roman Empire (AD 135–425)*. Translated by H. McKeating. Oxford: Littman Library of Jewish Civilization, 1996.

Jewish Believers in the Early Church
Skarsaune, Oskar, and Reidar Hvalvik, eds. *Jewish Believers in Jesus: The Early Centuries*. Peabody, MA: Hendrickson, 2007.

Pritz, Ray A. *Nazarene Jewish Christianity: From the End of the New Testament Period Until Its Disappearance in the Fourth Century*. Studia Post-biblica 37. Jerusalem: Hebrew University / Magnes Press, 1988.

BIBLIOGRAPHY

Al-Buheiri, Muhammad. "Egyptian Researcher Muhammad Al-Buheiri: Jews Still Use Christian Blood to Bake Passover Matzos," MEMRI TV, Clip #1393, 7:20, from excerpts [transcript included] from an interview with Egyptian researcher Muhammad Al-Buheiri, which aired on Nile Culture TV. Egypt on February 25, 2007, http://www.memritv.org/clip/en/1393.htm

Al-Zaafrani, Khaled. "Egyptian Politician Khaled Zaafrani: Jews Use Human Blood for Passover Matzos," MEMRI TV, Clip #3873, 2:27, from excerpts [transcript included] from a TV show with Khaled Al-Zaafrani, founder of the Egyptian Justice and Progress Party, which aired on Al-Hafez TV. Saudi Arabia/Egypt on May 12, 2013, http://www.memritv.org/clip/en/3873.htm.

Aland, Kurt, ed. *Synopsis of the Four Gospels: Greek-English Edition of the* Synopsis Quattuor Evangeliorum. 12th ed. Stuttgart: German Bible Society, 2001.

Angel, Marc D. הגדה של פסח כמנהג הספרדים; *A Sephardic Passover Haggadah: Translated with Commentary by Rabbi Marc D. Angel.* Hoboken, NJ: KTAV, 1988.

Arnow, David, Mary C. Boys, and Muhammad Shafiq. "What Role Does Washing Play in Our Traditions?" *Exodus Conversations.* n.d. (ca. October 2013). http://exodusconversations.org/questions/what-role-does-washing-play-in-our-traditions/.

Audet, Jean-Paul. "Affinités littéraire et doctrinales du 'Manuel de discipline.'" *Revue Biblique* 59 (1952): 219–38.

Audet, Jean-Paul. "Literary and Doctrinal Affinities of the 'Manual of Discipline.'" In *The* Didache *in Modern Research*, edited and translated by Jonathan A. Draper, 129–47. Leiden: Brill, 1996.

Babylonian Talmud. Judeo-Christian Research. http://juchre.org/talmud/pesachim/pesachim1.htm#4a.

Bacchiocchi, Samuele. *Anti-Judaism and the Origin of Sunday.* Rome: Pontifical Gregorian University Press, 1975.

Bacchiocchi, Samuele. *From Sabbath to Sunday: A Historical Investigation of the Rise of Sunday Observance in Early Christianity.* Rome: Pontifical Gregorian University Press, 1977.

Barrett, C. K. *The First Epistle to the Corinthians.* Black's New Testament Commentary. London: Adam & Charles Black, 1968.

Ben-Sasson, H. H. ed. *A History of the Jewish People,* coauthored by A. Malamat, H. Tadmor, M. Stern, S. Safrai, H. H. Ben-Sasson, and S. Ettinger. Cambridge: Harvard University Press, 1976.

Bengtsson, Per Å. *Passover in Targum Pseudo-Jonathan Genesis: The Connection of Early Biblical Events with Passover in Targum Pseudo-Jonathan in a Synagogue Setting.* Scripta Minora Regiae Societatis Humaniorum Litterarum Lundensis, 2000/2001, 1. Stockholm: Almqvist & Wiksell International, 2001.

Berlin, Adele, and Marc Zvi Brettler, eds. *The Jewish Study Bible.* New York: Oxford University Press, 2004.

Biblesoft's New Exhaustive Strong's Numbers and Concordance with Expanded Greek-Hebrew Dictionary. Seattle, WA: Biblesoft and International Bible Translators, 2006.

Blackman, Philip, trans. and ed. "Mishnah." *Mishnayoth: Pointed Hebrew Text, English Translation, Introductions, Notes, Supplement, Appendix, Indexes, Addenda, Corrigenda.* 7 vols. 2nd ed. Gateshead, UK: Judaica Press, 1963–64.

Blasz, Elijohu. *Code of Jewish Family Purity: A Condensation of the Nidah Laws in an Abridged Form.* Translated by Committee for the Preservation of Jewish Family Purity. 14th ed. Brooklyn, NY: Committee for the Preservation of Jewish Family Purity, 1987. http://www.israel613.com/books/TAHARAT_HAMISHPACHA-E.pdf.

Blumenkranz, Bernhard, and B. Mordechai Ansbacher. "Badge, Jewish." In *Encyclopaedia Judaica,* edited by Fred Skolnik and Michael Berenbaum, 3:45–48. 2nd ed. 22 vols. Detroit: Macmillan Reference USA, 2007.

Bock, Darrell. "Blasphemy and the Jewish Examination of Jesus." *Bulletin for Biblical Research* 17, no. 1 (2007): 53–114. https://www.ibr-bbr.org/files/bbr/bbr17a03.pdf.

Bock, Darrell. *Mark*. New Cambridge Bible Commentary. Cambridge: Cambridge University Press, 2015.

Bock, Darrell L. "Precision and Accuracy: Making Distinctions in the Cultural Context That Give Us Pause in Pitting the Gospels Against One Another." In *Do Historical Matters Matter to the Faith? A Critical Appraisal of Modern and Postmodern Approaches*, edited by James K. Hoffmeier, Dennis Magary, 367–82. Wheaton: Crossway, 2012.

Bokser, Baruch M. "Changing Views of Passover and the Meaning of Redemption According to the Palestinian Talmud." *AJS Review* 10, no. 1. 1985.

Bokser, Baruch M. *The Origins of the Seder: The Passover Rite and Early Rabbinic Judaism*. Berkeley: University of California Press, 1984.

Bokser, Baruch M. "Ritualizing the Seder." *Journal of the American Academy of Religion* 56, no. 3. 1988.

Bokser, Baruch M. "Was the Last Supper a Passover Seder?" *Bible Review* 3, no. 2 (1987): 24–33.

Bradshaw, Paul F. "The Origins of Easter," in *Passover and Easter: Origin and History to Modern Times*, edited by Paul F. Bradshaw and Lawrence A. Hoffman, 98–124. Two Liturgical Traditions 5. Notre Dame, IN: University of Notre Dame Press, 1999.

Broadhead, Edwin K. *Jewish Ways of Following Jesus: Redrawing the Religious Map of Antiquity*. Tübingen: Mohr Siebeck, 2010.

Brown, Michael L. *The Real Kosher Jesus*. Lake Mary, FL: FrontLine, 2012.

Brueggemann, Walter. *1 & 2 Kings*. Smyth & Helwys Bible Commentary. Macon, GA: Smyth & Helwys, 2000.

Brümmer, Vincent. "Atonement and Reconciliation." *Religious Studies* 28, no. 4, 1992.

Brunson, Andrew C. *Psalm 118 in the Gospel of John: An Intertextual Study on the New Exodus Pattern in the Theology of John*. Wissenschaftliche Untersuchungen zum Neuen Testament 2, 158. Tübingen: Mohr Siebeck, 2003.

Carmichael, Deborah Bleicher. "David Daube on the Eucharist and the Passover Seder." *Journal for the Study of the New Testament* 13, no. 42 (1991): 45–67. https://doi.org/10.1177/0142064X9101304203.

Carroll, M. Daniel. "Malachi." In *Eerdmans Commentary on the Bible*. Edited by James D. G. Dunn and John W. Rogerson. Grand Rapids: Eerdmans, 2003.

Carson, D. A. *The Gospel According to John*. Pillar New Testament Commentary. Leicester, UK: Inter-Varsity Press; Grand Rapids: Eerdmans, 1991.

Carson, D. A., and Douglas J. Moo. *An Introduction to the New Testament*. 2nd ed. Grand Rapids: Zondervan, 2005.

Cathcart, Kevin. Michael Maher, and Martin McNamara, eds., *The Aramaic Bible: Targum Neofiti 1: Exodus and Targum Pseudo-Jonathan: Exodus*. Translated by Martin McNamara, Michael Maher, and Robert Hayward. Vol. 2. Collegeville, MN: Liturgical Press, 1994.

Cernea, Ruth Fredman. *The Passover Seder: An Anthropological Perspective on Jewish Culture*. Lanham, MD: University Press of America, 1995. Originally published in 1981.

Cesari, Jocelyne. *The Awakening of Muslim Democracy: Religion, Modernity, and the State*. New York: Cambridge University Press, 2014.

Charles, R. H., trans. *The Book of Jubilees; or The Little Genesis*. Translations of Early Documents. London: SPCK; New York: Macmillan, 1917. Originally published in London by Adam and Charles Black in 1902.

Cohen, Jeremy. *Christ Killers: The Jews and the Passion from the Bible to the Big Screen*. Oxford: Oxford University Press, 2007.

Cohn-Sherbok, D. M. "A Jewish Note on τὸ ποτήριον τῆς εὐλογίας." *New Testament Studies* 27, no. 5 (1981): 704–9.

Constable, Thomas L. "Notes on John, 2017 Edition." *Sonic Light*. http://www.soniclight.com/constable/notes/pdf/john.pdf. PDF file. 419 pages.

Chazan, Robert. *Medieval Stereotypes and Modern Antisemitism*. Berkeley: University of California Press, 1997.

Danker, Frederick W., Walter Bauer, William F. Arndt, and F. Wilbur Gingrich, *Greek-English Lexicon of the New Testament and Other Early Christian Literature*, 3rd ed. Chicago: University of Chicago Press, 2000.

Daube, David. "The Earliest Structure of the Gospels," *New Testament Studies* 5, no. 3 (1959), 174–87.

Daube, David. *He That Cometh.* St. Paul's Lecture 5. London: Council for Christian-Jewish Understanding, 1966. Originally given as a lecture held in the Crypt of St. Paul's Cathedral, London, in October 1966.

Daube, David. *New Testament Judaism*, vol. 2 of *Collected Works of David Daube*, Edited by Calum M. Carmichael, Studies in Comparative Legal History. Berkeley: Robbins Collection Publications/University of California at Berkeley, 2000.

Dictionary.com Unabridged, s.v. "atonement," accessed February 2, 2016, http://www.dictionary.com/browse/atonement.

Edersheim, Alfred. *The Life and Times of Jesus the Messiah.* 2 vols. London, Longmans, Green: 1883.

Edersheim, Alfred. *The Temple: Its Ministries and Services.* London: Religious Tract Society, 1874.

Eisenberg, Joyce, and Ellen Scolnic. *Dictionary of Jewish Words.* Rev. ed. Philadelphia: Jewish Publication Society, 2006. Originally published in 2001.

Eisenstein, Judah David, and Emil G. Hirsch. "Wine." In *The Jewish Encyclopedia: A Descriptive Record of the History, Religion, Literature, and Customs of the Jewish People from the Earliest Times to the Present Day*, ed. Isidore Singer, 12:533. New York; London: Funk & Wagnalls, 1906. http://www.jewishencyclopedia.com/articles/14941-wine.

Eisler, Robert. "Das Letzte Abendmahl" (Part 1), *Zeitschrift für die neutestamentliche Wissenschaft und die Kunde der älteren Kirche* 24 (1925): 161–92.

Eisler, Robert. "Das Letzte Abendmahl" (Part 2), *Zeitschrift für die neutestamentliche Wissenschaft und die Kunde der älteren Kirche* 25 (1926): 5–37.

El Moneim, Ghada Abd. "Qualities of the Jews and the Impact of mating with them" [translation of Arabic; select See Translation], Facebook page, posted April 25, 2014, accessed February 3, 2017, https://www.facebook.com/photo.php?fbid=10151967027556533&set=a.4613338 66532.247979.619346532&type=1&theater.

Encyclopædia Britannica Online, s.v. "Code of Justinian," accessed August 31, 2015, http://www.britannica.com/topic/Code-of-Justinian.

Encyclopædia Britannica Online, s.v. "Council of Antioch," accessed August 31, 2015, http://www.britannica.com/event/Council-of-Antioch.

Encyclopaedia Judaica. "Badge, Jewish." Vol. 4, col. 62–74. In *Encyclopaedia Judaica.* Jerusalem: Keter, 1972.

Encyclopaedia Judaica. Edited by Fred Skolnik and Michael Berenbaum. 2nd ed. 22 vols. Detroit: Macmillan Reference USA, 2007.

Enns, Peter. *Exodus.* NIV Application Commentary. Grand Rapids: Zondervan, 2000.

Eusebius, *Ecclesiastical History. Nicene and Post-Nicene Fathers, Series 2.* Edited by Philip Schaff and Henry Wace. Vol. 1. Buffalo, NY: Christian Literature Company, 1890.

Evans, Craig A. "The Jewish Christian Gospel Tradition," in *Jewish Believers in Jesus: The Early Centuries,* edited by Oskar Skarsaune and Reidar Hvalvik, 121–52. Peabody, MA: Hendrickson, 2007.

Flannery, Edward H. *The Anguish of the Jews: Twenty-Three Centuries of Anti-Semitism,* rev. ed., Stimulus Book. New York: Paulist Press, 1985.

Foster, Lewis A. "The Chronology of the New Testament." In *Expositor's Bible Commentary: Introductory Articles,* edited by Frank E. Gaebelein and J. D. Douglas. Vol. 1. Grand Rapids: Zondervan, 1979.

Francis, Fred O. "The Baraita of the Four Sons." *Journal of the American Academy of Religion* 42, no. 2. (1974): 280–97.

Freund, Michael. "Passover Blood Libels, Then and Now," *The Jerusalem Post,* April 13, 2014, http://www.jpost.com/Jewish-World/Judaism/Passover-blood-libels-then-and-now-348382.

Glaser, Mitch, and Zhava Glaser. *The Fall Feasts of Israel.* Chicago: Moody Press, 1987.

Glaser, Richard. "The Greek Jews in Baltimore." *Jewish Social Studies* 38, no. 3/4 (1976): 321–36. http://www.jstor.org/stable/4466941.

Goitein, S. D., and Paula Sanders (vol. 6, indexes). *A Mediterranean Society: The Jewish Communities of the Arab World as Portrayed in the Documents of the Cairo Geniza.* 6 vols. Berkeley: University of California Press, 1967–93.

Goodman, Philip, ed. *The Passover Anthology*. JPS Holiday. Philadelphia: Jewish Publication Society of America, 1961.

Gottheil, Richard, Hermann L. Strack, and Joseph Jacobs, "Blood Accusation," in *Jewish Encyclopedia: A Descriptive Record of the History, Religion, Literature, and Customs of the Jewish People from the Earliest Times to the Present Day*, edited by Isidore Singer, 3:260–67. New York: Funk & Wagnalls, 1902. Accessed September 1, 2015. http://www.jewishencyclopedia.com/articles/3408-blood-accusation.

Grayzel, Solomon. *The Church and the Jews in the XIII Century: A Study of Their Relations During the Years 1198–1254,* Based on the Papal Letters and the Concillar Decrees of the Period. Philadelphia: Dropsie College, 1933.

Grayzel, Solomon. "Passover and the Ritual Murder Libel," in *The Passover Anthology,* ed. Philip Goodman, JPS Holiday. Philadelphia: Jewish Publication Society of America, 1961.

Greenburg, William H., trans. *The Haggadah According to the Rite of Yemen: Together with the Arabic-Hebrew Commentary*. London: David Nutt, 1896.

Greenspan, Ari, Ari Z. Zivotofsky, and Elli Wohlgelernter. "Matzah." In *Encyclopaedia Judaica*, Edited by Fred Skolnik and Michael Berenbaum, 13:689–70. 2nd ed. 22 vols. Detroit: Macmillan Reference USA, 2007.

Hall, S.G. *On Pascha and Fragments*, Oxford: Clarendon Press, 1979.

Hamilton, Victor P. *The Book of Genesis: Chapters 18–50*. New International Commentary on the Old Testament. Grand Rapids: Eerdmans, 1995.

Harris, R. Laird. "גָּאַל." *Theological Wordbook of the Old Testament*. Edited by R. Laird Harris, Gleason L. Archer, and Bruce K. Waltke. Vol. 1. Chicago: Moody Press, 1980.

Harris, R. Laird. "כָּפַר," *Theological Wordbook of the Old Testament*. Edited by R. Laird Harris, Gleason L. Archer Jr., and Bruce K. Waltke. Vol. 1. Chicago: Moody Press, 1999.

Hartley, John E. "שָׁמַר," *Theological Wordbook of the Old Testament*. Edited by R. Laird Harris, Gleason L. Archer, and Bruce K. Waltke. Vol. 2. Chicago: Moody Press, 1980.

Hauptman, Judith. "How Old Is the Haggadah?" *Judaism* 51, pt. 1. 2002: 5–18. http://www.globethics.net/gel/9770555.

Hauptman, Judith. "The Talmud's Women in Law and Narrative." *Nashim: A Journal of Jewish Women's Studies and Gender Issues* 28, no. 1. 2015: 30–50. http://www.jstor.org/stable/10.2979/nashim.issue-28.

Hoehner, Harold. *Chronological Aspects of the Life of Christ*. Grand Rapids: Zondervan, 1977.

Instone Brewer, David. *Techniques and Assumptions in Jewish Exegesis before 70 CE*. Texte und Studien zum antiken Judentum 30. Tübingen: J. C. B. Mohr. P. Siebeck, 1992.

Jaubert, Annie. *La date de la Cène: Calendrier biblique et liturgie chrétienne*. Paris: Lecoffre, 1957. English translation: Annie Jaubert, *The Date of the Last Supper*. Translated by Isaac Rafferty. Staten Island, NY: Alba House, 1965.

Jeremias, Joachim. *The Eucharistic Words of Jesus*. Translated by Norman Perrin. Rev. ed. New Testament Library. New York: Scribner, 1966. Scribner edition cited in chapters 5 and 7.

Jeremias, Joachim. *The Eucharistic Words of Jesus*. Translated by Norman Perrin. Rev. ed. New Testament Library. London: SCM Press, 1966. SCM Press edition cited in chapter 6.

The Jewish Theological Seminary of America, The Rabbinical Assembly, and United Synagogue of America. *Emet Ve'emunah: Statement of Principles of Conservative Judaism*. New York: Jewish Theological Seminary of America, 1988.

Josephus, Flavius. *Jewish War*. In *Josephus*. Translated by Henry St. John Thackeray. Loeb Classical Library. Cambridge: Harvard University Press, 1979.

Josephus, Flavius. *The Works of Flavius Josephus*. Translated by William Whiston. 4 vols. Grand Rapids: Baker, 1990. Originally published in 1974.

Josephus. *Josephus, the Essential Works: A Condensation of Jewish Antiquities and the Jewish War*. Translated and edited by Paul L. Maier. Rev. ed. Grand Rapids: Kregel, 1994. First published 1988.

Kaiser, Walter C., Jr. "Exodus." In *The Expositor's Bible Commentary: Genesis–Leviticus*. Rev. ed. Vol. 1. Grand Rapids: Zondervan, 2012.

Karo, Joseph ben Ephraim. *Code of Jewish Law. Kitzur Schulḥan Aruḥ: A Compilation of Jewish Laws and Customs.* Compiled by Solomon Ganzfried. Translated by Hyman E. Goldin. 4 vols. Rev. ed. New York: Hebrew Publishing Company, 1927.

Keener, Craig S. *The Gospel of John: A Commentary.* 2 vols. Peabody, MA: Hendrickson, 2003.

Kisber, Susie. "Midrashim and Prayer for Passover," Ritualwell. http://www.ritualwell.org/ritual/midrashim-and-prayer-passover.

Kitov, Eliyahu. *The Book of Our Heritage: The Jewish Year and Its Days of Significance.* Translated by Nachman Bulman. Rev. ed. 3 vols. Jerusalem: Feldheim Publishers, 1988. Originally published in Hebrew as *Sefer ha-Toda'ah* in 1962. First published in English in 1968.

Klawans, Jonathan. "Was Jesus' Last Supper a Passover?" *Bible Review* 17 (2001): 24–33, 47. http://www.biblicalarchaeology.org/daily/people-cultures-in-the-bible/jesus-historical-jesus/was-jesus-last-supper-a-seder/.

Klein, Isaac. *A Guide to Jewish Religious Practice.* New York: Jewish Theological Seminary of America, 1992. Originally published in 1979.

Klijn, A. F. J. and G. J. Reinink, *Patristic Evidence for Jewish-Christian Sects.* Supplements to Novum Testamentum 36. Leiden: Brill, 1973.

Koehler, Ludwig. Walter Baumgartner, and Johann J. Stamm. *The Hebrew and Aramaic Lexicon of the Old Testament.* Translated and edited under the supervision of Mervyn E. J. Richardson. 4 vols. Leiden: Brill, 1994–1999.

Kolatch, Alfred J. *The Jewish Book of Why.* Middle Village, NY: Jonathan David Publishers, 1981.

Konkel, August H. *1 & 2 Kings.* NIV Application Commentary. Grand Rapids: Zondervan, 2000.

Kulp, Joshua. "Mishnah Tosefta Pesahim." *Shiurim Online Beit Midrash.* Accessed December 2, 2015, http://learn.conservativeyeshiva.org/haggadah-and-the-seder-0-mishnah-tosefta-pesahim.

Langmuir, Gavin I. *Toward a Definition of Antisemitism.* Berkeley: University of California Press, 1990.

Lauterbach, Jacob Z., trans. *Mekilta de-Rabbi Ishmael: A Critical Edition on the Basis of the Manuscripts and Early Editions with an English Translation, Introduction and Notes.* 2 vols. 2nd ed. JPS Classic Reissues. Philadelphia: Jewish Publication Society of America, 2004. Originally published in 1933–35.

Leese, Arnold S. *My Irrelevant Defense Being Meditations Inside Prison and Out on Jewish Ritual Murder.* Birmingham, AL: Thunderbolt, 1962, https://archive.org/details/dudeman5685_yahoo_MID.   Originally published in 1938.

Leonhard, Clemens. *The Jewish Pesach and the Origins of the Christian Easter: Open Questions in Current Research.* Studia Judaica 35. Berlin: Walter de Gruyter, 2006.

Levine, Baruch A. *Leviticus.* JPS Torah Commentary. Philadelphia: Jewish Publication Society, 1989.

Levine, Lee I. *The Ancient Synagogue: The First Thousand Years.* New Haven; London: Yale University Press, 2005.

Levy, Richard S., comp. *Antisemitism in the Modern World: An Anthology of Texts.* Sources in Modern History. Lexington, MA: D.C. Heath and Company, 1991.

Levy, Richard S. "Marr, Wilhelm (1819–1904)." In *Antisemitism: A Historical Encyclopedia of Prejudice and Persecution.* Edited by Richard S. Levy. 2 vols. Santa Barbara, CA: ABC-CLIO, 2006.

Lewis, Jack P. "דַעֲ [see under דֵּעֶוֹם]," *Theological Wordbook of the Old Testament.* Edited by R. Laird Harris, Gleason L. Archer, and Bruce K. Waltke. Vol. 1. Chicago: Moody Press, 1980.

Licht, J. s.v. *"pesaḥ."* In *'Entsiklopediah Mikra'it.* Vol. 6. Jerusalem: Mosad Bialik, 1950–88.

Licona, Michael R. *The Resurrection of Jesus: A New Historiographical Approach.* Downers Grove, IL; Nottingham, England: IVP Academic; Apollos, 2010.

Long, George. "Codex Theodosianus." In *A Dictionary of Greek and Roman Antiquities.* Edited by William Smith, 302–3. London: John Murray, 1875.   http://penelope.uchicago.edu/Thayer/E/Roman/Texts/secondary/SMIGRA*/Codex_Theodosianus.html.

Lumpkin, Joseph B., trans. *The Book of Jubilees, [or], The Little Genesis, The Apocalypse of Moses*. Blountsville, AL: Fifth Estate, 2006.

Luomanen, Petri. *Recovering Jewish-Christian Sects and Gospels, Supplements to Vigiliae Christianae 110*. Leiden: Brill, 2012.

Luther, Martin. *Jesus Christ Was a Jew by Birth*. Wittenberg, 1523.

Luther, Martin. *Luther's Works, Volume 43: Devotional Writings II*. Edited by Helmut T. Lehmann and Martin O. Dietrich. Philadelphia: Fortress Press, 1968.

Luther, Martin. *Luther's Works. Volume 47, IV*. Edited by Franklin Sherman, and Helmut T Lehmann. Philadelphia: Fortress Press, 1971.

Lyons, Eric. "Did Jesus Rise 'On' or 'After' the Third Day?" *Apologetics Press*. 2004. http://apologeticspress.org/apcontent.aspx?category=6&article=756.

Maier, P. L. "Chronology." In *Dictionary of the Later New Testament and Its Developments*. Edited by Ralph P. Martin and Peter H. Davids. Downers Grove, IL: InterVarsity Press, 1997.

Maimonides, Moses and Aryeh Kaplan. *Maimonides' Principles: The Fundamentals of Jewish Faith*. New York: National Conference of Synagogue Youth, 2002.

Marcus, Joel. "Passover and Last Supper Revisited." *New Testament Studies* 59, no. 3 (2013): 303–24.

Marr, Wilhelm. *Der Sieg des Judenthums über das Germanenthum*. Bern: Rudolph Costenoble, 1879, http://sammlungen.ub.uni-frankfurt.de/urn/urn:nbn:de:hebis:30-180014998005.

Marr, Wilhelm. "The Victory of Jewry over Germandom." In *Antisemitism in the Modern World: An Anthology of Texts*. Compiled by Richard S. Levy. Sources in Modern History. Lexington, MA: D.C. Heath and Company, 1991.

Marshall, I. Howard. "The Last Supper." In *Key Events in the Life of the Historical Jesus: A Collaborative Exploration of Context and Coherence*. Edited by Darrell L. Bock and Robert L. Webb, 481–588. Wissenschaftliche Untersuchungen zum Neuen Testament 247. Tübingen: Mohr Siebeck, 2009.

Martin, John J. "The Nature of the Atonement," *The American Journal of Theology* 14, no. 3, (1910): 385.

Martin, M. "Communal Meals in the Late Antique Synagogue." *Byzantina Australiensa* 15 (2004): 55. http://www.aabs.org.au/byzaust/byzaus15/.

Martin, M. "Communal Meals in the Late Antique Synagogue." In *Feast, Fast or Famine: Food and Drink in Byzantium,* edited by W. Mayer and S. Trzcionka, 135–46. Byzantina Australiensia 15. Brisbane: Australian Associate for Byzantine Studies, 2005.

Mathews, K. A. *Genesis 11:27–50:26.* New American Commentary. Vol. 1B. Nashville: Broadman & Holman, 2005.

Melito of Sardis. *On Pascha and Fragments.* Edited by Stuart G. Hall. Oxford Early Christian Texts. Oxford: Clarendon Press, 1979.

Melito of Sardis. *On Pascha: With the Fragments of Melito and Other Material Related to the Quartodecimans.* Edited by John Behr. Translated by Alistair Stewart-Sykes. Popular Patristics Series 20. Crestwood, NY: St Vladimir's Seminary Press, 2001. See entry below for 2nd edition. All citations are to the 2001 edition.

Melito of Sardis. *On Pascha: With the Fragments of Melito and Other Material Related to the Quartodecimans.* Edited by John Behr. Translated by Alistair Stewart. 2nd ed. Popular Patristics 55. New York: St Vladimir's Seminary Press, 2017.

Milavec, Aaron. *The Didache: Text, Translation, Analysis, and Commentary.* Collegeville, MN: Liturgical Press, 2003.

Milgrom, Jacob. *Numbers.* JPS Torah Commentary. Philadelphia: Jewish Publication Society, 1990.

Morris, Leon. *The Gospel according to John,* New International Commentary on the New Testament. Grand Rapids: Eerdmans, 1971.

Nicholls, William. *Christian Antisemitism: A History of Hate.* Northvale, NJ: J. Aronson, 1993.

Niederwimmer, Kurt. *The Didache: A Commentary.* Translated by Linda M. Maloney. Edited by Harold W. Attridge. Hermeneia. Minneapolis: Fortress Press, 1998.

Nostra Aetate, Declaration on the Relation of the Church to Non-Christian Religions, proclaimed by Pope Paul VI on October 28, 1965, http://www.vatican.va/archive/hist_councils/ii_vatican_council/documents/vat-ii_decl_19651028_nostra-aetate_en.html.

Noy, Dov, and Joseph Tabory. "Afikoman." In *Encyclopaedia Judaica*. Edited by Fred Skolnik and Michael Berenbaum. 1:434. 2nd ed. 22 vols. Detroit: Macmillan Reference USA, 2007.

Ochs, Vanessa L. "What Makes a Jewish Home Jewish?" *CrossCurrents* 49, no. 4 (1999/2000): 491–510. http://www.crosscurrents.org/ochsv. htm.

Open Mishnah, Sefaria Community Translation. Sefaria. http://www.sefaria. org/Mishnah_Pesachim.10.

Oppenheimer, Aharon. *The 'Am Ha-aretz: A Study in the Social History of the Jewish People in the Hellenistic-Roman Period*. Translated from the Hebrew by I. H. Levine. Arbeiten zur Literatur und Geschichte des hellenistischen Judentums 8. Leiden: Brill, 1977.

Origen. *Treatise on the Passover and Dialogue of Origen with Heraclides and His Fellow Bishops on the Father, the Son, and the Soul*. Translated by Robert J. Daly. Ancient Christian Writers 54. Mahwah, NJ: Paulist Press, 1992.

Palomino, Michael. "Prosecution of the Jews: The Badge and Clothing Laws for Jews in the Middle Ages," *History in Chronology*, 2007. http://www. geschichteinchronologie.com/MA/judentum-EncJud_judenfleck-u-judenhut-im-MA-ENGL.html.

Parkes, James. *The Conflict of the Church and the Synagogue: A Study of the Origins of Antisemitism*. New York: Atheneum, 1977. Originally published by Soncino Press in 1934.

Payne, J. Barton. "תָּמַם," *Theological Wordbook of the Old Testament*. Edited by R. Laird Harris, Gleason L. Archer, and Bruce K. Waltke. Vol. 2. Chicago: Moody Press, 1980.

Peters, Ted. "Models of Atonement." In *Theological Brief for PLTS/ITE*. December 10, 2005, PDF file, 19, http://www.plts.edu/faculty-staff/documents/ite_models_atonement.pdf.

Petterson, Anthony R. *Haggai, Zechariah & Malachi*. Apollos Old Testament Commentary 25. Nottingham, UK: Apollos; Downers Grove, IL: InterVarsity Press, 2015.

Plato. *Lycis. Symposium. Gorgias*. Translated by W. R. M. Lamb. Vol. 3 of *Plato in Twelve Volumes*. Loeb Classical Library 166. Cambridge: Harvard University Press, 1925.

Pohle, Joseph. "The Real Presence of Christ in the Eucharist." In *The Catholic Encyclopedia*. Vol. 5. New York: Robert Appleton Company, 1909. Accessed February 3, 2017. http://www.newadvent.org/cathen/05573a.htm.

Poliakov, Léon. *The History of Anti-Semitism*. 4 vols. New York: Vanguard Press, 1965.

Prager, Dennis, and Joseph Telushkin. *Why the Jews? The Reason for Antisemitism*. New York: Simon and Schuster, 1983.

Pritz, Ray A. *Nazarene Jewish Christianity: From the End of the New Testament Period Until Its Disappearance in the Fourth Century*. Studia Post-biblica 37. Jerusalem: Hebrew University / Magnes Press, 1988.

Roberts, J. H. "The Lamb of God." *Neotestamentica* 2 (1968): 43, http://www.jstor.org/stable/43047704.

Robertson, A. T. *A Harmony of the Gospels for Students of the Life of Christ: Based on the Broadus Harmony in the Revised Version*. New York: George H. Doran, 1922.

Robinson, H. Wheeler. "Hebrew Sacrifice and Prophetic Symbolism." In *Journal of Theological Studies* 43, no. 171/172 (1942): 129–39. http://www.jstor.org/stable/23957190.

Rofé, A. *Mavo' le-sefer Devarim*. Jerusalem: Akademon, 1988.

Rooker, Mark F. *Leviticus*. New American Commentary. Vol. 3A. Nashville: Broadman & Holman, 2000.

Rosenblum, Jordan D. *Food and Identity in Early Rabbinic Judaism*. New York: Cambridge University Press, 2010.

Rovner, Jay. "An Early Passover Haggadah According to the Palestinian Rite." *Jewish Quarterly Review* 90, no. 3/4 (2000): 337–96.

Rubin, Miri. *Gentile Tales: The Narrative Assault on Late Medieval Jews*. Philadelphia: University of Pennsylvania Press, 2004. Originally published in 1999.

Sachar, Abram Leon. *A History of the Jews*. New York: Knopf, 1965.

Sacks, Jonathan. *Not in God's Name: Confronting Religious Violence*. New York: Schocken Books, 2015.

Safrai, Shmuel, and Peter J. Tomson, eds. *The Literature of the Sages. First Part: Oral Tora, Halakha, Mishna, Tosefta, Talmud, External Tractates.* Compendia Rerum Iudaicarum ad Novum Testamentum. Assen, Netherlands: Van Gorcum; Philadelphia: Fortress Press, 1987.

Sailhamer, John H. "Genesis." In *The Expositor's Bible Commentary: Genesis–Leviticus.* Rev. ed. Vol. 1. Grand Rapids: Zondervan, 2009.

Sarna, Nahum M. *Exodus.* JPS Torah Commentary. Philadelphia: Jewish Publication Society, 1991.

Schauss, Hayyim. *The Jewish Festivals: A Guide to Their History and Observance.* Translated by Samuel Jaffe. New York: Schocken Books, 1938.

Schechter, Solomon, and Wilhelm Bacher. "Judah I." In *Jewish Encyclopedia: A Descriptive Record of the History, Religion, Literature, and Customs of the Jewish People from the Earliest Times to the Present Day,* ed. Isidore Singer, 7:333–37. New York: Funk & Wagnalls, 1904. Accessed February 5, 2017. http://www.jewishencyclopedia.com/articles/8963-judah-i.

Schechtman, Joseph B. "The Repatriation of Iraq Jewry." *Jewish Social Studies* 15, no. 2 (1953): 151–72.

Scherman, Nosson, ed. *The Chumash: The Torah, Haftaros and Five Megillos.* ArtScroll Series. Brooklyn, NY: Mesorah Publications, 1993.

Scherman, Nosson, and Meir Zlotowitz, eds. חסף לש הדנה; *The Family Haggadah.* Translated by Nosson Scherman. ArtScroll Mesorah Series. Brooklyn, NY: Mesorah Publications, 1981.

Segal, Phillip. "Another Note to 1 Corinthians 10:16." *New Testament Studies* 29, no. 1 (1983): 134–39.

Sevener, Harold A., ed. *Messianic Passover Haggadah.* New York: Chosen People Ministries, 1994.

Shapiro, James. *Oberammergau: The Troubling Story of the World's Most Famous Passion Play.* New York: Vintage, 2007.

Sharf, Andrew. "Justinian I." In *Encyclopaedia Judaica,* edited by Fred Skolnik and Michael Berenbaum, 11:579–80. 2nd ed. 22 vols. Detroit: Macmillan Reference USA, 2007.

Shields, Harry E. "1 Kings," *The Moody Bible Commentary.* Edited by Michael Rydelnik and Michael Vanlaningham. Chicago: Moody Publishers, 2014.

Silberberg, Naftali. "Why Is Elijah the Prophet Invited to the Seder?" *Chabad. org.* http://www.chabad.org/holidays/passover/pesach_cdo/aid/504495/jewish/Why-Is-Elijah-the-Prophet-Invited-to-the-Seder.htm.

Silverstein, Mordechai, trans. "The Four Sons of the Haggadah—Introduction to Rabbinic Midrash." *Shiurim Online Beit Midrash.* Accessed December 2, 2015. http://learn.conservativeyeshiva.org/introduction-to-rabbinic-midrash-10-lesson-10-the-four-sons-of-the-haggadah.

Simon, Marcel. *Verus Israel: A Study of the Relations Between Christians and Jews in the Roman Empire (ad 132–425).* Translated by H. McKeating. London: Littman Library of Jewish Civilization, 1996. Originally published in 1986.

Sinclair, Julian. "Geulah." *The Jewish Chronicle,* March 6, 2009. https://www.thejc.com/judaism/jewish-words/geulah-1.8102.

Skarsaune, Oskar. "Evidence for Jewish Believers in Greek and Latin Patristic Literature." In *Jewish Believers in Jesus: The Early Centuries,* edited by Oskar Skarsaune and Reidar Hvalvik, 121–53. Peabody, MA: Hendrickson, 2007.

Skarsaune, Oskar. "The Ebionites." In *Jewish Believers in Jesus: The Early Centuries,* edited by Oskar Skarsaune and Reidar Hvalvik, 121–53. Peabody, MA: Hendrickson, 2007.

Skarsaune, Oskar. *In the Shadow of the Temple: Jewish Influences on Early Christianity.* Downers Grove, InterVarsity Press, 2002.

Slonim, Rivkah. "The Mikvah." *TheJewishWoman.org.* n.d. (ca. April 2004). http://www.chabad.org/theJewishWoman/article_cdo/aid/1541/jewish/The-Mikvah.htm.

Slutsky, Yehuda, and Dina Porat. "Blood Libel." In *Encyclopaedia Judaica,* edited by Fred Skolnik and Michael Berenbaum 3:774–80. 2nd ed. 22 vols. Detroit: Macmillan Reference USA, 2007.

Smeaton, George. *The Doctrine of the Atonement: As Taught by the Apostles; or, The Sayings of the Apostles Exegetically Expounded; with Historical Appendix.* Edinburgh: T&T Clark, 1870.

Stein, Siegfried. "The Influence of Symposia Literature on the Literary Form of the Pesaḥ Haggadah." In *Journal of Jewish Studies* 8, no. 1–2 (1957): 13–44.

Strack, H. L., and Günter Stemberger. *Introduction to the Talmud and Midrash*. Translated and edited by Markus Bockmuehl. Minneapolis: Fortress Press, 1996.

Strong, James. *Strong's Exhaustive Concordance of the Bible*, 1890. Peabody, MA: Hendrickson Publishers, 2007.

Stuart, Douglas K. *Exodus*. New American Commentary. Vol. 2. Nashville: B&H, 2006.

Sultan, Salah. "Salah Sultan," The Global Muslim Brotherhood Daily Watch, posted by "gmbwatch," January 17, 2015, https://www.globalmbwatch.com/wiki/salah-sultan/; "Blood Libel on Hamas TV - President of the American Center for Islamic Research Dr. Salah Sultan: Jews Murder Non-Jews and Use Their Blood to Knead Passover Matzos," MEMRI TV, Clip #2443, 1:03, from excerpts [transcript included] from an address by Dr. Salah Sultan, president of the American Center for Islamic Research, which aired on Al-Aqsa TV. Hamas/Gaza on March 31, 2010, http://www.memritv.org/clip/en/2443.htm.

Tabory, Joseph. *JPS Commentary on the Haggadah: Historical Introduction, Translation, and Commentary*. Philadelphia: Jewish Publication Society, 2008.

Tabory, Joseph. Review of *Passover in Targum Pseudo-Jonathan Genesis: The Connection of Early Biblical Events with Passover in Targum Pseudo-Jonathan in a Synagogue Setting*, by Per Å. Bengtsson. In *Jewish Quarterly Review* 93, no. 1 (2002): 317–19. http://muse.jhu.edu/article/390121/pdf.

Telushkin, Joseph. *Jewish Literacy: The Most Important Things to Know about the Jewish Religion, Its People, and Its History*. New York: W. Morrow, 1991.

Thiselton, Anthony C. *The First Epistle to the Corinthians: A Commentary on the Greek Text*. New International Greek Testament Commentary. Grand Rapids: Eerdmans, 2000.

Tigay, Jeffrey H. *Deuteronomy*. JPS Torah Commentary. Philadelphia: Jewish Publication Society, 1996.

Trachtenberg, Joshua. *The Devil and the Jews: The Medieval Conception of the Jew and Its Relation to Modern Anti-Semitism*, 2nd ed. Philadelphia: Jewish Publication Society, 2002.

Union of American Hebrew Congregations. *Reform-Liberal-Progressive Judaism Its Ideals and Concepts, as Set Forth in the Guiding Principles of Reform Judaism*; New York: Union of American Hebrew Congregations, 1937.

Valentin, Hugo. *Antisemitism: Historically and Critically Examined.* Translated by A. G. Chater. New York: Viking Press, 1936.

VanGemeren, Willem A. "Psalms." In *The Expositor's Bible Commentary.* Vol. 5. Grand Rapids: Zondervan, 1991.

Waltke, Bruce K., with Cathi J. Fredricks. *Genesis: A Commentary.* Grand Rapids: Zondervan, 2001.

Webster, Douglas Raymund. "St. William of Norwich." In *The Catholic Encyclopedia.* Vol. 15. New York: Robert Appleton Company, 1912. http://www.newadvent.org/cathen/15635a.htm.

Werner, Eric. "Melito of Sardes, the First Poet of Deicide." *Hebrew Union College Annual* 37 (1966): 191–210. http://www.jstor.org/stable/23503121.

Westermann, Claus. *Genesis.* Translated by David Green. New York: T&T Clark, 2004.

Westermann, Claus. *The Psalms: Structure, Content and Message.* Minneapolis: Augsburg, 1980.

Wilhite, David E. *The Gospel According to the Heretics: Discovering Orthodoxy through Early Christological Conflicts.* Grand Rapids: Baker Academic, 2015.

Wistrich, Robert S. *A Lethal Obsession: Antisemitism from Antiquity to the Global Jihad.* New York: Random House, 2010.

Wright, David F. "Ebionites." In *Dictionary of the Later New Testament and Its Development*, edited by Ralph P. Martin and Peter H. Davids, 313–17. Downers Grove, IL: InterVarsity Press, 1997.

Youngblood, Ronald F., ed. *Nelson's Illustrated Bible Dictionary.* Rev. ed. Nashville: Thomas Nelson, 2014.

Yuval, Israel J. "Easter and Passover as Early Jewish-Christian Dialogue." In *Passover and Easter: Origin and History to Modern Times*, edited by Paul F. Bradshaw and Lawrence A. Hoffman, 98–124. Two Liturgical Traditions 5. Notre Dame, IN: University of Notre Dame Press, 1999.

Zaklikowski, Dovid. "The Chair of Elijah and Welcoming the Baby."
    Chabad.org. ˙http://www.chabad.org/library/article_cdo/aid/144123/
    jewish/The-Chair-of-Elijah-and-Welcoming-the-Baby.htm.

Zivotofsky, Ari Z. "What's the Truth about . . . the Meaning of 'Pesach'?"
    Jewish Action. (Spring 2004): 58–59, https://www.ou.org/torah/
    machshava/tzarich-iyun/tzarich_iyun_the_meaning_of_pesach/.

INDEX OF SCRIPTURE

INDEX OF ANCIENT AND MEDIEVAL WRITINGS

INDEX OF RABBINIC WRITINGS

INDEX OF NAMES

INDEX OF SUBJECTS

INDEX OF HEBREW TERMS

INDEX OF GREEK TERMS

Also edited by Darrell L. Bock
& Mitch Glaser

In Celebration of Israel's 70th Anniversary

ISRAEL
THE
CHURCH
AND THE
MIDDLE
EAST

A BIBLICAL RESPONSE TO THE CURRENT CONFLICT

Darrell L. Bock and Mitch Glaser, Editors

Also edited by Darrell L. Bock & Mitch Glaser

The Gospel According to
Isaiah 53

ENCOUNTERING THE
SUFFERING SERVANT IN JEWISH
AND CHRISTIAN THEOLOGY

DARRELL L. BOCK
AND MITCH GLASER
EDITORS